Communication in Our Lives

From the Wadsworth Series in Communication Studies

Communication in Our Lives

Julia T. Wood

The University of North Carolina at Chapel Hill

Wadsworth Publishing Company

I(T)P   An International Thomson Publishing Company

Belmont • Albany • Bonn • Boston • Cincinnati • Detroit • London • Madrid • Melbourne
Mexico City • New York • Paris • San Francisco • Singapore • Tokyo • Toronto • Washington

Communication Studies Editor: Todd R. Armstrong

Editorial Assistant: Michael Gillespie

Project Development Editor: Lewis DeSimone

Marketing Manager: Mike Dew

Production Editor: Vicki Friedberg

Text and Cover Designer: Carolyn Deacy

Art Editor: Laura Murray

Print Buyer: Barbara Britton

Permissions Editor: Robert M. Kauser

Advertising Project Manager: Elaine Cline

Copy Editor: Melissa Andrews

Page Makeup: Rosa+Wesley Design Associates

Photo Researcher: Stephen Forsling

Illustrator: Seventeenth Street Studios

Compositor and Color Separation: York Graphic Services

Printer: Von Hoffman

Cover Photos: Top row: © Rieder & Walsh/Photonica; © Walter Hodges/Tony Stone Images. *Bottom row:* © Anne Dowie; © Russell Sparkman/Photonica; © Bob Daemmrich/Stock, Boston.
Frontmatter Photos: p. ix: © James Holland/Stock, Boston; *p. x:* © Goldberg/Monkmeyer; *p. xi:* © Tom Levy/Photo 20-20; *p. xii:* © Burns/Monkmeyer; *p. xiii:* Julia T. Wood; *p. xiv:* © Mark Antman/The Image Works; *p. xv:* © Craig Aurness/West Light; *p. xvi:* © Ron Sanford/Black Star; *p. xvii:* © Paula Lerner/Woodfin Camp & Associates, Inc.; *p. xviii:* © Bob Daemmrich/Stock, Boston; *p. xix:* © Arthur Rickerby/ Black Star.
Chapter Opening Photos: Introduction: © Tom Levy/Photo 20-20; *Ch. 1:* © Catherine Karnow/Woodfin Camp & Associates; *Ch. 2:* © Richard Younker/Tony Stone Images; *Ch. 3:* © Comstock; *Ch. 4:* © Paula Lerner/Woodfin Camp & Associates; *Ch. 5:* © Renee Lynn/Photo Researchers; *Ch. 6:* © Burns/Monkmeyer; *Ch. 7:* © Sharon Stewart/Impact Visuals; *Ch. 8:* © Comstock; *Ch. 9:* © William Thompson/National Geographic Image Collection; *Ch. 10:* © Bruce Ayers/Tony Stone Images; *Ch. 11:* © Ron Sanford/Black Star; *Ch. 12:* © Bob Daemmrich/Stock, Boston; *Ch. 13:* © Michael Grecco/Stock, Boston; *Ch. 14:* © Bob Daemmrich/Stock, Boston.

1 2 3 4 5 6 7 8 9 10

For more information, contact Wadsworth Publishing Company.

Wadsworth Publishing Company
10 Davis Drive
Belmont, California 94002, USA

International Thomson Publishing Europe
Berkshire House 168-173
High Holborn
London, WC1V 7AA, England

Thomas Nelson Australia
102 Dodds Street
South Melbourne 3205
Victoria, Australia

Nelson Canada
1120 Birchmount Road
Scarborough, Ontario
Canada M1K 5G4

International Thomson Editores
Campos Eliseos 385, Piso 7
Col. Polanco
11560 México D.F. México

International Thomson Publishing GmbH
Königswinterer Strasse 418
53227 Bonn, Germany

International Thomson Publishing Asia
221 Henderson Road
#05-10 Henderson Building
Singapore 0315

International Thomson Publishing Japan
Hirakawacho Kyowa Building, 3F
2-2-1 Hirakawacho
Chiyoda-ku, Tokyo 102, Japan

Library of Congress Cataloging-in-Publication Data
Wood, Julia T.
   Communication in our lives/Julia T. Wood.
     p. cm. — (Wadsworth series in communication studies)
   Includes bibliographical references (p.) and index.
   ISBN 0-534-50426-4
   1. Communication. I. Title. II. Series
P90.W618 1997
302.2—dc20   96-4333

For Carolyn

For so many reasons.

BRIEF CONTENTS

CONTENTS

CHAPTER 2

Perception and Communication 38

Communication and Personal Identity 64

Effective Listening 92

CHAPTER 5

The Verbal Dimension of Communication 120

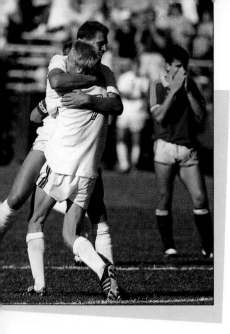

CHAPTER 6

The Nonverbal Dimension of Communication 148

CHAPTER 7

Communication and Cultures 176

Part Two   Contexts of Communication

wrote *Communication in Our Lives* to share with students my view of the importance of communication in our everyday lives. I have strived to make the book as interesting, substantive, and engaging as communication itself is. I use a conversational style of writing and weave into the chapters examples, reflections from students, artwork, and applications that invite students to become engaged personally with the ideas presented.

Communication in Our Lives provides insight into communication in a range of contexts and helps students develop concrete skills as communicators. This book is unique in its incorporation of social diversity and in its emphasis on theories, research, and skills developed by scholars of communication.

Integrated Attention to Social Diversity

Social diversity is one of the most significant features of life in the United States. Our culture includes people of different ethnicities, ages, genders, physical and mental abilities, and sexual orientations. The notion of America as a melting pot in which all differences are homogenized has given way to metaphors such as the family quilt. Just as a family quilt consists of squares with distinct integrity, so does our culture consist of people with unique histories and identities; just as the individual squares in a family quilt create an exquisite whole, so do the different people in America make up a glorious overall culture. We do not need to erase or dilute differences to have a vibrant, rich society.

Communication in Our Lives encourages students to appreciate social diversity as a strength of cultural life and weaves social diversity into the basic fabric of human communication. Rather than segregating diversity into sidebars that are set apart from the main text, I have infused every chapter with material on race, class, gender, sexual orientation, ethnicity, and other anchors of individual identity and communication style. For example, in Chapter 10 I note how cultural values affect communication in groups and teams. In discussing personal identity in Chapter 3, I point out how social views of race, class, gender, and sexual orientation affect self-concept.

In addition to weaving social diversity into my basic approach to communication, Chapter 7 is devoted exclusively to communication and culture as one of the foundations of effective interaction in today's world. This chapter provides a sustained and focused exploration of the reciprocal relationship between culture and communication.

Emphasis on Communication Theory, Research, and Skills

The first books written for the hybrid course in communication relied extensively on theories and research from disciplines such as psychology and sociology. Doing so made sense when communication was a young field without its own base of knowledge and theories. Although communication continues to contribute to and draw from other disciplines, it is a substantive field in its own right. Scholars of communication have developed an impressive range of theories and research that shed light on the dynamics of human interaction.

Communication in Our Lives highlights theories, research, and skills developed by scholars of communication. For example, Chapter 9 provides coverage of relational dialectics, a theory developed by Leslie Baxter, a professor of communication at the University of Iowa. Chapter 9 also discusses research conducted by communication scholars on the topic of negotiating safer sex in an era shadowed by HIV and AIDS. I emphasize the work of professionals in communication, both because that work is sound and valuable and because accenting it allows students to appreciate the substantive depth of the communication field.

Special Features of *Communication in Our Lives*

I've already noted two distinct features of this book: incorporation of social diversity into all chapters and emphasis on theories, research, and skills developed by scholars of communication. In addition to those two features, there are several other aspects of this book that make it interesting and valuable to students.

First, as I said earlier, I adopt a conversational style of writing, rather than the more distanced and formal style often employed by textbook authors. I share with students some of my experiences in communicating with others, and I invite them to think with me about important issues and difficult challenges surrounding communication in our everyday lives. The accessible, informal writing style encourages students to interact personally with the ideas that I present.

A second feature of this book is the student commentaries. Every chapter is enriched by reflections on experience that were written by students in my classes. The questions, insights, and concerns expressed by diverse students enlarge the viewpoints represented in this book. Further, they invite readers to reflect on their own experiences as communicators.

Communication in Our Lives also includes pedagogical features that promote learning and skill development. Punctuating each chapter are Everyday Applications, which help students apply concepts and develop skills that are discussed in the text. Each chapter also includes a number of Communication Highlights, which call attention to interesting communication research and examples of communication issues in everyday life. Focus Questions open each chapter so that students have a preview of the main ideas to be covered. Concluding each chapter are questions that encourage students to reflect on and discuss material that has been presented.

Additional Resources for Instructors

Accompanying the textbook are instructional resources that complement and extend its coverage. I have written an Instructor's Resource Manual that describes alternative approaches to teaching the basic course, provides a wealth of class-tested exercises, and suggests journal entries and films and panels. Also included in the manual are transparency masters and sample test items. Full-color transparency acetates and computerized testing are also available to instructors who adopt this text.

Two other pedagogical resources accompany *Communication in Our Lives*. One is the Student Companion, which I wrote to provide students with practical exercises and inventories that guide them in applying concepts and developing skills discussed in the book. The Student Companion includes exercises, observation forms, and other activities that instructors may assign either outside of class or as part of classroom activity. Pages in the Student Companion are perforated so that assigned activities may be turned in to instructors. Also accompanying *Communication in Our Lives* is the Wadsworth Basic Communication Videotape, which is available to instructors who adopt this text.

ACKNOWLEDGMENTS

All books grow out of more than one person's efforts, and *Communication in Our Lives* is no exception. Many people have helped this book evolve from an early vision to the final form you hold in your hands. My greatest debt is to my editor, Todd Armstrong. From start to finish he has been a full partner in the project, offering ideas, responding thoughtfully to initial drafts, working with me and others to design the overall book, and giving me the benefits of his personal insights and editorial expertise. Not only a superb editor, Todd is also a friend I cherish.

I am also indebted to the following individuals who reviewed drafts of *Communication in Our Lives* and who were extraordinarily generous in offering suggestions for improving the final book: Robert Bohlken, Northwest Missouri State University; Tamara L. Burk, The College of William and Mary; Jamie M. Byrne, Millersville University; Diane Casagrande, West Chester

University; April Chatham-Carpenter, University of Northern Iowa; Dennis Dufer, St. Louis Community College-Meramec; Lisa Goodnight, Purdue University-Calumet; Joanne Keyton, University of Memphis; Bobbie Klopp, Kirkwood Community College; Minh A. Luong, Purdue University; Kim Niemczyk, Palm Beach Community College; Nan Peck, Northern Virginia Community College-Annandale; Diane Prusank, University of Hartford; Ed Schiappa, University of Minnesota; and Ruth Wallinger, Frostburg State University.

I could not have written this book without the support of the Department of Communication Studies at the University of North Carolina at Chapel Hill. There I am blessed by generous and helpful colleagues who are always willing to discuss ideas and to share insights. In addition, the undergraduate and graduate students in my classes have allowed me to experiment with new approaches to communication and have helped me refine ideas and activities that appear in this book. Invariably, my students teach me at least as much as I teach them, and for that I am deeply grateful.

The professionals at Wadsworth have also contributed significantly to *Communication in Our Lives*. Along with Todd Armstrong, others have been remarkable in their creativity, attention to detail, and unflagging insistence on quality. Perhaps just as important is the patience they have shown in dealing with my quirks and weaknesses as a writer. I thank Vicki Friedberg, production editor; Melissa Andrews, copy editor; Carolyn Deacy, text and cover designer; Laura Murray, art editor; Stephen Forsling, photo researcher; Michael Gillespie, editorial assistant; Robert Kauser, permissions editor; Barbara Britton, print buyer; and Lewis DeSimone, project development editor.

Finally, and always, I acknowledge my partner Robbie Cox. As is the case with everything I do, this book has benefited from his presence in my life. Living with him for more than 20 years has enriched my appreciation of the possibilities for growth, kindness, love, and magic between people. He remains my best critic and greatest fan, and both his criticism and support have shaped the final form of this book.

Julia T. Wood

Communication in Our Lives

by Julia T. Wood

A STUDENT'S GUIDE TO LEARNING

Communication is relevant to virtually every aspect of your life, whether you're talking with others to sustain personal relationships, speaking to a group, or working through an idea by talking to yourself. *Communication in Our Lives* is written for anyone interested in human communication. It includes timely theories and research generated by scholars of communication, as well as practical advice and guidelines for your everyday interactions.

Each chapter highlights the experiences and orientations of diverse people and discusses the commonalities and differences among us. For instance, Chapter 7 focuses exclusively on communication and culture. This chapter is designed to heighten your awareness of the ways in which language expresses cultural values and how communication can shape and change the character of cultures.

Learning aids such as Student Commentaries, Communication Highlights, and Everyday Applications are included in every chapter. These features are designed to provide insight, spark discussion, highlight important information, and show you how the text material pertains to your everyday life.

I hope you'll take a few minutes to read the next five pages. They offer an overview of the special features of the book and help you understand how communication works—or doesn't—in a variety of situations. In short, they introduce you to ways in which this book will give you opportunities to strengthen your skills as a communicator!

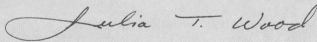

Wadsworth Publishing Company

I(T)P An International Thomson Publishing Company

INTEGRATING COMMUNICATION THEORY AND PRACTICE

Communication in Our Lives will show you how theories help us understand everyday experiences. This book demonstrates that effective practice is based on theory—the knowledge of how and why the communication process works and what is likely to result from different kinds of communication. You will see the importance of adapting your personal and professional communication to be effective with the variety of people who make up our society.

(Jane Golden, detail from *Ocean Park Pier* (1976). Ocean Park Boulevard and Main Street, Santa Monica, Calif. © Jane Golden, photo courtesy the artist and Social Public Art Resource Center, Venice, Calif.)

And he has no idea how to deal with a group that can't get on track. He and six other students have worked for 3 months to organize a student book co-op, but the group can't get its act together. By now everyone is really frustrated, and nobody listens to anyone else. When he checked his electronic mail earlier today, Mike found angry messages from three of the group members. He shrugs again and leaves to meet Coreen.

Like Mike, most of us communicate continuously in our daily lives. Effective communication is vital to long-distance friendships, romantic relationships, public speaking, interviewing, and productive group discussion. Communication opportunities and demands fill our everyday lives.

Mike and all of us continue to rely on communication long after the college years. Even if you don't pursue a career such as teaching or law, which require strong speaking skills, communication will be essential in your work. You may want to persuade your boss you deserve a raise, represent your neighborhood in a zoning hearing, or work with colleagues to develop company policies. You will have conflicts with co-workers, romantic partners, and friends. You may need to deal with superiors who tell racist jokes or harass you sexually. Each of these situations calls for communication skills. The ability to communicate effectively is vital to personal and professional well-being and to the health of our society.

WHY STUDY COMMUNICATION?

Because you've been communicating all of your life, you might be asking what is gained by formal study. One answer is that formal study can improve skill. Some individuals have a natural aptitude that enables them to play basketball fairly well. They could be even more effective, however, if they studied theories of offensive and defensive play. Likewise, even if you communicate well now, learning about communication can make you more effective.

Another reason to study communication is that theories and principles help us to make sense of what happens in our everyday lives, and they help us have personal impact. For instance, learning about different gender communication cultures would help Mike understand why Coreen, like many women, enjoys talking about relationships more than he and men in general do. If Mike had better insight into the communication that sustains

What Can Be Gained by Studying Communication?

This excerpt (left) from *Chapter 1: The World of Communication* shows you how studying communication theories can make you a better communicator and help you make sense of what happens in your everyday life.

ABBY

Until I took a course in women's studies, I didn't realize how biased textbooks are. We learned that a lot of textbooks use more examples and pictures with men than women and that men are described more actively. Once the teacher pointed this out, I noticed it in my chemistry and psychology books and in the texts for other classes. Now no matter what I read, I notice whether women are underrepresented.

What we select to notice is also influenced by who we are and what is going on inside us. Our motives and needs affect what we see and don't see. If you've just broken up with a partner, you're more likely to notice attractive people at a party than if you are in an established romantic relationship. Motives also explain the oasis phenomenon in which thirsty people stranded in a desert see an oasis although none really exists. Our expectations further affect what we notice. We are more likely to perceive what we expect to perceive and what others lead us to anticipate. This explains the phenomenon of **self-fulfilling prophecy** in which a person acts in ways that are consistent with how others describe her or him. A child who is told she is unlovable may perceive herself that way and notice rejecting but not affirming communication from others. We selectively tune in to only some stimuli, so that we simplify the complexities of the world in which we live.

Expectations greatly influence how we perceive others, particularly people who differ from us in some way. In an experiment, racially prejudiced and unprejudiced European Americans were asked to describe African Americans pictured in photographs. The prejudiced viewers "saw" stereotypical racial characteristics such as broad noses and full lips, even when those features were not present. The unprejudiced viewers didn't notice stereotypical racial qualities. This study demonstrates how powerfully expectations can mold what we see (Secord, Bevan, & Katz, 1956).

LEE TENG-HUI

Before I came to school here, I was told that Americans are very pushy, loud, and selfish. For my first few months here, I saw that was true of Americans just as I had been told it would be. It took me longer to see also that Americans are friendly and helpful, because I had not been taught to expect these qualities.

Organization

Once we have selected what to notice, we must make sense of it. We don't simply collect perceptions and string them together randomly; instead, we organize them in meaningful ways. The most useful theory for explaining how we organize perceptions is **constructivism**, which states that we organize and interpret experience by applying cognitive structures called **schemata**. Originally developed by George Kelly in 1955, constructivism

Perception: How We Make Sense of the World

This excerpt (right) from *Chapter 2: Perception and Communication* demonstrates how our expectations can be greatly influenced by how we perceive others.

TONE AND CONTENT TO ENHANCE YOUR UNDERSTANDING OF COMMUNICATION

A personal, conversational tone is used to make the content of *Communication in Our Lives* interesting and applicable to your life.

How Language Influences Cultural Views of Personal Identity

This excerpt (right) from *Chapter 7: Communication and Cultures* exemplifies the conversational tone used throughout the book. In this instance, a description is given for how language reflects cultural views of personal identity.

in specific circumstances. For instance, in the United States, salads are usually served before a main course, but they follow it in France and much of Europe. In China, defendants are presumed guilty, whereas in the United States, they are presumed innocent until proven guilty. In America, children are expected to grow up and leave their families of origin in order to start their own families. In some Asian societies, however, children are expected to live with or near their parents and to operate as a single large family. What we view as normal reflects the teachings of our particular culture, not absolute truths. The values endorsed by a culture are woven into communication, so that how people talk and interact nonverbally both reflect and perpetuate particular cultural values.

Norms are often rooted in cultural traditions. For example, in the United States and some other countries, women have assumed their husbands' names because of the tradition that a man is the head of a household. Although some couples now choose not to use the man's name for their identities, the tradition of regarding men as heads of families still prevails and, with it, the normative practice of women's symbolically becoming one with their husbands. Norms of communication may also reflect cultural values. In the United States, for instance, there are many norms that respect the values of individuals' privacy, property, and autonomy: knocking on closed doors, asking permission to borrow others' property, having separate utensils for eating and serving food and individual places for meals, and moving without consulting any authorities. In countries with collectivist values, however, different communicative norms prevail. Koreans do not set individual places, and they use the same utensils for serving and eating. In China, no citizen would change jobs or move without first getting approval from the local unit of the Communist Party (Ferrante, 1995).

Language Language shapes how we think about the world and ourselves. As we saw in Chapter 5, language is packed with values. Consequently, in the process of learning language, we learn our culture's values, beliefs, and norms. The value that most Asian cultures attach to age is structured into Asian languages. For instance, the Korean language makes fine distinctions among different ages, and any remark to another person must acknowledge the other's age (Ferrante, 1995). To say "I am going to school" in Korean, a teenager would say "hakkyo-eh gahndah" to a peer of the same age, "hakkyo-eh gah" to a parent, and "hakkyo-eh gahneh" to a grandparent (Park, 1979).

Language also reflects cultural views of personal identity. Western cultures tend to emphasize individuals, whereas many Eastern cultures place greater emphasis on family and community than on individuals. It's unlikely that an Eastern textbook on human communication would even include a chapter on self, which is standard in Western textbooks. If I were a Korean, I would introduce myself as Wood Julia to communicate the greater value placed on familial than personal identity.

EXASPERATED? TRY TO THINK OF YOUR MATE AS A CROSS-CULTURAL EXPERIENCE!

I AM NOT TRYING TO BE ALOOF-I'M A DAMNED CAT, OKAY?!

(© 1992 by Jennifer Berman. Reprinted by permission.)

Another general difference is what each sex regards as the primary basis of relationships. For men, activities tend to be a key foundation of close friendships and romantic relationships (Inman, 1996; Swain, 1989; Wood & Inman, 1993). Thus, men typically cement friendships through doing things together (playing soccer, working on cars, watching sports) and through doing things for one another (trading favors, washing a car, doing laundry). Many women see communication as the crux of relationships. It is not only a means to instrumental ends, but an end in itself. Thus women often regard talking about feelings, personal issues, and daily life as the way to build and continuously enrich relationships.

Given the differences between how women and men, in general, use communication, it's hardly surprising that the sexes often misunderstand one another. One clash between gender communication cultures occurs when women and men discuss problems. When women talk about something that is troubling them, they are often looking first for communication that expresses empathy and connection. Yet masculine socialization teaches men to use communication instrumentally, so they tend to offer advice or solutions (Tannen, 1990; Wood, 1994d, 1996b). Thus, women sometimes interpret men's advice as communicating lack of personal concern. On the other hand, men may feel frustrated when women offer empathy and support instead of advice for solving problems. In general, men also make fewer personal disclosures, whereas women regard sharing confidences as an important way to enhance closeness (Aries, 1987; Johnson, 1996).

Men and women, in general, also have different styles of listening. Socialized to be responsive and expressive, women tend to make listening noises such as "um hm," "yeah," and "I know what you mean" when others are talking (Tannen, 1990; Wood, 1996b). This is how they show they are following and interested. Masculine culture, however, doesn't emphasize affirming others vocally or verbally, so men tend to make fewer listening noises than women. Thus, women sometimes feel men aren't listening to them because men don't symbolize their attention in the ways women have learned to expect. Men may also misinterpret women's listening noises as indicating agreement (versus attention) and be surprised if women later disagree with their ideas.

Perhaps the most common complication in communication between the genders occurs when a woman says "Let's talk about us." To men this often means trouble, because they interpret the request as implying there is a problem in a relationship. For women, however, this is not the only—

Gender as a Co-Culture: How Communication Practices Differ

This excerpt (left) from Chapter 7 describes common differences in the ways women and men communicate and shows how these differences can cause misunderstandings.

THE FOUNDATION OF EFFECTIVE COMMUNICATION

Communication in Our Lives shows you that by studying and practicing the ideas presented, you will become a more confident and competent communicator.

Planning a Public Speech That Has Impact

In this excerpt (left) from *Chapter 12: Planning Public Speaking,* you learn the importance of analyzing your audience before giving a speech. In order to entertain, inform, or persuade people with a speech, the views and perspectives of your listeners need to be considered.

A thesis statement refines what you've already done in limiting your topic and defining your purpose. Chris's thesis statement for his speech was this: Donating blood is painless, quick, and lifesaving for others. Although Chris's listeners may have forgotten many of the specific points in his speech, they remembered his main idea, which is the purpose of a thesis statement.

The foundation of effective public speaking is choosing and clarifying the focus of communication. As we've seen, this requires you to select and narrow a topic, define a primary purpose, and develop a clear, concise thesis statement. We're now ready to consider how listeners shape the goals, content, and style of public speaking.

ANALYZING YOUR AUDIENCE

In one of my classes, a student named Odell gave a persuasive speech designed to convince listeners to support affirmative action. He was personally compelling and dynamic in his delivery, and his ideas were well organized. The only problem was that his audience had little background on affirmative action, and he didn't explain exactly what the policy involves. He assumed listeners understood how affirmative action works, and he focused on its positive effects. His listeners weren't persuaded because Odell failed to give them information necessary to their support. Odell's speech also illustrates our earlier point that speeches often combine more than one speaking purpose—in this case giving information was essential to Odell's larger goal of persuading listeners.

In another class, a student named Christie spoke passionately about the morality of vegetarianism. She provided dramatic evidence of the cruelty animals suffer as they are raised and slaughtered. When we polled students after her speech, only two had been persuaded to consider vegetarianism. Why was Christie ineffective? She didn't recognize and address listeners' beliefs that vegetarianism wasn't healthy and that vegetarian foods are unappetizing. Christie mistakenly assumed that listeners would know it's easy to get sufficient protein, vitamins, and minerals without consuming meat, and she assumed they would understand vegetarian foods can be delicious. However, her listeners *didn't* know that, and they weren't about to consider a diet that they thought wasn't nutritious or palatable.

The mistake that Christie and Odell made was not adapting to their audiences. It's impossible to entertain, inform, or persuade people if we don't consider their perspectives on our topics. Speakers need to understand what listeners already know and believe and what reservations they might have about what we say (McGuire, 1989). To paraphrase the advice of an ancient Greek rhetorician, "The fool persuades me with his or her reasons, the wise person with my own." That is, effective speakers understand and work with listeners' reasons, values, knowledge, and concerns. This advice is as wise today as it was over 2,000 years ago.

POSITIVE SELF-FULFILLING PROPHECY

Georgia Tech's Challenge program is a bridge course designed to help disadvantaged, primarily minority students succeed academically. Yet for years, students who enrolled in Challenge did no better than disadvantaged students who didn't attend.

Norman Johnson, a special assistant to the president of Tech, explained that Challenge failed because the program was based on the idea that disadvantaged students were dumb. The whole program was set up on a deficit model. Knowing the power of self-fulfilling prophecy, Johnson revamped the program by telling instructors that Challenge students were unusually bright and were quick learners.

Once Challenge teachers expected success from their students, they communicated this expectation by the way they acted toward the students. The results were impressive: In 1992, 10% of the first-year Challenge students had perfect 4.0 averages for the academic year. By comparison, only 5% of the white students who didn't participate in Challenge had perfect averages. That 10% was more than all of the minority students who had achieved 4.0 averages in the entire 1980–1990 decade. When teachers expected Challenge students to do well and communicated those expectations, the students in fact did well—a case of a positive self-fulfilling prophecy.

Source: Raspberry, W. (1994, July 5). Major gains in minorities' grades at Tech. *Raleigh News and Observer*, p. A9.

---

children, so daughters are told "Nice girls don't play rough," "Be kind to your friends," and "Don't mess up your clothes." Sons, on the other hand, are more likely to be told "Go out and get 'em," "Stick up for yourself," and "Don't cry." As we hear these messages, we pick up our parents' and society's gender expectations.

Family members provide direct communication about many aspects of who we are through statements they make. Positive labels enhance our self-esteem: "You're so responsible," "You are smart," "You're sweet," "You're great at soccer." Negative labels can damage children's self-esteem: "You're a troublemaker," "You're stupid," and "You're impossible" are messages that demolish a child's sense of self-worth.

Direct definition also takes place as family members respond to children's behaviors. If a child clowns around and parents respond by saying "What a cut-up; you really are funny," the child learns to see herself or himself as funny. If a child dusts furniture and receives praise ("You're great to help me clean the house"), being helpful to others is reinforced as part of the child's self-concept. From direct definition, children learn what parents value, and this shapes what they come to value. For instance, in my family, reading was considered very important. I was great at outdoor activities such as building tree houses and leading "jungle expeditions" through the woods behind our home. Yet my parents were indifferent to my aptitudes for adventures and physical activity. What they stressed was learning and reading. I still have vivid memories of being shamed for a "B"

The Importance of Groups and Teams

This excerpt (right) from *Chapter 10: Foundations of Group and Team Communication* discusses the strengths of group communication—starting with greater resources, and moving on to more thoroughness and creativity and greater commitment to decisions.

---

resist co[...]
ng and t[...]
s that m[...]
iverse id[...]
discussion o[...]
is relevant to[...]

Conform[...]
extremely ch[...]
members. Ev[...]
the status to[...]
doesn't inten[...]
status, howe[...]
ple, often tri[...]
so highly tha[...]
ing and agree[...]
trates, often [...]
of pressures [...]
against the p[...]

LAN[...]

I used to belong to a creative writing group where all of us helped each other improve our writing. We were all equally vocal, and we had a lot of good discussions and even disagreements when the group first started. But then one member of the group got a story of hers accepted by a big magazine, and all of a sudden we thought of her as a better writer than any of us. She didn't act any different, but we saw her as more accomplished, so when she said something everybody listened and nobody disagreed. It was like a wet blanket on our creativity because her opinion just carried too much weight once she got published.

Strengths of Groups

The primary potential strengths of groups in comparison to individuals are that groups generally have greater resources, are more thorough, are more creative, and generate greater commitment to decisions (Wood, 1992a).

Greater Resources   A group obviously exceeds any individual's in the number of ideas, perspectives, experiences, and expertise it can bring to bear on solving a problem. Especially in teams, the different resources of individual members are a key to effectiveness. One member may know the technical aspects of a product, another understands market psychology, a third is talented in advertising, and so forth. Health care teams consist of specialists who combine their knowledge to care for a patient. When my father was hospitalized after a series of strokes, we had a health care team that included a neurologist, a cardiologist, a physical therapist, a social worker, and a registered nurse. Each member of the team had a different expertise, and they coordinated their specific skills and knowledge to provide him with integrated care.

How Family Members Affect Our Self-Concepts

This excerpt (above) from Chapter 3 explains that family members influence our self-concepts by how they describe us and respond to our behavior.

USEFUL TOOLS FOR IMPROVED COMMUNICATION SKILLS

Two learning tools are used liberally throughout *Communication in Our Lives*—Communication Highlights and Everyday Applications. They are designed to help you understand how learning about communication and learning to communicate are important skills for effective living.

Communication Highlights

Offering springboards for class discussion, Communication Highlight boxes illuminate ideas that merit special attention and highlight interesting findings from communication research. This box from *Chapter 6: The Nonverbal Dimension of Communication* illustrates the power of nonverbal communication.

Communication Highlight

CLEVER HANS

In the 1900s, Herr von Osten trained his horse Hans to count by tapping his front hoof. Hans learned quickly and was soon able to multiply, add, divide, subtract, and perform complex mathematical calculations. He could even count the number of people in a room or the number of people wearing eyeglasses. Herr von Osten took Hans on a promotional tour. At shows he would ask Hans to add 5 and 8, divide 100 by 10, and do other computations. In every case Hans performed flawlessly, leading others to call him "Clever Hans." Because some doubters thought Clever Hans's feats involved deceit, proof of his mathematical abilities was demanded.

The first test involved computing numbers that were stated on stage by people other than von Osten. Using his hoof, Hans pounded out the correct answers. However, he didn't fare so well on the second test in which one person whispered a number into Hans's left ear and a different person whispered a number into his right ear. Hans was told to add the two numbers and pound out the sum, an answer not known by anyone present. Hans couldn't solve the problem. On further investigation, it was deduced that Hans could solve problems only if someone he could see knew the answer. When Hans was given numbers and asked to compute them, viewers leaned forward and tensed their bodies as Hans began tapping his hoof. When Hans tapped the correct number, onlookers relaxed their body postures and nodded their heads, which was Hans's signal to stop tapping. Hans was clever, not because he could calculate, but because he could read nonverbal communication.

Source: Sebeok, T. A., & Rosenthal, R. (Eds.). (1981). *The Clever Hans phenomenon: Communication with horses, whales, apes and people.* New York: New York Academy of Sciences.

For good reason, poets call the eyes "the mirrors of the soul." Our eyes communicate some of the most important and complex messages about how we feel. If you watch infants, you'll notice that they focus on others' eyes. Babies become terrified if they can't see their mothers' eyes, but they aren't bothered when other parts of their mothers' faces are hidden (Spitz, 1965). As adults, we often look at eyes to judge emotions, honesty, interest, and self-confidence. This explains why strong eye contact tends to heighten the credibility of public speakers.

Haptics

Haptics, or touch, refers to nonverbal communication involving physical touch. Touch is the first of our five senses to develop (Leathers, 1976), and many communication scholars believe touching and being touched are essential to a healthy life. Research reveals that mothers in dysfunctional families touch babies less often and less affectionately than mothers in

attending meetings, interacting with superiors on the job, clerks, and relaxing with friends. We use scripts to organi[ze] into lines of action.

Prototypes, personal constructs, stereotypes, and scrip[ts] schemata that we use to organize how we think about pe[ople and situa]tions. They help us make sense of what we notice and an[ticipate how we] and others will act in particular situations. The cognitive [schemata that] reflect how our culture and specific social groups organize [thinking. When] we interact with others, we internalize their ways of classi[fying experience] and predicting norms for acting in various situations.

Social perspectives are not always accurate or constru[ctive, so we] shouldn't accept them unreflectively. For instance, if your [family engaged] in bitter, destructive quarreling, you may have learned a s[cript for conflict] that will undermine your relationships. Similarly, many W[esterners have] negative and inaccurate perceptions of some groups of pe[ople. We should] assess these views critically before using them to organize [our percep]tions and direct our own activities.

Everyday Application

PERCEIVING OTHERS

Pay attention to the cognitive schemata you use the next time you meet a new person. First, notice how you classify the person. Do you categorize her or him as a potential friend, date, bureaucrat, neighbor? Next, identify the constructs you use to assess the person. Do you focus on physical characteristics (attractive–unattractive), mental qualities (intelligent–unintelligent), psychological features (secure–insecure), and/or interpersonal qualities (eligible–committed)? Would different constructs be prominent if you used a different prototype to classify the person? Now, note how you stereotype the person. What do you expect him or her to do based on the prototype and constructs you've applied? Finally, identify your script—how you expect interaction to unfold between the two of you.

Interpretation

People, interactions, and situations have no intrinsic meaning. Instead, we assign meaning by interpreting what we have noticed and organized. **Interpretation** is the subjective process of explaining perceptions in ways that let us make sense of them. To interpret the meaning of others' actions, we construct explanations for what they say and do.

Everyday Applications

Everyday Application sections show you how the material in this book pertains to your everyday life. In this example from Chapter 2, you learn to become more aware of your perceptions when you meet a new person.

ADDITIONAL LEARNING AIDS

The following learning aids are designed to expand on the ideas in the book and spark further discussion in your classroom and elsewhere.

Student Commentaries

Communication in Our Lives includes excerpts from students' journals in every chapter. These commentaries enhance the material in the text by adding to the voices and views it represents. This example (left) from Chapter 8 illustrates how expressing awareness of another's perspective in a work setting can improve employee morale and retention.

DAN

My supervisor did an excellent job of letting me know I was valued even when I got passed over for a promotion last year. I'd worked hard and felt I had earned it. Jake, my supervisor, came to my office to talk to me before the promotion was announced. He told me that both I and the other guy were qualified, but that the other person had seniority and also field experience I didn't have. Then Jake told me he was assigning me to a field position for 6 months so that I could get the experience I needed to get promoted the next time a position opened up. Jake communicated that he understood how I felt and that he was supporting me, even if I didn't get the promotion. His talk made all the difference in how I felt about staying with the company.

Self-Disclose When Appropriate

As we noted earlier, self-disclosure allows people to know each other in greater depth. For this reason, it's an important communication skill, especially in the early stages of relationships. Research indicates that appropri-

230

For Further Reflection and Discussion

Each chapter closes with a "For Further Reflection and Discussion" section designed to help you reflect on the material you've read and become more aware of your own beliefs. Item 2 (left) from *Chapter 13: Researching and Developing Support for Public Speeches* asks you to explain how the process of researching a speech has affected your understandings, beliefs, and speaking goal.

SUMMARY

This chapter extended the previous one by considering ways to research speeches and support ideas to be presented. Just as when you are first planning a speech, your listeners should influence how you research and support it. Thus, you need to ask yourself what kinds of research and what forms of support your particular listeners are most likely to find interesting and credible.

The process of researching a speech includes reviewing your personal experiences and knowledge relevant to your topics, interviewing experts who can expand your insight into the subject, scouting libraries for evidence, and conducting surveys to find out about others' beliefs, practices, and knowledge that are relevant to your topic. It isn't unusual for speakers to revise the focus of a speech in the course of conducting research. This is appropriate when information that you discover modifies or alters your knowledge or even your position.

Research for a speech provides speakers with different kinds of evidence that may be used to clarify, dramatize, and energize a speech. The five types of evidence we discussed are statistics, examples, analogies, quotations, and visual aids. These are effective forms of support when they are used thoughtfully and are adapted sensitively to the attitudes, values, and knowledge of listeners.

Now that you've gone through the phases of planning, researching, and finding support for public speaking, we're ready to consider the final steps in designing effective presentations. Chapter 14 explains how to organize and present public speeches. Before you move on to Chapter 14, take a moment to fill in the checklist on the next page for researching and supporting your speech.

FOR FURTHER REFLECTION AND DISCUSSION

1. After you've interviewed two experts on your topic, reflect on what you learned. What did they explain, reveal, or show you that added to your knowledge of the topic? What did you learn from lines of talk that they initiated?

2. With others in your class, discuss how the process of researching your speech affected your understandings, beliefs, and speaking goal. Explain what changed and why it did.

3. Construct a mind map to record evidence you discover while researching your speech. Does this method seem more holistic and helpful than a traditional listing of evidence?

4. During the next week, pay attention to evidence that others cite in public presentations. You might notice what evidence is used on news programs, by professors in classes, and by special speakers on your campus. Evaluate the effectiveness of evidence that others use. Are visuals clear and uncluttered? Do speakers explain the qualifications of sources they cite, and are those sources adequately unbiased? What examples and analogies are presented, and how effective are they?

5. Notice the use of stories to add to interest and impact to public presentations. Describe a speaker who uses a story effectively and one who uses a story ineffectively. What are the differences between the two cases? What conclusions can you draw about the effective use of stories in public presentations?

KEY TERMS

credibility
initial credibility
derived credibility
terminal credibility
survey research
evidence
statistics
examples
comparisons
similes
analogies
quotations
halo effect
visual aids

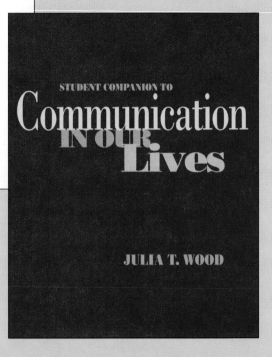

STUDENT COMPANION TO

Communication
IN OUR
Lives

JULIA T. WOOD

Student Companion

This comprehensive study guide (right) will complement and expand your understanding of the concepts discussed in the book. It includes a summary of each chapter, lists of vocabulary terms for key concepts, activities on perforated pages, and self-test questions.

Communication in Our Lives

PART ONE

Foundations
of Communication

Focus Questions

1 Which aspects of your life are affected by communication?

2 How does the author's identity shape this book?

3 How does social diversity influence how people communicate and how we think about communication?

Introduction

A friend comes to you with a problem, and you aren't sure how to comfort and support him.

You've been invited to interview for your dream job, and getting it depends on communicating effectively in the interview.

A group you belong to is working on recycling programs for the campus, but you don't know how to make group discussion productive.

At the end of the term, your romantic partner will graduate and take a job in a city that's 1,000 miles away, and you wonder how to communicate across the distance.

The major project in one of your courses is an oral research report, so your grade depends on your public speaking ability.

Julia T. Wood. (© Billy Barnes)

Situations such as these illustrate the importance of communication in our everyday lives. Unlike some of the subjects you study, communication is relevant to virtually every aspect of your life. We communicate with ourselves when we work through ideas, psych ourselves up for big moments, and talk ourselves into or out of various adventures. We communicate with others to build and sustain personal relationships, perform our jobs and advance in our careers, and participate in social and civic activities. Every facet of life involves communication.

Although communication is pervasive, it isn't always effective. People who have inadequate communication knowledge and skills are handicapped in their efforts to achieve personal, professional, and social goals. On the other hand, individuals who communicate well have a keen advantage in accomplishing their objectives. This suggests that learning about communication and learning how to communicate are keys to effective living.

Communication in Our Lives is designed to help you understand how communication works in personal, professional, and social life. To open the book, I'll introduce myself and describe the basic approach and special features of *Communication in Our Lives*.

INTRODUCTION TO THE AUTHOR

As an undergraduate, I enrolled in a course much like the one you're taking now. It was an introductory class in which we studied a variety of communication forms and contexts. In that course, I began a love affair with the field of communication—one that has endured for more than 20 years. Today I am still in love with the field—more, in fact, than ever. I see communication as the basis of cultural life and a primary tool for social change. This makes communication one of the most dynamic and important areas of study in higher education. It is a field that is both theoretically rich and pragmatically useful. I know of no discipline that offers more valuable insights, skills, and knowledge than communication.

Because communication is central to our lives, I feel I am fortunate to be able to teach communication courses and conduct research in the field. Working with students allows me to help them improve their communication skills and, thus, their effectiveness in many arenas. Research and writing continuously enlarge my understanding of communication and let me share what I learn with others like you.

Since you will be reading this book, you should know something about the person who wrote it. I am a 45-year-old middle-class Caucasian heterosexual who has strong spiritual beliefs. For more than 20 years I have been married to Robbie Cox, who is also a professor of communication at my university. As is true for all of us, who I am affects what I know, and how I think, act, communicate, and feel. For instance, many of the examples I share in the chapters that follow reflect my teaching and research

(Shi-Ling Hsiang, *Dance Before Dusk*, acrylic on canvas, 32 × 26". Courtesy and © Shi-Ling Hsiang.)

in the areas of gender, personal relationships, and communication. I draw from my knowledge of these areas to illustrate concepts and principles of communication.

Other facets of my identity also influence what I know and how I write. My race, gender, social class, and sexual orientation have given me certain kinds of insight and obscured others. As a woman, I understand discrimination based on sex, since I've personally experienced it. I do not, however, have personal knowledge of racial discrimination, since Western culture confers privilege on European Americans. Being middle class has shielded me from personal experience with hunger, poverty, and class bias, and being heterosexual has spared me from homophobic prejudice. Who you are also influences your experiences and knowledge.

Although our identity limits what we personally know and experience, it doesn't completely prevent insight into people and situations different from our own. From conversations with others and from reading, I have gained some understanding of kinds of discrimination that I haven't personally experienced. In our increasingly diverse world, all of us need to learn about a variety of people, lifestyles, and cultures. We need to understand and communicate effectively with people whose communication styles differ from our own. What we learn by studying and interacting with people of diverse cultural heritages expands our appreciation of the richness and complexity of humanity. In addition, learning about and forming relationships with people different from ourselves enlarges our own repertoire of communication skills. *Communication in Our Lives* includes much of what I've learned about different cultural groups and how they communicate.

The majority of my time is spent teaching and writing, both of which I enjoy greatly. I find teaching particularly gratifying because it allows me to open students' eyes to the wonder and value of communication and to share in their pleasure as they refine their skills as communicators. Writing is another way I share my passion for communication and the knowledge I've acquired over the past two decades. I hope that you'll enjoy reading *Communication in Our Lives* as much as I enjoyed writing it. To provide a context for your reading, let me share my vision of this book.

INTRODUCTION TO THE BOOK

Communication in Our Lives introduces you to many forms and functions of communication in modern life. The title reflects my belief that communication is an important part of our everyday lives.

Coverage

Because communication is a continuous part of life, we need to understand how it works—or doesn't—in a range of situations. Thus, this book covers a broad spectrum of communication encounters, from communication with yourself to communication with friends and romantic partners and communication in group and public situations.

Because this book surveys many types of communication, it cannot provide great depth in any area. Your instructor and the people in your class may choose to extend and elaborate specific topics that are especially important to you. The breadth of communication issues and skills presented in this book can be adapted to the interests, needs, and preferences of individual classes and instructors.

The many forms and contexts of communication that you will explore in this book are visually reinforced by a range of artwork on the pages that follow. You'll find diagrams that illustrate the concepts discussed and photographs of diverse people engaged in informal and formal communication, personal and public interaction, and relaxed and tense encounters. Each chapter also features a fine art selection that invites you to consider and appreciate metaphorical and artistic perspectives on human communication. I hope you will feel, as I do, that the artwork in this book provides a visual text that complements and enhances the written one.

Students

Communication in Our Lives is written for anyone who is interested in human communication. It is equally appropriate for majors and nonmajors. If you are a communication major, this book and the course it accompanies will provide you with a firm foundation for more advanced study. If you are majoring in another discipline, *Communication in Our Lives* and the course you are taking will give you a sound basic understanding of communication and opportunities to strengthen your skills as a communicator.

Learning should be enjoyable, not a chore. Textbooks don't have to be dry, and specialized jargon is seldom necessary. I've written this book in an informal, personal style; for instance, I refer to myself as "I" rather than "the author," and I use contractions ("can't" and "you're" instead of the more formal "cannot" and "you are") as we do in normal conversation. To heighten interest, I punctuate chapters with concrete examples and insights from students at my university and other campuses around the country.

Every facet of life involves communication. (©Tom Levy/Photo 20-20)

Theory and Practice

Communication in Our Lives reflects my conviction that theory and practice are natural allies. Years ago, the renowned scholar Kurt Lewin said, "There is nothing so practical as a good theory." His words remain true today. In this book, I've blended theory and practice so that each draws on and enriches the other. Effective practice is theoretically informed—it must be based on knowledge of how and why the communication process works and what is likely to result from different kinds of communication. At the same time, effective theories have pragmatic value—they help us understand experiences and events in our everyday lives. Each chapter in this book is informed by the impressive theories and research generated by scholars of communication. For this reason, the perspectives and skills recommended reflect current knowledge of effective communication practices.

FEATURES

Accenting this book are five features that I want to call to your attention.

Focus Questions

Each chapter opens with several focus questions that highlight important topics that will be covered. Reading the questions helps you focus your attention as you study the chapter. Rereading the questions after completing the chapter allows you to check your understanding of ideas and issues that have been discussed.

Integrated Attention to Cultural Diversity

Diversity is woven into the fabric of this book. The United States and the world are culturally diverse, and they always have been. However, the diversity of human beings and the lives we lead have been inadequately recognized and represented in much popular and academic writing. Some books reflect the narrow perspective of white, middle-class Western heterosexuals who are educated and able-bodied. This restrictive focus ignores a great many people who don't fit into that category. In recent years, a number of textbooks have dealt with diversity by adding comments about various groups onto general discussions. For instance, a chapter on leadership might examine how Western, middle-class, Caucasian males lead, and then add a few paragraphs about female leadership. A chapter on communication in personal relationships might focus on interaction patterns between heterosexuals, and only briefly mention communication in gay and lesbian commitments.

This approach to diversity is an important first step in the effort to broaden our understandings of the social world. Yet, we need to do more than append information about people and activities that fall outside of mainstream Western society. In this book, I try to extend these efforts to recognize social diversity by weaving attention to diversity into our basic understandings of human communication.

Awareness of diversity is integral to how we think about communication; it is not something to be tacked on as an afterthought. I integrate cultural diversity into the text in two ways. First, each chapter includes the experiences and orientations of diverse people and highlights commonalities and differences among us. For example, Chapter 9 on personal relationships identifies differences in how women and men generally communicate and provides clues about how the sexes can translate each other's language. Early chapters trace the impact of ethnicity, sexual orientation, gender, and other facets of identity on self-concept and communication practices.

In addition to incorporating diversity into the book as a whole, I focus exclusively on communication and culture in Chapter 7. There you will learn about cultures and co-cultures (distinct groups within a single society) and the ways cultural values and norms shape how we view and practice communication. Just as important, Chapter 7 will heighten your awareness of the power of communication to shape and change the character of cultures. This chapter will extend your insight into the intricate relationships among culture, identity, and communication. In addition, it will enhance your ability to participate effectively in a culturally diverse world.

Student Commentaries

Communication in Our Lives also features commentaries from students. In my classes, students teach me and each other through their insights, experiences, and questions. Because I view students as teachers, I've included reflections written by students at my university and other campuses. As you read the student commentaries, you'll probably identify with some, disagree with others, and be puzzled by still others. Whether you agree, disagree, or are perplexed, I think you'll find that the student commentaries valuably expand the text by adding to the voices and views it represents. In the students' words you will find much insight and much to spark thought and discussion in your class and elsewhere.

Communication Highlights

Communication in Our Lives also includes inserts that highlight particularly important or interesting information about communication. I use Communication Highlight boxes to call your attention to ideas that merit special attention and to highlight particularly interesting findings from communication research. The Communication Highlights offer springboards for class discussions.

Everyday Applications

Finally, there are Everyday Applications, which bring the concepts we discuss to life by showing you how material in the text pertains to your everyday life. They invite you to apply communication principles and skills as you interact with others. Some of the Everyday Applications suggest ways to develop a particular communication skill by practicing it in your daily life. Others encourage you to discover how a specific communication principle or theory shows up in your interactions.

I hope you will enjoy reading this book as much as I've enjoyed writing it. If so, then both of us have spent our time well.

FOR FURTHER REFLECTION AND DISCUSSION

1.   How does your identity shape how you think, act, feel, and communicate? How has it influenced what you know? Recall my discussion of how my identity affects my knowledge and behavior. Using my discussion as a guide, reflect on how your identity shapes your beliefs and practices.

2.   Think about the various forms and contexts of communication: intrapersonal (communication with yourself), personal relationships, groups, public speaking. In which contexts is your communication most effective? In which contexts do you wish to become more skillful? At the outset of the course, you might make a contract with yourself to focus on improving in one or two areas.

3.   Do you agree that theory and practice are "natural allies"? As a class, discuss the importance of theories in everyday life. How do they affect your behavior and your interpretation of people, situations, and events?

4.   Media today often comment on the emergence of multiculturalism in the present era. Yet, in this introduction I claim that the United States and the world have always been multicultural, but that this has not been widely recognized. Do you agree that multiculturalism is not new but only recently acknowledged? Do you think the current emphasis on multiculturalism is appropriate and valuable?

Focus Questions

1 Why study communication when you've been communicating for years without formal study?

2 What do communication scholars study and teach?

3 What is communication?

4 What issues unify the field of communication?

5 What are the levels of meaning in communication?

6 What careers are open to people who have strong backgrounds in communication?

CHAPTER 1

The World of Communication

Mike hangs up the phone and shakes his head. Talking with Chris is awkward now that they live 800 miles apart. They were buddies in high school but drifted apart once they enrolled in different universities. Mike wishes he knew how to keep the friendship going now that they can't hang out together. Shrugging, he turns the radio on while he finishes dressing for his date with Coreen. He hopes she won't want to talk about the relationship again tonight. Unless something is wrong, he can't see the point of always analyzing and discussing their relationship, but it seems to matter to Coreen. As he dresses, Mike thinks about his oral research presentation for Thursday's sociology class. He has some good ideas, but he doesn't know how to turn them into a speech. He vaguely remembers that the professor talked about how to organize a speech, but he wasn't listening. Mike also wishes he knew how to impress someone in an interview, since next week he has a big interview for a great summer internship.

(Jane Golden, detail from *Ocean Park Pier* (1976). Ocean Park Boulevard and Main Street, Santa Monica, Calif. © Jane Golden; photo courtesy the artist and Social Public Art Resource Center, Venice, Calif.)

And he has no idea how to deal with a group that can't get on track. He and six other students have worked for 3 months to organize a student book co-op, but the group can't get its act together. By now everyone is really frustrated, and nobody listens to anyone else. When he checked his electronic mail earlier today, Mike found angry messages from three of the group members. He shrugs again and leaves to meet Coreen.

Like Mike, most of us communicate continuously in our daily lives. Effective communication is vital to long-distance friendships, romantic relationships, public speaking, interviewing, and productive group discussion. Communication opportunities and demands fill our everyday lives.

Mike and all of us continue to rely on communication long after the college years. Even if you don't pursue a career such as teaching or law, which require strong speaking skills, communication will be essential in your work. You may want to persuade your boss you deserve a raise, represent your neighborhood in a zoning hearing, or work with colleagues to develop company policies. You will have conflicts with co-workers, romantic partners, and friends. You may need to deal with superiors who tell racist jokes or harass you sexually. Each of these situations calls for communication skills. The ability to communicate effectively is vital to personal and professional well-being and to the health of our society.

WHY STUDY COMMUNICATION?

Because you've been communicating all of your life, you might be asking what is gained by formal study. One answer is that formal study can improve skill. Some individuals have a natural aptitude that enables them to play basketball fairly well. They could be even more effective, however, if they studied theories of offensive and defensive play. Likewise, even if you communicate well now, learning about communication can make you more effective.

Another reason to study communication is that theories and principles help us to make sense of what happens in our everyday lives, and they help us have personal impact. For instance, learning about different gender communication cultures would help Mike understand why Coreen, like many women, enjoys talking about relationships more than he and men in general do. If Mike had better insight into the communication that sustains long-distance relationships, he might be able to revive the intimacy with Chris. Mike might also be able to organize his group if he knew about discussion agendas and effective group communication. Studying public speaking could help Mike design a good presentation for his class report, and learning about interviewing would clue him how to impress the interviewer. Learning to be a better listener would help Mike retain information, like his professor's tips on organizing oral reports. Knowledge of communication theory and principles would help Mike maximize his effectiveness in all of the communication activities in his life.

Everyday Application

YOUR COMMUNICATION ACTIVITIES

To find out how important communication is in your life, monitor your activities for the next 24 hours. Keep a record of the following (the activities may overlap, so you may have a total greater than 100%):

1. What percentage of time do you spend listening to others?
2. What percentage of time do you spend talking with yourself about ideas, plans, and options?
3. What percentage of your time do you spend communicating with friends and romantic partners?
4. How much of your time is devoted to group and public communication?
5. How much time do you spend on the job communicating with others?
6. How much time do you spend interacting with people of cultures different from yours?

Communication in Our Lives will help you become a more confident and competent communicator. Part 1 clarifies how communication works (or doesn't) and how perception, personal identity, language, nonverbal communication, listening, and culture affect the overall communication process. In Part 2, we'll look at communication in three specific contexts: personal relationships, small groups, and public settings. Studying and practicing the ideas in this book will enhance your effectiveness in all spheres of your life.

This chapter builds foundations for studying communication. To do this, we'll first discuss the values of communication. Next, we'll explain what communication involves and how the process works. The third section of the chapter describes the breadth of the communication field and careers for communication specialists.

Values of Communication

We spend more time communicating than doing anything else. We talk, listen, have dialogues with ourselves, participate in group discussions, interview or are interviewed, and so forth. From birth to death, communication shapes our personal, professional, relationship, and social lives.

Personal Values

George Herbert Mead (1934)* said humans are talked into humanity. He meant that we gain personal identity as we communicate with others. In the earliest years of our lives, our parents tell us who we are. "You're so smart." "You're so strong." "You're such a funny one." We first see ourselves through the eyes of others, so their messages form important foundations of self-concept. Later we interact with teachers, friends, romantic partners, and co-workers who communicate their views of us. Thus, how we see ourselves reflects the views of us that others communicate.

The profound connection between identity and communication is dramatically evident in children who are deprived of human contact. Case studies of children who were isolated from others reveal that they seem to have no self-concept and their mental and psychological development is severely hindered by lack of language.

Communication with others not only affects our sense of identity, but also directly influences our physical well-being. Consistently, research shows that communicating with others promotes health, whereas social isolation is linked to stress, disease, and early death (Crowley, 1995). People who lack close friends have greater levels of anxiety and depression than people who are close to others (Hojat, 1982; Jones & Moore, 1989). Heart disease is also more common among people who lack strong interpersonal relationships (Ruberman, 1992). Women with metastatic breast cancer double their average survival time when they belong to support groups in which they talk with others (Crowley, 1995). Steve Duck (1992), a scholar of interpersonal communication, reports that people in disturbed relationships tend to have low self-esteem, headaches, alcoholism, cancer, sleep disorders, and other physical problems. Clearly, healthy interaction with others is important to our physical and mental health.

Relationship Values

Communication is also a key foundation of relationships. We build connections with others by revealing our private identities, listening to learn about them, working out problems, remembering shared history, and planning a future. Marriage counselors have long emphasized the importance of communication for healthy, enduring relationships (Beck, 1988;

*I am using the American Psychological Association's (APA) method of citation. This means that in the text if you see "Mead (1934)," I am referring to a work by Mead that was written in 1934. If you see "Mead (1934, p. 10)" or "(Mead, 1934, p. 10)," I am specifically citing page 10 of Mead's 1934 work. The full bibliographic citations for all works may be found in the references at the end of the book.

GHADYA KA BACHA

Ghadya Ka Bacha, or "the wolf boy," was found in 1954 outside of a hospital in Balrampur, India. He had calloused knees and hands as if he moved on all fours, and he had scars on his neck, suggesting he had been dragged about by animals. Ramu, which was the name the hospital staff gave the child, showed no interest in others, but became very excited when he saw wolves on a visit to the zoo. Ramu lapped his milk from a glass instead of drinking as we do, and he tore apart his food. Most of the doctors who examined Ramu concluded he was a wolf boy who had grown up with wolves and who acted like a wolf, not a person.

Source: Shattuck, T. R. (1980). *The forbidden experiment: The story of the wild boy of Aveyron.* New York: Farrar, Straus, & Giroux.

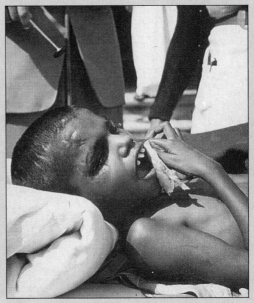

(Archive Photos/APA)

Gottman & Carrere, 1994; Scarf, 1987). They point out that the failure of some marriages is not due primarily to troubles and problems, since all relationships encounter these. A major distinction between relationships that endure and those that collapse is effective communication. Couples who learn how to express love and manage conflict constructively tend to sustain intimacy over time.

Communication is, however, important for more than solving problems or making disclosures. For most of us, everyday talk and nonverbal interaction are the very essence of relationships (Barnes & Duck, 1994; Duck, 1994a,b; Spencer, 1994). Routine talk between intimates continuously weaves their lives together. More than the big moments, such as declarations of love or major crises, it is unremarkable, everyday interaction that sustains the "conversation of marriage" (Berger & Kellner, 1964). Through making small talk, sharing news about mutual acquaintances, discussing clothes or furniture, and talking about other mundane topics, partners keep up the steady pulse of their relationship. For this reason, couples involved in long-distance romances say the biggest problem is not being able to share small talk (Gerstel & Gross, 1985).

SANDY

When my boyfriend moved away, the hardest part wasn't missing big moments in each other's life. What really bothered us was not being able to talk about little stuff or just be together. It was like we weren't part of each other's normal life when we couldn't talk about all the little things that happened or about our feelings.

Professional Values

Communication skills affect professional success. The importance of communication is obvious in professions such as teaching, business, law, sales, and counseling where talking and listening are primary. Many attorneys, counselors, business people, and teachers major or minor in communication before pursuing specialized training.

In other fields, the importance of communication is less obvious, but nonetheless present. Even highly technical jobs such as computer programming, accounting, and systems design require a variety of communication skills. Specialists have to be able to get along with others, listen carefully, and explain technical ideas to people who lack their expert knowledge. Thus, the information in this book is relevant to you, no matter what your career goals may be.

Cultural Values

Communication skills are also important for the health of our society. To be effective, citizens in a democracy have to be able to express ideas and to evaluate the ideas of others. A routine event in presidential elections is one or more debates between candidates. To make informed judgments, viewers need to listen critically to candidates' arguments and responses to criticism and questions.

Verbal and nonverbal communication styles reflect cultural backgrounds and understandings. We learn how to express ourselves by interacting with others in our social groups.
(© Bonnie Kamin/PhotoEdit)

Good communication skills are necessary to participate in social life, in general. In pluralistic cultures such as ours, we interact with people who differ from us and we need to know how to understand and work with them. Both civic and social life depend on our ability to listen thoughtfully to a range of perspectives and to communicate in a variety of ways.

LESLIE

I feel so awkward trying to talk with people from China or Mexico or other countries. They act different, and I don't understand them or how to talk with them. With so many people from other countries around, it seems nobody can get by without learning how to relate to people from other cultures.

Leslie is right. When she was a student in one of my courses, she and I talked several times about the concern she expresses in her commentary. Leslie realized she needs to learn to interact with people who differ from her if she is to be a full participant in today's world. She has learned a lot about communicating with diverse people, and no doubt she will learn more in the years ahead. Like Leslie, you can learn how to interact effectively with the variety of people who make up our society.

Communication, then, is important for personal, relationship, professional, and cultural reasons. Because communication is a cornerstone of human life, your choice to study it will serve you well. To understand what's involved in communication, let's now define the process.

DEFINING COMMUNICATION

So far we've been using the word *communication* as if we agree on what it means. Yet, there are many different definitions of communication. In 1970, Frank Dance, a communication theorist, counted over 100 distinct definitions of communication proposed by experts in the field. In the two and a half decades since that survey, even more definitions have surfaced. By drawing from these multiple definitions, we can define **communication**** as a *systemic process in which individuals interact with and through symbols to create and interpret meanings.*

**Boldfaced terms are defined in the glossary at the end of the book.

Features of Communication

The first important idea in this definition is that communication is a **process,** which means it is ongoing and always in motion. It's hard to tell when communication starts and stops, since what happened long before we talk with someone may influence interaction and what occurs in a particular encounter may have repercussions in the future. The fact that communication is a process means it is always in motion, moving ever forward, and changing continuously. We cannot freeze communication at any one moment.

Communication is also systemic, which means that it occurs in a **system** of interrelated parts that affect one another. In family communication, for instance, each member of the family is part of the system. In addition, the physical environment and the time of day are elements of the system that affect interaction. People interact differently in a formal living room than they do on a beach, and we may be more alert at certain times of day than others. Communication is also affected by the history of a system. If a family has a history of listening sensitively and working out problems constructively, then saying "There's something we need to talk about" is unlikely to raise defensiveness. On the other hand, if the family has a record of nasty conflicts and bickering, then the same comment might arouse strong defensiveness. A lingering kiss might be an appropriate way to show affection in a private setting, but the same action would raise eyebrows in an office. To interpret communication, we have to consider the system in which it takes place.

Our definition of communication also includes **symbols,** which are abstract, arbitrary, and ambiguous representations of other things. Symbols include all of language and many nonverbal behaviors, as well as art and music. Anything that abstractly signifies something else can be a symbol. We might symbolize love by giving a ring, saying "I love you," or embracing. Later in this chapter, we'll have more to say about symbols. For now, just remember that human communication involves interaction with and through symbols.

Finally, our definition focuses on meanings, which are the heart of communication. Meanings are the significance we bestow on phenomena— what they signify to us. Meanings are not in experience itself. Instead, we use symbols to create meanings. We ask others to be sounding boards so that we can clarify our own thinking; we talk to them to figure out what things mean; we listen to them to enlarge our own perspectives; and we label feelings to give them reality. In all of these ways, we actively construct meaning by working with symbols.

There are two levels of meaning in communication. The **content level of meaning** is the literal message. For example, if someone says "You're crazy," the content level of meaning is that you are crazy. The **relationship level of meaning** expresses the relationship between communicators. In our example, if the person who says "You're crazy" is a friend and is smiling, then you would probably interpret the relationship level of meaning as indicating the person likes you and is kidding around. On the other hand,

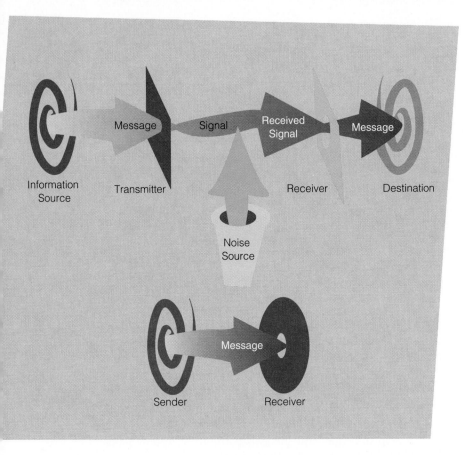

if the person who says "You're crazy" is your supervisor responding to your request for a raise, then you might interpret the relationship level of meaning as indicating that your supervisor regards you as inferior and dislikes your work.

In communicating, we use symbols to construct meanings. In later parts of this book, we will elaborate the connections between symbols and meanings.

Models of Communication

Theorists create models to describe how things work. Over the years, scholars in communication have developed a number of models, which reflect increasingly sophisticated understandings of the communication process.

FIGURE 1.1
Linear Model of Communication

Source: Adapted from Shannon, C., & Weaver, W. (1949). *The mathematical theory of communication*. Urbana, IL: University of Illinois Press.

Linear Models   Harold Laswell (1948) advanced an early model of communication, which described it as a linear or one-way process in which one person acted on another person. This was a verbal model that consisted of five questions that described early views of how communication worked (Laswell, 1948).

Who?
Says what?
In what channel?
To whom?
With what effect?

A year later, Claude Shannon and Warren Weaver (1949) extended Laswell's idea by adding that noise, or interferences, occur and may distort understanding between communicators. Figure 1.1 shows Shannon and Weaver's model. Although these early models were useful starting points, they were too simplistic to capture the complexity of human communication.

Interactive Models   The major shortcoming of linear models was that they portrayed communication as flowing in only one direction—from a sender to a receiver. This suggests that listeners only listen; they never send messages. Further, it suggests that listeners passively absorb senders'

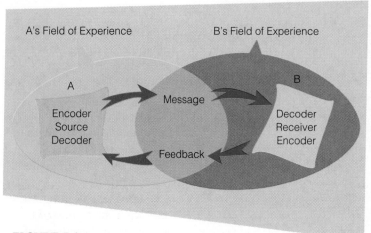

A's Field of Experience

B's Field of Experience

A

Encoder
Source
Decoder

Message

Feedback

B

Decoder
Receiver
Encoder

FIGURE 1.2
Interactive Model of Communication

Source: Adapted from Schramm, W. (1955). *The process and effects of mass communication.* Urbana, IL: University of Illinois Press.

messages and do not respond. Clearly, this isn't how communication occurs. As you talk to friends, you notice whether they seem interested or bored. If they nod, you're likely to continue talking; if they yawn or turn away from you, you might stop. In other words, what others do affects how we communicate.

The idea that listeners respond to senders led communication theorists to add a new feature to models. Responses to a message are called **feedback.** Feedback may be verbal, nonverbal, or both, and it may be intentional or unintentional. Wilbur Schramm (1955) depicted feedback as a second kind of message in the communication process. In addition, Schramm pointed out that communicators create and interpret messages within personal fields of experience. The more communicators' fields of experience overlap, the better they can understand each other. Adding fields of experience to models clarifies why misunderstandings sometimes occur. You jokingly put a friend down, and he takes it seriously and is hurt. You offer to help someone, and she feels patronized. Adding fields of experience and feedback allowed Schramm and other communication scholars to develop models that portrayed communication as an interactive process in which both senders and receivers participate actively (see Figure 1.2).

L O R I   A N N

I was born in Alabama, and all my life I've spoken to people whether I know them or not. I say hello or something to a person I pass on the street just to be friendly. When I went to a junior college in Pennsylvania, I got in trouble for being so friendly. When I spoke to guys I didn't know, they thought I was coming on to them or something. And other girls would just look at me like I was odd. I'd never realized that friendliness could be misinterpreted.

Transactional Models   Although interactive models are an improvement over linear ones, they still don't fully capture the dynamism of human communication. A serious limitation of interactive models is that they portray communication as a sequential, linear process. One person communicates to another who then sends feedback to the first person. This view doesn't recognize that people may communicate simultaneously, instead of taking turns. Also, the interactional model designates one person as a

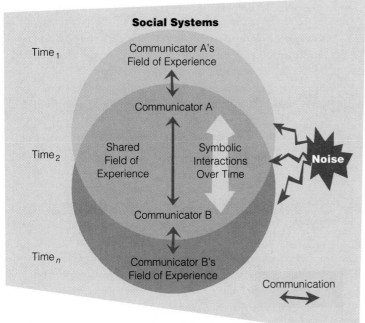

Social Systems

Time₁ — Communicator A's Field of Experience

Communicator A

Time₂ — Shared Field of Experience | Symbolic Interactions Over Time

Noise

Communicator B

Timeₙ — Communicator B's Field of Experience

Communication

FIGURE 1.3
Transactional Model of Communication

Source: Adapted from Wood, J. T. (1996a). *Everyday encounters: An introduction to interpersonal communication.* Belmont, CA: Wadsworth.

sender and another person as a receiver. In reality, everyone who is involved in communication both sends and receives messages. While making a press release, a speaker watches reporters to see if they express interest—both the speaker and the reporters are "listening," and both are "speaking."

A final shortcoming of the interactional model is that it doesn't really capture the process quality of communication. To do this, a model would need to show that communication changes over time as a result of what happens between people. For example, Mike and Coreen communicated in more reserved and formal ways on their first date than they do after months of seeing each other. What they talk about and how they talk have changed as a result of interacting. An accurate model would include the feature of time and would depict features of communication as varying, rather than as constant. Figure 1.3 is a transactional model of communication that highlights these features and others we have discussed.

Consistent with what we've covered in this chapter, our model includes **noise** that can distort communication. Noise is anything that interferes with the intended communication. This includes sounds such as a lawn mower or others' conversations, as well as noises inside of communicators, such as mental biases and preoccupation, that hinder effective listening. In addition, our model emphasizes that communication is a continuous and constantly changing process. The feature of time underlines this by reminding us that how people communicate varies over time.

The outer lines on our model emphasize that communication occurs within systems that affect what and how people communicate and what meanings are created. Those systems, or contexts, include shared systems of both communicators (shared campus, town, and culture) as well as the personal systems of each person (family, religious associations, friends). Also notice that our model, unlike previous ones, portrays each person's field of experience and the shared field of experience between communicators as changing over time. As we encounter new people and grow personally, we alter how we interact with others. Finally, our model doesn't label one person a "sender" and the other a "receiver." Instead, both individuals are defined as communicators who participate equally, and often simultaneously, in the communication process. This means that at a given moment in communication, you may be sending a message (speaking or nodding your head), receiving a message (listening), or doing both at the same time (interpreting what someone says while nodding to show you are interested).

Now that we have a shared understanding of what communication is, let's explore the breadth of the field.

BREADTH OF THE COMMUNICATION FIELD

The study and teaching of communication dates back more than 2,000 years. Originally, the field focused almost exclusively on public communication. Aristotle, a famous Greek philosopher, believed effective public speaking was essential to citizens' participation in civic affairs. He taught his students how to develop and present persuasive speeches to influence public life. Although public speaking remains a vital skill, it is no longer the only focus of the communication field. The modern discipline can be classified into eight areas.

Intrapersonal Communication

Intrapersonal communication is communication with ourselves, or self-talk. You might be wondering whether intrapersonal communication is just jargon for thinking. In one sense, yes. Intrapersonal communication does involve thinking, since it is a cognitive process that goes on inside of us. Yet, because thinking relies on language to name and reflect on ideas and people, it is also a kind of communication. Donna Vocate's (1994) recent book, devoted entirely to intrapersonal communication, reflects the importance of this area of study and teaching.

One school of counseling focuses on enhancing self-esteem by changing how we talk to ourselves (Ellis & Harper, 1977; Rusk & Rusk, 1988; Seligman, 1990). For instance, you might say to yourself, "I blew that test, so I'm really stupid. I'll never graduate and, if I do, nobody will hire a klutz like me." This kind of talk lowers self-esteem by convincing you that a single event (blowing one test) proves you are totally worthless. Therapists who realize that what we say to ourselves affects our feelings urge us to challenge negative self-talk by saying, "Hey, wait a minute. One test is hardly a measure of my intelligence. I did well on the other test in this course, and I have a decent overall college record. I shouldn't be so hard on myself." What we say to ourselves can enhance or diminish self-esteem.

ANALYZING YOUR SELF-TALK

Pay attention to the way you talk to yourself for the next day. When something goes wrong, what do you say to yourself? Do you put yourself down with negative messages that blame you for what happened? Do you generalize beyond the specific event to describe yourself as a loser or as inadequate?

The first step in changing negative self-talk is to become aware of it. We'll say more about how to change negative self-talk in Chapter 3.

We engage in self-talk to plan our lives, rehearse different ways of acting, and prompt ourselves to do or not do particular things. For example, you can use self-talk to motivate yourself to listen attentively in your classes. Intrapersonal communication is how we remind ourselves to eat in healthy ways ("No saturated fats"), show respect to others ("I need to show interest in grandmother's story"), and check impulses that might be destructive ("I'll wait until I've cooled off to say anything").

CHIQUELLA

I talk to myself all the time. That's how I figure out a lot of things—by thinking them through in my head. It's like having a trial run without risk. Usually after I think through different ideas or ways of approaching someone, I can see which one would be best.

Intrapersonal communication also helps us rehearse alternative scenarios so that we can determine how each might turn out. To control a disruptive group member named Nelson, Cass might consider (1) telling him to shut up, (2) suggesting the group adopt a rule that everyone should participate equally, and (3) taking Nelson out for coffee and privately asking him to be less domineering. She'll think through the various ways of approaching Nelson, weigh the likely consequences of each, and then choose one to put into practice. We engage in internal dialogues continuously as we reflect on experiences, sort through ideas and options for communicating, and test out alternative ways of acting.

Interpersonal Communication

A second major emphasis in the field of communication is **interpersonal communication,** which deals with communication between people. In one sense, everything except intrapersonal communication is interpersonal.

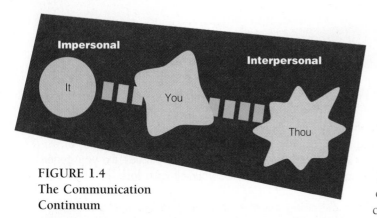

FIGURE 1.4
The Communication
Continuum

Such a broad definition, however, doesn't create useful boundaries for the area of study. There is growing consensus that interpersonal communication is not a single thing, but rather exists on a continuum from very impersonal to highly interpersonal (Wood, 1995b). Figure 1.4 illustrates the communication continuum. The more we know and interact with another person as a distinct individual, the more interpersonal the communication is. Using this criterion, we would say that a deep conversation with a friend is more interpersonal than a casual exchange with a sales clerk.

Since the 1960s, interest in interpersonal communication has mushroomed, making it one of the most vibrant branches of the field today. Scholars focus on how communication creates and sustains relationships and how partners communicate to deal with the normal and extraordinary challenges of maintaining intimacy over time (Canary & Stafford, 1994; Duck & Wood, 1995; Spencer, 1994; Wood & Duck, 1995a,b).

Of particular concern to scholars of interpersonal communication are the ways romantic partners and close friends use communication to create and sustain intimacy. Research indicates that communication is the lifeblood of close relationships, since it is how friends and couples develop intimacy and how they continuously refashion relationships to meet their changing needs and identities. Intimates who learn how to listen sensitively and talk with each other have the greatest chance of enduring over time.

Interpersonal communication researchers study how communication is influenced by gender (Wood, 1986, 1993b,c,d, 1994b,c,d, 1996b; Wood & Inman, 1993), ethnicity (Gaines, 1995; Houston, 1994; Houston & Wood, 1996), and sexual preference (Huston & Schwartz, 1995; Wood, 1994c). In later chapters, we'll discuss research on the communication goals and styles that different social groups tend to use. Knowledge about diverse communication patterns yields principles for teaching about effective interaction between people who differ from one another.

Group Communication

A third important branch of communication study is small group communication, including social groups, decision-making committees, and work teams. Small group communication includes leadership, member roles, group features, an agenda for achieving group goals, and conflict management. Research that we will consider in Chapters 10 and 11 helps us understand how communication affects each of these aspects of group life and how we can participate effectively in groups and teams.

Public speaking is part of most people's lives, and when done well, it's a powerful way to communicate information, beliefs, and ideas and to foster understanding, build commitment, and motivate action.
(left: © Gerd Ludwig/Woodfin Camp & Associates; right: © Bob Daemmrich/The Image Works)

Dennis Gouran (1982), a scholar of group communication, emphasizes the importance of rational group decision making. He believes that effective group work is based on careful communication to discover and analyze information and to reason from information to conclusions. Gouran has identified forms of communication that advance and interfere with rational decision making, and he has developed discussion strategies that help group members avoid impediments to effective group work.

Other scholars of small group communication have concentrated on communication processes that transform a collection of individuals into a cohesive group. In this area, the work of Ernest Bormann and his associates is particularly important (Bormann, 1975; Bormann, Putnam, & Pratt, 1978). According to Bormann's line of study, group cohesion and identity often crystallize through **fantasy themes,** which are chains of ideas that spin out in a group and capture its social and task themes. The talk of politicians often suggests that they view their parties as warring opponents. When politicians speak of "attacking" the "other side's" plan, "defending" their agenda, and "refusing to give ground," they create a fantasy chain that defines the parties as warring factions. Fantasy themes frame how group members think and talk about what they are doing. A compromise is less attractive if group members talk about themselves as at war so that only one side can win, than if they talk about collaborating to develop solutions that work for everyone.

Public Communication

Although public speaking no longer defines the scope of the field, it remains an important branch of communication theory, research, and practice. Even though most of us may not seek careers that call for extensive formal speaking, most of us will have opportunities to speak to others. In addition, we all will be in situations where speaking up is a responsibility. My editor speaks to his sales representatives to explain what his books are about and how to spotlight important features to potential purchasers. I recently coached my doctor who was asked to address her colleagues on a development in treatment of renal disease. My plumber presents workshops to his staff to inform them of new developments in plumbing products and to teach them how to communicate effectively with customers. My sister relies on public speaking skills when she's trying cases in court and when she's raising funds to support a battered women's center. A friend of mine recently took a leading role in organizing a union in her company. My editor, doctor, plumber, sister, and friend don't consider themselves public speakers, but public speaking is a part of their lives, and doing it effectively is important to their success.

Scholars of public communication focus on critical evaluation of speeches and on principles for speaking effectively. Rhetorical critics study important communication events such as the Reverend Martin Luther King, Jr.'s "I Have a Dream" speech and public arguments for and against reproductive freedom. Critics often take a role in civic life by evaluating political debates and speeches to help voters understand how well candidates support their positions and respond to challenges from opponents.

Scholars of public communication are also interested in discovering and teaching principles of effective public speaking. As we will see in Chapters 12–14, we know a great deal about what makes speakers seem credible to listeners and how credibility affects persuasion. Research has also enlightened us about the kinds of argument, methods of organizing ideas, and forms of proof that listeners find effective. If Mike studied this body of research, he could glean useful guidelines for his oral report in class.

Media and New Technologies of Communication

One of the most exciting areas of the modern field of communication is media and new technologies. For some time, communication scholars have studied mediated communication such as films, radio, and television. More recently, scholars have also begun to study new forms of communication that are emerging in our technological era. From substantial research, we understand a great deal about how media work and how they represent and influence cultural values. For instance, the cultural feminine ideal, which centers on youth and beauty, is perpetuated by use of young, beautiful women as models in ads and as news reporters and anchors. Several women newscasters who were in their mid-thirties were replaced by younger women.

Media sometimes reinforce cultural stereotypes about race and ethnicity. For example, African Americans are most often cast in supporting roles, rather than principal roles. In addition, black males are frequently portrayed as lazy and unlawful and are typically cast as athletes or entertainers (Evans, 1993; "Sights, Sounds, and Stereotypes," 1992). Robert Entman (1994), a communication professor at Northwestern University, points out that major networks are more likely to show black defendants in mug

"Dennis, I would like to talk to you for a minute—off line."

(Drawing by Mort Gerberg; © 1994 The New Yorker Magazine, Inc.)

shots without names, but to offer multiple pictures and names of white defendants. This difference may contribute to perceptions of blacks as an undifferentiated group.

FRANKLIN

I hate the way television shows African Americans. Most of the time they are criminals, welfare cases, drunks, or Uncle Toms. The only positive African Americans are on the TV show Cosby, but that wasn't realistic either. When I watch TV, I understand why so many people still think blacks are dumb, uneducated, and criminal. We're not, but you'd never know it from watching television.

Although Asian Americans have tripled their population since 1970 and now number 8 million, they seldom appear in prime-time shows (Wong, 1994). Hispanics and Asians who do appear in prime time usually appear in the roles of villains or criminals (Lichter, Lichter, Rothman, & Amundson, 1987). One important contribution of communication scholars is heightening awareness of how media shape—and sometimes distort—our perceptions of ourselves and society.

A more recent focus in the area of media is new and converging technologies of communication. We are in the midst of a technological revolution, which provides us with the means to communicate in more ways at faster speeds with greater numbers of people throughout the world. How do new technologies and the accompanying acceleration of the pace of interaction influence how we think, work, and form relationships? Some scholars caution that new technologies may undermine human community (Hyde, 1995), whereas others celebrate the increased social contact and productivity technology allows (Lea & Spears, 1995). Still others claim that new communication technologies will fundamentally transform how we think and process information (Chesebro, 1995).

CHUCK

I live through my modem. That's how I stay in touch with friends at other schools, and I even "talk" daily with my mom who has an e-mail system in her office. I think if I couldn't communicate with these people, the relationships would deteriorate or completely die. I think that's what happened to a lot of relationships before we had modems.

Clearly, the verdict on media's effects is not in and will not be for some time. Meanwhile, all of us struggle to keep up with our increasingly technological world. When I was an undergraduate student, I typed my papers on a typewriter. Today any student without access to a computer is at an academic disadvantage. Five years ago, we relied on letters and phone calls to communicate across distance. Today, FedEx, faxes, and electronic mail make it possible for us to communicate almost immediately with people on the other side of the world. As a student and for the first decade of my career, I had to go to libraries and find books and articles to do research. Today's students conduct much of their research on the World Wide Web or specialized information networks on the Internet. Video-conferencing now makes it possible to have discussions among people who are separated by many miles. Communication scholars will continue to study whether emerging technologies merely alter how we communicate or whether they actually change how we think about interaction and what kinds of connections we build.

Everyday Application

YOUR MEDIATED WORLD

How do new technologies of communication affect your interactions? If you use the Internet, how are your electronic exchanges different from face-to-face interactions? Have you made any acquaintances or friends through electronic communication? Did those relationships develop differently than ones formed through personal contact? Do you feel differently about people whom you haven't ever seen than ones you see face to face?

Organizational Communication

Communication in organizations is another growing area of interest in the field of communication. As we saw earlier in this chapter, communication skills facilitate advancement in most careers. Communication scholars have identified communication skills that enhance professional success, and they have traced the impact of various kinds of communication on morale, productivity, and commitment in organizations. For many years, scholars of organizational communication have studied aspects of work life such as interviewing, listening, organizational structure, making presentations, leadership, and decision making.

In addition to continuing to study these topics, organizational scholars have begun to focus substantial attention on organizational culture and

A "CAN DO" CULTURE

In July of 1994, a Colorado wildfire became a raging inferno in which 14 firefighters lost their lives. A detailed investigation revealed that a primary contributor to the loss of lives was a "can do" culture among firefighters. Trained to believe that they can do what others cannot and that they can perform heroic feats, the firefighters didn't observe critical safety regulations. Ironically, the "can do" culture essential for such a dangerous job also led to disregard for important cautions and the subsequent loss of 14 lives.

personal relationships in professional settings in organizations. **Organizational culture** refers to understandings about identity and codes of thought and action that are shared by members of an organization. Some organizations think of themselves as families. From this understanding of who they are emerge rules for how to interact with each other and how fully to commit to work.

Studies of organizational culture also shed light on the continuing problem of sexual harassment. Some institutions have developed cultures that treat sexual harassment as the normal way "we do things around here" (Strine, 1992). A number of communication scholars have analyzed how some institutions trivialize complaints about sexual harassment and sustain an organizational culture that implies sexual harassment is normal and acceptable (Bingham, 1994; Clair, 1993; Conrad, 1995; Strine, 1992; Taylor & Conrad, 1992).

Another area of increasing interest among organizational scholars is personal relationships among co-workers. As we expand the hours we spend on the job, it is natural for personal relationships among co-workers to increase. Further, since the majority of women work full-time or part-time today, there is increased opportunity for romantic and sexual relationships to unfold. Obviously, this adds both interest and complications to life in organizations.

In one example of a study in the area of personal relationships among co-workers, communication scholar Ted Zorn (1995) studied "bosses and buddies," relationships in which one friend is the boss of the other. Zorn discovered a number of ways people cope with the often contradictory rules for communication between friends and between superiors and subordinates. He also points out both potential values and hazards of friendships in which one person has formal power over another.

MELBOURNE

It was a real hassle when my supervisor and I started going out. Before, he gave me orders like he did all the other wait staff, and none of us thought anything about it. But after we started dating, he would sort of ask me, instead of tell me, what to do, like saying "Mel, would you help out in section 7?" Another problem was that if he gave me a good station where tips run high, the other waits would give me trouble because they thought he was favoring me because we go out. And when he gave me a bad station, I'd feel he was being nasty. It was a mess being his employee and his girlfriend at the same time.

Personal relations on the job also require that women and men learn to understand each other's language. In a number of ways, women and men communicate differently, and they frequently misunderstand one another (Wood, 1993b, 1994d, 1995a,b, 1996b). For example, women tend to make more "listening noises," such as "um," "uh huh," and "go on," than men do. If men don't make these noises when communicating with women colleagues, the women may think the men aren't listening. Conversely, men are likely to misinterpret the listening noises women make as signaling agreement, rather than just interest. Such misunderstandings can strain professional relations and performance. Some scholars of organizational communication study and conduct workshops on effective communication between the sexes (Murphy & Zorn, 1996).

Intercultural Communication

Intercultural communication is an increasingly important focus of research, teaching, and training. Although intercultural communication is not a new area of study, it is one whose importance has grown in recent years. The United States always has been a culture made up of many peoples, and demographic shifts in the last decade have increased this tendency, making our country richly pluralistic. Increasing numbers of Asians, Indians,

Eastern Europeans, Latinas and Latinos, and people of other nations are immigrating to the United States and making their homes here. With them, they bring cultural values and styles of communicating that differ from those of citizens whose ancestors are native-born U.S. citizens.

Scholars of intercultural communication increase awareness of different cultures' communication styles and meanings. For example, a Taiwanese woman in one of my graduate classes seldom spoke up and wouldn't enter the heated debates that typically characterize graduate classes. One day after class I encouraged Mei-Ling to argue for her ideas when others challenged them. She replied that would be impolite. Her culture, unlike the West, considers it disrespectful to argue or assert oneself and even more disrespectful to contradict others. Understood in terms of the communication values of her culture, Mei-Ling's deference did not mean she lacked confidence.

MEIKKO

What I find most odd about Americans is their focus on themselves. Here everyone wants to be an individual who is so strong and stands out from everyone else. In Japan, it is not like that. We see ourselves as parts of families and communities, not as individuals. Here I *and* my *are the most common words, but they are not often said in Japan.*

A particularly important recent trend in the area of intercultural communication is research on different communication cultures within a single society. Cultural differences are obvious in communication between a Nepali and a Canadian. Less obvious are cultural differences in communication between people who speak the "same" language. Within the United States, there are distinct communication cultures based on race, gender, sexual preference, and other factors. Larry Samovar and Richard Porter (1994) have identified distinctive styles of communication used by women, men, blacks, whites, Native Americans, gays, individuals with disabilities, and other groups in our country. For example, women more than men tend to disclose personal information and to engage in emotionally expressive talk in their friendships (Wood, 1993b, 1994a,d). African Americans belong to a communication culture that encourages dramatic talk, verbal duels, and other communication routines that have no equivalents in Caucasian speech communities (Houston, 1994; Houston & Wood, 1996). Recognizing and respecting different communication cultures increases effectiveness in a pluralistic society.

Ethics and Communication

A final area of study and teaching in the field focuses on relationships between ethics and communication. Because all forms of communication involve ethical issues, this area of interest infuses all other areas in the discipline. For instance, ethical dimensions of intrapersonal communication include the influence of stereotypes on judgments we make and beliefs we hold. In the realm of interpersonal communication, scholars who focus on ethics are concerned with issues such as honesty, compassion, and fairness in relationships. Conformity pressures that sometimes operate in groups are another concern of scholars who specialize in ethics and communication. Steve May, an organizational communication scholar at Chapel Hill, raises ethical questions about the ways in which institutional policies intrude on individuals' personal lives. For instance, do companies have a right to refuse to purchase health insurance for employees who smoke, sky dive, or race cars when they are off the job? Ethical issues also surface in public communication. Linda Alcoff (1991) is concerned that people who speak for others who are oppressed may misrepresent others' experiences or even reinforce oppression by keeping others silent.

In all communication situations, ranging from interpersonal to public, there are ethical considerations such as whether people misrepresent information, conveniently neglect to mention evidence contrary to their positions, or misquote statistics. Another ethical issue relevant to a range of communication contexts concerns attitudes and actions that encourage or hinder freedom of speech: Are all members of organizations equally empowered to speak? What does it mean when audiences shout down a speaker with unpopular views? How does the balance of power between relationship partners affect each person's freedom to express himself or herself? Because ethical issues infuse all forms of communication, we will discuss ethical themes in each chapter of this book.

After reading about the major branches of the modern field of communication, you might think that the field is a collection of separate and unrelated areas of interest. Actually, this isn't the case. The field of communication is unified by a persisting interest in language, nonverbal behavior, and the processes by which we construct meaning for ourselves and our activities.

Unifying Themes in the Field

Seemingly disparate areas such as intrapersonal, organizational, and relational communication are unified by central concerns with symbolic activities and meaning. These two themes underlie research and teaching in different branches of the communication field.

Symbolic Activities

Symbols are the basis of language, thinking, and much of our nonverbal behavior. Symbols are arbitrary, ambiguous, and abstract representations of other phenomena. For instance, a wedding band is a symbol of marriage in Western culture, the name *Julia* is a symbol for me, a smile is a symbol of friendliness, and the word *cat* is a symbol for one species of animal. Because symbols are abstract, they allow us to lift experiences and ourselves out of the concrete world of here and now and reflect on our experiences and ourselves. Because symbols let us represent ideas and feelings, we can share experiences with others, even if they have not had those experiences themselves.

Whether we are interested in intrapersonal, interpersonal, organizational, mediated, group, public, or intercultural communication, symbols are central to what happens. Thus, symbols and the mental activities they allow are a unifying focus of study and teaching about all forms of communication. We will discuss symbols in greater depth in Chapter 5, which deals with verbal communication.

Meaning

Closely related to interest in symbols is the communication field's persisting concern with meaning. The human world is one of meaning. We don't simply exist, eat, drink, sleep, and go through motions. Instead, we imbue every aspect of our lives with significance, or meaning. When I feed my cat, Scrambles, she eats her food and then returns to her feline adventures. For her, eating is a necessary and enjoyable activity. We humans, however, layer food and eating with significance. Food often symbolizes special events or commitments. For example, kosher products reflect commitment to Jewish heritage; turkey is commonly associated with commemorating the first Thanksgiving in the United States (though vegetarians symbolize their commitment by *not* eating turkey); eggnog is a Christmas tradition; and Mandel Brot is a Hanukkah staple. Birthday cakes celebrate an individual, and we may fix special meals to express love for others.

Some families consider meals an occasion to come together and share their lives, while in other families meals are battlefields where family tensions are played out. A meal can symbolize business negotiations (power lunches, for instance), romance (candles, wine), a personal struggle to stick to a diet, or an excuse to spend 2 hours talking with a friend. For humans, eating and other activities take on value beyond their physical or functional qualities. Our experiences gain significance as a result of how we define what we are doing and what it means.

Because we are symbol users, we actively interpret events, situations, experiences, and relationships. We don't react passively to the world. Instead, we use symbols to construct what it means (Wood, 1992a, 1995b). Symbols are the foundation of meaning, because they enable us to name, evaluate, and reflect, and to share experiences, ideas, and feelings with others. Through the process of communicating with others, we define our relationships: Do we have a friendship or something more? How serious are we? Do we feel the same way about each other? Is this conflict irresolvable, or can we work it out and stay together?

B E N I T A

It's funny how important a word can be. Nick and I had been going out for a long time and we really liked each other, but I didn't know if this was going to be long term. Then we said we loved each other, and that changed how we saw each other and the relationship. Just using the word love *transformed who we are.*

To study communication, then, is to study how we use symbols to create meaning in our lives. Communication scholars see friendship, group cohesion, and organizational culture as relationships that individuals collaboratively create in the process of interaction (Andersen, 1993; Wood, 1992a, 1995b). Leslie Baxter (1987, p. 262) says that "relationships can be regarded as webs of significance" spun as partners communicate. By extension, all human activities are webs of significance spun with symbols and meaning.

CAREERS IN COMMUNICATION

Studying communication prepares you for a wide array of careers. As we've seen, communication skills are essential to success in most fields. In addition, there are a number of careers for people who major in communication.

Research

Communication research is a vital and growing field of work. A great deal of study is conducted by academics who combine teaching and research in faculty careers. In this book, you'll encounter much academic research, and you'll be able to evaluate what we learn from doing it.

In addition to academic research, communication specialists do media research on everything from message production to marketing (SCA, 1995). Companies want to know how people respond to different kinds of advertisements, logos, and labels for products. Before naming a new cereal or beer, various names are test marketed. Retailers' success depends on understanding how customers will respond to different communication strategies. In addition, businesses research the audiences reached by different media such as newspapers, magazines, radio, and television. Individuals who understand communication and who have research skills are qualified for careers in communication research.

Education

Teaching others about communication is another exciting career path for individuals with extensive backgrounds in the field. Clearly, I am biased toward this profession, since I've had a 20-year love affair with teaching communication. I find nothing more exciting than opening students' eyes to the power of communication and to working with them to improve their skills. Across the nation there are growing opportunities for communication teachers at all levels. There are communication classes and often whole curricula in secondary schools, junior colleges, colleges, universities, technical schools, and community colleges.

The level at which a person is qualified to teach depends on how extensively she or he has pursued the study of communication. Generally, a B.A. in communication education plus certification by the Board of Education are required to teach in elementary and secondary schools. A master's

A consultant is making a presentation to a group of clients. What do you notice about her nonverbal communication? Does it suggest she is confident, competent, relaxed?
(© Walter Hodges/Tony Stone Images)

degree in communication qualifies a person to teach at community colleges, technical schools, and some junior colleges and colleges. The Ph.D., or doctoral degree, in communication is generally required for a career in university education, although some universities offer short-term positions to individuals with master's degrees (SCA, 1995).

Although generalists are preferred for many teaching jobs, at the college level individuals can focus on areas of communication that particularly interest them. For instance, my research and teaching focus on interpersonal communication and gender and communication. My partner, who is also on the faculty in my department, specializes in environmental advocacy and social movements. Other college faculty concentrate in areas such as oral traditions, intercultural communication, family communication, organizational dynamics, and performance of literature.

Communication educators are not restricted to communication departments. In recent years, more and more individuals with advanced degrees in communication have taken positions in medical and business schools. Good doctors have not only specialized medical knowledge, but also good communication skills. They know how to listen sensitively to patients, how to explain complex problems and procedures, and how to provide comfort, reassurance, and motivation. Similarly, good business people not only know their business, but also know how to explain it to others, how to present themselves and their company or product favorably, and so on. Because communication is essential for doctors and business people, increasing numbers of medical and business schools are creating permanent positions for communication specialists.

Training and Consulting

Consulting is another field that increasingly welcomes individuals with backgrounds in communication. Businesses want to train employees in effective group communication skills, interview techniques, and interpersonal interaction. Some large corporations such as IBM have entire departments devoted to training and development. Individuals with communication backgrounds often join these departments and work with the corporation to design and teach courses or workshops that enhance employees' communication skills.

In addition, communication specialists may join or form consulting firms, which provide particular kinds of communication training to government and businesses. One of my colleagues consults with corporations to teach men and women how to understand each other's language and work together. Another of my colleagues consults with organizations to help them develop work teams that interact effectively. I sometimes prepare workshops for educators who want to learn how to use communication to stimulate students' interest and learning. Other communication specialists work with politicians to improve their presentational style and sometimes to write their speeches. I consult with attorneys on cases involving charges of sexual harassment and sex discrimination. I help them understand how particular communication patterns create hostile, harassing environments, and I collaborate with them to develop trial strategy. In addition, I sometimes testify as an expert witness on whether sexual harassment or sex discrimination occurred. Other communication consultants work with attorneys on jury selections and advise attorneys how dress and nonverbal behaviors might affect jurors' perceptions of clients.

Human Relations and Management

Because communication is the foundation of human relations, it's no surprise that many communication specialists build careers in human development or human relations departments of corporations. Individuals with solid understandings of communication and good personal communication skills are effective in careers such as public relations, personnel, grievance management, negotiations, customer relations, and development and fund raising (SCA, 1995). In each of these areas, communication skills are the primary requirements.

Communication degrees may also open the door to careers in management. The most important qualifications for management are not technical skills, but abilities to interact with others and to communicate effectively. Good managers are skilled in listening, expressing their ideas, building consensus, creating supportive work environments, and balancing task and interpersonal concerns in dealing with others. Developing skills such as these gives communication majors a firm foundation for effective management.

SUMMARY

In this chapter, we took a first look at human communication. We discussed the pervasiveness of communication and explored the many contexts and ways in which communication is part of our everyday lives. Next, we defined communication and considered a series of models, the most accurate of which is transactional. The transactional model emphasizes that communication is a systemic process in which individuals interact to create and share meanings.

Like most fields of study, communication has developed over the years. The original focus on public speaking, although still important, no longer defines the boundaries of the field. Today, communication

scholars and teachers are interested in intrapersonal, group, interpersonal, public, organizational, intercultural, electronically mediated, and public forms of communication. In addition, the relationship between ethics and communication permeates study and teaching about all contexts in which communication takes place. This broad range of areas is held together by abiding interests in symbolic activities and meanings, which together form the foundation of personal, interpersonal, and social life.

In the final section of this chapter, we considered some of the many career opportunities open to individuals who choose to specialize in communication. The modern field of communication is growing, and it offers an array of exciting career paths for people who enjoy interacting with others and who want the opportunity to be part of a dynamic discipline that evolves to meet changing needs and issues in our world.

FOR FURTHER REFLECTION AND DISCUSSION

1. Using each of the models discussed in this chapter, describe interaction and transaction in your class. What does each model highlight and obscure? Which model best describes and explains communication in your class?

2. Keep a log of your activities for the next 2 days. Record how much time you spend engaging in intrapersonal, interpersonal, group, intercultural, technological, and public communication. What do you conclude about the importance of communication in your life?

3. Interview a professional in the field you plan to enter to discover what kinds of communication skills she or he thinks are most important for success. Which of those skills do you already have? Which skills do you need to develop or improve? How can you use this book and the course it accompanies to develop the skills you will need to be effective in your career?

4. As a class, discuss particular topics and skills that interest you. How might you highlight these during the course of the term? You might agree to have project groups that study and make presentations to the class on communication topics that you consider especially important.

5. Go to the placement office on your campus and examine descriptions for available positions. Record the number of job notices that call for "excellent written and oral communication skills."

KEY TERMS

communication
process
system
symbols
content level of meaning
relationship level of meaning
feedback
noise
intrapersonal communication
interpersonal communication
fantasy themes
organizational culture

Focus Questions

1 How does perception affect human communication?

2 How does communication affect our perceptions?

3 Do people from different cultures perceive and communicate differently?

4 Can we change how we perceive people, relationships, and situations?

5 How does mindreading influence communication?

6 How does the self-serving bias affect perception?

CHAPTER 2

Perception and Communication

Recently, my sister Carolyn visited me with her 4-year-old daughter, Michelle, and 15-month-old son, Daniel. My partner and I had spent the better part of the day cleaning the house and fixing up their rooms with flowers. As Carolyn walked through the house, she picked up a glass paperweight, two small sculptures, a set of darts Robbie and I use for dartthrowing, and a saber knife from Nepal. "I'm babyproofing the house," Carolyn explained. She moved the flowers in their room to the top of a tall bureau, saying, "Your rugs don't need all this water spilled on them." She perceived our home in terms of dangers to her children (the saber and darts) and objects that youngsters might accidentally damage (crystal, sculptures). Because we don't have young children, Robbie and I hadn't noticed potential hazards that were obvious to Carolyn. Our perceptions differed because we had different interests and experiences. Perceptions—and differences among people's perceptions—are major influences on human communication.

This chapter focuses on meaning, which is the heart of communication. To understand how humans create meanings for themselves and their activities, we need to explore the relationship between perception and communication. As we will see, these two processes interact so that each affects the other in an ongoing cycle of influence. In other words, perception shapes how we understand others' communication and how we ourselves communicate. At the same time, communication influences our perceptions of people and situations. The two processes are intricately intertwined.

Our words profoundly affect how we perceive others, situations, and ourselves. At the same time, our perceptions, which are always incomplete and subjective, shape what things mean to us and the labels we use to describe them. We communicate with others according to how we perceive and define them, and we may miss opportunities when our labels limit what we perceive. In the pages that follow, we unravel the complex relationship between perception and communication.

To understand how perception and communication interact, we will first discuss the three-part process of perception. Next, we'll consider factors that affect our perceptions. Finally, we will explore ways to improve our abilities to perceive and communicate effectively.

Human PERCEPTION

The external world and our experiences gain meaning only when we perceive and attach significance to them. Perception concerns how we make sense of the world and what happens in it. **Perception** is an active process of selecting, organizing, and interpreting people, objects, events, situations, and activities. The first thing to notice about this definition is that perception is an active process. We don't passively receive stimuli. Instead, we actively work to make sense of ourselves, others, and interactions. To do so, we focus on only certain things, and then we organize and interpret what we have selectively noticed. What anything means to us depends on which aspects of it we attend to and how we organize and interpret what we notice. Thus, perception is not simply a matter of noting what exists. Instead, we interact actively with phenomena to construct meanings.

Perception consists of three processes: selecting, organizing, and interpreting. These processes are continuous, so they blend into and influence one another. They are also interactive, so each of them affects the other two.

Selection

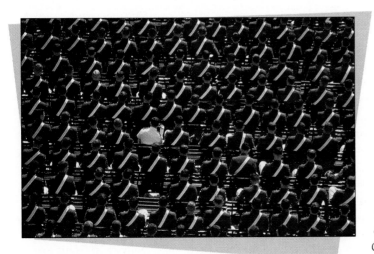

We notice things that stand out or vary from their surroundings.
(© James Holland/Stock, Boston)

Stop for a moment and notice what is going on around you right now. Is there music in the background or perhaps several different kinds of music from different places? Is the room warm or cold, messy or clean, large or small, light or dark? Is there laundry in the corner waiting to be washed? Can you smell anything—food being cooked, the stale odor of cigarette smoke, traces of cologne? Who else is in the room and nearby? Do you hear other conversations? Is the window open? Can you hear muted sounds of activities outside? Now think about what's happening inside you: Are you alert or sleepy, hungry, comfortable? Do you have a headache or an itch anywhere? On what kind of paper is your book printed? Is the type large, small, easy to read? How do you like the size of the book, the colors used, the design for features in the text?

Chances are that you weren't conscious of most of these phenomena when you began reading the chapter. Instead, you focused on reading and understanding the material in the book. You narrowed your attention to what you defined as important in this moment, and you were unaware of many other things going on around you. This is typical of how we live our lives. We can't attend to everything in our environment, because there is simply far too much there and most of it isn't relevant to us at a particular time.

Which stimuli we notice depends on a number of factors. First, some qualities of external phenomena draw attention. For instance, we notice things that **STAND OUT** because they are immediate, relevant, or intense. We're more likely to hear a loud voice than a soft one and to notice a bright shirt than a drab one. Change or variation also compels attention, which is why we may take for granted all of the pleasant interactions with a friend and notice only the tense moments.

Sometimes we deliberately influence what we notice by indicating things to ourselves (Mead, 1934). Indicating occurs when we point out certain things by naming them so that they are called to our attention. In many ways, education is a process of learning to indicate to ourselves things we hadn't seen. Right now you're learning to indicate to yourself that you perceive selectively, so in the future you will be more aware of selectivity in your perceptions. In English courses, you learn to notice how authors craft characters and use words to create images. Women's Studies classes heighten awareness of the consistent absence of women in most recorded history. In every case, we learn to perceive things that previously we didn't notice.

ABBY

Until I took a course in women's studies, I didn't realize how biased textbooks are. We learned that a lot of textbooks use more examples and pictures with men than women and that men are described more actively. Once the teacher pointed this out, I noticed it in my chemistry and psychology books and in the texts for other classes. Now no matter what I read, I notice whether women are underrepresented.

What we select to notice is also influenced by who we are and what is going on inside us. Our motives and needs affect what we see and don't see. If you've just broken up with a partner, you're more likely to notice attractive people at a party than if you are in an established romantic relationship. Motives also explain the oasis phenomenon in which thirsty people stranded in a desert see an oasis although none really exists. Our expectations further affect what we notice. We are more likely to perceive what we expect to perceive and what others lead us to anticipate. This explains the phenomenon of **self-fulfilling prophecy** in which a person acts in ways that are consistent with how others describe her or him. A child who is told she is unlovable may perceive herself that way and notice rejecting but not affirming communication from others. We selectively tune in to only some stimuli, so that we simplify the complexities of the world in which we live.

Expectations greatly influence how we perceive others, particularly people who differ from us in some way. In an experiment, racially prejudiced and unprejudiced European Americans were asked to describe African Americans pictured in photographs. The prejudiced viewers "saw" stereotypical racial characteristics such as broad noses and full lips, even when those features were not present. The unprejudiced viewers didn't notice stereotypical racial qualities. This study demonstrates how powerfully expectations can mold what we see (Secord, Bevan, & Katz, 1956).

LEE TENG-HUI

Before I came to school here, I was told that Americans are very pushy, loud, and selfish. For my first few months here, I saw that was true of Americans just as I had been told it would be. It took me longer to see also that Americans are friendly and helpful, because I had not been taught to expect these qualities.

Organization

Once we have selected what to notice, we must make sense of it. We don't simply collect perceptions and string them together randomly; instead, we organize them in meaningful ways. The most useful theory for explaining how we organize perceptions is **constructivism,** which states that we organize and interpret experience by applying cognitive structures called **schemata.** Originally developed by George Kelly in 1955, constructivism

THE WESTERN PROTOTYPE OF LOVE

Beverly Fehr and her colleagues have studied North American prototypes of love. For most of us, the prototype of love centers on five qualities: trust, caring, honesty, friendship, and respect. Passionate feelings and qualities, although often desired and appreciated, are not central to the cultural prototype of love. Instead, companionship seems to be the essence of what love means to us.

Sources: Fehr, B. (1993). How do I love thee: Let me consult my prototype. In S. W. Duck (Ed.), *Understanding relationship processes, 1: Individuals in relationships* (pp. 87–122). Newbury Park, CA: Sage. Fehr, B., & Russell, J. A. (1991). Concept of love viewed from a prototype perspective. *Journal of Personality and Social Psychology, 60,* 425–438.

has been elaborated by scholars in communication and psychology. We use four kinds of cognitive schemata to make sense of perceptions: prototypes, personal constructs, stereotypes, and scripts.

Prototypes **Prototypes** are knowledge structures that define the most clear or representative examples of some category (Fehr, 1993, p. 89). For example, you probably have prototypes of great teachers, unreasonable bosses, true friends, and perfect romantic partners. Each of these categories is exemplified by a person who is the ideal case—that's the prototype. We use prototypes to place others in categories—Jane is a friend, Martin is a romantic interest, Marge is a work associate. One way we classify people is by figuring out which of our prototypes they most closely resemble. Prototypes organize our perceptions by placing people and other phenomena in broad categories that are defined by prototypes. We may then consider how close a phenomenon is to the prototype for that category.

Personal Constructs **Personal constructs** are "mental yardsticks" that allow us to measure people and situations along bipolar dimensions of judgment (Kelly, 1955). Examples of personal constructs are intelligent–unintelligent, responsible–irresponsible, kind–unkind, and attractive–unattractive. To size up an individual, we measure her or him by personal constructs that we use to distinguish among people. How intelligent, kind, responsible, and attractive is this person? Whereas prototypes help decide into which broad category a person or event fits, personal constructs let us make more detailed assessments of particular qualities of phenomena we have indicated to ourselves. Our personal constructs shape our perceptions, because we define something only in terms of how it measures up on the constructs we use. Thus, we may not notice qualities of people that aren't covered by the constructs we apply.

Stereotypes call our attention to what members of a group have in common and obscure awareness of their differences. What stereotypes do you have about the people in this photograph?
(© Phil McCarten/PhotoEdit)

Stereotypes   **Stereotypes** are predictive generalizations about people and situations. Based on the category in which we place a phenomenon and how it measures up against personal constructs we apply, we predict what it will do. For instance, if you define someone as conservative, you might stereotype the person as likely to vote Republican, be against social programs, and so forth. You may have stereotypes of fraternity and sorority members, athletes, middle managers, and other groups of people.

Stereotypes may be accurate or inaccurate. They are generalizations, which are sometimes based on facts that are generally true of a group. In other cases, stereotypes are based on prejudice or assumptions, not facts. Even if we have accurate understandings of a group, they may not apply to particular individuals in it. Although most environmentalists don't smoke, a few do. Although college students, as a group, are more liberal than the population as a whole, some college students are very conservative. A particular individual may not conform to what is typical of her or his group as a whole. Thus, stereotypes are both necessary and troublesome: We need to have predictive generalizations, but they can distort our perceptions. Consequently, it's a good idea to remind ourselves that stereotypes are only generalizations.

SCOTT

The stereotype that really ticks me off is "dumb jock." I'm a fullback on the team, and I'm tall and big just like any good fullback. But I'm also a good student. I'm smart, I study, and I put a lot into papers and homework for classes. But a lot of the professors here and the students, too, assume I'm dumb just because I'm an athlete. Sometimes I say something in class, and you can just see surprise all over everyone's face because I had a good idea. When you think about it, athletes have to be smart to do all of their schoolwork plus practice and work out about 30 hours a week.

Scripts   To organize perceptions, we also use **scripts,** which are guides to action based on what we've experienced and observed. Scripts consist of a sequence of activities that define what we and others are expected to do in specific situations. Many of our daily activities are governed by scripts, although we're often unaware of them. You have a script for greeting casual acquaintances ("Hey, how ya doing?" "Fine. See ya around"). You also have scripts for going on first dates, managing conflict, talking with professors, attending meetings, interacting with superiors on the job, dealing with clerks, and relaxing with friends. We use scripts to organize perceptions into lines of action.

Prototypes, personal constructs, stereotypes, and scripts are cognitive schemata that we use to organize how we think about people and situations. They help us make sense of what we notice and anticipate how we and others will act in particular situations. The cognitive schemata we use reflect how our culture and specific social groups organize perceptions. As we interact with others, we internalize their ways of classifying, measuring, and predicting norms for acting in various situations.

Social perspectives are not always accurate or constructive, so we shouldn't accept them unreflectively. For instance, if your parents engaged in bitter, destructive quarreling, you may have learned a script for conflict that will undermine your relationships. Similarly, many Westerners have negative and inaccurate perceptions of some groups of people. We should assess these views critically before using them to organize our own perceptions and direct our own activities.

Everyday Application

PERCEIVING OTHERS

Pay attention to the cognitive schemata you use the next time you meet a new person. First, notice how you classify the person. Do you categorize her or him as a potential friend, date, bureaucrat, neighbor? Next, identify the constructs you use to assess the person. Do you focus on physical characteristics (attractive–unattractive), mental qualities (intelligent–unintelligent), psychological features (secure–insecure), and/or interpersonal qualities (eligible–committed)? Would different constructs be prominent if you used a different prototype to classify the person? Now, note how you stereotype the person. What do you expect him or her to do based on the prototype and constructs you've applied? Finally, identify your script—how you expect interaction to unfold between the two of you.

Interpretation

People, interactions, and situations have no intrinsic meaning. Instead, we assign meaning by interpreting what we have noticed and organized. **Interpretation** is the subjective process of explaining perceptions in ways that let us make sense of them. To interpret the meaning of others' actions, we construct explanations for what they say and do.

TABLE 2.1 Dimensions of Interpersonal Attributions		
Locus	Internal	External
Stability	Stable	Unstable
Scope	Global	Specific
Responsibility	Within personal control	Beyond personal control

Attributions Attributions are causal accounts that explain why things happen and why people act as they do (Heider, 1958; Kelley, 1967). Attribution is an active process, since we attribute causes to what we observe. It's good to remind ourselves that the attributions we make aren't always correct. Attributions have four dimensions (see Table 2.1). The first is internal/external locus, which attributes what a person does to either internal factors (he's sick) or external factors (the traffic jam frustrated him). The second dimension is stable/unstable, which explains actions as resulting from either stable factors that won't change (she's a Type A person) or temporary occurrences (she was irritable because she just had a fight with the boss). Global/specific is the third dimension, and it defines behavior as the result of a general pattern (he's a mean person) or a specific instance (he gets angry about sloppy work). Finally, there is the dimension of responsibility, which attributes behaviors either to factors people can control (she doesn't try to control her outbursts) or to ones they cannot (she has a chemical imbalance that makes her moody). In judging whether others can control their actions, we decide whether to hold them responsible for what they do.

Investigations have shown that happy and unhappy couples have distinct attributional styles. Happy couples make relationship-enhancing attributions. Individuals attribute nice things a partner does to internal, stable, and global reasons that the partner controls. "She got the film because she is a good person who always does sweet things for us." Unpleasant things a partner does are attributed to external, unstable, and specific factors and sometimes to influences beyond personal control. "He yelled at me because all of the stress of the past few days made him not himself." In contrast, unhappy couples make relationship-diminishing attributions. They explain nice actions as results of external, unstable, and specific factors. "She got the tape because she had some time to kill this particular day." Negative actions are seen as stemming from internal, stable, and global factors. "He yelled at me because he is a nasty person who never shows any consideration for anybody else." This suggests we should be mindful of the attributions we make, since they influence how we experience our relationships (Bradbury & Fincham, 1990; Fletcher & Fincham, 1991).

REVISING ATTRIBUTIONS

Think about an attribution you recently made about another person's behavior. Did you explain it as internally or externally caused? Did you label the behavior as stable or unstable, global or specific, and within control or not? Now experiment with changing your attribution. If you attributed the behavior to internal causes (mood, personality), try thinking about it as externally caused (circumstance). If you labeled the behavior as a specific occurrence, try thinking about it as part of a larger pattern. How do changes in your attributions affect how you feel about the behavior and the person?

Self-Serving Bias   Research indicates that we tend to construct attributions that serve our personal interests (Hamachek, 1992; Sypher, 1984). Thus, we are inclined to make internal, stable, and global attributions for our positive actions and our successes. We're also likely to claim that good results come about because of personal control we exerted. On the other hand, people tend to avoid taking responsibility for negative actions and failures by attributing them to external, unstable, and specific factors that are beyond personal control. In other words, we may perceive that our misconduct results from outside forces that we can't help, but all the good we do reflects our personal qualities and effort. This **self-serving bias** can distort our perceptions, leading us to take excessive personal credit for what we do well and to abdicate responsibility for what we do poorly. When we make faulty attributions for our behaviors, we form an unrealistic image of ourselves and our abilities.

NADINE

My mom wrote the book on self-serving bias. She likes to experiment with cooking, so she tries a lot of new dishes. When one turns out well, she grabs the credit, saying she used just the right touch on spices or knew how to adapt something in the original recipe. But when a dish is bad, she says the recipe was wrong or the store sold her tough meat or the stove didn't hold an even temperature. She feels proud when her dishes turn out well, but she never thinks it's her fault when one is a loser.

We've seen that perception involves three interrelated processes. The first of these, selection, allows us to notice certain things and ignore others. The second process is organization, where we use prototypes, personal constructs, stereotypes, and scripts to order what we have selectively perceived. Finally, we engage in interpretation to make sense of the perceptions we have gathered and organized. Attributions are a primary way we

Communication reflects the perspectives we have developed throughout our lives.
(© Craig Aurness/West Light)

explain what we and others do. Although we discussed each of these processes separately, in reality they may occur in different orders and they interact continuously. Thus, our interpretations can reverberate into the knowledge schemata we use to organize experiences, and the ways we order perceptions can affect what we notice. Now that we understand the complex processes involved in perception, we are ready to consider a range of factors that influence what and how we perceive.

INFLUENCES ON PERCEPTION

In opening this chapter, I mentioned an incident in which my sister's perceptions differed from mine. Her experience as a parent led her to perceive objects that could be dangerous to children or could be damaged by children. Not being a parent, I didn't perceive what she did. Similarly, able-bodied people might not notice the lack of elevators or ramps in a building, but someone with a physical disability would immediately perceive the building as inaccessible. European American students often don't notice that few people of color are in classes at many colleges, but the ethnic majority is very obvious to African Americans, Asians, Native Americans, and others who are not European Americans. As these examples illustrate, people differ in how they perceive situations and people. Let's consider some of the influences on our perceptions.

Physiology

The most obvious reason perceptions vary among people is that we differ in our sensory abilities and physiologies. The five senses are not the same for all of us. Music that one person finds deafening is barely audible to another. Salsa that is painfully hot to one diner may seem mild to someone else. On a given day on my campus, students wear everything from shorts and sandals to jackets, indicating they have different sensitivities to cold. Some people have better vision than others, and still others are color-blind. Differences in sensory abilities affect our perceptions.

Our physiological states also influence perception. If you are tired, stressed, or sick, you're likely to perceive things negatively that might not bother you when you feel rested and healthy. For instance, a criticism from a co-worker might anger you if you're feeling down, but wouldn't bother you if you felt good. Also, if you interact with someone who is sick, you might attribute negative behaviors to unstable and specific causes rather than to enduring personality. Each of us has our own biorhythm, which influences the times of day when we tend to be alert and fuzzy. I'm a morning person, so that's when I prefer to teach classes and write. I am less alert and creative late in the day. Thus, I perceive things in the morning that I simply don't notice when my energy level declines.

IT USED TO BE THAT IF A CLIENT WANTED SOMETHING DONE IN A WEEK, IT WAS CONSIDERED A RUSH JOB, AND HE'D BE LUCKY TO GET IT.

NOW, WITH MODEMS, FAXES, AND CAR PHONES, EVERYBODY WANTS EVERYTHING INSTANTLY! IMPROVED TECHNOLOGY JUST INCREASES EXPECTATIONS.

THESE MACHINES DON'T MAKE LIFE EASIER — THEY MAKE LIFE MORE HARASSED.

SIX MINUTES TO MICROWAVE THIS?? WHO'S GOT THAT KIND OF TIME?!

IF WE WANTED MORE LEISURE, WE'D INVENT MACHINES THAT DO THINGS *LESS* EFFICIENTLY.

(©1995 Watterson. Dist. by Universal Press Synd. Reprinted by permission.)

Age is another factor that influences our perceptions. The older we get, the more rich a perspective we have for perceiving life and people. Thus, compared to a person of 20, a person of 60 has a more complex fund of experiences to draw on in perceiving. Perhaps you think nothing of paying 50 or 75 cents for a can of soda, but I recall paying a dime when I was younger. To me, the current prices seem high in comparison to what a soft drink cost 20 years ago. The extent of discrimination still experienced by women and minorities understandably discourages many college students. I am more hopeful that our society is increasingly accepting of differences than some of my students because I have seen so many changes in my lifetime. When I attended college, women weren't admitted on an equal basis with men and almost all students of color attended minority colleges. The substantial progress made during my life leads me to perceive current inequities as changeable.

Culture

The influence of culture is so pervasive that it's hard to realize how powerfully it shapes our perceptions. A **culture** consists of beliefs, values, understandings, practices, and ways of interpreting experience that are shared by a number of people. It is a set of taken-for-granted assumptions that form the pattern of our lives and that guide how we think, feel, and act. One of the best ways to recognize the values and structures of a culture is to travel to places with different values, understandings, and codes of behavior.

Consider a few aspects of modern Western culture that influence our perceptions. One characteristic of our culture is the emphasis on technology and its offspring, speed. We expect things to happen fast—almost instantly. Whether it's instant photos, 5-minute copying, or 1-hour martinizing, we live at an accelerated pace (Wood, 1995b). We FedEx letters, jet across the country, correspond by electronic mail, and microwave meals. Social commentators suggest that the cultural emphasis on speed may diminish patience and thus our willingness to invest in long-term projects, such as relationships (Toffler, 1970, 1980). In countries such as Nepal and Mexico, life proceeds at a more leisurely pace and people spend more time talking, relaxing, and engaging in low-key activity.

North America is also a fiercely individualistic culture in which personal initiative is expected and rewarded. Other cultures, particularly many Asian ones, are more communal and identity is defined in terms of one's family, rather than as an individual quality. Because families are more valued in communal cultures, elders are given greater respect and care than they often receive in the United States. The difference between communal and individualistic cultures is also evident in child-care policies. Communal countries have policies that reflect the value they place on families. In every developed country except the United States, new parents, including adoptive parents, are given at least 6 weeks of subsidized parental leave, and some countries provide nearly a year's paid leave (Wood, 1994d).

Everyday Application

NOTICING INDIVIDUALISM

How do the individualistic values of our culture influence our perceptions and activities? Check it out by observing the following:

> How is seating arranged in restaurants? Are there large, communal eating areas or private tables and booths for individuals or small groups?

> How are living spaces arranged? How many people live in the average house? Do families share homes?

> How many people share a car in your family? How many cars are there in the United States?

How does the Western emphasis on individualism affect your day-to-day perceptions and activities?

In recent years, scholars have realized that we are affected not only by the culture as a whole, but also by our particular location within the culture (Haraway, 1988; Harding, 1991). **Standpoint theory** claims that a culture includes a number of social groups and each one distinctively shapes the perceptions, identities, and opportunities of its members. Race–ethnicity, gender, class, religious commitment, age, and sexual orientation are primary ways that Western culture groups people. Although we may all realize our society attaches unequal value to different social groups, each of us is only one race, class, sex, and so forth. The way we perceive the world and ourselves is shaped by our experiences as members of the particular groups to which we belong. This is why an African American is likely to notice the absence of people of color in a campus group and European Americans are less likely to perceive the imbalance.

Caregiving is a skill we learn through socialization. (© Margaret Miller/Photo Researchers, Inc.)

In the earliest writing on standpoint, the philosopher Georg William Frederick Hegel (1807) pointed out that standpoints reflect power positions in social hierarchies. To illustrate, he noted that the system of slavery is perceived very differently by masters and slaves. Extending Hegel's point, we can see that those in positions of power have a vested interest in preserving the system that gives them privileges. Thus, they are unlikely to perceive its flaws and inequities. On the other hand, those who are disempowered by a system are most able to discern inequities and discrimination (Harding, 1991).

Women and men, as social groups, have different standpoints. For instance, the caregiving often associated with women is not due primarily to maternal instinct, but rather to socialization that teaches women to care for others, notice who needs what, and defer their own needs (Ruddick, 1989). Researchers have discovered that men who are primary caregivers become nurturing, accommodative, and sensitive to others' needs as a consequence of being in the role of caregiver (Kaye & Applegate, 1990).

JACOB

When Ellen and I married, we agreed to take equal responsibility for everything from earning income to housework and taking care of kids. When our twins were born, at first I felt like Ellen should be the primary parent, but she insisted that I be as involved as she was. Taking care of the twins really changed me—made me more aware of what others need, more patient, and more flexible about adjusting my own priorities to accommodate those of others. I think everyone would benefit by taking care of children.

Gendered standpoints are also evident in communication during marital conflict. Researchers have found that conflict erodes wives' love for husbands more than it affects husbands' love for wives (Huston, McHale, & Crouter, 1986; Kelly, Huston, & Cate, 1985). This makes sense in light of research demonstrating that husbands generally exercise more power over decision making, so they usually prevail in conflict. Naturally, the winners of conflicts are more satisfied than losers!

Gendered standpoints are also obvious in the difference between the amount of effort that women and men in general invest in communication that maintains relationships. Socialized into the role of "relationship expert," women are expected by others and themselves to take care of relationships (Tavris, 1992; Wood, 1993b, 1994d). They are supposed to know when something is wrong and to take the lead in resolving any tension. This may explain why women tend to be more aware than men of problems in relationships and to be more willing to discuss them (Brehm, 1992). It may also shed light on the reasons for women's tendency to exercise leadership in personal and relationship-oriented ways (Helgesen, 1990; Natalle, 1996).

Both your membership in an overall culture and your standpoint as a member of particular social groups are communication contexts that shape how you perceive people, situations, events, social life, and yourself.

Social Roles

Our perceptions are also shaped by social roles that others communicate to us. Both messages that tell us we are expected to fulfill particular roles and the actual demands of those roles affect how we perceive and communicate. I perceive my classes in terms of how interested students seem, whether they appear to have read material, and whether they find what they're learning to be useful in their lives. Students have told me that they think about classes in terms of number and difficulty of tests, whether papers are required, and whether the professor is interesting. We have different perspectives on what classes are. In working on this book, I concentrated on ideas, information, and organization. In addition to noticing those aspects of a book, my editor, Todd, also focused on layout, design features, and marketing issues that don't occur to me.

The careers people enter influence what they notice and how they think and act. Prior to her professional training, my sister Carolyn had not developed skill in analytic thinking. After law school, however, she was extremely analytic, and her conversational style shifted to be more argumentative, logical, and probing. Doctors are trained to be highly observant of physical symptoms, and they may detect a physical problem before a person knows that she or he has it. For example, at a social gathering, a friend of mine who is a doctor asked me how long I had had a herniated disk. Shocked, I told him I didn't have one. "You do," he insisted, and sure enough, a few weeks later a disk ruptured. His medical training enabled him to perceive subtle changes in my posture and walk that I hadn't noticed.

Cognitive Abilities

In addition to physiological, cultural, and social influences, perception is also shaped by our cognitive abilities. How elaborately we think about situations and people and the extent of our personal knowledge of others affect how we select, organize, and interpret experiences.

Cognitive Complexity People differ in the number and type of knowledge schemata they use to organize and interpret people and situations. **Cognitive complexity** refers to the number of constructs used, how abstract they are, and how elaborately they interact to shape perceptions. Most

(René Magritte, *The False Mirror* (1928). Oil on canvas, 21¼ × 31⅞". The Museum of Modern Art, N.Y. Purchase. Photograph © 1996 The Museum of Modern Art, N.Y. © 1996 C. Herscovici/ Artists Rights Society (ARS), N.Y.)

children have fairly simple cognitive systems. They rely on few schemata, focus more on concrete categories than abstract ones, and often don't perceive relationships among different perceptions. For instance, infants may call any and every adult male "Daddy," because they haven't learned more complex ways to distinguish among men.

Adults also differ in cognitive complexity, and this affects their perceptions and styles of communicating. If you can think of people only as nice or mean, you have a limited range for perceiving others. Similarly, people who focus on concrete data tend to have less sophisticated understandings than people who also perceive psychological data. For example, you might notice that a co-worker is assertive, tells jokes, and talks to others easily. These are concrete perceptions. At a more abstract, psychological level, you might reason that the concrete behaviors you observe reflect a secure, self-confident personality. This is a more sophisticated cognition because it integrates three perceptions to develop an explanation of why the person acts as she or he does.

Now what if you later find out that the person is very quiet in one-to-one situations? Someone with low cognitive complexity would have difficulty integrating the new information into prior observations. Either the new information would be dismissed because it doesn't fit or the most recent data would replace the former perception and the person would be redefined as shy. A more cognitively complex person would integrate all of the information into a coherent account. Perhaps a cognitively complex individual would conclude that the person is very confident in social situations, but less secure in more personal ones.

Research has shown that cognitively complex individuals tend to be relatively flexible in interpreting complicated phenomena and in integrating new information into how they think about people and situations. More cognitively simple individuals are likely to ignore discrepant information that doesn't fit neatly with their impressions or to use it to supplant the impressions they have already formed (Delia, Clark, & Switzer, 1974). Either way, they fail to recognize some of the nuances and inconsistencies that are part of human nature. The complexity of our cognitive systems affects the fullness and intricacy of our perceptions of people and interpersonal situations. Cognitively complex individuals also tend to communicate in more flexible, appropriate ways with a range of others. This probably is due to their ability to recognize differences in people and to adapt their own communication accordingly.

Person-Perception   Person-perception is related to cognitive complexity, since it requires abstract thinking and a breadth of schemata. Person-perception refers to the ability to perceive another as a unique and distinct individual apart from social roles and generalizations. Our ability to perceive others as unique depends both on general ability to make cognitive distinctions and on how well we know particular others. As we get to know individuals, we gain insight into how they differ from others in their groups ("Rob's not like most campus politicos"; "Janet's more flexible than most managers"). The more we interact with another and the greater variety of experiences we have together, the more insight we gain into that individual's motives and perspective. As we come to understand others, we fine-tune our perceptions of them in a process that continues throughout the life of relationships.

D A V E

First dates are the pits. It's so awkward to keep up a conversation with somebody you don't really know. You try one line of talk and it flops, so you try another. Then she starts something up, but you can't really get into that. It usually takes about three dates with a new girl before I feel comfortable about how to interact. I wish there were some easier way to get to know new people.

Person-perception is not the same as empathy. **Empathy** is the ability to feel with another person—to feel what she or he feels in a situation. Feeling with another is an emotional response. Because feelings are guided by our own emotional tendencies and experiences, it may be impossible to feel exactly and completely what another person feels. A more realistic goal is to try to recognize another's perspective and adapt your communication to how she or he perceives situations and people (Phillips & Wood, 1983; Wood, 1982, 1995b). With commitment and effort, we can learn a lot about how others see the world, even if that differs from how we see it.

When we take the perspective of others, we try to grasp what something means to them and how they perceive things. This requires suspending judgment at least temporarily. We can't appreciate someone else's perspective when we're imposing our evaluations of whether it is right or wrong, sensible or crazy. Instead, we have to let go of our own perspective and perceptions long enough to enter the mind-set of another person. Doing this allows us to understand issues from the other person's point of view, so that we can communicate more effectively. You might learn why your boss thinks something is important that you've been disregarding. You might find out how a friend interprets your behavior in ways inconsistent with what you intend to communicate. You might discover why a person on your project team places greater priority on an issue than you do. At a later point in interaction, we may choose to express our own perspective or to disagree with another's views. This is appropriate and important in honest communication, but voicing our own views is not a substitute for the equally important skill of recognizing another's perspective.

Taking the perspective of others is a foundation of effective communication. (© Lawrence Migdale/Stock, Boston)

In sum, we've seen that many factors influence perception and account for variation among people's perceptions. Differences based on physiology, culture, standpoint, social roles, and cognitive abilities affect what we perceive and how we interpret others and experiences. In the final section of the chapter, we consider ways to improve the accuracy of our perceptions.

ENHANCING COMMUNICATION COMPETENCE

Perceptions are a key foundation of communication. To be a competent communicator, you need to realize how perception and communication affect one another. We'll elaborate the connection between perception and communication and then discuss guidelines for enhancing communication competence.

Perceptions, Communication, and Abstraction

Words crystallize perceptions. When we name feelings and thoughts, we create precise ways to describe and think about them. But just as words crystallize experiences, they can also freeze thought. Once we label our perceptions, we may respond to our own labels rather than actual phenomena.

In our own lives, the labels we use can affect our perceptions of what is happening. Consider this situation. Suppose you get together with five others in a study group and a student named Andrea monopolizes the whole meeting with her questions and concerns. Leaving the meeting, one person says, "Gee, Andrea is so selfish and immature! I'll never work with her again." Another person responds, "She's not really selfish. She's insecure about her grades in this course, so she was hyper in the meeting." Chances are these two people will perceive and treat Andrea differently depending

WHAT YOU SAY IS WHAT YOU GET

The effect of labels on perception is dramatically evident in eyewitness testimony. Studies show that witnesses' perceptions are shaped by the language attorneys use to describe phenomena.

In one experiment, viewers were shown a film of a traffic accident and then asked "How fast were the cars going when they *smashed* into each other?" Other viewers were asked how fast the cars were going when they *bumped* or *collided*. Viewers testified to significantly different speeds depending on which word was used in the question.

In a separate experiment, viewers were shown a film of a traffic accident and then filled out a questionnaire that included questions about things that had not actually been on the film. Viewers who were asked "Did you see *the* broken headlight?" more frequently testified they saw it than did viewers who were asked "Did you see *a* broken headlight?" The accidents that viewers "saw" were shaped by the words used to describe them.

Source: Trotter, R. J. (1975, October 25). "The truth, the whole truth, and nothing but . . ." *Science News, 108,* 269.

on whether they label her selfish or insecure. The point is that the two people don't respond to Andrea herself, but to how they label their perceptions of her.

Communication is based on a process of abstracting from complex stimuli. Our perceptions are not equivalent to the complex reality on which they are based, since total reality can never be fully described, nor even apprehended. This means that what we perceive is a step removed from stimuli, since perceptions are always partial and subjective. We move a second step from stimuli when we label a perception. We move even further from the stimuli when we respond not to behaviors or our perceptions of them, but to the judgments we associate with the label we have imposed. This process can be illustrated as a ladder of abstraction as shown in Figure 2.1 (Hayakawa, 1962, 1964; Korzybski, 1948).

Guidelines for Enhancing Competence

Thinking of communication as a process of abstracting suggests ways to enhance competence in interaction. Five guidelines help us avoid problems abstraction may invite.

Recognize That All Perceptions Are Subjective   Our perceptions are partial and subjective because we perceive from a personal perspective that is shaped by physiology, culture, standpoint, social roles, and cognitive abili-

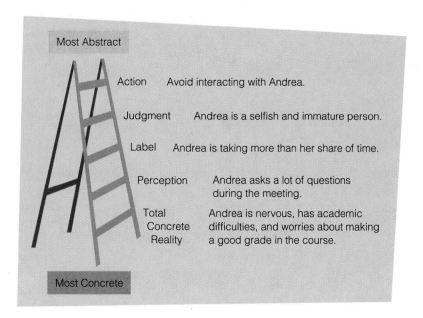

FIGURE 2.1
Perception, Communication,
and Abstraction

ties. Phenomena have no meaning until we perceive them and define what they mean. A party perceived as fun by one person may seem boring to another. A class you find exciting may put another student to sleep. Writing is a creative, enjoyable activity for some of us and a tedious grind for others. There is no truth or falsity to perceptions—they represent what things mean to individuals. Thus, when you and another person disagree about something, it's likely that differences in your social, cultural, and physiological backgrounds influence the disparity in your perceptions. Effective communicators realize that perceptions are subjective and don't assume their own perceptions are the only valid ones.

Avoid Mindreading   One of the most common problems in communication is **mindreading,** which is assuming we understand what another person thinks or perceives. When we mindread, we don't check with another person to see what he or she is thinking. Instead, we act as if we know what's on another's mind, and this can get us into considerable trouble. Marriage counselors identify mindreading as one of the behaviors that contributes to interpersonal tension (Gottman, 1993). According to communication scholar Fran Dickson (1995), one exception may be mindreading between spouses in long-lasting marriages. After living together for so long, partners may be able to mindread with considerable accuracy.

For the most part, however, mindreading is more likely to harm than help communication. We risk misreading others, such as supervisors, co-workers, and friends, when we assume we know what they are thinking. Mindreading invites problems when we say things such as "I know why you're upset" (Has the person said she or he is upset?) or "You don't care about me" (maybe the other person is too preoccupied or worried to be as attentive as usual). We also mindread when we tell ourselves we know how somebody else will feel or react, or what they'll do. The truth is we don't really know—we're only guessing. When we mindread, we impose our perspectives on others instead of letting them define their feelings. This can lead to resentment as well as misunderstandings, since most of us prefer to speak for ourselves.

PAT

I got into a lot of trouble mindreading my girlfriend. When we first started dating, I made a lot of assumptions about what Anne would or wouldn't like and then acted as if what I assumed was a fact. For example, once I got tickets for a concert that I "knew" she'd want to go to, but she had to go out of town that weekend. Another time, I "knew" she'd want to take a study break during exam week, so I got a pizza and stopped by. She was really irritated because she had eaten early and was settled in for a heavy review session. It took me a while, but I finally realized I should ask her what she wants instead of assuming I know. We've gotten along a lot better since I figured that out.

Check Perceptions with Others Because perceptions are subjective and mindreading is ineffective, we need to check our perceptions with others. Perception checking is an important communication skill because it helps people arrive at mutual understandings of each other and their relationships. To check perceptions, you should first state what it is that you have noticed. For example, a person might say, "Lately you've seemed less attentive to me." Second, the person should check to see whether the other perceives the same thing: "Do you feel you've been less attentive?" Third, it's appropriate to offer alternative explanations of your perceptions ("It might be that you are annoyed with me or that you're stressed out at work or that you're focused on other things"). Finally, you may ask the other person to clarify how she or he perceives the behavior and the reasons for it ("What do you think is going on?"). If the other person doesn't share your perceptions, ask him or her to explain the behaviors on which your perception is based ("Why have you wanted to be together less often and seemed distracted when we've talked lately?").

It's important to speak tentatively when you're checking perceptions. This minimizes defensiveness and encourages open dialogue. Just let the other person know you've noticed something and would like him or her to clarify his or her perceptions of what is happening and what it means. It's also a good idea to check perceptions directly with the other person. It is more difficult to reach a shared understanding with another person when we ask someone else to act as a go-between or when we ask others if they agree with our perceptions of a third person.

(©1994 by Matt Groening. All rights reserved. Reprinted by permission of Acme Features Syndicate.)

PERCEPTION CHECKING

Becoming skillful at checking perceptions requires practice. Enhance your skill by doing the following:

1. The next time you catch yourself mindreading, stop. Tell the other person what you are noticing and invite her or him to explain how she or he perceives what's happening. Does the person agree with you about what you noticed? If you agree, then find out how the other person interprets what you've noticed.

2. Focus on perception checking for 3 days so that you have lots of chances to see what happens. Keep a tally of the times your mindreading was inaccurate.

Distinguish Between Facts and Inferences Competent communicators know the difference between facts and inferences. A fact is a statement based on observation or other data. An inference involves an interpretation that goes beyond the facts. For example, it is a fact that my partner, Robbie, forgets a lot of things. Based on that fact, I might infer that he is thoughtless. Defining Robbie as thoughtless is an inference that goes beyond the facts. The "fact" of his forgetfulness could equally well be explained by preoccupation or general absentmindedness.

DISTINGUISHING FACTS FROM INFERENCES

Identify whether each of the following statements is a fact or an inference.

1. There are 50 states in the United States.
2. HIV/AIDS is caused by immoral sexual activity.
3. Women have a maternal instinct.
4. German Shepherds have a tendency to suffer hip dysplasia.
5. Students who come to class late are disrespectful.
6. Acid rain destroys trees.
7. College students earn money for dating and clothes.
8. Older students aren't career oriented.

9. Evelyn made 378 on the LSAT exam.

10. Evelyn would not do well in law school.

Numbers 1, 4, 6, and 9 are facts; 2, 3, 5, 7, 8, and 10 are inferences.

It's easy to confuse facts and inferences because we sometimes treat the latter as the former. When we say "He is irresponsible," we make a statement that sounds factual, and we may then regard it that way ourselves. To avoid this tendency, substitute more tentative words for *is*. For instance, "Robbie's behaviors seem thoughtless" is more tentative than "Robbie is thoughtless." Tentative language helps us resist the tendency to treat inferences as facts.

USING TENTATIVE LANGUAGE

For the next 24 hours, listen carefully for language that blurs facts and inferences. Listen for words like *is* and *are,* which imply factual knowledge. When others say someone or something "is" a certain way, are they making a factual statement or an inference? When you use *is*-words, do you have a factual foundation for your statements?

Substitute tentative language for *is*-language. How does this affect your perceptions and judgments?

Monitor the Self-Serving Bias   Earlier in this chapter, we discussed the self-serving bias. You'll recall it involves attributing our successes and nice behaviors to internal, stable qualities that we control and attributing our failures and bad behaviors to external, unstable factors beyond our control. Because this bias can distort perceptions, we need to monitor it carefully.

Monitoring the self-serving bias also has implications for how we perceive others. Just as we tend to judge ourselves generously, we may also be inclined to judge others too harshly. Monitor your perceptions to see whether you attribute others' successes and admirable actions to external factors beyond their control and their shortcomings and blunders to internal factors they can (should) control. If you do this, substitute more generous explanations for others' behaviors and notice how that affects your perceptions of them.

Perceiving accurately is neither magic nor an ability that some people just naturally have. Instead, it is a communication skill that can be developed. Following the five guidelines we have discussed will allow you to perceive more carefully and accurately.

SUMMARY

In this chapter, we've explored human perception, which involves selecting, organizing, and interpreting experiences. These three processes are not separate in practice; instead, they interact so that each one affects the others. What we selectively notice affects what we interpret and evaluate. In addition, our interpretations act as lenses that influence what we notice in the world around us. Selection, interpretation, and evaluation interact continuously in the process of perception.

Perception is shaped by many factors. Our sensory capacities and our physiological condition affect what we notice and how astutely we recognize stimuli around us. In addition, our cultural backgrounds and standpoints in society shape how we see and interact with the world. Social roles are another influence on perception. Thus, professional training and roles in families affect what we notice and how we organize and interpret it. Finally, perception is influenced by cognitive abilities including cognitive complexity, person-perception, and perspective taking.

Thinking about communication as a process of abstracting helps us understand how perception works. We discussed five guidelines for avoiding the problems abstraction sometimes causes. First, realize that all perceptions are subjective, so there is no absolutely correct or best understanding of a situation or a person. Second, because people perceive differently, we should avoid mindreading or assuming we know what others are perceiving. Third, it's a good idea to check perceptions, which involves stating how you perceive something and asking how another person does. A fourth guideline is to distinguish facts from inferences. Finally, avoiding the self-serving bias is important, since it can lead us to perceive ourselves too charitably and to perceive others too harshly.

When we label our selective perceptions, we abstract for notice only some of the stimuli around us. Consequently, we can't see aspects of ourselves and others that our labels don't highlight. Realizing this encourages us to be more sensitive to the power of language and to make more considered choices about how we use it.

FOR FURTHER REFLECTION AND DISCUSSION

1. Identify a positive and negative self-fulfilling prophecy in your life. Describe how communication from and with others created these prophecies. How did they affect your behaviors and your beliefs about yourself?

2. To understand how your standpoint influences perceptions, enter a culture different from the one you are used to. If you are Caucasian, you might attend services at a black church or a meeting of an African American community group. Do you notice your whiteness more in this context? If you are not Caucasian, reflect on the differences in how you perceive situations in which Caucasians are the majority and situations in which your own race is the majority. With others in your class, discuss the impact of standpoint on perceptions and communication.

3. Use the ladder of abstraction to analyze your perceptions and actions in a specific communication encounter. First, identify the concrete reality, what you perceived from the totality, the labels you assigned, and the resulting inferences and judgments. Second, return to the first level of perception and substitute different perceptions—other aspects of the total situation you might have selectively perceived. What labels, inferences, and judgments do the substitute perceptions invite? With others in the class, discuss the extent to which our perceptions and labels influence "reality."

KEY TERMS

perception	attributions
self-fulfilling prophecy	self-serving bias
constructivism	culture
schemata	standpoint theory
prototypes	cognitive complexity
personal constructs	person-perception
stereotypes	empathy
scripts	mindreading
interpretation	

Focus Questions

1 How does your self-concept affect your communication?

2 How does your communication affect your self-concept?

3 How do cultural perspectives influence how you perceive yourself and others?

4 How can you improve your self-concept?

5 What is self-sabotage, and how do you avoid it?

CHAPTER 3

Communication and Personal Identity

Who are you? That's a question that you've pondered time and again throughout your life. We answer the question one way at one time, then change our answer as we ourselves change. When you were 5 or 6 you probably defined yourself as your parents' son or daughter. In doing so, you implicitly recognized sex, race, and social class as parts of your identity. In high school you may have described yourself in terms of academic abilities ("I'm better at math than history"), athletic achievements ("I'm on the track team"), leadership positions ("I'm president of the club"), your social circle ("I'm in the college-bound group"; "My best friend is Cindy"), or future plans ("I'm going to study business in college next year").

If you entered college shortly after completing high school, it's likely you're starting to see yourself in terms of a major, career path, and perhaps a relationship you hope will span the years ahead. If you have worked and established a family, you probably already have a sense of yourself as a professional, and you may see the student role as only one of many in your life. By now you've probably made some decisions about your sexual orientation, religious commitments, and political beliefs. Now and throughout your life, you'll be engaged in the unending process of sculpting your personal identity.

As you think about the different ways you've defined yourself over the years, you'll realize that the self is not fixed firmly at one time and constant thereafter. Instead, the self is a process that evolves and changes throughout our lives. Among the experiences that have the greatest impact on how we see ourselves are interactions with others. In this chapter, we will explore how the self develops continuously through communication with others.

WHAT IS THE SELF?

The **self** is a complex process that involves internalizing and acting from social perspectives that we learn as we communicate. At first this may seem like a complicated way to define self. As we will see, however, this definition directs our attention to some important propositions about what, in fact, is very complicated—the self.

The Self Arises in Communication with Others

The most basic proposition about the self is that communication is essential to developing a self. Infants aren't born with selves. Instead, we develop selves in the process of communicating with particular others and participating in social life in general. As we internalize others' perspectives, we come to share their perceptions of the world, people, situations, and ourselves.

From the moment we enter the world, we interact with others. As we do, we learn how they see us, and we take their perspectives inside ourselves. Once we have internalized the views of particular others and the society in general, we engage in internal dialogues in which we remind ourselves of social perspectives. It is through the process of internal dialogues, or conversations with ourselves, that we enforce the social values we have learned and the views of us that others communicate. How we perceive ourselves reflects the image of us that is reflected in others' eyes. We'll return to this idea later in the chapter.

Self-Fulfilling Prophecy   One particularly powerful way in which communication shapes the self is self-fulfilling prophecy, which is acting in ways that bring about expectations or judgments of ourselves. If you have done poorly in classes where teachers didn't seem to respect you and done well with teachers who thought you were smart, then you know what self-fulfilling prophecy is. Perhaps you have been more effective on the job when you had a supervisor who expressed confidence in you and your abilities. The prophecies that we act to fulfill are usually first communicated by

How we see ourselves is strongly influenced by our family interactions.
(© David M. Grossman/Photo Researchers, Inc.)

others. Because we internalize others' perspectives, however, we may label ourselves as they do and then act to fulfill our own labels. We may try to live up or down to the ways others define us and the ways we define ourselves. A friend of mine constantly remarks that he is unattractive. As a child, he was overweight and his family constantly called him "fatty" and "tubby." Later he had to wear braces and endure the nickname "silvermouth." Now my friend is slender and physically attractive, but he can't see that. He still sees himself in terms of outdated labels. As a result, he won't buy nice clothes, saying "What's the point?" He accepted others' judgments that he was unattractive and continues to fulfill the prophecy by being less attractive than he could be.

Like my friend, many of us believe things about ourselves that are inaccurate. Sometimes labels that were once true aren't any longer, but we continue to believe them and to communicate in ways that reflect those labels. In other cases, the labels were never valid, but we are trapped by them anyway. Unfortunately, children are often called slow or stupid when the real problem is that they have physiological difficulties such as impaired vision or hearing. Even when the true source of difficulty is discovered, it may be too late—the children have already bought into a destructive self-fulfilling prophecy. If we accept others' judgments, they may become self-fulfilling prophecies.

Communication with three kinds of others is especially influential in shaping self-concept.

Communication with Family Members   For most of us, family members are the first and most important influence on how we see ourselves. Because family interaction dominates our early years, it usually establishes the foundations of our self-concepts. Parents and other family members communicate who we are and what we are worth through direct definitions, identity scripts, and attachment styles.

Direct definition, as the name implies, is communication that explicitly tells us who we are by labeling us and our behaviors. Parents and other family members define us by how they describe us. For instance, parents might say "You're my little girl" or "You're a big boy," and thus communicate to the child what sex it is. Having been labeled boy or girl, the child then pays attention to other communication about boys and girls to figure out what it means to be a certain sex. Family members guide our understandings of gender by instructing us in what boys and girls do and don't do. Parents' own gender stereotypes are typically communicated to

POSITIVE SELF-FULFILLING PROPHECY

Georgia Tech's Challenge program is a bridge course designed to help disadvantaged, primarily minority students succeed academically. Yet for years, students who enrolled in Challenge did no better than disadvantaged students who didn't attend.

Norman Johnson, a special assistant to the president of Tech, explained that Challenge failed because the program was based on the idea that disadvantaged students were dumb. The whole program was set up on a deficit model. Knowing the power of self-fulfilling prophecy, Johnson revamped the program by telling instructors that Challenge students were unusually bright and were quick learners.

Once Challenge teachers expected success from their students, they communicated this expectation by the way they acted toward the students. The results were impressive: In 1992, 10% of the first-year Challenge students had perfect 4.0 averages for the academic year. By comparison, only 5% of the white students who didn't participate in Challenge had perfect averages. That 10% was more than all of the minority students who had achieved 4.0 averages in the entire 1980–1990 decade. When teachers expected Challenge students to do well and communicated those expectations, the students in fact did do well—a case of a positive self-fulfilling prophecy.

Source: Raspberry, W. (1994, July 5). Major gains in minorities' grades at Tech. *Raleigh News and Observer,* p. A9.

children, so daughters are told "Nice girls don't play rough," "Be kind to your friends," and "Don't mess up your clothes." Sons, on the other hand, are more likely to be told "Go out and get 'em," "Stick up for yourself," and "Don't cry." As we hear these messages, we pick up our parents' and society's gender expectations.

Family members provide direct communication about many aspects of who we are through statements they make. Positive labels enhance our self-esteem: "You're so responsible," "You are smart," "You're sweet," "You're great at soccer." Negative labels can damage children's self-esteem: "You're a troublemaker," "You're stupid," and "You're impossible" are messages that demolish a child's sense of self-worth.

Direct definition also takes place as family members respond to children's behaviors. If a child clowns around and parents respond by saying "What a cut-up; you really are funny," the child learns to see herself or himself as funny. If a child dusts furniture and receives praise ("You're great to help me clean the house"), being helpful to others is reinforced as part of the child's self-concept. From direct definition, children learn what parents value, and this shapes what they come to value. For instance, in my family, reading was considered very important. I was great at outdoor activities such as building tree houses and leading "jungle expeditions" through the woods behind our home. Yet my parents were indifferent to my aptitudes for adventures and physical activity. What they stressed was learning and reading. I still have vivid memories of being shamed for a "B"

Parents show and tell us how to be masculine or feminine.
(© Spencer Grant/Stock, Boston)

in reading on my first-grade report card. Just as keenly I recall the excessive praise heaped on me when I won a reading contest in fourth grade. By then I had learned how to get my parents' approval. Through explicit labels and responses to our behaviors, family members provide direct definitions of who we are and—just as important—who we are supposed to be.

Identity scripts are another way family members communicate who we are. Psychologists define identity scripts as rules for how we are supposed to live and who we are supposed to be (Berne, 1964; Harris, 1969). Like the scripts for plays, identity scripts define our roles, how we are to play them, and basic elements in the plot of our lives. Usually, identity scripts reflect the values and heritage of our family. Think back to your childhood to identify some of the principal scripts that operated in your family. Did you learn "We are responsible people," "Save your money for a rainy day," "Always help others," "Look out for yourself," or "Live by God's word"? These are examples of identity scripts people learn in families.

Most psychologists believe that the basic identity scripts for our lives are formed very early, probably by age 5. This means that fundamental understandings of who we are and how we are supposed to live are forged when we have virtually no control. We aren't allowed to co-author or even edit our initial identity scripts, because adults have power and children aren't conscious of learning scripts. The process by which we internalize scripts that others write is largely unconscious and we absorb them with little, if any, awareness. As adults, however, we are no longer passive tablets on which others can write out who we are. We have the capacity to review the identity scripts that were given to us and to challenge and change those that do not fit the selves we now choose to be.

Everyday Application

REFLECTING ON YOUR IDENTITY SCRIPTS

Try to recall explicit scripts your parents communicated about who you were or were supposed to become. Can you hear them saying "Our people do . . ." or "our people don't . . ."? Can you recall messages that told you what and who they expected you to be? As a youngster, did you hear "You'll go to college" or "You're going to be a doctor"?

Now review key identity scripts. Which ones make sense to you today? Are you still following any that are irrelevant to your present life or that are at odds with your personal values and goals? If so, then commit to changing scripts that aren't productive for you or that conflict with values you hold. You can rewrite identity scripts now that you're an adult.

Finally, parents communicate who we are through their **attachment styles,** which are patterns of parenting that teach us who we and others are and how to approach others and relationships. From extensive studies of interaction between parents and children, John Bowlby (1973, 1988) developed a theory that we learn attachment styles in our earliest relationships. In these formative relationships, others communicate how they see us, others, and relationships. In turn, we are likely to learn their views and internalize them as our own.

Most children form their first human bond with a parent, usually the mother, since women do more of the caregiving in our society (Wood, 1994e). Clinicians who have studied attachment styles believe that the first bond is especially important because it forms expectations for later relationships (Bartholomew & Horowitz, 1991; Miller, 1993). Four distinct attachment styles have been identified.

Secure attachment styles develop when the primary caregiver responds in a consistently attentive and loving way to a child. In response, the child develops a positive sense of self-worth ("I am lovable") and a positive view of others ("People are loving and can be trusted"). People with secure attachment styles tend to be outgoing, affectionate, and able to handle the challenges and disappointments of close relationships without losing self-esteem.

Fearful attachment styles are cultivated when the caregiver in the first bond communicates in negative, rejecting, or even abusive ways to a child. Children who are treated this way often infer that they are unworthy of love and that others are not loving. Thus, they learn to see themselves as unlovable and others as rejecting. Not surprisingly, people with fearful attachment styles are apprehensive about relationships. Although they often want close bonds with others, they fear others will not love them and that they are not lovable. Thus, close relationships are sources of apprehension and mistrust.

Dismissive attachment styles are also promoted by caregivers who are disinterested, rejecting, or abusive toward children. Yet, people who develop this style do not accept the caregiver's view of them as unlovable. Instead, they dismiss others as unworthy. Consequently, children develop a positive view of themselves and a low regard for others and relationships. This pattern leads them to regard relationships as unnecessary and undesirable.

A final pattern is the anxious/resistant attachment style, which is the most complex of the four. Each of the other three styles results from some consistent pattern of treatment by a caregiver. The anxious/resistant style, however, is fostered by *inconsistent* treatment from the caregiver. Sometimes

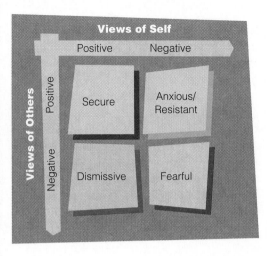

FIGURE 3.1
Styles of Attachment

the adult is loving and attentive, yet at other times she or he is indifferent or rejecting. The caregiver's communication is not only inconsistent, but also unpredictable. He or she may respond positively to something a child does on Monday and react negatively to the same behavior on Tuesday. An accident that results in severe punishment one day may be greeted with indulgent laughter on another day. Naturally, this unpredictability creates great anxiety in a child who depends on the caregiver (Miller, 1993). Because children tend to assume others are right and they are wrong, they believe they are the source of any problem—they are unlovable or deserve others' abuse.

In adult life, individuals who have anxious/resistant attachment styles tend to be preoccupied with relationships. On one hand, they know others can be loving and affirming. On the other hand, they realize that others can hurt them and be unloving. Reflecting the pattern displayed by the caregiver, people with anxious/resistant attachment styles are often inconsistent themselves. One day they invite affection, the next day they rebuff it and deny needing closeness. Figure 3.1 shows the four attachment styles.

The attachment styles we learned in our first close relationship tend to persist (Bartholomew & Horowitz, 1991; Belsky & Pensky, 1988; Bowlby, 1988). However, this is not inevitable. We can modify our attachment styles by challenging unconstructive views of us communicated in our early years and by forming relationships that foster secure connections today.

Communication with Peers   A second major influence on our self-concepts is communication with peers. From childhood playmates to work associates, friends, and romantic partners, we interact with peers throughout our lives. As we do, we gain further information about how others see us, and this refines how we see ourselves. As we communicate with peers, we engage in **social comparison**, which involves comparing ourselves with others to form judgments of our own talents, professional abilities, leadership skills, and so forth. We gauge ourselves in relation to others in two ways. First, we compare ourselves to others to decide whether we are like them or different from them. Are we the same age, color, religion? Do we socialize with the same kinds of people? Do we have similar backgrounds, political beliefs, and social commitments? Are we equally attractive? Assessing similarity and difference allows us to decide with whom we fit. Research has shown that people generally are most comfortable with others who are like them, so we tend to gravitate toward those we regard as similar (Whitbeck & Hoyt, 1994). This can, however, deprive us of diverse perspectives of people whose experiences and beliefs differ from our own. When we interact only with people who are like us, we impoverish our understandings of ourselves and the world.

We also use social comparison to gauge ourselves in relation to others. Because there are no absolute standards of beauty, intelligence, musical talent, athletic ability, career success, speaking ability, and so forth, we measure ourselves in relation to others. Am I as good a batter as Jenny? Do I play the guitar as well as Sam? Am I advancing as quickly as others who were hired when I was? How do other members of my team judge my communication skills? We form and continuously refine our self-image based on how we compare in relation to others on various criteria of judgment. This is normal and necessary if we are to develop realistic self-concepts. We should, however, be wary of using inappropriate standards of comparison. It isn't realistic to judge our attractiveness in relation to movie stars and models or our athletic ability in relation to professional players.

KEVIN

I learned more about myself and about being white when I was assigned to room with a black guy my freshman year. I'd never interacted much with blacks, and I'd never been friends with a black, but I got really close with my roommate. Carl helped me see a lot of things I take for granted that he can't because of his skin. For example, people assume I'm here because I earned a good record in high school, but a lot of people think Carl got in just because he's black and the college had to meet its minority quota. His SAT was higher than mine and so are his grades, but people believe I'm smart and he's a quota admission.

Communication with Society   The third influence on our self-concepts is interaction with society in general. As members of a shared social community, we are influenced by the values, judgments, and perspectives that the community holds and expresses to us. The perspectives of society are revealed to us in two ways. First, they surface in the communication of others who have internalized cultural values and express them to us. In the course of conversations, we learn how society regards our sex, race, and class, and what society values in personal identity. We also learn what others regard as effective public speaking and skillful group leadership. As we interact with others, we encounter not just their particular perspectives, but also the perspective of the generalized other as they reflect it. For example, Western families often teach children to stand up for themselves and be individuals. Asian families, in contrast, reflect their culture's emphasis on collective identity and accommodating others. Many Western families also communicate the cultural emphasis on competition, whereas many Asian families teach children to place priority on cooperation and teamwork.

Broadly shared social perspectives are also communicated to us through media and institutions that reflect cultural values. For example, when we read popular magazines and go to movies, we are inundated with messages about how women and men are supposed to look and act. The desirable women are invariably thin, young, beautiful, and deferential, while attractive men are strong, in charge, and successful (Faludi, 1991).

Mediated communication infuses our lives, telling us over and over again how we are supposed to be, talk, and appear and providing us with a basis for assessing ourselves.

The institutions that organize our society further communicate social perspectives by the values they uphold. For example, our judicial system reminds us that as a society we value laws and punish those who break them. The institution of marriage communicates society's view that when people marry they become a single unit, which is why joint ownership of property is assumed for married couples. The number of schools and the levels of education inform us that as a society we value learning. At the same time, institutional processes reflect prevailing social prejudices. For instance, we may be a lawful society, but wealthy defendants can often buy better "justice" than poor ones. Similarly, although we claim to offer equal educational opportunities to all, students whose families have money and influence can often get into better schools than students whose families are without such resources. These and other values are woven into the fabric of our culture, and we learn them with little effort or awareness.

The Self Is Multidimensional

There are many dimensions, or aspects, of the human self. You have an image of your physical self—how large, attractive, and athletic you are; what color your skin is; and whether you are male or female. In addition, you have perceptions of your cognitive self, including your intelligence and interests. You also have an emotional self-concept. Are you sensitive or not? Are you easily hurt? Are you generally optimistic or cynical? Then there is your social self, which involves views of how you are with others. Some people are extroverted and joke around a lot or dominate interactions, whereas others are more quiet. Our social selves also include our social roles—daughter or son, student, worker, parent, and partner in a committed relationship. Finally, each of us has a moral self consisting of ethical and spiritual principles we believe in and use as codes for conduct. Although we use the word *self* as if it referred to a single entity, in reality the self has many dimensions.

The Self Is a Process

The second proposition about the self is that it develops over time and, therefore, is a process. Virtually all researchers and clinicians who have studied human identity conclude that we are not born with selves, but instead we acquire them. Humans do not come into the world with a clear sense of themselves. Babies literally have no **ego boundaries,** which define where an individual stops and the rest of the world begins. An infant perceives being held by a father as a unified sensation in which it and the father are blurred. A baby perceives no boundaries between its mouth and a nipple or its foot and the tickle by a mother. As infants have a range of experiences and as others respond to them, they gradually begin to see themselves as distinct from the external environment. This is the beginning of a self-concept—the realization that one is a separate entity.

MICHELLE

My daughter is 11 months old, and she's just beginning to realize she is a distinct person. Until the last month or so, she didn't recognize her hands or feet as hers. I used to point to her foot and say "Lynne's foot," and then she'd point to my hand and my arm and say "Lynnefoot." She thought she was part of whatever was around her. Now she doesn't. If I ask where Lynne's foot is, she points to her foot. If I point to my foot and say Lynne's foot, she shakes her head no or giggles.

Within the first year or two of life, infants begin to differentiate themselves from the rest of the world and the self starts to develop. Babies, then toddlers, then children devote enormous energy to understanding who they are. They listen to and observe others to define themselves and to become competent in the identities they claim (Kohlberg, 1958; Piaget, 1932/1965). For instance, children start working early on being competent females and males, respectively. They identify females and males and use them as models for their own performances of gender. In like manner, children figure out what it takes to be smart, strong, pretty, and responsible, and they work to become competent at being those things. Throughout our lives, we continuously rely on communication to define ourselves and enact our identities. The ways we define ourselves, of course, vary as we mature. Struggling to be a good mudcake maker at age 4 gives way to striving for popularity in high school and succeeding in professional and family roles later in life. A person who was anxious about speaking at age 16 may become a confident speaker by age 25. If you're interested in reducing communication anxiety, you may wish to read the section in Chapter 12 that discusses it.

Some people feel uneasy with the idea that the self is a process, not a thing. We want to believe there is some stable, enduring core that is our essence—our true, unchanging identity. Of course, we all enter the world with certain biological abilities and limits, which constrain the possibilities of who we can be. Someone without the genes to be tall and coordinated, for instance, is probably not going to be a star forward in basketball, and a person who has poor fine-motor control is unlikely to become a renowned pianist. Beyond genetic and biological limits, however, we have considerable freedom to create who we will be. We change again and again during our lives because we are self-renewing and ever-growing beings.

The Self Internalizes and Acts from Social Perspectives

In studying how infants acquire selves, Mead realized that we internalize, or take inside ourselves, social perspectives on who we are. We take in both general and particular social perspectives to define ourselves and to guide how we think, act, and feel.

(Pablo Picasso, *Girl Before a Mirror* (Boisgeloup, March 1932). Oil on canvas, 64 × 51¼". The Museum of Modern Art, N.Y. Gift of Mrs. Simon Guggenheim. Photograph © 1996 The Museum of Modern Art, N.Y. © 1996 Artists Rights Society (ARS), N.Y./SPADEM Paris.)

Particular Others We first encounter the perspectives of **particular others,** who are part of our early lives. As the term implies, these are the viewpoints of specific individuals who are significant to us. Mothers, fathers, siblings, and often day-care providers are particular others who are significant to most infants. In addition, some families, particularly those of people of color, include aunts, uncles, grandparents, and others who live together or in the same community. Hispanic and African American families, in general, are extended, so children in these families often have a great many particular others who affect how they come to see themselves (Gaines, 1995).

SHENNOA

My grandmother was the biggest influence on me. I lived with her while my mamma worked, and she taught me to take myself seriously. She's the one who told me I should go to college and plan a career so that I wouldn't have to depend on somebody else. She's the one who told me to stand up for myself and not let others tell me what to do or believe in. But she did more than just tell me to be a strong person. That's how she was, and I learned just by watching her. A lot of who I am is modeled on my grandmother.

As babies interact with particular others, they learn how others see them. This is the beginning of a self-concept. Notice that the self starts from outside—from others' communicating their views of who we are. Recognizing this, Mead said that we must first get outside ourselves to get into ourselves. By this he meant that the only way we can see ourselves is from the perspectives of others as those are communicated to us. We first see ourselves in terms of how particular others define us. If parents communicate to a child that she or he is special and cherished, the child will come to see herself or himself as worthy of love. On the other hand, children whose parents communicate that they are not wanted or loved may come to think of themselves as unlovable.

The process of seeing ourselves through others' eyes and words is called **reflected appraisal.** It means that we see ourselves in terms of the appraisals of us that reflect in others' eyes. The process has also been called the "looking glass self," since others are mirrors who reflect who we are (Cooley, 1912). Reflected appraisals are not confined to childhood, but continue throughout our lives. Sometimes a teacher first sees potential that students have not recognized in themselves. When the teacher communicates that a student is smart, the student may come to see himself or herself that way. In professional life, co-workers and supervisors reflect their appraisals of us when they communicate that we're on the fast track, average, or not suited to our position. When we present public speeches, audience responses reflect appraisals of our effectiveness. The appraisals of us that others communicate shape how we see ourselves. In turn, how we see ourselves affects how we communicate. Thus, if you see yourself as a skillful speaker, you're likely to communicate that confidence when you give a presentation.

Everyday Application

YOUR LOOKING GLASS SELF

Identify five individuals who have been or are particularly important in your life. For each person, identify one positive and one negative self-perception you have that reflects the appraisal of you communicated by that individual.

Now, imagine that you'd never known each of the five people. Describe how you would be different if those individuals had not been part of your life. How would your self-image change? For instance, Shennoa (see commentary) might think she would be less independent if her grandmother had not influenced how she sees herself.

Trace how you see yourself to the appraisals of you that particular others reflected.

Generalized Other   The second social perspective that influences how we see ourselves is called the **perspective of the generalized other.** The generalized other is the collection of rules, roles, and attitudes endorsed by the whole social community in which we live (Mead, 1934). In other words, the generalized other is the views of society that are communicated to us. The process of socialization is one in which individuals internalize the perspective of the generalized other and thus come to share that perspective. In North American culture, the perspective of the generalized other views murder, rape, robbery, and embezzlement as wrong, and each of us learns that perspective as a result of communicating with others in the society. In addition, communication with others tells us which aspects of identity society considers important, how society views various social groups, and by extension, how it views us as members of specific groups. Modern Western culture emphasizes gender, race, affectional preference,

We see ourselves in the looking glass of others' eyes.

(Leigh M. Wilco)

and socioeconomic class as central to personal identity (Andersen & Collins, 1992; Wood, 1995b, 1996a,b). Each of these social groupings represents a standpoint, which we discussed in Chapter 2.

In North America, race is considered a primary aspect of personal identity. The race that has been historically favored and privileged in the United States is Caucasian. In the early years of this country's life, it was considered normal and right for white men to own black women, men, and children and to require them to work for no wages and in poor conditions. Later, it was considered "natural" that white men could vote but black men could not. White men had rights to education, professional jobs, ownership of property, and other basic freedoms that were denied to blacks. Even today, Caucasian privilege continues: White children often have access to better schools with more resources than do people of color. The upper levels of government, education, and business are dominated by Caucasian men, while people of color and women continue to fight overt and covert discrimination in admission, hiring, and advancement. The color of one's skin makes a difference in how society perceives and treats us and, by extension, in how we perceive ourselves and the opportunities open to us.

WEN-SHU

I was born in Korea, and my family moved here when I was 9 years old. Because I look Asian, people make assumptions about me. They assume I am quiet (true), I am good at math (not true), and I defer to men and elders (true with regard to elders, but not men). People also see all Asians as the same, but Taiwanese are as different from mainland Chinese as French Caucasians are from U.S. Caucasians. The first thing people notice about me is my race, and they make too many assumptions about what it means.

Gender, another important category in Western culture, also is communicated through social practices and institutions. Historically, men, particularly white men, have been seen as more valuable and entitled to privileges than women. In the 1800s, women weren't allowed to own property, attend colleges, or vote. Society viewed it as appropriate for a husband to beat his wife; the phrase "rule of thumb" comes from the law that stated a man could beat his wife as long as he used a stick no larger than the size of his thumb. Even today, in some respects women and men are not considered or treated as equal.

Many scholars argue that gender is the most important aspect of personal identity in Western culture (Fox-Genovese, 1991). From pink and blue blankets that hospitals wrap around newborns to differential salaries earned by women and men, gender discrimination is a persisting fact of modern life. Given the importance our society places on gender, it is no wonder that one of the first ways children learn to identify themselves is by sex (Wood, 1996b). When I asked my then 4-year-old niece, Michelle, who she was, her immediate response was "I'm a girl." Only after naming sex as the most important aspect of her identity did she describe her family, likes and dislikes, and other parts of herself.

Western cultures have strong gender prescriptions. Girls and women are expected to be caring, deferential, and cooperative, while boys and men are supposed to be independent, assertive, and competitive (Wood, 1994d). Consequently, women who assert themselves or compete are likely to receive social disapproval, to be called "bitches," and to be reprimanded in other ways for violating gender prescriptions. Men who refuse to conform to social views of masculinity and who are gentle and caring risk being labeled "wimps." Our sex, then, makes a great deal of difference in how others view us and how we come to see ourselves.

MANDY

One of the worst things about being female is knowing that others see you as vulnerable and easy to attack. All of my girlfriends are afraid to walk across campus alone at night if we want a pizza break or need to go to the library. The guys I know never think about that. If they want to go out, they just do it. In this society if you're female, you're seen as a target.

A third aspect of identity that cultural communication establishes as salient is sexual orientation. Historically, heterosexuality has been considered as the normal sexual orientation, and even today many people view lesbians, bisexuals and gays as abnormal. Society communicates this viewpoint not only directly, but also through privileges given to heterosexuals but denied to gays, lesbians, and bisexuals. For example, a woman and man who love each other can be married and have their commitment recognized religiously and legally. Two men or two women who love each other and want to be life partners are denied social and legal recognition of their commitment (Wood, 1995b). Heterosexuals can cover their partners on insurance policies and will them tax-free money, but people with other sexual preferences cannot.

SANDI

I've known I was lesbian since I was in high school, but only in the last year have I come out with others. As soon as I tell someone I'm lesbian, they see me differently. Even people who have known me a long time act like I've developed spots or something. Some of my girlfriends don't want to hug or touch me anymore like they think I'm suddenly going to come on to them. Guys act as if I'm from another planet. It's really strange that sexual orientation makes so much difference in how others see you. I mean, relative to other things like character, personality, and intelligence, who you sleep with is pretty unimportant.

A fourth dimension of identity in our society is socioeconomic class. Because North America is a class-conscious society, the class we belong to affects everything from how much money we make, to the kinds of schools, jobs and lifestyle choices we see as possibilities for ourselves. Our class even affects which needs are most important to us. For example, people with economic security have the resources and leisure time to contemplate higher level needs such as personal growth. They can afford therapy, yoga, spiritual development, and elite spas to condition their bodies. These are not feasible for people who are a step away from poverty. Members of the middle and upper classes assume they will attend college and enter good professions, yet people from the working class are often directed toward vocational training, regardless of their academic abilities (Langston, 1992). In such patterns, we see how the perspective of the generalized other shapes our identities and our concrete lives.

ROCHELLE

I got so mad in high school. I had a solid "A" average and ever since I was 12, I had planned to go to college. But when the guidance counselor talked with me at the start of my senior year, she encouraged me to apply to a technical school that is near my home. When I said I thought my grades should get me into a good college, she did this double take like "Your kind doesn't go to college." My parents both work in a mill and so do all my relatives, but does that mean that I can't have a different future? What really burned me was that a lot of girls who had average grades but came from "the right families" were told to apply to colleges.

Race, gender, sexual orientation, and class are primary in our society's views of individuals and their worth. Other social classifications that society communicates to us include age, (dis)ability, and religious commitments. In thinking about the ways society creates and communicates identity, it's important to realize that the classifications interact with one another. Race intersects gender, so that women of color often experience double oppression and devaluation in our culture (Higginbotham, 1992; Lorde, 1992). Class and sexual orientation also interact: Homophobia, or fear of homosexuals, is particularly pronounced in the working class, so a lesbian or gay man in a poor community may be socially ostracized (Langston, 1992). Race and class also tend to intersect. For instance, a working-class person of a socially devalued race may suffer greater discrimination than a working-class individual of a privileged race. Class and gender are also interlinked, with women being far more likely to live at the poverty level than men (Stone, 1992). Intersections between race and class mean that minority persons who belong to the working class are often treated less well than whites who are working class. Race, class, gender, and sexual orientation are facets of our identity that interact in complex ways.

Although race, gender, sexual orientation, and socioeconomic class are especially salient in social views of identity and worth, there are many other views of the general society that we learn and often internalize. For instance, Western societies clearly value intelligence, ambition, rugged individualism, and competitiveness. People who don't conform to these social values often receive less respect than those who do. The social emphasis on slenderness in women sheds light on the finding that eating disorders are epidemic. As many as 80 out of 100 fourth-grade girls diet—and most of them are well within normal weight limits (Wolf, 1991). Society imposes physical requirements on men as well. Strength and sexual prowess are two expectations of "real men," which may explain why increasing numbers of men are having pectoral implants and penis enlargement surgery. A great many people are willing to pay substantial money and endure pain to reconstruct their bodies to meet cultural ideals.

Communication from particular others and society in general (the generalized other) teaches us what and whom our society values. Social perspectives, however, do not remain outside of us. We internalize many of them, and we come to share many of the views and values generally endorsed in our society. Shared understandings are useful, even essential, for collective life. If we all made up our own rules about when to stop and go at traffic intersections, the incidence of accidents would skyrocket. If each of us operated by our own morals, there would be no shared standards regarding rape, murder, robbery and so forth. Life would be chaotic.

Yet not all social views are as constructive as traffic rules and criminal law. The generalized other's unequal valuing of different races, genders, and sexual preferences fosters discrimination against whole groups of people just because they don't fit what society defines as normal or good. In a related way, social perspectives affect how we see ourselves relative to what our society currently defines as normal and right. Each of us has an ethical responsibility to exercise critical judgment about which social views we personally accept and use as guides for our own behaviors, attitudes, and values. This suggests a third proposition about the self.

THE THREE GENDERS

The Navajo and Mohave Indian tribes gave special respect to *nadles,* who were considered neither male nor female, but a combination of the two sexes. The identity of nadle was sometimes conferred at birth on babies born with ambiguous genitals. Nadle was also an identity that individuals could choose later in life. When working on weaving or other tasks assigned to women, nadles dressed and acted as women. When engaged in male activities, nadles dressed and acted as males. Nadles could marry either women or men. Within their tribes, nadles were regarded as very wise and were given special privileges and deference.

Source: Olien, M. (1978). *The human myth.* New York: Harper & Row.

Social Perspectives on the Self Are Constructed and Variable

We come to understand ourselves and our society as we interact with others and internalize the social perspectives of particular others and the generalized other. However, this doesn't mean that fixed social values determine how we see ourselves and what opportunities are open to us. Social views are constructed and variable, so they can be changed.

Constructed   Social perspectives are constructed in particular cultures at specific times. What a society values in any particular era doesn't reflect divine law or absolute truth. Actually, the values a society endorses are arbitrary and designed to support dominant ideologies, or the beliefs of those in power. For example, it was advantageous to white plantation owners to define Africans as slaves and as inferior human beings. Doing so supported the privileges that white landowners enjoyed. Similarly, it was to men's advantage to deny women the right to vote, since doing so preserved men's power to control the laws of the land and to elect the people who ran the country. When we reflect on widely endorsed social values, we realize that they are arbitrary and tend to serve the interests of those who benefit by prevailing values.

Variable   The constructed and arbitrary nature of social values becomes especially obvious when we consider how widely values differ among cultures. For example, in Sweden, Denmark, and Norway, marriages between members of the same sex are given full legal recognition. Prescriptions for femininity and masculinity also vary widely among different cultures. In some places, men are emotional and dependent, and women are assertive and emotionally controlled. Some cultures even recognize more than two

Committed relationships between members of the same sex are viewed differently today than they were years ago.
(© Donna Binder/Impact Visuals)

genders and allow people to choose whether to live as women or as men! In many countries south of the United States, race is less consequential than in North America, and mixed-race marriages are common and accepted. The individualistic ethic so prominent in the United States is discouraged in many countries, particularly Asian and African ones.

Social meanings also vary across time within single cultures. For example, in the 1700s and 1800s, women in the United States were defined as too delicate to engage in hard labor. During the World Wars, however, women were expected to do "men's work" while men were at war. When the men returned home, society once again decreed that women were too weak to perform in the labor market, and they were reassigned to home and hearth. The frail, pale appearance considered feminine in the 1800s gave way to robust, fleshy ideals in the 1940s as embodied by Marilyn Monroe. Today a more athletic body is one of the ideals prescribed for women.

Social prescriptions for men also have changed. The rugged he-man who was the ideal in this country's early years used his six-shooter to dispose of unsavory rustlers and relied on his physical strength to farm wild lands. After the Industrial Revolution, physical strength and bravado gave way to business acumen, and money replaced muscle as a sign of manliness. Today, as our society struggles with changes in women, men, and families, the ideals of manhood are being revised yet again. Increasingly, men are expected to be involved in caring for children and to be sensitive as well as independent and strong.

The meaning of homosexuality has also been revised over time in Western culture. Until fairly recently, our society strongly disapproved of gays, lesbians, and bisexuals, so most nonheterosexuals did not publicly acknowledge their affectional preference. Although much prejudice still exists, it is gradually diminishing. Laws protecting lesbians and gays against housing and job discrimination are also being enacted. As social views of gender, race, class, and homosexuality evolve, individuals' views of others and their own self-concepts will also change.

Changeable   Our discussion implies that social perspectives change over time. Social perspectives are fluid and respond to individual and collective efforts to weave new meanings into the fabric of common life. From 1848 until 1920, many individuals fought to change social views of women, and they succeeded in gaining rights for women to vote, attend college, and so forth. In the 1960s, civil rights activism launched nationwide rethinking of actions and attitudes toward nonwhites. The battle to recognize and value gays and lesbians is more recent, yet already it has altered social perspectives. Each of us has the responsibility to speak out against social perspectives that we perceive as wrong or harmful. By doing so, we participate in the ongoing process of refining social perspectives.

JANINE

My husband and I have really worked to share equally in our marriage. When we got married 8 years ago, we both believed women and men were equal and should have equal responsibilities for the home and family and equal power in making decisions that affect the family. But it's a lot harder to actually live that ideal than to believe in it. Both of us have struggled against our socialization that says I should cook and clean and take care of the kids and he should make big decisions about our lives. I think we've done a pretty good job of creating and living an egalitarian marriage. A lot of our friends see us as models.

Because social views of identity are created and arbitrary, they vary across time and cultures. This highlights the power of individuals and groups to shape social understandings that make up the generalized other.

To review, we've seen that the self arises in communication. From interaction with family members, peers, and society as a whole, we are taught the prevailing values of our culture and of particular others who are significant in our lives. These perspectives become part of who we are. In addition, we are given general and specific lenses through which to view and evaluate ourselves. As well as arising in communication, the self is a process that imports and acts from social perspectives that are constructed and, therefore, changeable. In the final section of this chapter, we consider the important topic of how to improve our self-concepts.

ENHANCING SELF-CONCEPT

What we've discussed so far explains how we form our self-concepts in the process of communicating with others. Building on that knowledge, we now want to explore guidelines for encouraging personal growth as communicators.

Make a Strong Commitment to Improve Your Self-Concept

The first principle for changing self-concept is the most difficult and important. You must make a firm commitment to cultivating personal growth. This isn't as easy as it might sound. A firm commitment involves more than saying "I want to listen better" or "I want to be less judgmental." Saying these sentences is simple, but actually investing effort to bring change about is difficult. Self-esteem doesn't increase just because we want it to or think it should. Instead, it grows out of accomplishments and positive changes. A firm commitment requires that we keep trying even if we don't see dramatic effects immediately.

It is difficult to change self-concept for two reasons. First, doing so requires continuous effort. Because the self is a process, it is not formed in one fell swoop, and it cannot be changed in a moment of decision. We have to be willing to invest effort in an ongoing way. In addition, we must realize at the outset that there will be setbacks, and we can't let them derail our resolution to change. Last year a student said she wanted to be more assertive, so she began speaking up more often in class. When a professor criticized one of her contributions, her resolution folded.

DANICA

I have always been shy, and I am more so here than I was when I lived in Croatia. But I did not like being shy, and I decided to change myself. I took a course in social dance, and I made myself carry on the conversations with other people. Next, I pushed myself to start conversations. It was very hard at first, but it is not so hard now. Now that I am not so shy, I am making many friends.

A second reason it is difficult to change our self-concepts is that the self resists change. Morris Rosenberg (1979), a psychologist who has studied self-concept extensively, says that the two most basic principles of self-concept are that it resists change and it seeks esteem. The good news is that we want to think well of ourselves; the bad news is that we find it difficult to change, even in positive directions. Interestingly, Rosenberg found that we are as likely to hold onto negative self-images as we are to keep positive ones. Apparently, consistency itself is comforting. If you realize in advance that you may struggle against change, you'll be prepared for the tension that accompanies personal growth. Because change is a process and the self resists change, a firm and continuous commitment to improving your self-concept is essential. It's also advisable to strive for incremental, gradual improvements, rather than attempting to radically alter yourself at once.

Gain Knowledge as a Basis for Personal Change

Commitment alone is insufficient to spur changes in who you are. In addition, you need knowledge of several types. First, you need to understand how your self-concept was formed. In this chapter, we've discussed values and views of different groups that our culture encourages us to adopt. You may not wish to go along with all of the prevailing social views of race, gender, sexual preference, and class. You have the right and the responsibility to embrace only those values that you consider worthy.

C H R I S T I N A

My parents taught me that homosexuality is a crime against nature and God, and I believed that until I came to college. Now that I've met a lot of people who are homosexuals, I just can't buy the idea that they're bad or sinful. One of my best friends is a gay man, and I think he has more integrity than most straight guys. I'm also really close to a lesbian couple, and they are as loving and normal as my boyfriend and I are. My parents grew up in a different time, and their views about homosexuals aren't going to change. But I don't have to accept their views as my own.

Second, you need to know what changes are desirable and how to bring them about. Vague goals for self-improvement usually lead nowhere because they don't invite concrete work toward change. For instance, "I want to be better at intimate communication" is a very vague objective. You can't do anything to meet such a fuzzy goal until you know something about the talk that enhances and impedes intimacy. Books such as this one will help you pinpoint concrete skills that facilitate healthy intimate communication. For instance, Chapter 4 will help you develop empathic listening skills, and Chapters 8 and 9 will explain how communication affects personal and social relationships. Another example of an overly vague objective is "I want to be a more effective team leader." To achieve that fuzzy goal, you need to understand the communication responsibilities of group leadership and the ways to build good work teams. We will learn about these in Chapters 10 and 11.

In addition to reading this book and learning from your class, there are other ways to gain knowledge to help you set and achieve goals of personal improvement. One very important source of knowledge is other people. Talking with others is a way to learn about relationships and what people want in them. Perhaps you recall a time when you began a new job and didn't know the norms for interaction. If you were fortunate, you found a mentor who explained the ropes to you so that you could learn how to communicate effectively in your work context.

Others can also provide useful feedback on your interpersonal skills and your progress in the process of change. Feedback that I receive in my annual conference with the chair of my department helps me understand how he perceives my work and how I might improve my teaching and research. Finally, others can provide models. If you know someone you think is particularly skillful in supporting others, observe her or him carefully to identify particular communication skills. Observing will make you more aware of concrete skills involved in supporting others. You may choose to tailor some of the skills others display to suit your personal style.

Set Realistic Goals

Although it is true that willpower can do marvelous things, it does have limits. We need to recognize that changing how we see ourselves requires setting realistic goals. If you are shy and want to be more extroverted, it is reasonable to try to speak up more and socialize more often. On the other hand, it may not be reasonable to try to be the life of every party. Effective goal setting requires you to target specific changes you seek.

Realistic goals require realistic standards. Often dissatisfaction with ourselves stems from unrealistic expectations. In a culture that emphasizes perfectionism, it's easy to be trapped into expecting more than is humanly possible. If you define a goal of being a totally perfect communicator in all situations, you set yourself up to fail. It's more constructive to establish a series of realistic small goals. You might focus first on improving one communication skill. When you're satisfied with your ability at that skill, you can work on another one.

Everyday Application

SETTING REALISTIC GOALS FOR CHANGE

Apply the skills we've discussed so far by completing these sentences:

One important goal I have for myself is to _____

_____ .

Specific changes in behavior that are evidence of this change would be

_____ , _____ , and

_____ . So that I do not set an unrealistic goal, I

will not try to _____ or _____ .

With regard to our discussion of social comparison, it's also important to select reasonable measuring sticks for yourself. It isn't realistic to compare your academic work to that of a certified genius. It is reasonable to measure your academic performance against others similar to you in intelligence and circumstances. It isn't realistic to compare your public speaking

Learning to communicate effectively enhances self-confidence and self-esteem. This woman is claiming a voice for a cause that matters to her.
(© Frank Siteman/The Picture Cube)

skill to that of someone who has made public presentations for years. It is reasonable to measure your public speaking ability against others who have speaking experience that is similar to yours. Setting realistic goals and selecting appropriate standards of comparison are important to bring about change in yourself.

MIKE

For a long time I put myself down for not doing as well academically as a lot of my friends. They ace courses and put mega hours into studying and writing papers. I can't do that because I work 30 hours a week. Now I see that it's unfair to compare myself to them. When I compare myself to students who work as much as I do, my record is pretty good.

Accept Yourself as in Process

A key foundation for improving self-concept is to accept yourself as in process. Earlier in this chapter, we saw that one characteristic of the human self is that it is continuously in process, always becoming. This implies several things. First, it means you need to accept who you are now as a starting point. You don't have to like or admire everything about yourself, but it is important to accept who you are today as a basis for going forward (Wood, 1992a). The self that you are results from all of the interactions, reflected appraisals, and social comparisons you have made during your life. You cannot change your past, but neither do you have to be bound by it forever. Only by realizing and accepting who you are now can you move ahead.

Accepting yourself as in process also implies that you realize you can change. Who you are is not who you will be in 5 or 10 years. Because you are in process, you are always changing and growing. Don't let yourself be hindered by defeating self-fulfilling prophecies or the mindtrap that you cannot change (Rusk & Rusk, 1988). You can change if you set realistic goals, make a genuine commitment, and then work for the changes you want. Just remember that you are not fixed as you are; rather, you are always in the process of becoming.

Create a Supportive Context for Change

Just as it is easier to swim with the tide than against it, it is easier to change our views of ourselves when we have some support for our efforts. You can do a lot to create an environment that supports your growth by choosing contexts and people who help you realize your goals.

UPPERS, DOWNERS, AND VULTURES

Uppers are people who communicate positively about us and who reflect positive appraisals of our self-worth. They notice our strengths, see our progress, and accept our weaknesses and problems without discounting us. When we're around uppers, we feel more upbeat and positive about ourselves. Uppers aren't necessarily unconditionally positive in their communication. A true friend can be an upper by recognizing our weaknesses and helping us work on them. Instead of putting us down, an upper believes in us and helps us believe in ourselves and our ability to grow.

Downers are people who communicate negatively about us and our self-worth. They call attention to our flaws, emphasize our problems, and deride our dreams and goals. When we're around downers, we tend to feel down about ourselves. Reflecting their perspectives, we're more aware of our weaknesses and less confident of what we can accomplish when we're around downers.

Vultures are an extreme form of downers. They not only communicate negative images of us, but also attack our self-concepts just as actual vultures prey on their victims (Simon, 1977). Sometimes vultures harshly criticize us. They say, "That outfit looks dreadful on you" or "You're hopeless." In other cases, vultures pick up on our own self-doubts and magnify them. They pick us apart by focusing on our weak spots. By telling us we are inadequate, vultures demolish our self-esteem.

First think about settings. If you want to improve your physical condition, it makes more sense to go to intramural courts than to hang out in bars. If you want to lose weight, it's better to go to restaurants that serve healthy foods and offer light choices than to go to cholesterol castles. If you want to become more extroverted, put yourself in social situations, rather than in libraries. But libraries are a better context than parties if your goal is to improve academic performance.

JAN

I never cared a lot about clothes until I joined a sorority where the labels on your clothes are a measure of your worth. The girls compete with each other to dress the best and have the newest styles. When one of the sisters wears something out of style she gets a lot of teasing, but really it's pressure on her to measure up to the sorority image. At first I adopted my sisters' values, and I spent more money than I could afford on clothes. For a while I even quit making contributions at church so that I could have more money for clothes. When I finally realized I was becoming somebody I didn't like, I tried to change, but my sisters made me feel bad anytime I wasn't dressed well. Finally, I moved out rather than face that pressure all the time. It just wasn't a good place for me to be myself.

Because how others view us affects how we see ourselves, you can create a supportive context by consciously choosing to be around people who believe in you and encourage your personal growth without being dishonest about your limitations. It's also important to steer clear of people who put you down without reason or say you can't change. In other words, people who reflect positive appraisals of us enhance our ability to improve who we are.

Others aren't the only ones whose communication affects our self-concepts. We also communicate with ourselves, and our own messages influence our esteem. One of the most crippling kinds of self-talk we can engage in is **self-sabotage.** This involves telling ourselves we are no good, we can't do something, there's no point in trying to change, and so forth. We may be repeating judgments others made of us, or we may be inventing negative self-fulfilling prophecies ourselves. Either way, self-sabotage defeats us because it undermines belief in ourselves. Self-sabotage is poisonous; it destroys our motivation to change and grow. We can be downers or even vultures, just as others can be. In fact, we probably can do more damage to our self-concepts than others can because we are most aware of our vulnerabilities and fears. This may explain why vultures were originally described as people who attacked and put themselves down (Simon, 1977).

We can also be uppers for ourselves. We can affirm our worth, encourage our growth, and fortify our sense of self-worth. Positive self-talk builds motivation and belief in yourself. It is also a useful strategy to interrupt and challenge negative messages from yourself and others. The next time you hear yourself saying "I can't do . . ." or someone else says "You'll never change," challenge the self-defeating message with self-talk. Say out loud to yourself, "I can do it. I will change." Use positive self-talk to resist counterproductive communication about yourself.

Before leaving this discussion, we should make it clear that improving your self-concept is not facilitated by uncritical positive communication. None of us grows and improves when we listen only to praise, particularly if it is less than honest. The true uppers in our lives offer constructive criticism as a way to encourage us to reach for better versions of ourselves. In sum, improving your self-concept requires being in contexts that support growth and change. Seek out experiences and settings that foster belief in yourself and the changes you desire. Also, recognize uppers, downers, and vultures in yourself and others, and learn which people and which kinds of communication assist you in achieving your own goals for self-improvement.

SUMMARY

In this chapter, we explored the self as a process that evolves as we communicate with others over the course of our lives. As we interact with others, we learn and internalize social perspectives, both those of particular others and those of the generalized other, or society as a whole. Reflected appraisals, direct definitions, and social comparisons are key communication processes that shape how we see ourselves and how we change over time. The perspective of the generalized other includes social views of key aspects of identity, including gender, race, and sexual orientation. These, however, are arbitrary social constructions that we may challenge and resist once we are adults. When individuals resist counterproductive social views, they promote change in both society and themselves.

The final section of the chapter focused on ways to enhance communication competence by improving self-concept. Guidelines for this are to make a firm commitment to personal growth, gain knowledge about desired changes and the skills they involve, set realistic goals, accept yourself as in process, and create contexts that support the changes you seek. Transforming how we see ourselves is not easy, but it is possible. We can make amazing changes in who we are and how we feel about ourselves when we commit to doing so.

FOR FURTHER REFLECTION AND DISCUSSION

1. As part of taking this course, set one specific goal for personal growth as a communicator. Goals you could establish are to be a better listener, be more assertive, or learn about communication cultures that differ from your own. As you study different topics during the semester, apply what you learn to your personal goal.

2. Discuss society's views (the generalized other) of women and men. What are current social expectations for each sex? What behaviors, appearances, and attitudes violate social prescriptions for gender? Do you agree or disagree with these social expectations?

3. Imagine you have the authority to establish social values. Would you dictate that people be categorized by race, class, gender, or affectional preference? How would you define people and differences among them? How would existing social institutions and practices have to change in response to the values you would establish?

4. Think about the influence of settings on intellectual development and involvement. To what extent does your college promote intellectual growth and engagement? How might contexts on your campus be changed to enhance the intellectual atmosphere?

5. What ethical issues do you perceive in the process of developing and continuously refining self-concepts, both your own and those of people around you?

KEY TERMS

self
direct definition
identity scripts
attachment styles
social comparison
ego boundaries
particular others
reflected appraisal
perspective of the
   generalized other
uppers
downers
vultures
self-sabotage

Focus Questions

1 What's the difference between receiving communication and listening?

2 What are the most common barriers to effective listening?

3 What are the differences among listening for information, listening critically, listening to support others, and listening for pleasure?

4 How can we improve our listening?

5 Is it a good idea to express positive judgments of others when we listen to them?

Effective Listening

Do you have a minute to talk?" Suzanne asks her roommate, Elly.

"Sure," Elly agrees without looking up from the letter she is writing to her mother. Lately her mother has been criticizing her for not studying enough, and Elly's trying to explain that college is more than academics.

"I'm worried about what's happening between Drew and me," Suzanne begins. "He takes me for granted all the time. He never asks what I want to do or where I'd like to go. He just assumes I'll go along with whatever he wants."

"Yeah, I know that routine. Barton does it to me, too," Elly says with exasperation. "Last weekend he insisted we go to this stupid war movie that I wouldn't have chosen to see in a million years. But what I wanted didn't seem to make a lot of difference to him."

"That's exactly what I'm talking about," Suzanne agrees. "I don't like it when Drew treats me that way, and I want to know how to get him to be more considerate."

(Richard Diebenkorn, *Man and Woman, Seated* (1958). Oil on canvas, 70¾ × 83½". Palmer Museum of Art, The Pennsylvania State University.)

"What I told Barton last weekend was that I'd had it, and from now on we decide together what we're doing or we don't do it together," Elly says forcefully. "We've had this talk before, but this time I think I really got through to him that I was serious."

"So are you saying that's what I should do with Drew?"

"Sure. You have to stand up for your rights, or he'll walk all over you. Take it from me, subtlety won't work. Remember last year when I was dating Larry? Well, he started this routine, and I tried to be subtle and hint that I'd like to be consulted about things. What I said to him went in one ear and out the other. If you're not firm, they'll run over you."

"But Drew's not like Larry or Barton. He's not trying to run over me. I think he just doesn't understand how I feel when he makes all the decisions."

"Well, I really don't think Barton's 'like that' either. He's just as good a guy as Drew."

"That's not what I meant. I just meant that I don't think I need to hit Drew over the head with a two-by-four."

"And I suppose you think Barton does need that?"

"I don't know. He's not my boyfriend. I'm just thinking that maybe our relationships are different."

How would you describe the communication between Elly and Suzanne? Is Elly a good communicator? Is she sensitive and responsive to Suzanne? Usually, when we think about communication, we focus on talking. Yet, talking is not the only or even the greatest part of communication. For people to interact meaningfully, they must also listen to one another. As obvious as this is, few of us devote as much energy to listening as we do to talking.

In the conversation between Elly and Suzanne, several poor listening habits surface. The first obstacle to effective listening is Elly's preoccupation with the letter she's writing to her mother. If she really wants to listen to Suzanne, she should put the letter aside. A second problem is Elly's tendency to monopolize the conversation, turning it into an occasion to discuss *her* problems and her boyfriends, instead of Suzanne's concerns about the relationship with Drew. Third, Elly listens defensively, taking offense when Suzanne suggests their relationships may differ. Elly isn't alone in having ineffective listening habits. Most of us often listen less well than we could. When we listen poorly, we are not communicating well.

Effective listening begins with a decision to focus on another person. (© Anne Dowie)

If you think about your normal day, you'll realize that listening—or trying to—is the single greatest communication activity in which you engage. Studies of people, ranging from college students to professionals, indicate that the average person spends between 45% and 53% of waking time listening to others (Barker, Edwards, Gaines, Gladney, & Holley, 1981; Weaver, 1972). If we add in the time we are listening while also doing other things, the total for listening time would be even greater. If we don't listen effectively, we're communicating poorly more than half of the time!

Ineffective listening can be very costly. When people don't listen carefully on the job, they often miss important information that affects their work and their advancement. Ineffective listening in the classroom diminishes what students learn, as well as how they perform on tests. In personal relationships, poor listening can lead us to misunderstand people we care about and to respond to them with less sensitivity than possible. Becoming a better listener enhances personal, academic, and professional effectiveness.

This chapter explores what listening is and how to listen effectively. First, we'll consider what's involved in listening, which is more than most of us realize. Next, we'll discuss obstacles to effective listening and how to minimize these. We'll also consider common forms of nonlistening. The third section of the chapter explains different types of listening and the skills required for each. To wrap up the chapter, we'll identify principles for improving listening effectiveness.

THE LISTENING PROCESS

Although we often use the words *listening* and *hearing* as if they were synonyms, actually they're not. **Hearing** is a physiological activity that occurs when sound waves hit our eardrums. As we will see, listening involves considerably more than just hearing. Further, not everyone receives messages through hearing. We also receive messages through sight, as when we notice nonverbal behaviors or when people with hearing impairments read lips or use ASL (American Sign Language). Listening has psychological dimensions that aren't part of physically receiving messages. **Listening** is a complex process that involves being mindful, physically receiving messages, selecting and organizing information, interpreting communication, responding, and remembering.

Being Mindful

The first step in listening is making a decision to be mindful. **Mindfulness** means being fully engaged in the moment. To be mindful is to keep your mind on what is happening in the here and now. When you are mindful, you don't let your thoughts wander from the present situation. You don't think about what you did yesterday or about a letter you're writing to your mother; nor do you focus on your own feelings and issues. Instead, when you listen mindfully, you tune in fully to another person and try to hear that person without imposing your own ideas, judgments, or feelings on him or her. You demonstrate mindfulness by paying attention and indicating interest in what another expresses (Bolton, 1986).

Mindfulness enhances communication in two ways. First, attending mindfully to others increases our understanding of how they feel about what they are saying. In addition, mindfulness enhances the other person's communication. When we really listen to others, they engage us more fully, elaborate their ideas, and express themselves in more depth.

Being mindful is a choice we make. It is not a talent that some people have and others don't. Instead, mindfulness is a personal commitment to attend fully and without diversion to another person. No amount of skill will make you a good listener if you do not choose to attend mindfully to others. Thus, your own choice of whether to be mindful is the foundation of how you listen—or fail to.

Everyday Application

BEING MINDFUL

Mindfulness is a skill that develops with commitment and practice. Zen Buddhists, who emphasize mindfulness as a way of being in relation to others, offer these guidelines for becoming more mindful:

1. Empty your mind of thoughts, ideas, and plans so that you are open to listening to another.
2. Concentrate on the person with whom you are communicating. Say to yourself, "I want to focus on this person and what she or he is saying and feeling."
3. If your mind does wander, don't criticize yourself. Instead, just refocus your mind on the person you are with and what she or he is saying.
4. Don't be surprised if distracting thoughts come up or if you find yourself thinking about your responses instead of what the other person is saying. This is natural. Just push away diversionary thoughts and refocus on the person with whom you are talking.

5. Evaluate how well you listened when you were focusing on being mindful. If you aren't as fully engaged as you want to be, remind yourself that mindfulness is a habit of mind and a way of living. Developing it requires considerable practice.

Physically Receiving Messages

In addition to being mindful, listening involves physically receiving a message. We might receive it by hearing sounds or by reading lips or seeing ASL. As we noted earlier, hearing is a physiological process in which sound waves hit our eardrums so that we become aware of noises, such as music or human voices. Similarly, reading lips and ASL occurs when our eyes register light waves and images. Sometimes we physically receive a message first, and this causes us to become mindful; in other instances, choosing to be mindful allows us to receive communication we might otherwise not notice. Unlike listening, physical reception of communication is a relatively passive process: We simply have to be present when vibrations are in the air or when visual stimuli convey communication.

Most of us take hearing for granted. However, individuals with hearing difficulties may have trouble actually receiving oral messages. When we speak with someone who has a hearing impairment, we should face her or him and check to make sure we are coming across clearly. In addition to being affected by physiological limitations, our ability to receive messages may decline when we are fatigued or when we have to be attentive for extended times without breaks. You may have noticed that it's harder to sustain attention in long classes than in shorter ones. Physical reception of messages may also be impeded by background noises, such as a blaring television or others talking nearby, or by competing visual cues. Thus, it's a good idea to control distractions that hinder listening.

JIMMY

It's flat out impossible to listen well in my apartment. Four of us live there, and at least two different stereos are on all the time. Also, a TV is usually on, and there may be conversations or phone calls, too. It's crazy when we try to talk to each other in the middle of all the racket. We're always asking each other to repeat something or skipping over whatever we don't hear. If we go out to a bar or something, the noise there is just as bad. Sometimes I think we don't really want to talk with each other and all the distractions protect us from having to.

Other physiological factors influence how and how well we listen. Women and men seem to differ in how they listen. As a rule, women are more fully receptive than men to what is happening around them. Thus, men tend to focus, shape, and direct their hearing in instrumental ways, while women are more likely to attend to the whole of communication, noticing details, tangents, and major themes (Weaver, 1972). Judy Pearson

(1985), a communication researcher, suggests this could be due to different hemispheric specialization of brains. Women usually have more developed right lobes, which govern creative and holistic thinking, whereas men typically have more developed left lobes, which control analytic and linear processing of information. The difference in listening styles is a source of much frustration in interaction between women and men. Often men think women's communication is unfocused and burdened with irrelevant details, but to many women the details and sideline topics are part of the overall interaction. Women, on the other hand, frequently find that the linear, undetailed communication more typical of men is too bare bones to give them a real grasp of the topics and how men feel about them. Later in this and other chapters, we'll discuss ways to improve communication between the sexes.

Selecting and Organizing Material

The third element of listening is selecting and organizing material. As we noted in Chapter 2, we don't perceive everything around us. Instead, we selectively attend to some messages and elements of our environments and we disregard others. What we select to attend to depends on many factors, including our interests, cognitive structures, and expectations. If we realize that our own preoccupations can hamper listening, we can curb interferences. Once again, mindfulness comes into play. Choosing to be mindful doesn't necessarily mean our minds won't stray when we try to listen, but it does mean that we will bring ourselves back to the present moment. We have to remind ourselves to focus attention and concentrate on what another is saying.

We can monitor our tendencies to attend selectively by remembering that we are more likely to notice stimuli that are intense, loud, or unusual. Thus, we may overlook communicators who don't call attention to themselves with strong volume and strong gestures. If we're aware of this tendency, we can guard against it so that we don't miss out on people and messages that may be important. Some researchers (Gabriel & Smithson, 1990; Sadker & Sadker, 1986; Spender, 1989) claim that teachers unintentionally give more attention and encouragement to male students than to female students because men communicate more assertively.

Once we've selected what to notice, we then organize the stimuli to which we've attended. As you'll recall from Chapter 2, we use cognitive schemata to organize our perceptions. As you listen to others, you decide how to categorize them by asking which of your prototypes they most closely resemble—good friend, person in trouble, professional rival, teacher, and so forth. You then apply personal constructs to define others and their messages more fully. You evaluate whether they are smart or not smart, upset or calm, reasonable or unreasonable, open to advice or closed, and so on. Based on how you construct others, you apply stereotypes to predict what they will do. Finally, based on the meanings that you have constructed, you choose which script to follow in interaction.

When a friend is clearly distraught, you can reasonably predict he needs to ventilate and may not want advice until he has first had a chance to clarify his feelings. On the other hand, when a co-worker comes to you with a problem that must be solved quickly, you assume she might welcome concrete advice or collaboration. Your script for responding to the distraught friend might be to say, "Tell me more about what you're feeling" or "You sound really upset—let's talk." With a work team that is facing a deadline, you might adopt a more directive script and say, "Here's what we need to do to stay on schedule" or "Maybe we can work together and get it all done." In a public speaking situation, you might follow a script that specifies you should compliment listeners and engage their interest before you move into the substance of your speech.

PATRICIA

I always thought that listening was just taking in what others say. But what we've talked about in class helps me see how much I do to affect the meaning of what others say. I'd never thought about how my listening influences the meaning of communication.

Patricia's insight is important. She's realized that listeners play active roles in constructing the meaning of interaction. The schemata we use to create meaning help us figure out how to respond to others and what they say. When we decide someone is angry and needs to spout off, we're likely to rely on a script that tells us to back off and let her air her feelings. If, on the other hand, we perceive someone as confused, we might follow a script that says we should help him clarify his feelings and options. It's important to remember that *we construct others and their communication* by the schemata we use to organize perceptions. In other words, the meaning we perceive depends on how we select and organize communication. This reminds us to keep our perceptions tentative. In the course of interaction, we may revise the meanings we initially formed.

Interpreting Communication

The fourth process involved in listening is interpreting others' communication. When we interpret, we put together all that we have selected and organized to make sense of the overall situation. The most important principle in this process is to interpret others on their own terms. Certainly, you won't always agree with other people and how they see themselves, others, issues, and situations. Recognizing others' viewpoints doesn't mean you have to share their perspectives; it does, however, require you to make an earnest effort to understand others' perspectives. This is one of the ethical responsibilities of mindful listening.

To interpret someone with respect for their perspective is one of the greatest gifts we can give another. What we give is regard for another person and a willingness to open ourselves to his or her perspective. Too often we impose our meanings on others, we try to correct or argue with

THE IMPACT OF RESPONSIVE LISTENING

To test the impact of responsive listening, researchers taught students in a college psychology course to give different responses to their professor. The professor in the class was a boring lecturer who read his notes in a monotone voice, seldom gestured, and did little to engage students. After the first few minutes of class, the students changed their postures, kept greater eye contact, nodded their interest, and so forth. Shortly after the students began responding, the lecturer started using gestures, increased speaking rate and inflection, and began interacting with students visually and verbally. Then, at a prearranged signal, the students stopped showing interest. Within a few minutes, the lecturer lapsed back into his old lecture style. The students' responses influenced the professor's effectiveness.

Source: Bolton, R. (1986). Listening is more than merely hearing. In J. Stewart (Ed.), *Bridges, not walls*, 4th ed. (pp. 159–179). New York: Random House.

them about what they feel, or we crowd out their words with our own. As listening expert Robert Bolton (1986, p. 167) has observed, good listeners "stay out of the other's way" so that they can learn how the speaker views his or her situation. Good communicators try to grasp how others think and feel. Interpreting others on their own terms is equally important in professional and personal relationships. Just as it's desirable to try to understand a friend's point of view, it's also advisable to attempt to interpret co-workers within their frames of reference. Doing this allows us to understand how they see situations so that we can decide how to respond most effectively to them and their ideas.

MAGGIE

Don and I didn't understand each other's perspective, and we didn't even understand that we didn't understand. Once I told him I was really upset about a friend of mine who needed money for an emergency. Don told me she had no right to expect me to bail her out, but that had nothing to do with what I was feeling. He would have seen the situation in terms of rights, but I didn't and he didn't grasp my view. Only after we got counseling did we learn to really listen to each other instead of listening through ourselves.

Responding

Effective listening also involves **responding**, which is communicating attention and interest, as well as voicing our own views. As we noted in Chapter 1, communication is not a linear procedure in which one person speaks at another. Rather, it is a transactional process in which we simultaneously listen and speak. Skillful listeners give outward signs that they are following and involved in the interaction even though they are not speaking.

We don't respond only when others finish speaking, but throughout interaction. This is what makes listening such an active process. Nonverbal behaviors such as looking out a window, making notes to ourselves, and slouching signal that we aren't involved. We also indicate disinterest if we appear bored or uninvolved (Ernst, 1973).

Good listeners show they're engaged. The only way that others know we are listening is through our feedback. Indicators of engagement include postures of involvement, head nods, eye contact, and vocal responses such as "um hmm," "okay," and "go on." When we respond with interest, we communicate that we care about the other person and what she or he says.

Everyday Application

RESPONSIVE LISTENING

Test the impact of responsive listening. The next time a friend talks to you, signal interest by removing distractions, keeping eye contact, nodding your head, and so forth. How does your friend react? How is her or his communication affected by your responsiveness?

Repeat this exercise in a team situation. When other members of the team speak, express your interest and attention through nonverbal communication that signals involvement. How do various members of the group respond?

Remembering

Many listening experts regard the final part of listening as **remembering**, which is the process of retaining what you have heard. According to communication professors Ron Adler and Neil Towne (1993, p. 246), we remember less than half of a message immediately after we hear it. As time goes by, retention decreases further so that we recall only about 35% of most messages 8 hours after we hear them. Because we forget about two-thirds of what we hear, it's important to make sure we hang on to the most important third. Effective listeners retain basic ideas and general impressions (Fisher, 1987). By being selective about what to remember, we enhance our listening competence. Selective focusing of attention is particularly important when we are listening to public speeches, which often present a great deal of information in a short period of time. Later in this chapter, we'll discuss more detailed strategies for retaining material in communication.

Full listening is a complex process that involves being mindful, physically receiving communication, organizing, interpreting, responding, and remembering. Next, we'll consider hindrances to our ability to enact the processes that make up effective listening.

OBSTACLES TO EFFECTIVE LISTENING

There are two broad types of obstacles to good listening—ones in communication situations and ones in us.

Hindrances in Communication Situations

There are many interferences to effective listening in communication situations. Although we can't always control external obstacles, knowing what situational factors hinder effective listening can help us guard against them or compensate for the interference they create.

Message Overload   The sheer amount of communication in our lives makes it difficult to listen fully to all of it. We simply aren't able to be mindful and totally involved in all of the listening we do. Instead, we have to screen the talk around us, much as we screen calls on our answering machines, to decide when to listen carefully. Message overload often occurs in academic settings in which readings and class discussions are laden with detailed information. Message overload may also occur in situations where communication occurs simultaneously in two channels. For instance, you might suffer information overload if a speaker is presenting information verbally while also showing a visual aid that depicts complex statistical data. In such a situation, it's difficult to know where to focus your listening energy—on the visual message or on the verbal one.

Message Complexity   Listening is also impeded by complex messages. The more detailed and complicated ideas are, the more difficult it is to follow and retain them. Many jobs today are highly specialized so that communication among co-workers involves complex messages. It's tempting to tune out people who use technical vocabularies, focus on specifics, and use complex sentences. When we have to listen to messages that are dense with information, taking notes can improve retention.

Environmental Distractions   Effective listening is also impeded by distractions in the environment. Sounds around us can divert our attention or even make it difficult to hear clearly. Perhaps you've been part of a crowd at a rally or a game. If so, you probably had to shout to the person next to you just to be heard. Although most sounds aren't as overwhelming as the roar of crowds, there is always some noise in communication situations. It might be music or television in the background, side conversations during a conference, or muffled traffic sounds from outside.

We can't listen mindfully when our attention is divided. How might the man on the right create a better listening situation?
(© Anne Dowie)

Good listeners try to reduce environmental distractions. It's considerate to cut off a television or turn down music if someone wants to talk with you. Similarly, when meeting with others it's advisable to defer private comments until after a meeting so that they don't interfere with listening. Professionals often instruct secretaries to hold their calls when they want to give undivided attention to a conversation with a client or business associate. It's also appropriate to suggest moving from a noisy area in order to cut down on distractions. Even if we can't always eliminate distractions, we can usually reduce them or change our location to one that is more conducive to good communication.

Internal Obstacles to Effective Listening

In addition to external interferences, listening is also hindered by things we do or don't do. We'll discuss four psychological obstacles to effective listening.

Preoccupation   One of the most common hindrances to listening is preoccupation. When we are absorbed in our own thoughts and concerns, we can't focus on what someone else is saying. Perhaps you've attended a class right before taking a test in another class and later realized you got virtually nothing out of the first class. That's because you were preoccupied with the upcoming test. If you are preoccupied with a report you need to prepare, you may not listen effectively to what a colleague says. When we are preoccupied with our own thoughts, we aren't being mindful.

AUTURRO

Last week I got a letter from my family in which my mother said the monsoons had hurt their crops and so they would not make much money at the market. I was very worried because my family does not have savings—we live year to year and crop to crop. After a couple of days, I realized that I did not know what had happened in any of my classes. I read my notebooks and I had good notes, but I didn't remember ever hearing the lectures in class.

Prejudgments   Another reason we don't always listen effectively is that we prejudge others or their communication. Sometimes we think we already know what is being said, so we don't listen carefully. In other cases, we decide in advance that others have nothing to offer us, so we tune them out. This can be a serious impediment to effective listening on the job. If someone with whom you work has not had ideas that impressed you in the past, you might assume nothing of value will be in a present conversation. The risk here is that you might miss a good idea simply because you prejudged the other person. It's also important to keep an open mind when listening to public speeches that present ideas about which you already have opinions. You might miss out on important information and perspectives if you don't suspend prejudgments about the topic.

A third kind of prejudgment occurs when we impose our preconceptions about a message on the person who is communicating. When this happens, we assume we know what another feels, thinks, and is going to say, and we then assimilate her or his message into our preconceptions. Naturally, this often leads us to misunderstand what the person means, since we haven't really listened on her or his own terms.

KEITH

My parents need a course in listening! They are so quick to tell me what I think and feel or should think and feel that they never hear what I do feel or think. Last year I approached them with the idea of taking a year off from school. Before I could even explain why I wanted to do this, Dad was all over me about being responsible and getting ahead in a career. Mom jumped on me about looking for an easy out and not having the gumption to stick with my studies. The whole point was that I wanted to work as an intern to get some hands-on experience in media production, which is my major. It had nothing to do with wanting an easy out or not trying to get ahead, but they couldn't even hear me through their own ideas about what I felt.

Prejudgments disconfirm others because we deny them their own voices. Instead of listening openly to them, we force their words into our own preconceived mind-set. This devalues others and their messages. When we impose our prejudgments on others' words, at the relational level of meaning we express a disregard for them and what they say. Prejudgments also affect the content level of meaning, since we may not grasp important content when we decide in advance that someone has nothing of value to say. This can be costly on the job when we are expected to pay attention and understand information, even when it is very complex.

Lack of Effort   It takes considerable effort to listen well, and sometimes we don't invest the necessary energy. It's hard work to be mindful—to focus closely on what others are saying, try to grasp their meanings, ask questions, and give responses so that they know we are interested and involved. In addition to these activities, we have to control distractions inside ourselves, monitor external noise, and perhaps fight against fatigue, hunger, or other physiological conditions that can impede listening.

Because active listening requires so much effort, we're not always able or willing to do it well. Sometimes we make a decision not to listen fully, perhaps because the person or topic isn't important to us. In other cases,

Different cultures have different norms for communication. These Nepalese villagers have been socialized to be deferential and quiet. (Julia T. Wood)

initially we may be mindful, but then our thoughts detour to tangents or private planning and we cease to focus on what another is saying. There are also instances in which we really want to listen, but have trouble marshaling the energy required because we are tired, ill, or overloaded with other matters. When this happens, an effective strategy is to suggest postponing interaction until a time when you will have the energy to listen mindfully. If you explain to the other that you want to defer communication because you really are interested and want to be able to listen well, she or he is likely to appreciate your honesty and commitment to listening.

Not Recognizing Diverse Listening Styles   A final way in which we sometimes hinder our listening effectiveness is by not respecting and adjusting to different listening styles that reflect diverse communication cultures. The more we understand about different people's rules for listening, the more effectively we can signal our attention in ways they appreciate. For example, Nepalese citizens give little vocal feedback to people who are speaking. In that culture it's considered disrespectful to make sounds while someone else is talking. Cultures also vary in what they teach about eye contact. In the United States, it is considered polite to make frequent, but not constant eye contact with others. Yet in some cultures, continuous eye contact is normative, and in others virtually any eye contact is disapproved of.

Even within our country, there are differences in listening rules based on membership in racial, gender, and other communication cultures. In general, African Americans engage in a more participative listening style than European Americans. Thus, blacks are more likely to call out responses to a speaker as a way of showing their interest. A speaker who doesn't understand that this is a compliment in the African American speech community is likely to misinterpret responses as rude interruptions. Because feminine communication cultures regard talking as a way to form and develop relationships, responsive listening is emphasized. Thus, women, in general, make more eye contact, give more vocal and verbal feedback, and use head nodding and facial expressions to signal interest (Tannen, 1990; Wood, 1994d).

LAVONDA

My boyfriend is the worst listener ever. Whenever I try to tell him about some problem I have, he becomes Mr. Answer Man. He tells me what to do or how to handle a situation. That doesn't do anything to help me with my feelings or even to let me know he hears what I'm feeling.

Masculine culture, with its more instrumental orientation and greater focus on emotional control, places less emphasis on personal responsiveness. For this reason, men typically provide fewer verbal and nonverbal clues about their interest and attentiveness. If you understand these general differences, you can adapt your listening style to particular individuals with whom you communicate. In addition, understanding gendered listening styles will improve your accuracy in interpreting what others mean by the ways they listen and signal interest.

JERRY

I wish my girlfriend were a better listener. For example, she asks me how an interview went and I tell her it was fine or not so good or whatever. Then she starts in on all the questions about how do I feel and what happened. I told her what happened. The details are boring. What does she want?

Forms of Nonlistening

Now that we've discussed obstacles to effective listening, let's consider some forms of nonlistening. As you read about these six types of nonlistening, they may seem familiar, since you and others probably engage in them at times.

Pseudolistening **Pseudolistening** is pretending to listen. When we pseudolisten, we appear to be attentive, but really our minds are elsewhere. We engage in pseudolistening when we think we should appear conscientious, but we really aren't interested. Sometimes we pseudolisten because we don't want to hurt a friend who is sharing experiences, even though we are preoccupied with other things. We also pseudolisten when communication bores us, but we have to appear interested. Superficial talk in social situations and boring lectures are two communication situations in which we may consciously choose to pseudolisten so that we seem polite even though we really aren't involved. Similarly, on the job we often have to appear interested in what others say because of their positions.

Monopolizing **Monopolizing** is hogging the stage by continuously focusing communication on ourselves instead of the person who is talking. Two tactics are typical of monopolizing. One is conversational rerouting in which a person shifts the topic of talk to himself or herself. For example, if Ellen tells her friend Marla that she's having trouble with her roommate, Marla should respond by showing interest in Ellen's problem and feelings. Instead, however, Marla might reroute the conversation by saying, "I know

(Reprinted by permission of United Feature Syndicate, Inc.)

what you mean. My roommate is a real slob." Then Marla would go off on an extended description of her own roommate problems. In work situations, people with higher status are sometimes guilty of monopolizing. They habitually shift conversations to themselves and their accomplishments and, as a result, they don't listen to others. Whether in personal or work relationships, rerouting takes the conversation away from the person who is talking and focuses it on the self.

Another monopolizing tactic is interrupting to divert attention to ourselves. Interrupting can occur in combination with rerouting, so that a person interrupts and then directs the conversation to a new topic. In other cases, diversionary interrupting involves questions and challenges that are not intended to support the person who is speaking. Monopolizers may fire questions that express doubt about what a speaker says ("What makes you think that?" "How can you be sure?" "Did anyone else see what you did?") or prematurely offer advice to establish their own command of the situation and possibly to put down the other person ("What you should do is . . . " "You really blew that," "What I would have done is . . . "). Both rerouting and diversionary interrupting are techniques to monopolize a conversation. They are the antithesis of good listening.

It's important to realize that not all interruptions are attempts to monopolize communication. We also interrupt the flow of others' talk to show interest, voice support, and ask for elaboration. Interrupting for these reasons doesn't divert attention from the person speaking; instead, it affirms that person and keeps the focus on her or him. Research indicates that women tend to interrupt to show interest and support, while men interrupt more often to gain control of the talk stage (Aries, 1987; Beck, 1988; Mulac, Wiemann, Widenmann, & Gibson, 1988).

Selective Listening   A third form of nonlistening is **selective listening,** which involves focusing on only particular parts of communication. We listen selectively when we screen out parts of a message that don't interest us or with which we disagree. We also listen selectively when we isolate for attention those parts of communication that especially interest us or with which we agree.

Chapter 4 / Effective Listening   **107**

One form of selective listening is focusing only on aspects of communication that interest us or correspond with our own opinions and feelings. Listeners screen out message content that doesn't interest them or square with their ideas. If you are worried about a storm, you will listen attentively to weather reports while disregarding news, talk, and music on the radio. Students often become highly attentive in classes when teachers say "This is important for the test." We also listen selectively when we tune in only to topics that interest us and tune out the rest of what others say. For example, we might give only half an ear to a friend until the friend mentions spring break, and then we zero in because that topic interests us. In the workplace, we may become more attentive when communication addresses topics such as raises, layoffs, and other matters that may directly affect us.

Selective listening also occurs when we reject communication that bores us or makes us uncomfortable. Many smokers, for instance, selectively block out reports on the dangers of smoking and of secondhand smoke. We may also choose not to attend to requests we don't want to meet. We sometimes don't listen when others criticize us or our work, because we don't like what they say. We may also screen out communication that makes us uncomfortable. For months I tried to suggest good investment strategies to one of my friends who has no retirement savings or investments. She became inattentive whenever I offered advice, and she diverted our conversation to other topics. Finally, we talked about what was happening between us, and she explained that the topic made her feel like a failure, since she hadn't already developed an investment program. We all have subjects that bore or bother us, and we may be tempted to avoid listening to communication about them.

Defensive Listening **Defensive listening** involves perceiving personal attacks, criticisms, or hostile undertones in communication where none are intended. When we listen defensively, we assume others don't like, trust, or respect us, and we read these motives into whatever they say, no matter how innocent their communication actually is. Some individuals are generally defensive, expecting insults and criticism from all quarters (a global, stable attribution). They hear threats and negative judgments in almost anything said to them. Thus, an innocent remark such as "Have you finished your report yet?" may be perceived as criticism for not having completed the report earlier or as suspicion that you aren't doing your work.

In other instances, defensive listening is confined to areas where we judge ourselves inadequate or times when we feel negative about ourselves. A man who is defensive about money may perceive phone solicitations as reproaches for his lack of earning ability; a woman who fears she is selfish may interpret offers of help as proof others don't think of her as helpful; a person who feels unattractive may hear genuine compliments as false; someone who just failed a test may perceive questioning of his intelligence in benign comments; a worker who has been laid off may perceive work-related communication by others as personal criticism.

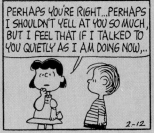

(Reprinted by permission of United Feature Syndicate, Inc.)

Ambushing   **Ambushing** is listening carefully for the purpose of attacking a speaker. Unlike the other kinds of nonlistening we've discussed, ambushing involves very careful listening, but it isn't motivated by openness and interest in another. Instead, ambushers listen intently to gather ammunition, which they then use to attack a speaker. They don't mind bending or even distorting what you say in order to advance their combative goals. Political candidates routinely do this. Each person listens carefully to the other for the sole purpose of later undercutting the opponent. Similar ambushing sometimes plagues work life when employees feel they must compete with and outdo one another in order to stand out. There is no openness, no effort to understand the other's meaning, no interest in recognizing value in what another says, and no interest in genuine dialogue.

ERIC

One of the brothers at my house is a real ambusher. He's a prelaw major, and he loves to debate and win arguments. No matter what somebody talks about, this guy just listens long enough to mount a counterattack. He doesn't care about understanding others, just about beating them. I've quit talking when he's around.

Literal Listening   The final form of nonlistening we'll discuss is **literal listening**, which involves listening only to the content level of meaning and ignoring the relationship level of meaning. All communication includes both content, or literal, meaning and relational meaning that pertains to the power, responsiveness, and liking between individuals. When we listen literally, we attend to only the content meaning and overlook what's being communicated about the other person or our relationship with that person. When we listen only literally, we are insensitive to others' feelings and to our connections with them.

In this section, we have seen that there are many obstacles to effective listening. Ones that inhere in messages and situations include message overload, difficulty of messages, and environmental distractions. In addition to these, there are four potential interferences inside of us: preoccupation, prejudgment, lack of effort, and failure to recognize and adapt to diverse expectations of listening. The obstacles to effective listening combine to create six types of nonlistening. These are pseudolistening, ambushing speakers, monopolizing the stage, responding defensively, attending selectively, and listening literally. Learning about hindrances to mindful listening and learning to recognize forms of nonlistening enable you to exercise greater control over how you listen and, thus, how fully you enter into relationships with other unique individuals.

ADAPTING LISTENING TO COMMUNICATION GOALS

Now that you recognize some of the common pitfalls to effective listening, let's focus on how to listen well. The first requirement is to determine your reason for listening. **Informational listening, critical listening,** and **relational listening** require different listening styles and behaviors. We'll discuss the specific attitudes and skills that support each type of listening.

Informational and Critical Listening

Much of our listening has the purpose of gaining and evaluating information. We listen for information in classes, at political debates, in professional meetings, when important news stories are reported, and when we need guidance on everything from medical treatment to directions to a new place. In all of these cases, the primary purpose of listening is to gain and understand information.

Closely related to informational listening is critical listening in which we listen to form opinions, make judgments, or evaluate people and ideas. Critical listening is related to informational listening because both require attending closely to information. Yet critical listening goes beyond just gaining information and requires us to analyze and evaluate information and people who express it. We decide whether a speaker is credible and ethical by judging the thoroughness of a presentation, the accuracy of quotes and statistics, and the carefulness of reasoning. In Chapter 13, we discuss ways of evaluating evidence in depth. Informational and critical listening call for similar skills in organizing and retaining information. Critical listening also calls for skill in evaluating information.

Be Mindful   Our discussion of obstacles to listening suggests some important clues for how we can listen critically to information. First, it's important to make a decision to be mindful, choosing to attend carefully even if material is complex and difficult. Don't let your mind wander if information gets complicated or confusing. Avoid detouring onto tangents. Instead, stay focused on gaining as much information as you can. Later you may want to ask questions if material isn't clear even when you listened mindfully.

Control Obstacles   You can also minimize distractions in communication situations. You might shut a window to block out traffic noises or adjust a thermostat so that the room temperature is comfortable. In addition, you

A park ranger is communicating important information about safety. Visitors who listen well will gain the knowledge they need to enjoy a mishap-free visit to the park. (© James D. Wilson/Woodfin Camp & Associates)

should minimize psychological distractions by emptying your mind of the many concerns and ideas that can divert your attention from the communication at hand. This means you should try to let go of preoccupations as well as prejudgments that can interfere with effective listening.

Ask Questions   Also important is posing questions to speakers. Asking speakers to clarify or elaborate their message allows you to gain understanding of information you didn't grasp at first and enhances insight into content that you did comprehend. Recently, I listened to a speech on national economic issues. After what was a fairly technical speech, these questions were posed: "Could you explain what you meant by the M2 money supply?" "Could you simplify your explanation of economic trends?" and "Can you clarify the distinction between the national debt and the deficit?" Questions allow listeners to gain further information to clarify content. Questions compliment a speaker because they indicate you are interested and want to know more.

Critical listening often calls for more probing questions of speakers and their content. "What is the source of your statistics on the rate of unemployment?" "Is a 7-year-old statistic on welfare current enough to tell us anything about welfare issues today?" "Have you met with any policy-makers who hold a point of view contrary to yours? What is their response to your proposals?" "I noticed that all of the sources you quoted were fiscal conservatives. Does this mean your presentation and your conclusions are biased?"

It's especially important and appropriate for nonnative speakers to ask questions if they don't understand language (Lee, 1994). The English language is ambiguous, and it contains many colloquial phrases and slang expressions. People whose native language is not English may not understand idioms such as "in a heartbeat" (fast), "not on your life" (very unlikely), or "kick the bucket" (die). Sensitive communicators will explain any idioms they use if nonnative speakers are present. If speakers don't offer explanations, listeners should request them.

Use Aids to Recall   To understand and remember important information, we can apply the principles of perception we discussed in Chapter 2. For instance, we learned that we tend to notice and recall stimuli that are repeated. To use this principle in everyday communication, repeat important ideas to yourself immediately after hearing them. This moves the ideas from short-term to long-term memory (Estes, 1989). Repetition can save you the embarrassment of having to ask people you just met to repeat their names.

Chapter 4 / Effective Listening   **111**

Another way to increase retention is to use mnemonic (pronounced new-monic) devices, which are memory aids that create patterns for what you've heard. You probably already do this in studying. For instance, you could create the mnemonic MPSIRR, which is made up of one word for each of the six parts of listening (*M*indfulness, *P*hysical reception, *S*electing and organizing, *I*nterpreting, *R*esponding, *R*emembering). You can also invent mnemonics to help you recall personal information in communication. For example, KIM is a mnemonic to remember that *K*aya from *I*owa is going into *M*edicine.

Organize Information   A third technique to increase retention is to organize what you hear. When communicating informally, most people don't order their ideas carefully. The result is a flow of information that isn't coherently organized and therefore is hard to retain. We can impose order by regrouping what we hear. For example, suppose a friend tells you he is confused about long-range goals, then says he doesn't know what he can do with a math major, wants to locate in the Midwest, wonders if graduate school is necessary, likes small towns, needs some internships to try out different options, and wants a family eventually. You could regroup this stream of concerns into two categories: academic information (careers for math majors, graduate school, internship opportunities) and lifestyle preferences (Midwest, small town, family). Remembering those two categories allows you to retain the essence of your friend's concerns, even if you forget many of the specifics. Repetition, mnemonics, and regrouping are ways to enhance retention.

Everyday Application

IMPROVING RECALL

Apply the principles we've discussed to enhance memory.

1. The next time you meet someone, repeat his or her name to yourself three times after you are introduced. Do you find the name sticks better?

2. After your next communication class, take 15 minutes to review your notes in a quiet place. Read them aloud so that you hear as well as see the main ideas. Does this increase your retention of material?

3. Invent mnemonics to create patterns that help you remember basic information in communication.

4. Organize complex ideas by grouping them into categories. To remember the main ideas of this chapter, you might use major subheadings to form categories: listening process, obstacles to listening, and listening goals. Then the mnemonic LOG (*Listening, Obstacles, Goals*) could help you remember those topics.

We can increase our understanding and retention of informational communication by being mindful, minimizing distractions, asking questions, repeating and organizing ideas, and using mnemonic devices.

Relational Listening

Listening for information focuses on the content level of meaning in communication. Yet, often we're as concerned or even more concerned with the relational level of meaning that has to do with another's feelings and perceptions. We engage in relational listening when we listen to a friend's worries, let a romantic partner tell us about problems, counsel a co-worker, or talk with a parent about health concerns. Whenever supporting a person is the primary goal of listening, specific attitudes and skills are appropriate.

Be Mindful   The first requirement for effective relational listening is to be mindful. You'll recall this was also the first step in informational listening. When we're interested in relational meanings, however, a different kind of mindfulness is needed. Instead of focusing our minds on information, we need to concentrate on understanding feelings that may not be communicated explicitly. Thus, mindful relational listening calls on us to pay attention to what lies "between the words," the subtle clues to feelings and perceptions. As listening scholar Gerald Egan (1973, p. 228) notes, "Total listening is more than attending to another person's words. It is also listening to the meanings that are buried in the words and between the words and in the silences in communication."

Suspend Judgment   When listening to help another person for the purpose of providing support, it's important to avoid excessively judgmental responses. Although Western culture emphasizes evaluation, often we really don't need to judge others or what they feel or do. Judgments add our evaluations to the others' experiences. When we do this, we move away from them and their feelings. Our judgments may also lead others to become defensive and to be wary of talking further with us. To curb evaluative tendencies, we can ask whether we really need to pass judgment in the present moment.

In Chapter 8, we will discuss in detail how judgmental responses can create defensive communication climates. For now, you need only realize that evaluations, even positive evaluations ("That's a good way to approach the problem"), can make others uneasy and less willing to communicate openly with us. The other person may reason that if we make positive judgments, we could also make negative ones. Only if someone asks for our judgment should we offer it when we are listening to support. Even if our opinion is sought, we should express it in a way that doesn't devalue others. Sometimes people excuse strongly judgmental comments by saying "You asked me to be honest" or "I mean this as constructive criticism." Too often, however, the judgments are not constructive and are more harsh than candor requires. Good relational listening includes responses that support others.

JOSÉ

My best friend makes it so easy for me to tell whatever is on my mind. She never puts me down or makes me feel stupid or weird. Sometimes I ask her what she thinks, and she has this way of telling me without making me feel wrong if I think differently. What it boils down to is respect. She respects me and herself, so she doesn't have to prove anything by acting better than me.

Understand the Other's Perspective   One of the most important principles for effective relational listening is to concentrate on grasping the other person's perspective. This means we have to step outside of our own point of view, at least long enough to understand another's perceptions. We can't respond sensitively to others until we understand their perspective and meanings. To do this, we must put aside preconceptions about issues and how others feel and try to focus on their words and nonverbal behaviors for clues about how they feel and think.

Paraphrasing is a method of clarifying another's meaning or needs by reflecting our interpretations of his or her communication back to him or her. For example, a friend might confide, "I'm really scared my kid brother is messing around with drugs." We could paraphrase this way: "It sounds as if you think your brother may be experimenting with drugs." This paraphrase allows us to clarify whether the friend has any evidence of the brother's drug involvement. The response might be, "No, I don't have any real reason to suspect him, but I just worry because drugs are so pervasive in high schools now." This tells us that the friend's worries are more the issue than any evidence her brother is experimenting with drugs. Paraphrasing also helps us figure out what others feel. If someone screams, "I can't believe he did that to me!" it's not clear whether he is angry, hurt, or upset. We could find out what he's feeling by saying, "You seem really angry." If anger is the emotion, the speaker could agree; if not, he could clarify what he is feeling. Paraphrasing also allows us to check whether we understand another person's meaning: "Let me see if I followed you. What you're saying is that . . ."

PRACTICING PARAPHRASING

Developing skill in paraphrasing others' messages is important in effective communication. Practice your paraphrasing skill by creating paraphrases of the following comments:

1. "I don't know how they expect me to get my work done when they don't give me the information I need and there's no training on how to use this new software program."

2. "I've got three midterms and a paper due next week and I'm behind in my reading."

3. "Can you believe it? This is the fifth rejection letter I've received. I thought all of the time I spent interviewing would produce better results."

4. "My parents don't understand why I need to go to summer school, and they won't help with the expenses."

5. "My son wants to go to summer school and expects us to come up with the money. Doesn't he understand what we're already paying for the regular school year?"

Another strategy for understanding another's thoughts and feelings is to use **minimal encouragers.** These are responses that express interest in hearing more and thus gently invite another person to elaborate. Examples of minimal encouragers are "Tell me more," "Really?" "Go on," "I'm with you," "Then what happened?" "Yeah?" and "I see." We can also use nonverbal minimal encouragers such as a raised eyebrow to show we're involved, a nod to indicate we understand, or widened eyes to indicate we're fascinated. Minimal encouragers indicate we are listening, following, and interested. They encourage others to keep talking so that we can more fully understand what they mean. Keep in mind that these are *minimal* encouragers. They shouldn't interrupt or take the focus away from another. Effective minimal encouragers are very brief interjections that prompt, rather than interfere with, the flow of another's talk.

A third way to enhance understanding of what another feels or needs is to ask questions. For instance, we might ask "How do you feel about that?" "What do you plan to do?" or "How are you working this through?" Another reason we ask questions is to find out what a person wants from us. Sometimes it isn't clear whether someone wants advice, a shoulder to cry on, or a safe place to vent feelings. If we can't figure out what's wanted, it's appropriate to ask. "Are you looking for advice or a sounding board?" "Do you want to talk about how to handle the situation, or do you just want to air the issues?" Asking directly signals that we really want to help and allows others to tell us how we can best do that.

Express Support   Once you have understood another's meanings and perspective, then relational listening should focus on communicating support. This doesn't necessarily require us to agree with another's perspective or ideas. What it does call on us to do is to communicate support for the person. To illustrate how we can support a person even if we don't agree with her or his position, consider the following between a son and his father.

Son: Dad, I'm changing my major from business to acting.

Father: Oh.

Son: Yeah, I've wanted to do it for some time but I kept holding back because acting isn't as safe as accounting.

Father: That's certainly true.

Son: Yeah, but I've decided to do it anyway. I'd like to know what you think about the idea.

Father: The idea worries me. Starving actors are a dime a dozen. It just won't provide you with any economic future or security.

Son: I understand acting isn't as secure as business, but it is what I really want to do.

Father: Tell me what you feel about acting—why it matters so much to you.

Son: It's the most creative, totally fulfilling thing I do. I've tried to get interested in business, but I just don't love that like I do acting. I feel like I have to give this a try or I'll always wonder if I could have made it. If I don't get somewhere in 5 or 6 years, I'll rethink my career options.

Father: Couldn't you finish your business degree and get a job and act on the side?

Son: No. I've got to give acting a full shot—give it everything I have to see if I can make it.

Father: Well, I still have reservations, but I guess I can understand having to try something that matters this much to you. I'm just concerned that you'll lose years of your life to something that doesn't work out.

Son: Well, I'm kinda concerned about that too—but I'm more worried about wasting years of my life in a career that doesn't turn me on than about trying to make a go of the one that does.

Father: That makes sense. I wouldn't make the choice you're making, but I respect your decision and your guts for taking a big gamble.

This dialogue illustrates several principles of effective relational listening. First, notice that the father's first two comments are minimal encouragers that invite his son to elaborate thoughts and feelings. The father also encourages his son to explain how he feels. Later, the father suggests a compromise solution, but his son rejects that and the father respects the son's position. Importantly, the father makes his own position clear, but he

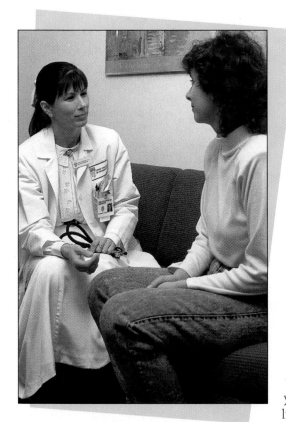

Listening to discriminate is vital when doctors communicate with patients. (© Frank Siteman/The Picture Cube)

separates his personal stance from his respect for his son's right to make his own choices. Sometimes it's difficult to listen openly and nonjudgmentally, particularly if we don't agree with the person speaking, as in the example. However, if your goal is to support another person, then sensitive, responsive involvement without evaluation is the ideal listening style.

Other Purposes of Listening

Listening for information and to make critical evaluations and listening to support others are two major listening purposes. In addition, there are other listening goals that we will discuss briefly.

Listening for Pleasure Sometimes we listen for pleasure, as when we attend concerts or play CDs. Listening for enjoyment is also a primary purpose when we go to comedy shows or pay attention to jokes an acquaintance tells. When we are listening for pleasure, we don't need to concentrate on organizing and remembering as much as when we listen for information, although retention is important if you want to be able to tell a joke to someone else later. Yet, listening for pleasure does require mindfulness, hearing, and interpretation.

Listening to Discriminate In some situations, we listen to make fine discriminations in sounds in order to draw valid conclusions and act appropriately in response. For example, doctors listen to discriminate when they use stethoscopes to diagnose heart functioning or chest congestion. Parents listen to discriminate between a baby's cries for attention, food, or a diaper change. Subtle differences in the crying signal distinct needs in infants, and parents need to be able to discriminate accurately. Skilled mechanics can distinguish among engine sounds that most people cannot detect. Mindfulness and keen hearing abilities are particularly important when listening to discriminate.

There are different purposes for listening. Mindfulness is a prerequisite for effective listening regardless of specific purpose. With the exception of mindfulness, each listening purpose tends to emphasize particular aspects of the listening process and to put less weight on others. Whereas evaluating content is especially important in listening critically, it is less crucial when listening for pleasure. Hearing acoustic nuances is important when listening to discriminate but not vital to listening for information. Selecting, organizing, and retaining information matter more when we are listening for information than when we are listening for pleasure. Deciding on your purpose for listening allows you to enact the particular communication skills that are most pertinent.

SUMMARY

According to Zeno of Citium, an ancient philosopher, "We have been given two ears and but a single mouth, in order that we may hear more and talk less." Thousands of years later, we can still learn from his comment. Listening is a major and vital part of communication, yet too often we don't consider it as important as talking. In this chapter, we've explored the complex and demanding process of listening.

We began by distinguishing the processes of physically receiving messages and listening. The former is a straightforward physiological process that doesn't require effort on our part. Listening, in contrast, is a complicated process involving being mindful, hearing, selecting and organizing, interpreting, responding, and remembering. Listening well requires commitment and skill.

To understand what interferes with effective listening, we discussed both hindrances in situations and messages and obstacles in ourselves. Listening is complicated by message overload, complexity of material, and external noise in communication contexts. In addition, listening can be hampered by our preoccupations and prejudgments, lack of effort, and failure to recognize differences in listening styles. These obstacles to careful listening give rise to various types of nonlistening, including pseudolistening, monopolizing, selective listening, defensive listening, ambushing, and literal listening. Each of these forms of nonlistening signals that we aren't fully present in interaction.

We also discussed different purposes for listening and identified the skills and attitudes that advance each purpose. Informational and critical listening requires us to adopt a mindful attitude and to think critically, organize and evaluate information, clarify understanding through asking questions, and develop aids to retention of complex material. Relational listening also requires mindfulness, but it calls for other, distinct listening skills. Suspending judgment, paraphrasing, giving minimal encouragers, and expressing support enhance the effectiveness of relational listening.

FOR FURTHER REFLECTION AND DISCUSSION

1. Review the forms of nonlistening discussed in this chapter. Do any of them describe ways in which you attend (or don't attend) to others? Select one type of nonlistening in which you engage, and work to minimize its occurrence.

2. Apply the strategies for remembering discussed in this chapter to aid your retention of material covered in one of your classes. Work out ways to organize material, create mnemonics, and review material immediately after each class. Do you find this increases your understanding and retention?

3. What do you see as ethical principles that guide different listening purposes? What different moral goals and responsibilities accompany listening informationally and critically and listening relationally?

4. As a class discuss the idea of mindfulness. As we saw in the chapter, mindfulness isn't a technique or a specific skill, but rather is a commitment to attentiveness. Is it possible to learn mindfulness? Is it something we can improve with practice?

5. Keep a record of your listening for 2 days. How much of your listening is informational, critical, relational, for pleasure, and to discriminate?

KEY TERMS

hearing	defensive listening
listening	ambushing
mindfulness	literal listening
responding	informational listening
remembering	critical listening
pseudolistening	relational listening
monopolizing	paraphrasing
selective listening	minimal encouragers

Focus Questions

1 Can words really hurt people?

2 How does using symbols distinguish humans from other creatures?

3 Why is bias inevitable in language?

4 Do we need symbols to have a self-concept?

5 How do indexing and I-language improve communication?

CHAPTER 5

The Verbal Dimension of Communication

"I do."

"You're terrible."

"He's a drunk."

"She was date raped."

"The war on the environment threatens our children's future."

The five sentences you just read give us a quick introduction to the power of words. Words name experiences, shape attitudes, and define our identities.
The two little words "I do," for instance, have the power to change
individuals' lives personally, legally, and spiritually. Parents who say
"You're terrible" (or "You're stupid" or "You're a problem") can devastate a child's self-concept so that she or he never develops healthy
self-esteem. It's more dramatic and memorable to give a speech on
the "war on the environment" than to speak about efforts to open
public lands to mining and drilling. Likewise, the phrase "threatens
our children's future" is more powerful than saying "Environmental
losses will have long-range consequences."

(David Hockney, *Domestic Scene, Broadchalke, Wilts* (1963). Oil on canvas, 72 × 72". © David Hockney.)

You may also have noticed that the opening examples illustrate difficulties in abstraction, which we discussed in Chapter 2. "You're terrible," for instance, is a high-level abstraction that expresses a general conclusion. We don't know what concrete behaviors or qualities underlie the abstract statement, "You're terrible." "He's a drunk" is also a very abstract generalization, based on concrete behaviors that may or may not justify the label. Further, it is more harsh to say "He's a drunk" than to say "He's an alcoholic" or "Sometimes he drinks too much."

Finally, consider the significance of the term *date rape*. Only in recent years has that phrase entered popular language. Although unwanted and forced sexual activity between people who were dating occurred before the 1980s, we had no language to describe what happened as a crime. Instead, we said "He went too far" or "Things got out of hand." These phrases didn't capture the betrayal and violation of trust that occur when a date forces sex. The impact of the term *date rape* illustrates the power of naming and humans' ability to create language to reflect their experiences, two themes we will explore in this chapter. As the opening examples reveal, language is a major dimension of communication and of our lives.

The human world is one of words and meanings. We use words to express ourselves and to give meaning to our lives and activities. In this chapter, we take a close look at the verbal dimension of communication and how it affects our personal identity and our interaction with others. We begin by defining symbols. Second, we explore principles of verbal communication. Next, we consider what using symbols allows us to do. The final section of the chapter focuses on guidelines for using language effectively.

SYMBOLS AND MEANING

As we discovered in our discussion of perception, seldom, if ever, do we interact with phenomena in their complete, concrete detail. Instead, we abstract only certain parts of phenomena to notice and label. After we label experiences, we tend to respond to our labels, not the original experiences themselves. This means that our perceptions and experiences are shaped by symbols. To appreciate how this affects our lives, we need to explore what symbols are.

Symbols represent phenomena. For instance, your name is a symbol that represents you. *House* is a symbol that stands for a type of building. *Big government* is a phrase politicians often use to disparage incumbents whose positions they seek. *Total quality management* is a symbol that represents a new managerial philosophy. All language and much nonverbal behavior is symbolic, but not all symbols are language. Art, music, company logos, and objects also can be symbols that stand for feelings, thoughts, and experiences. Symbols are arbitrary, ambiguous, and abstract ways of representing other things.

The high-tech industry provides dramatic examples of the ways in which symbols function as private codes that are understood by insiders and that exclude outsiders. (© Michael Grecco/Stock, Boston)

Symbols Are Arbitrary

Symbols are **arbitrary,** which means they are not intrinsically connected to what they represent. For instance, the word *Julia* has no necessary or natural connection to me. We could substitute a different symbol/word as long as we agreed it referred to me. A friend of mine changed her name from Rita to Eliza because she had always disliked Rita. Certain words seem right because as a society we agree to use them in particular ways, but they have no natural correspondence with their referents.

Because language is arbitrary, we can create private codes that only we and certain others know. For example, in most organizations employees have specialized jargon that they understand but that is not understood by outsiders. Similarly, most couples have a private language that is not understood, and not meant to be understood, by people outside of the relationship. Their code language allows them to pass private messages in public settings. Coded language also allows users to communicate secret, confidential information that could be dangerous if understood by outsiders. Two of the primary tasks of military intelligence are to invent secret codes that cannot be broken and to break the secret codes used by others.

Language and meanings also change over time. In the 1950s, *gay* meant lighthearted and merry; today it is generally understood to mean men whose sexual preference is men. Similarly, the majority of publishers and dictionaries no longer allow male-generic language, which uses male terms (for example, *chairman, postman, mankind*) to represent both women and men. Our language also changes as we invent new words. African Americans began using *disrespect* as a verb (instead of a noun) as an active

CODE TALKERS

During World War II, a special group of soldiers serving in Iwo Jima developed a private code that was never broken by enemy intelligence. Because all of the soldiers in this group were Navajo Indians, the code they devised was based on the Navajo language, which was an oral language that was not written down and was not understood by non-Navajos. Dubbed the "code talkers," this group of soldiers invented a 400-word code that was extremely secure. Drawing on the strong nature theme in Navajo life and language, the code included the Navajo words for owl (observer), hawk (dive bomber), and egg (bomb).

way to describe behaviors that demean someone. *Disrespect* and its abbreviated form *diss*, have now entered the general language. Disrespectful conduct might as easily be termed *meanspeak* or *badspeak*, had we chosen to use those words to represent the idea of demeaning behavior.

Many new words that have entered the general vocabulary were coined in response to changes in business and professional contexts. The term *downsizing* didn't exist a decade ago, yet today it is commonly used and widely understood. *Networking* once meant making contacts in a field; today it is equally likely to mean being hooked up (another recently coined term) via computer to other people. We used to hear that people got fired; today they are *laid off*. My partner conducts his work in a *virtual office*, a term that nobody had heard of in the 1980s.

Politics is another rich source of new words. In 1994, Newt Gingrich proposed *the contract with America*, a phrase that symbolized the newly elected Republican majority's plans to restrict or reverse many of the results of Democratic leaders. *The moral majority, big spending liberals*, and *gridlock* are other terms that were coined by politicians and that have entered into popular language.

Symbols Are Ambiguous

Symbols are also **ambiguous**, which means their meanings aren't clear-cut or fixed. There are variations in what words mean, even ones we have agreed to use in specific ways. *Government regulation* may mean positive assistance to citizens who are suffering from pollutants emitted by a chemical factory. To owners of the chemical company, however, *government regulation* may mean costly and undesired requirements to control pollution. To one person, a *good friend* means someone to hang out with, and to another person it means someone to confide in. Christmas, Hanukkah, and Thanks-

But you didn't say to hand you the bread, you said to pass the bread."

(*Dennis the Menace®* used by permission of Hank Ketcham and © by North America Syndicate.)

giving carry distinct connotations for people who have families and those who don't. The *new year* begins in September for Jewish people and in January for Christians and nondenominational Westerners. *Affirmative action* means different things to people who have experienced discrimination and ones who haven't. Although the words are the same, what they mean varies as a result of individuals' identities and experiences.

Although words don't mean exactly the same thing to everyone, within a culture many symbols have an agreed-on range of meanings (Mead, 1934). In learning language, we learn not only words but the meanings and values of our society. Thus, we all understand that dogs are four-footed creatures, but each of us also has personal meanings for the word based on dogs we have known and our experiences with them. We've all experienced dynamic speakers, yet we may differ in the concrete attitudes and behaviors that lead us to label a speaker *dynamic* (remember the abstraction ladder in Chapter 2).

The ambiguity of symbols explains why misunderstandings so often occur in communication between people. At work, team members may have different referents and meanings for the same words, and public speakers and audiences may not share vocabularies. In personal relationships, too, the ambiguity of words is a source of frequent misunderstandings. Recently, a friend of mine told her 3-year-old daughter to be more responsible about putting away her toys. Later, we discovered stuffed animals tucked into beds around the house. The little girl had her own notion of what being responsible meant.

Ambiguity frequently surfaces in friendships and romantic relationships. Martina tells her boyfriend that he's not being attentive, meaning that she wants him to listen more closely to what she says. However, he infers that she wants him to call more often. The word *love* means different things to people brought up in different kinds of families. Similarly, spouses often have different meanings for "doing their share" of home chores. To most women it means doing half of the work, but men tend to see it as doing more than their fathers did (Hochschild with Machung, 1989).

Ambiguous language is a common problem between intimates (Beck, 1988). Friends and romantic partners often have different meanings for the same words and don't even realize that their meanings differ. To minimize

SOMETHING LOST IN TRANSLATION

When the U.S. manufacturer of Fresca soft drink decided to export the product to Mexico, sales were dismal. It turned out the word *fresca* in Spanish is sometimes used to describe a woman who is aggressive, brash, or unfeminine in her behavior.

When General Motors exported its popular Nova model to South America, there were problems. In Spanish, *no va* means "does not go"—not a particularly good advertisement for a car!

the problems of ambiguity, we should be as clear as possible in communication. In the earlier example, Martina asked her boyfriend to be more attentive, but she and he had different ideas about what being more attentive means. Thus, it's more effective to say "I would like for you to look at me and give feedback when I'm talking" than to say "I wish you'd be more attentive."

CLARIFYING MEANING

The next time someone with whom you're close uses a "fuzzy" word like *successful* or *thoughtful,* ask what she or he means by the word. Invite the person to tell you in concrete terms what she or he would see as loving, thoughtful, or so forth. Is that what it meant to you?

Now apply the same principle to your own communication. When you use a fuzzy word, ask whomever you're talking with what he or she thinks it means. Are your meanings the same?

The ambiguity of language may also cause problems in groups, organizational communication, and public speaking. A team leader who asks members to be "more responsible" may get a variety of responses, depending on what the ambiguous term *responsible* means to different members. The term *restructuring* may be interpreted to mean firing employees, closing locations, or reducing bonuses and salaries. Your supervisor tells you it's important to be "a team player," which you assume means you should cooperate with co-workers. Your supervisor, however, may mean that you are expected to initiate and participate in project teams on the job. After you give a public presentation, someone suggests you should be "more forceful," but what that means isn't clear. Should you use more facial expressions, greater vocal inflection, stronger evidence, more motion? The word *forceful* is ambiguous, and what it means is not transparent. Recognizing the ambiguity of language allows us to be sensitive to the different meanings that people may have for the same words.

Symbols Are Abstract

Finally, symbols are **abstract,** which means they are not concrete or tangible. They stand for ideas, people, events, objects, feelings, and so forth, but they are not the things they represent. In Chapter 2, we discussed the abstraction ladder whereby we move farther and farther away from concrete reality. The symbols we use vary in abstractness. *Managerial potential* is a very abstract term. *Organizational and presentational skill* is less abstract. Experience in *collaborating with others, public speaking,* and *organizing project teams* are even more concrete expressions.

A D I V A

Nonnative speakers have much difficulty with abstract language. My resident assistant told us we must observe "quiet hours" from 7 to 10 each night so that people can study. But everyone on my hall plays music and talks during quiet hours. My adviser told me I needed to take courses in "social diversity," so I took a class in oral traditions of Asian cultures. Then my adviser told me that is a non-Western civilization course, not one in social diversity.

As our symbols become increasingly abstract, the potential for confusion mushrooms. One of the ways this happens is overgeneralization. Public speakers sometimes make very abstract claims that critical listeners won't accept without clarification. For example, the assertion that "environmentalists despise big business" is fallacious because it is so general. Few environmentalists dislike all big business; many respect the goals and the efforts to protect the environment made by a substantial number of large businesses and industries. Overly abstract language can also complicate personal relationships. Couple counselor Aaron Beck (1988) reports that overly general language distorts how partners think about a relationship. They may make broad, negative statements such as "You never go along with my preferences" or "You always interrupt me." In most cases, such statements are overgeneralizations that are not entirely accurate. Yet the symbols partners use frame how they think about their experiences. Researchers have shown that we are more likely to recall behaviors that are consistent with how we've labeled people than ones that are inconsistent (Fincham & Bradbury, 1987). When we say a relative is intrusive, we're likely to remember times the relative seemed to interfere in our lives and to forget all the times when he or she respected our independence.

JARGON AND GOBBLEDYGOOK

Make a list of ambiguous and abstract language in your workplace or a place in which you have worked. List words that are jargon, or specialized terms that are clear to professionals in the area. Next list words and phrases that aren't necessary for specialized concepts but seem only to cause confusion and ambiguity.

Do you see the following phrases as clear or as ambiguous, inviting confusion and lack of shared understanding among employees?

Cash-flow problems	Team work
Negative budget decisions	Management material

Being aware that symbols are arbitrary, ambiguous, and abstract helps us understand their power to represent complex ideas and feelings in ways that allow us to share our ideas with others. At the same time, symbols have the potential to create misunderstandings. When we understand that symbols are ambiguous, arbitrary, and abstract, we can guard against their potential to hinder communication.

PRINCIPLES OF VERBAL COMMUNICATION

Now that we understand what symbols are, we can consider three principles that further explain the ways we use verbal communication and the impact it has.

Interpretation Creates Meaning

Because symbols are abstract, ambiguous, and arbitrary, their meanings aren't self-evident or absolute. Instead, we have to interpret the meaning of symbols. We construct meanings in the process of interacting with others and through dialogues we carry on in our own heads (Duck, 1994a,b; Shotter, 1993). The process of constructing meaning is itself symbolic, since we rely on words to think about what things mean.

Interpretation is an active, creative process we use to make sense of words. If a work associate says "Let's go to dinner after work," the suggestion could mean a variety of things. It could be an invitation to explore transforming the work relationship into a friendship. It could be a veiled request for a strategy session regarding some issue in the workplace. It might also indicate that the person issuing the invitation is interested in a romantic relationship. "Let's go to dinner after work" doesn't mean one fixed, exact thing. Words are ambiguous and layered with multiple possible

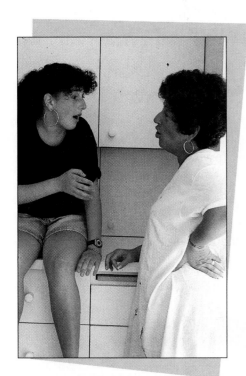

When managed effectively, conflict can allow people to understand one another and to grow closer. Does the nonverbal communication between this mother and daughter suggest they are listening to each other and managing conflict constructively? (© Ann Chwatsky/ The Picture Cube)

meanings. Although we're usually not conscious of the effort we invest to interpret words, we continuously engage in the process of constructing meanings.

When somebody says "Blow off," you have to think about the comment and the person who made it to decide whether it's an insult, a friendly needling, or a colloquial way to say you are out of line. If you are not a native English speaker, then the idiom *blow off* may make no sense to you. What the words mean also depends on the self-esteem and previous experiences of the individual who is told to blow off. Individuals who have high self-esteem are not as likely to be hurt as individuals who have less self-confidence. The systemic character of communication means that we have to consider who is speaking and the context of interaction to decide what words mean. Because symbols require active interpretation, communication is an ongoing process of creating meanings. This implies that good communication involves being alert to possible misunderstandings and checking with others to see if their meanings for language match our own.

Communication Is Rule-Guided

Verbal communication is patterned by unspoken but broadly understood rules (Argyle & Henderson, 1985; Shimanoff, 1980). **Communication rules** are shared understandings of what communication means and what behaviors are appropriate in various situations. For the most part, rules aren't explicit or intentionally constructed. Nonetheless, they can strongly influence how we communicate. In the course of interacting with our families and others, we unconsciously absorb rules that guide how we communicate and how we interpret others' communication. Children begin to understand and follow communication rules by the time they are 1 to 2 years old (Miller, 1993).

Two kinds of rules govern communication (Cronen, Pearce, & Snavely, 1979; Pearce, Cronen, & Conklin, 1979). **Regulative rules** regulate interaction by specifying when, how, where, and with whom to talk about certain things. For instance, we follow rules for turn taking in conversation. In formal contexts, we usually know not to interrupt when someone else is speaking, but in more informal settings interruptions may be appropriate. Yet, talking during formal speeches is appropriate in some contexts, such as in African American churches and meetings, where feedback is regarded as evidence of interest. Some families have a rule that people can't argue at the dinner table. Families also teach us rules about how to manage conflict (Honeycutt, Woods, & Fontenot, 1993; Jones & Gallois, 1989).

Regulative rules also define when, where, and with whom it's appropriate or required to show affection, demonstrate respect, and disclose private information. Some people have the rule that it's okay to kiss intimates in private but not in public and it's inappropriate to kiss strangers even in private. On the job, there are often regulative rules that specify individuals with higher positions may interrupt subordinates, but subordinates may not interrupt organizational superiors. There may also be regulative rules in the workplace that stipulate employees are expected to show interest and respect when higher-ups communicate.

Constitutive rules, the second type of rule, define what communication means by telling us how to count certain kinds of communication. We learn what counts as showing respect (paying attention), demonstrating affection (giving kisses, hugs), and being rude (ignoring). We also learn what communication is expected of a friend (showing support, being loyal), a professional (being assertive and confident, taking on extra projects), and a romantic partner (demonstrating respect, trust, and fidelity; sharing confidences). We learn constitutive and regulative rules from both particular others and the generalized other.

COMMUNICATION RULES IN FAMILIES

Identify constitutive and regulative rules you follow when interacting with your family.

Constitutive Rules

What counts as being attentive?

What counts as being respectful of parents?

What counts as being responsible?

What counts as showing affection?

Regulative Rules

When is it appropriate to interrupt?

What topics are appropriate during dinner conversation?

With whom can you talk about personal issues?

With whom do you talk about money problems?

Everyday interaction is guided by rules that tell us when to speak, what to say, and how to interpret others' communication. Social interactions tend to adhere to rules that are widely shared in our society. Interaction between intimates also follows rules, but these may not be shared by the culture as a whole. Intimate partners negotiate private rules to guide how they communicate and what certain things mean (Wood, 1982, 1995b). Couples craft personal rules that specify how to argue, express love, make decisions, and spend time together (Beck, 1988; Fitzpatrick, 1988).

It's important to understand that we don't have to be aware of communication rules in order to follow them. Most of the time we're not conscious of the rules that guide how, when, where, and with whom we communicate about various things. New employees learn the rules for communicating with each other and superiors as they interact with members and internalize the organizational culture. They learn whether or not supervisors are open to suggestions, whether teamwork or individual initiatives are rewarded, and what degree of socializing is expected on the job. We may not realize we have rules until one is broken and we become aware that we had an expectation. A study by Victoria DeFrancisco (1991) revealed that between spouses there was a clear pattern in which husbands interrupted wives and were unresponsive to topics wives initiated. The couples were unaware of the rules, but their communication nonetheless followed the pattern. Becoming aware of communication rules empowers you to change ones that don't promote healthy interaction and relationships.

MILAN

There's this funny pattern with the guys I hang out with. It starts when one of us says "Let's go get something to eat." Then somebody suggests Mexican food, and someone else says he hates it. Another guy says we should get a pizza, and someone else says they're too expensive. Somebody says burgers, and one of the others groans. Then we decide to fix something at the apartment. Honestly, we go through this routine two or three times a week, and it's always the same.

Punctuation Affects Meaning

We use **punctuation** in communication to interpret meaning. This isn't the kind of punctuation you study in grammar classes, although punctuation of communication is also a way of marking a flow of activity into meaningful units. In writing, we use periods to define where ideas stop and start. Similarly, in interpersonal communication, punctuation is mentally marking beginnings and endings of particular interactions to assign meaning to them (Watzlawick, Beavin, & Jackson, 1967). For example, when a teacher steps to the front of a classroom, you probably punctuate that as the beginning of the class. When the CEO enters a room, you punctuate that as the beginning of a meeting. When a speaker says "Thank you for your attention" and folds notes, you punctuate that as the end of the formal speech.

To decide what communication means, we must establish its boundaries. Usually this involves deciding who started the interaction. When we don't agree on punctuation, problems may arise. If you've ever heard children arguing about who started a fight, you understand the importance of punctuation. A common instance of conflicting punctuation is the demand-withdraw pattern (Bergner & Bergner, 1990) (Figure 5.1). This

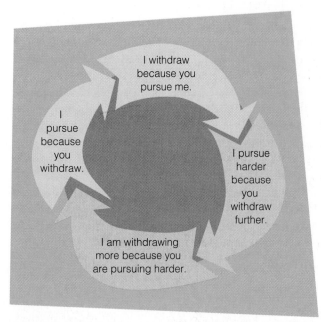

FIGURE 5.1
The Demand–Withdraw Pattern

occurs when one person tries to express closeness, and the other strives to maintain autonomy by avoiding interaction. The more one pushes for personal talk, the further the other withdraws. Each partner punctuates interaction as starting with the other's behavior. Thus, the demander thinks "I pursue because you withdraw," and the withdrawer thinks "I withdraw because you pursue."

It's not useful to judge the accuracy of punctuation, since it involves subjective perceptions. It is useful to understand that people don't always agree on punctuation. When they punctuate differently, they ascribe different meanings for what is happening between them. To break out of unconstructive cycles, such as demand–withdraw, partners need to discuss how each of them is punctuating the experience. This reminds us of a guideline discussed earlier: Effective communication requires perspective taking. Steven's comment illustrates the demand–withdraw pattern and a lack of perspective taking between him and his parents.

STEVEN

My parents say I am irresponsible if I don't tell them about something I do. So then they probe me and call more often to check up on me. I hate that kind of intrusion, so I don't return their calls and I sidestep questions. That makes them call more and ask more questions. That makes me clam up more. And it just keeps going in circles.

The meaning of verbal communication arises out of personal interpretations, communication rules, and punctuation. These three principles highlight the creativity involved in constructing meaning. We're now ready to consider how verbal communication affects identities and relationships.

Symbolic abilities

The human ability to use symbols allows us to live in a world of ideas and meanings. Instead of just reacting to our concrete environments, we think about them and sometimes transform them. Philosophers of language have identified five ways symbolic capacities affect our lives (Cassirer, 1944; Langer, 1953, 1979). As we discuss each, we'll consider how to realize the constructive power of symbols and minimize the problems they can generate.

LANGUAGE SHAPES OUR REALITIES

Studies by anthropologists reveal that language shapes perceptions. The language of the Hopi Indians makes no distinction between stationary objects and moving processes, whereas English uses nouns and verbs, respectively.

The English word *snow* is the only word we have to define frozen, white precipitation that falls in the winter. In Arctic cultures where snow is a major aspect of life, there are many words to define snow that is powdery, icy, dry, wet, and so forth. The distinctions are important to designate which snows allow safe travel.

Source: Whorf, B. (1956). *Language, thought, and reality.* New York: MIT Press/Wiley.

(Reprinted from *The Chronicle of Higher Education.* By permission of Mischa Richter and Harald Bakken.)

"Well, then, if 'commandments' seems too harsh to me, and 'guidelines' seems too wishy-washy to you, how about 'The 10 Policy Statements'?"

Symbols Define

The most basic symbolic ability is definition. We use symbols to define experiences, people, relationships, feelings, and thoughts (Blumer, 1969; Cassirer, 1944; Wood, 1992a). As we saw in Chapter 2, the definitions we impose on phenomena shape what they mean to us. When we label people, we focus attention on particular aspects of them and we necessarily obscure other aspects of who they are. We might define a person as an environmentalist, a teacher, a gourmet cook, and a father. Each way of classifying the person directs our attention to certain and not other aspects of identity. We might discuss wilderness legislation with the environmentalist, talk about testing with the teacher, swap recipes with the chef, and exchange stories about children with the father. We tend to interact with people according to how we define and classify them.

Totalizing occurs when we respond to a person as if one label totally represents who he or she is. We fixate on one symbol to define someone and fail to recognize many other aspects of who she or he is. Some individuals totalize gay men and lesbians as if sexual preference is the only important facet of a person. Interestingly, we don't totalize heterosexuals on the basis of *their* sexuality. Totalizing also occurs when we dismiss people by saying "He's a Republican," "She's old," "She's preppy," or "He's a jock." When we totalize others, we negate most of who they are by spotlighting a single aspect of their identity.

NANYA

I'm Indian and that's all a lot of people here see in me. They see that my skin is dark and I wear a sari, and they put me in the category "foreigner" or, if they are observant, "Indian." They mark me off as different, foreign, not like them, and they can't see anything else about me. How would they feel if I categorized them as "Americans" and didn't see their individual qualities?

Symbols influence how we think and feel about experiences and people. Perhaps you remember the 1991 Senate hearings regarding charges that Clarence Thomas, a nominee to the Supreme Court, had sexually harassed Anita Hill. At one dramatic point in the hearings, Thomas described the process as "a high-tech lynching." That phrase influenced many people to perceive the hearings as a racist attack on a black man. Symbols also affect perceptions in private relationships. In a recent study, my colleagues and I asked romantic couples how they defined differences between them (Wood, Dendy, Dordek, Germany, & Varallo, 1994). We found that some individuals define differences as positive forces that energize a relationship and keep it interesting. Others define differences as problems or barriers to closeness. There was a direct connection between how partners defined differences and how they dealt with them. Partners who viewed differences as constructive approached disagreements with curiosity and a belief that they would grow by discussing differences. On the other hand, partners who labeled differences as problems tended to deny differences or avoid talking about them.

A number of communication scholars point out that how we think about relationships directly affects what happens in them (Duck, 1985, 1994a,b; Honeycutt, Woods, & Fontenot, 1993; Spencer, 1994). People who dwell on negative thoughts about relationships heighten awareness of relationship flaws and diminish perceptions of strengths (Cloven & Roloff, 1991). Conversely, partners who focus on good facets of their relationships are more conscious of virtues in partners and relationships and less bothered by imperfections (Bradbury & Fincham, 1990; Fletcher & Fincham, 1991).

CHERYL

About 3 years ago, my husband and I were seriously considering divorce. We decided to try marital counseling first, and that saved our marriage. The counselor helped us see that we noticed problems, aggravations, and faults in each other and didn't see all of the good qualities in each other and our rela-

"COME IN. THIS PLACE IS FOR EVERYONE."

Adopted by the World Congress in 1969, the stylized wheelchair has become the international symbol of access for persons with disabilities. As critics point out, however, it may not be the ideal symbol.

One problem with the wheelchair symbol is that it doesn't represent many forms of disabilities; a visually impaired person couldn't even see the symbol. According to graphic designer Brendan Murphy, another problem is that the stylized wheelchair depicts a disabled person who is dependent and helpless.

Murphy has proposed an alternative new symbol that he thinks communicates, "Come in. This place is for everyone." Everyone includes the 49 million Americans who currently have disabilities, as well as those who will develop disabilities during their lives.

Mr. Murphy's open-door symbol applies to all impairments—ones that affect sight, hearing, physical motion, and learning.

Source: Pierson, J. (1995, February 17). Form + function. *Wall Street Journal*, p. B1.

tionship. Now we have a "warts and all" philosophy, which means we accept each other, warts and all. Changing how we think about our marriage really has changed what it is for us.

As Cheryl's commentary indicates, our definitions of relationships can create self-fulfilling prophecies. Because verbal language is ambiguous, arbitrary, and abstract, there are multiple ways we can define any experience, person, relationship, policy, or idea. Once we select a label, we tend to see what our label spotlights and to overlook what the label doesn't highlight. This suggests an ethical principle for using and interpreting language: We should consider what language we and others use includes, as well as what it excludes.

Symbols Evaluate

Symbols are not neutral, but laden with values. This is an intrinsic quality of symbols. In fact, it's impossible to find words that are completely neutral or objective. We tend to describe people we like with language that accents their good qualities and downplays their flaws. Just the reverse is generally true of descriptions for people we don't like. "The contract with America" implies a response to the public, whereas "the Republican agenda" would sound partisan and self-interested. Restaurants use positive words to

The power of symbols to define and evaluate phenomena is evident in the nonverbal communication at public events such as this one to gain respect and civil rights for gays and lesbians. (© Les Stone/Sygma)

heighten the attractiveness of menu items. "Tender lobster accented with drawn butter" sounds more appetizing than "a crustacean murdered by being boiled alive and then drenched in saturated fat"!

Of course, there are degrees of evaluation in language. We might describe people who speak their minds as assertive, outspoken, courageous, or dominating. Each word has a distinct connotation. In recent years, we have become more sensitive to how the evaluative nature of symbols can hurt people. Most individuals with disabilities prefer not to be called disabled, since that tends to totalize them in terms of a disability. The term *African American* emphasizes cultural heritage, whereas *black* focuses on skin color. Designations for homosexuals are currently in transition. The term *homosexual* has negative connotations and even more so do words like *fairy, queer,* and *dyke.* Some gays and lesbians use the term *sexual orientation* to suggest they didn't choose their sexuality. Others use the term *sexual preference* to indicate that their sexuality is a matter of choice, not genetics. Still others speak of *affectional preference* to signal that their commitment concerns the entire realm of affection, not just sexual activity. An ethical guideline for using language is to try to learn and respect others' preferences for describing their identities.

The term **loaded language** refers to words that strongly slant perceptions and, thus, meanings. For example, television and radio commentator Rush Limbaugh labels people who support women's rights as *feminazis* and *fembots.* Loaded language also encourages negative views of older citizens. Terms such as *geezer* and *old fogies* incline us to regard older people with contempt or pity. Alternatives such as *senior citizen* and *mature person* encourage more respectful attitudes.

Symbols Organize Perceptions

We use symbols to organize our perceptions. As we saw in Chapter 2, we rely on cognitive schemata to classify and evaluate experiences. How we organize experiences affects what they mean to us. For example, your prototype of a good friend affects how you judge particular friends. When we place someone in the category of friend, the category influences how we interpret that individual and his or her communication. An insult is likely to be viewed as teasing if made by a friend, but a call to battle if made by an enemy. The words don't change, but what they mean varies depending on how we classify the person uttering them.

The organizational quality of symbols also allows us to think about abstract concepts, such as the work ethic, morality, good citizenship, and healthy family life. We use broad concepts to transcend specific, concrete activities and to enter the world of conceptual thought and ideals. Because we think abstractly, we don't have to consider every specific object and experience individually. Instead, we can think about broad ideas.

Our capacity to abstract can also distort thinking. A primary way this occurs is stereotyping, which is thinking in broad generalizations about a whole class of people or experiences. Examples of stereotypes are "Sorority women are yuppies," "Ph.D.s are smart," "Jocks are dumb," "Republicans favor business," "Everyone who votes is a good citizen," and "Conflict is bad." Notice that stereotypes can be positive or negative.

REGGIE

People say racism no longer exists, but I know it does. If I'm out walking at night, white girls cross the street because they think I'll mug them. They don't cross the street if they see a white guy. One of the guys on my hall asked me whether I thought the Bridge Program was helpful. I didn't go through it because I had a good high school record. Does he think every black needs special help?

Common to all stereotypes is classifying experiences or people into a single category based on general knowledge or beliefs about a group. When we do this, we obscure the uniqueness of the individual person or a specific experience. Clearly, we have to generalize. We can't think about each thing in our lives as a specific instance. Stereotypes can, however, blind us to important differences among phenomena we lump together. Thus, we have an ethical responsibility to reflect on stereotypes and to stay alert to differences among things we place in any category.

Everyday Application

ASSESSING YOUR STEREOTYPES

Pick a stereotype you use, and consider 10 individuals to whom you might apply it. Identify differences among the individuals. At first this may be difficult, since stereotypes gloss over differences. What do you discover as you look for individual variations in the people you lumped together in a group?

Symbols Allow Hypothetical Thought

What do you expect to be doing 10 years from now? Who was your first date? What would you do if you won the lottery? To answer these questions, you must think hypothetically, which means to think about experiences and ideas that are not part of your concrete, present situation. Because we can think hypothetically, we can plan, dream, remember, fantasize, set goals, and weigh alternative courses of action.

Hypothetical thought is possible because we use symbols. When we symbolize, we name ideas so that we can hold them in our minds and reflect on them. We can contemplate things that currently have no real existence, and we can remember ourselves in the past and project ourselves into the future. Our ability to live simultaneously in all three dimensions of time explains why we can set goals and work toward them even though there is nothing tangible about them in the moment (Dixson & Duck, 1993). For example, you've invested many hours studying and writing papers because you imagine having a college degree. The degree is not real now, nor is the self that you will become once you have the degree. Yet the idea is sufficiently real to motivate you to work hard for many years.

Close relationships rely on ideas of history and future. One of the strongest glues for intimacy is a history of shared experiences (Bellah, Madsen, Sullivan, Swindler, & Tipton, 1985; Wood, 1995b). Just knowing that they have weathered rough times in the past helps partners get through current trials. Belief in a future also sustains intimacy. We interact differently with people we don't expect to see again than with ones who are continuing parts of our lives. Talking about the future also enhances intimacy because it suggests that more lies ahead (Acitelli, 1993; Duck, 1990).

Thinking hypothetically helps us improve who we are. In Chapter 3 we noted that improving self-concept begins with accepting yourself as in process. This requires you to remember how you were at an earlier time, to appreciate progress you've made, and to create an image of how you want to be to motivate your continued growth.

Symbols Allow Self-Reflection

Just as we use symbols to reflect on what goes on outside of us, we also use them to reflect on ourselves. Humans don't simply exist and act. Instead, we think about our existence and reflect on our actions. Self-reflection is a basis for human identity. If we weren't able to reflect on ourselves and our activities, civilized society would be impossible.

There are two aspects to the self (Mead, 1934). First, there is the I, which is the spontaneous, creative self (see Table 5.1). The I acts impulsively in response to inner needs and desires, regardless of social norms. The ME is the socially conscious part of the self that monitors and moderates the I's impulses. The ME reflects on the I from the social perspectives of others. The I is impervious to social conventions and expectations, but the ME is keenly aware of them. In an argument, your I may want to hurl

Self-reflection is a foundation of personal identity and communication. (Carolyn C. Wood)

a biting insult at a co-worker who has criticized you, but your ME censors that impulse and reminds you that it's impolite to put others down and that doing so might create future problems with that co-worker.

The ME is the reflective part of the self. The ME reflects on the I, so we simultaneously author our lives and reflect on them. This means we can think about who we want to be and set goals for becoming the self we desire. We can feel shame, pride, and regret for our actions—emotions that are possible because we self-reflect. We can control what we do in the present by casting ourselves forward in time to consider how we might later feel about our actions.

Self-reflection also empowers us to monitor ourselves by observing and judging how we're doing. When we monitor ourselves, we (the ME) notice and evaluate our (the I's) actions and may modify them based on our judgments (Phillips & Wood, 1983; Wood, 1992a). For instance, while giving a speech, you might notice that quite a few members of the audience are looking around or slouching. You think to yourself, "They seem bored. Perhaps I've been using too many statistics and straight information. Maybe I could regain their interest by mentioning some personal examples." In this case, monitoring allowed you to gauge your speaking effectiveness and make adjustments. It's necessary to notice how listeners respond to you (reflected appraisal) and to adapt your self-presentation in the process of speaking. Self-reflection allows us to monitor our communication and adjust it to enhance our effectiveness.

TABLE 5.1 Two Aspects of the Self	
I	ME
Impulsive	Reflective
Individualistic	Social
Creative	Conventional
Active	Analytical
Spontaneous	Controlled
Socially naive	Socially sophisticated
Motivated by urges	Edits urges

I–ME DIALOGUES

Monitor your I–ME dialogues as you talk with a close friend and a person with whom you work. What creative ideas and desires does your I initiate? What social controls does your ME impose? What whims occur to your I? What social norms does your ME remind you of?

How do the I and the ME work together? What would be lost if your I became silent? What would be missing if your ME disappeared?

Self-reflection also allows us to manage our image, or the identity we present to others. Because we reflect on ourselves from social perspectives, we are able to consider how we appear in others' eyes. Our ability to manage how we appear is sometimes called "facework," since it involves controlling the face we present to others. When talking with teachers, you may consciously present yourself as respectful, attentive, and a serious student. When interacting with parents, you may repress some of the language and topics that surface in discussions with your friends. When communicating with someone you'd like to date, you may choose to be more attentive and social than you are in other circumstances. In work situations, you may do facework to create an image of yourself as responsible, ambitious, and dependable. Continuously, we adjust how we present ourselves so that we sculpt our image to fit particular situations and people.

Summing up, we use symbols to define, evaluate and organize experiences, think hypothetically, and self-reflect. Each of these abilities helps us create meaning in our personal, social, and professional lives.

ENHANCING EFFECTIVENESS IN VERBAL COMMUNICATION

We've explored what symbols are and how they may be used differently in distinct communication cultures. Building on these understandings, we can now consider ways to improve the effectiveness of our verbal communication.

Engage in Dual Perspective

The single most important guideline for effective verbal communication is to engage in **dual perspective.** Dual perspective involves recognizing another person's perspective and taking that into account as you communicate. Effective interpersonal communication is not a solo performance, but a relationship between people. Awareness of others and their viewpoints should be reflected in how we speak. For instance, a person whose standard vocabulary includes profanity should modify her or his communica-

Dual perspective promotes communication that acknowledges the viewpoints of others.
(© Mark Antman/The Image Works)

tion when talking with someone who is offended by cursing. Similarly, instead of giving advice when a woman tells him about a problem, a man using dual perspective might realize that empathy and supportive listening are more appreciated by many women.

We don't need to abandon our own perspectives to recognize those of others. In fact, it would be just as unconstructive to stifle your own views as to ignore those of others. Dual perspective, as the term implies, consists of two perspectives. It requires understanding both our own and another's point of view and acknowledging each when we communicate. For example, you and your supervisor may disagree about a performance review. It's important that you understand why your supervisor assigns the ratings he or she does, even if you don't share his or her perceptions. By understanding the supervisor's perceptions and ratings, you enhance your ability to perform in ways that will be noticed and valued. Most of us can accept and grow from differences, but we don't feel affirmed if we are unheard or disregarded. Acknowledging others' viewpoints in your communication paves the way for affirming relationships.

Own Your Feelings and Thoughts

We often use verbal language in ways that obscure our responsibility for how we feel and what we think. For instance, people say "You made me mad," "You made me feel inadequate about my job performance," or "You hurt me" as if what they feel is caused by someone else. On a more subtle level, we sometimes blame others for our responses to what they say. "You're so demanding" really means that you feel put upon by what someone else wants or expects. The sense of feeling pressured by another's expectations is in you; it is not created by the other person. In reality, others seldom directly cause our feelings.

Our feelings and thoughts result from how we interpret others' communication. Although how we interpret what others say may lead us to feel certain ways, others do not directly cause our responses. Telling others that they make you feel some way is likely to arouse defensiveness, which doesn't facilitate healthy interpersonal relationships. We need to qualify this idea by noting that in unhealthy relationships, others sometimes exert a great deal of influence on how we feel and how we see ourselves. Although others can't directly cause our feelings, they can behave in ways that affect and sometimes harm us. In relationships with manipulative or dysfunctional individuals, it's necessary either to communicate in ways that don't enable the other and that do preserve your integrity, or to leave the relationship before it jeopardizes your own well-being.

TABLE 5.2 You- and I-Language

You-Language	I-Language
You hurt me.	I feel hurt when you ignore what I say.
You make me feel small.	I feel small when you tell me that I'm selfish.
My boss intimidates me.	When my boss makes demands, I feel intimidated.
You're really domineering.	When you shout, I feel dominated.
The guest speaker made me feel dumb.	I felt uninformed when the guest speaker discussed such complex information.
You humiliated me.	I felt humiliated when you mentioned my problems in front of our friends.

Effective communicators take responsibility for themselves by using language that owns their thoughts and feelings. They claim their feelings and do not blame others for what happens in themselves. To take responsibility for your own feelings, rely on I-language, rather than you-language. Table 5.2 gives examples of the difference.

There are two differences between I- and you-language. First, I-statements own responsibility, whereas you-statements project it onto another person. Second, I-statements offer considerably more description than you-statements. You-statements tend to be abstract accusations, which is one reason they're ineffective in promoting change. I-statements, on the other hand, provide concrete descriptions of behaviors and feelings without directly blaming another person for how we feel.

Some people feel awkward when they first start using I-language. This is natural, since most of us have learned to rely on you-language. With commitment and practice, however, you can learn to communicate with I-language. Once you feel comfortable using it, you will find that I-language has many advantages. It is less likely than you-language to make others defensive, so I-language opens the doors for dialogue. I-language is also more honest. We deceive ourselves when we say "You made me feel . . ." since others don't control how we feel. Finally, I-language is more empowering than you-language. When we say you did this or you made me feel that, we give control of our emotions to others. This reduces our personal sense of agency and, by extension, our motivation to change what is happening. Using I-language allows us to own our feelings while also explaining to others how we interpret their behaviors.

R O T H

I never realized how often I use you-language. I'm always saying my girlfriend makes me feel happy or my father makes me feel like a failure. What I'm beginning to see is that they really don't control my feelings. I do.

ON NOT SPEAKING FOR OTHERS

Marsha Houston (1994), a communication scholar, notes that European American women often say they understand the experiences of African American women. As an African American woman, Houston believes that "my experience of prejudice is erased when you identify it as 'the same' as yours." White women may have suffered sexism, but they have not felt the double whammy of sexism and racism.

Respect What Others Say About Their Feelings and Ideas

Has anyone ever said to you, "You shouldn't feel that way"? If so, you know how infuriating it can be to be told that your feelings aren't valid, appropriate, or acceptable. It's equally destructive to be told our thoughts are wrong. When someone says, "How can you think something so stupid?" we feel disconfirmed. Effective communicators don't disparage what others say about what they feel and think. Even if you don't feel or think the same way, you can still respect another person as the expert on her or his perspective.

One of the most disconfirming forms of communication is speaking for others when they are able to speak for themselves. Recently, I had a conversation with a couple at a party in which one person spoke for another. In response to questions that I asked the man, the woman said, "He's having trouble balancing career and family responsibilities," "He's proud of sticking with his exercise program," and "He's worried about how to take care of his parents now that their health is declining." She didn't allow her husband to speak for himself. By automatically answering questions I addressed to her husband, she left him voiceless. The same pattern occurs when parents speak for children by responding to questions the children could answer. Generally, it's arrogant and disempowering to speak for others.

Just as we should not speak for others, we also should not assume we understand how they feel or think. We referred to this as mindreading in Chapter 2, and it is relevant to this discussion as well. As we have seen, our distinct experiences and ways of interpreting life make each of us unique. We seldom, if ever, completely grasp what another person feels or thinks. Although it is supportive to engage in dual perspective, it isn't supportive to presume we fully understand someone else's feelings or thoughts, especially when he or she differs from us in important ways.

It's particularly important not to assume we understand people from other cultures, including ones within our society. Recently, an Asian woman in one of my classes commented on discrimination she faces, and a Caucasian man in the class said, "I know what you mean. Prejudice

Politicians often communicate using abstract language to avoid alienating voters by taking specific stands on controversial issues. (© Comstock)

really hurts." Although he meant to be supportive, his response angered the woman who retorted, "You have no idea how I feel, and you have no right to act like you do until you've been female and nonwhite." When we claim to understand what we haven't experienced, others may feel we're taking away from their lives and identities.

Respecting what others say about what they feel and think is a cornerstone of effective communication. We also grow when we open ourselves to perspectives, feelings, and thoughts that differ from our own. If you don't understand what others say, ask them to elaborate. This shows you are interested and respect their expertise or experience.

Strive for Accuracy and Clarity

Because symbols are arbitrary, abstract, and ambiguous, the potential for misunderstanding always exists. In addition, individual and cultural differences foster varying interpretations of words. Although we cannot eliminate misunderstandings, we can minimize their likelihood.

Be Aware of Levels of Abstraction   Misunderstanding is less likely when we are conscious of levels of abstraction. Much confusion results from language that is excessively abstract. For instance, assume a professor says "Your papers should demonstrate a sophisticated conceptual grasp of material and its pragmatic implications." Would you know how to write a paper to satisfy the professor? You probably would not, because the language is very abstract and unclear. Here's a more concrete description: "Your papers should include definitions of the concepts and specific examples that show how they apply in real life." With this less abstract statement, you would have a better idea of what the professor expected.

Abstract language is not always inadvisable. As we have seen, abstract language allows us to generalize, which is necessary and useful. The goal is to use a level of abstraction that suits particular communication objectives and situations. Abstract words are appropriate when speakers and listeners have similar concrete knowledge about what is being discussed. For example, a couple that has been dating might talk about "feel good movies" and "heavy movies" as shorthand ways to refer to two film genres. Because they have seen many movies together, they have shared referents for the abstract terms *feel good* and *heavy*, so confusion is unlikely. Similarly, long-term friends can say "Let's just hang out," and they will each understand the kinds of concrete activities implied by the abstract term *hang out*.

More concrete language is useful when communicators don't have shared experiences and interpretations. For example, early in a friendship the suggestion to "hang out" would be more effective if it included specifics: "Let's hang out today—maybe watch the game and go out for pizza." In a new dating relationship, it would be clearer to say, "Let's get a *feel good* movie like *Four Weddings and a Funeral*. I don't want to see anything *heavy* like *The Piano* or *Schindler's List*." Providing examples of general terms clarifies meanings.

Abstract language is particularly likely to lead to misunderstandings when people talk about changes they want in one another. Concrete language and specific examples help individuals have similar understandings of which behaviors are unwelcome and which ones are wanted. For example, "I want you to be more responsible about your job" does not explain what would count as being more responsible. Is it arriving on time, taking on extra assignments, or something else? It isn't clear what the speaker wants unless more concrete descriptions are supplied. Likewise, "I want to be closer" could mean the speaker wants to spend more time together, talk about the relationship, do things together, have a more adventurous sex life, or any number of other things. Vague abstractions promote misunderstanding if individuals don't share concrete referents.

Qualify Language   Another strategy for increasing the clarity of communication is to qualify language. Two types of language require qualification. First, we should qualify generalizations so that we don't mislead ourselves or others into mistaking a general statement for an absolute one. "Politicians are crooked" is a false statement because it overgeneralizes. A more accurate statement would be "A number of politicians have been shown to be dishonest." Qualifying reminds us of limitations on what we say.

We should also qualify language when describing and evaluating people. The term **static evaluation** refers to assessments that suggest something is unchanging or frozen in time. These are particularly troublesome when applied to people. Ann is selfish. Don is irresponsible. Bob is generous. Vy is dependent. Whenever we use the word *is*, we suggest something is inherent and fixed. In reality, we aren't static, but continuously changing. A person who is selfish at one time may not be at another. An individual who is irresponsible on one occasion may be responsible in other situations. **Indexing** is a technique developed by early communication scholars that allows us to note that our statements reflect only specific times and circumstances (Korzybski, 1948). To index, we would say Ann$_{\text{June 6, 1997}}$ acted selfishly, Don$_{\text{on the task committee}}$ was irresponsible, Bob$_{\text{in college}}$ was generous, and Vy$_{\text{in her relationships with men in high school}}$ was dependent. See how indexing ties description to a specific time and circumstance? Mental indexing reminds us that we and others are able to change in remarkable ways.

ROY

I had a couple of accidents right after I got my driver's license. Most teenagers do, right? But to hear my father, you'd think I am a bad driver today. Those accidents were 5 years ago, and I haven't even had a ticket since then. But he still talks about "reckless Roy."

We've considered four principles for improving the effectiveness of verbal communication. Engaging in dual perspective is the first principle and a foundation for all others. A second guideline is to take responsibility for our own feelings and thoughts by using I-language. Third, we should respect others as the experts on what they feel and think and not presume we know what they mean or share their experiences. The fourth principle is to strive for clarity by choosing appropriate degrees of abstraction, qualifying generalizations, and indexing evaluations, particularly ones applied to people.

SUMMARY

In this chapter, we've discussed the world of words and meaning, which make up the uniquely human universe that we inhabit because we are symbol users. Because symbols are arbitrary, ambiguous, and abstract, they have no inherent meanings. Instead, we actively construct meaning by interpreting symbols based on perspectives gleaned through interaction with others and our personal experiences. We also punctuate to create meaning in communication.

Instead of existing only in the physical world of the here and now, we use symbols to define, evaluate, and organize our experiences. In addition, we use symbols to think hypothetically so that we can consider alternatives and simultaneously inhabit all three dimensions of time. Finally, symbols allow us to self-reflect so that we can monitor our own behaviors. Communication is most effective and satisfying when individuals share meanings for symbols.

We can improve the likelihood of sharing meanings by being sensitive to levels of abstraction and the many opportunities for misunderstanding that are possible because symbols are arbitrary, ambiguous, and abstract. The final section of this chapter discussed principles for improving effectiveness in verbal communication. Because words can mean different things to various people, misunderstandings may occur. To minimize

the likelihood of misunderstandings, we should engage in dual perspective, own our thoughts and feelings, respect what others say about how they think and feel, and monitor abstractness, generalizations, and static evaluations.

In the next chapter, we continue our discussion of the world of human communication by exploring the fascinating realm of nonverbal behavior.

FOR FURTHER REFLECTION AND DISCUSSION

1. To appreciate the importance of symbolic capacities, try to imagine the following: living only in the present without memories or hopes and plans; thinking only in terms of literal reality, not what might be; having no broad classifications to organize experience. With others in the class, discuss how your life would be different without the symbolic abilities discussed in this chapter.

2. In this chapter, we learned that language names experiences and is continuously evolving. For instance, terms such as *date rape* and *disrespect* (as a verb) are recent additions to our language. Can you think of experiences, feelings, or other phenomena for which

we don't currently have names? What might we call a lesbian or gay couple with children—are both parents mommies in lesbian couples and daddies in gay ones? What is a good term for describing someone with whom you have a serious romance? *Boyfriend* and *girlfriend* no longer work for many people. Do you prefer one of these options: significant other, romantic partner, special friend, lover?

3. Pay attention to I- and you-language in your communication and that of others. What happens when you switch a you-statement to an I-statement? Does it change how you feel or what happens in interaction?

KEY TERMS

arbitrary	punctuation
ambiguous	totalizing
abstract	loaded language
communication rules	dual perspective
regulative rules	static evaluation
constitutive rules	indexing

Focus Questions

1 How does nonverbal communication announce identity?

2 Is nonverbal communication learned or instinctual?

3 Can we learn to read others' nonverbal behaviors?

4 How does nonverbal communication convey power between people?

CHAPTER 6

The Nonverbal Dimension of Communication

Ben Thompson had traveled to Japan to negotiate a joint business venture with Haru Watanabe. They seemed to see the mutual benefit of combining their resources, yet Thompson felt something was wrong in their negotiations. Every time they talked, Watanabe seemed uneasy and refused to hold eye contact. Thompson wondered if Watanabe was trying to hide something. Meanwhile, Watanabe wondered why Thompson was so rude if he wanted them to work together.

Maria noticed a nice-looking guy who was studying two tables away from hers in the library. When he looked up at her, she lowered her eyes. After a moment, she looked back at him just for a second. A few minutes later he came over, sat down beside her, and introduced himself.

Luanne Fitzgerald gave a final glance to be sure the dining room table was just right for dinner: The placemats and blue linen napkins were out; the silver and the crystal glasses sparkled; the bowl

(Robert Birmelin, *Hands (Interlocked)*
(1987). Acrylic on canvas, 48 × 78".
Courtesy Claude Bernard Gallery, N.Y.)

of flowers in the middle of the table added color; and the serving dishes were warmed and ready to be filled with roast, buttered new potatoes, and rice pilaf. Luanne whisked balsamic vinegar and olive oil together, added a trace of basil, and sprinkled it on the spinach salad just before calling the family to dinner.

Across town, Benita Bradsher was also preparing dinner for her family. She put a big spoon in the pot of mashed potatoes and transferred it from the stove to the kitchen table. Next, she piled paper napkins, knives, spoons, and forks in the middle of the table for her husband and kids. She took the ground beef casserole from the oven, put it on a potholder on the table, and called her family to dinner.

These three examples illustrate the power of nonverbal communication. In the first case, Thompson and Watanabe have difficulty because of different nonverbal norms in Japan and the United States. Ben Thompson has learned that eye contact is a sign of honesty and respect, so he looks directly at Haru Watanabe when they talk. In Watanabe's culture, however, direct eye contact is considered rude and intrusive, so he doesn't meet Thompson's gaze and feels uncomfortable when Thompson looks directly at him.

In the library scene, we see a clear example of gendered patterns of nonverbal communication. Maria follows feminine communication norms by indirectly signaling her interest and by waiting for the man to initiate contact. In turn, he enacts the rules of masculine communication culture by gazing directly at her and moving to her table.

In the final example, nonverbal communication reflects differences in socioeconomic class. Whereas Luanne Fitzgerald sets her table with cloth napkins, placemats, silver, crystal, and a vase of flowers, Benita Bradsher sets her table with pans off the stove and a pile of utensils and paper napkins that people can take. Notice also the different foods the two women serve: roast, new potatoes, rice pilaf, and spinach salad for the Fitzgerald family and mashed potatoes and casserole for the Bradsher family. What each woman serves and how she sets her table reflect the teachings of the social group to which she belongs.

Gender, ethnicity, sexual orientation, and socioeconomic class are not passive aspects of who we are. They are identities that we perform day in and day out in our lives. Recognizing this, Candice West and Don Zimmerman (1987) note that we "do gender" all the time by behaving in ways that announce we are feminine or masculine. We also perform, or "do," race, class, and sexual orientation by nonverbally communicating those facets of identity. In this sense, nonverbal communication, like language, is a primary way that we announce who we are. The intricate system of nonverbal communication helps us establish identity, negotiate relationships, and create environments we enjoy.

Nonverbal behavior is a major dimension of human communication. The nonverbal system accounts for 65% to 93% of the total meaning of communication (Birdwhistell, 1970; Mehrabian, 1981). This suggests that nonverbal behaviors often have more impact than verbal ones on how we communicate and perceive others' communication. The nonverbal system also includes a great range of communication, from dress and eye contact to body posture and vocal inflection.

In this chapter, we explore the fascinating realm of nonverbal interaction. We will identify principles of nonverbal communication and then discuss types of nonverbal behavior and guidelines for nonverbal effectiveness.

PRINCIPLES OF NONVERBAL COMMUNICATION

Nonverbal communication is all aspects of communication other than words themselves. It is more than gestures and body language. In addition, nonverbal communication includes *how* we utter words (inflection, volume), features of environments that affect meaning (temperature, lighting), and objects that affect personal images and interaction patterns (dress, jewelry, furniture). Like verbal communication, nonverbal behavior is ambiguous, abstract, and arbitrary. Thus, we can't be sure what a smile or gesture means, and we can't guarantee that others understand the meanings we intend to express with our actions.

Different cultures prescribe different styles of dress.
(© Christina Dameyer/Photo 20-20)

Also like verbal communication, our nonverbal behavior and our interpretations of others' nonverbal behaviors are governed by cultural rules. For this reason, our actions tend to reflect and reproduce understandings and values of the particular cultures to which we belong. For instance, dress considered appropriate for women varies across cultures, with some women in the United States wearing miniskirts and women in other countries wearing veils. Dress also reflects organizational identities: Bankers, attorneys, and many other professionals are expected to wear business suits or dresses, whereas companies such as Apple encourage employees to wear jeans and other informal attire. Each way of dressing reflects a particular organizational ethos.

Four principles of nonverbal behavior provide insight into how it affects meaning in interpersonal interaction.

Nonverbal Behavior Can Supplement or Replace Verbal Communication

Communication researchers have identified five ways in which nonverbal behaviors interact with verbal communication (Malandro & Barker, 1983). First, nonverbal behaviors may repeat verbal messages. For example, you might say "yes" while nodding your head. In making a public presentation, a speaker might hold up one, two, and three fingers to signal to listeners that she or he is moving from the first to the second to the third points of a speech. Second, nonverbal behaviors may highlight verbal communication, as when you use inflection to emphasize certain words—"This is the *most serious* consequence of the policy I'm arguing against." Third, we use nonverbal behaviors to complement or add to words. When you see a friend, you might say "I'm glad to see you" and underline the verbal message with a smile. Speakers often emphasize verbal statements with forceful gestures and increases in volume and inflection. Fourth, nonverbal behaviors may contradict verbal messages, as when a group member says "Nothing's wrong" in a hostile tone of voice. Finally, we sometimes substitute nonverbal behaviors for verbal ones. For instance, you might roll your eyes to indicate you disapprove of something. In all of these ways, nonverbal behaviors augment or replace verbal communication.

CULTURAL RULES OF GIFT GIVING

Giving gifts can be confusing and even offensive when the giver and the recipient are from different cultures. An American might offend a Chinese person with the gift of a clock, since clocks symbolize death in China. Giving a gift to an Arab person on first meeting would be interpreted as a bribe. Bringing flowers to a dinner hosted by a person from Kenya would puzzle the host, since in Kenya flowers are given only to express sympathy over a loss. And in Switzerland giving red roses is interpreted as indicating romantic interest. Also, the Swiss consider even numbers of flowers bad luck, so giving a dozen is inappropriate.

Sources: Axtell, R. (1990a). *Dos and taboos around the world* (2nd ed.). New York: Wiley; Axtell, R. (1990b). *Dos and taboos of hosting international visitors.* New York: Wiley.

Nonverbal Communication Can Regulate Interaction

You generally know when someone else is through speaking, when a professor welcomes discussion from students, and when someone expects you specifically to speak. Seldom do explicit, verbal cues tell us when to speak and keep silent. When talking, friends typically don't say "It's your turn to talk," work associates don't point to one another to switch speaking roles in a conference, and professors don't hold up signs saying "I am through now." Instead, conversations are usually regulated nonverbally (Malandro & Barker, 1983). For example, we use our eyes and body posture to indicate we wish to enter conversations, and speakers step back from a podium to indicate they are through with a speech. Although we're usually unaware of how nonverbal actions regulate interaction, we rely on them to know when to speak and when to remain silent.

DARCY

I know one guy who dominates every conversation. I'd never noticed this until we studied how nonverbal behaviors regulate turn taking. This guy won't look at others when he's talking. He looks out into space or sometimes he gives you a hard stare, but he doesn't ever look at anyone like he's saying, "Okay, your turn now."

From informal conversations to business meetings, we use nonverbal behaviors to regulate interaction. To signal that we don't want to be interrupted, we avert our eyes or increase our speaking volume and rate. When we're through talking, we look back to others to signal "Okay, now someone else can speak." We invite specific individuals to speak by looking directly at them, often after asking a question (Wiemann & Harrison, 1983).

Nonverbal Communication Can Establish Relational Level Meanings

You'll recall that there are two levels of meaning in communication. To review, the content level of meaning concerns actual information or literal meaning. The relational level of meaning defines individuals' identities and relationships between people. Nonverbal communication is often more powerful than verbal language in conveying relational level meanings (Keeley & Hart, 1994). In fact, some communication scholars refer to nonverbal communication as the "relationship language," because it so often expresses the overall feeling about relationships (Burgoon, Buller, Hale, & deTurck, 1984; Sallinen-Kuparinen, 1992).

Nonverbal communication is used to convey three dimensions of relationship level meanings: responsiveness, liking, and power (Mehrabian, 1981). Yet how we convey relationship meanings and what specific nonverbal behaviors mean to us and others depends on the communication rules we've learned in our particular cultures.

Posture often communicates how people feel toward one another. (© Ariel Skelley/The Stock Market)

Responsiveness One facet of relational level meaning is responsiveness. We use eye contact, facial expressions, and body posture to indicate interest in others as Maria did in one of the examples that opened this chapter. We signal interest by holding eye contact and assuming an attentive posture. As the example with Haru Watanabe and Ben Thompson reveals, however, eye contact doesn't mean the same thing in all cultures. To express disinterest, Westerners tend to avoid or decrease visual contact and adopt a passive body position or turn away from another person. Also, harmony between people's postures and facial expressions may reflect how comfortable they are with each other (Berg, 1987; Capella, 1991). We sense others are involved with us if they look at us, nod, and lean forward rather than gazing around the room. This nonverbal pattern is evident in group and team contexts. In a cohesive group, there is typically a great deal of nonverbal communication indicating responsiveness, inclusion, and involvement. Less cohesive groups include fewer nonverbal indicators of solidarity.

MARYAM

Americans do more than one thing at a time. In Nepal, when we talk with someone, we are with that person. We do not also write on paper or have the television on. We talk with the person. It is hard for me to accept the custom of giving only some attention to each other in conversation.

As Maryam's observation indicates, different communication cultures teach members distinct rules for showing responsiveness. In the West, feminine culture emphasizes sensitivity to others, so women generally display greater emotional responsiveness and interest in relationships than do men (Montgomery, 1988). In addition to communicating their own feelings nonverbally, women are generally more skilled than men in interpreting others' emotions (Hall, 1978; Noller, 1986, 1987). In general, African Americans are more skilled than European Americans in reading emotions. Prisoners also develop astute abilities to decode subtle nonverbal behaviors (Wood, 1994e). Decoding may be a survival strategy for those who have historically had subordinate standpoints (for example, women and minorities). The well-being and sometimes physical safety of those with low power depend on being able to decipher the feelings and intentions of those with greater power.

ELLEN

Secretaries are the best decoders. They can read their bosses' moods in a heartbeat. I am a secretary, part-time now that I'm taking courses, and I can tell exactly what my boss is thinking. Sometimes I know what he feels or will do before he does. I have to know when he can be interrupted, when he feels generous, and when not to cross his path.

Liking A second dimension of relational meaning is liking. Nonverbal behaviors are keen indicators of whether we feel positive or negative about others. Smiles and friendly touching usually indicate positive feelings, while frowns and belligerent postures express antagonism (Keeley & Hart, 1994). Have you ever noticed how continuously political candidates shake hands, slap backs, and otherwise touch people whose votes they want? In addition to these general rules shared in Western society, more specific rules are instilled by particular communication cultures. Masculine cultures tend to emphasize emotional control and independence, so men are less likely than women to use nonverbal behaviors that reveal how they feel. Reflecting the values of feminine culture, women generally sit closer to others and engage in more eye contact than men (Montgomery, 1988; Reis, Senchak, & Solomon, 1985). Women are also more likely than men to initiate hand-holding and affectionate touches. Happy couples sit closer together and engage in more eye contact than unhappy couples (Miller & Parks, 1982; Noller, 1986, 1987). Similarly, in work settings, individuals who like one another often sit together, exchange eye contact, and smile at one another.

Power A third aspect of relational level meanings is power. We use nonverbal behaviors to assert dominance and to negotiate status and influence (Henley, 1977). In general, men assume more space and use greater volume and more forceful gestures to assert their ideas (Hall, 1987; Major, Schmidlin, & Williams, 1990). Men are also more likely than women to move into others' space, as the man in the library moved to Maria's table in the example at the beginning of this chapter. In addition, men tend to use gestures and touch to exert control (Henley, 1977; Leathers, 1986). Powerful people such as bosses touch those with less power such as secretaries more than vice versa (Spain, 1992).

RAMONA

In my home, my father sits at the head of the table, and he has his chair in the family room, and his workroom. My mother does not have her chair anywhere in the house, and she has no room of her own either. This accurately reflects the power dynamics between them.

As Ramona observes, space also expresses power relations. The amount of space a person has often directly reflects her or his power. The connection between power and space is evident in the fact that CEOs usually have large, spacious offices, while entry- and mid-level professionals have smaller offices, and secretaries frequently have minuscule workstations, even though secretaries often store and manage more material than those higher in the organizational chain of command. Regulative communication rules also tacitly specify that individuals with status or power have the right to enter the space of people with less power, but the converse is not true. Space also reflects power differences among family members. Adults usually have more space than children, and men, like Ramona's father, more often than women have their own rooms and sit at heads of tables.

Control can also be exerted through silence, a powerful form of nonverbal communication. We sometimes use silence to stifle others' conversation. Silence accompanied by a glare is doubly powerful in conveying disapproval. Research indicates that people sometimes respond with silence to discourage others from speaking and to allow them to talk about topics they prefer (DeFrancisco, 1991). In extreme form, power is nonverbally enacted through physical violence and abuse, activities that men are more likely than women to commit (Wood, 1994d).

Responsiveness, liking, and power are dimensions of relational level meanings that are communicated primarily through nonverbal behaviors.

Nonverbal Communication Reflects Cultural Values

Like verbal communication, nonverbal patterns reflect communication rules of specific cultures. This implies that most nonverbal actions aren't instinctual, but are learned in the process of socialization. We've already noted a number of differences between nonverbal behaviors encouraged in Western feminine and masculine communication cultures. Nonverbal behaviors vary among cultures within our country and also among geographically distinct societies.

Have you ever seen the bumper sticker that says "If you can read this, you're too close"? That slogan proclaims North Americans' fierce territoriality. We value our private spaces, and we resent, and sometimes fight, anyone who trespasses on what we consider our turf. We want to have private homes, and many people want large lots to protect their privacy. On the job, having a private office with a door is valued and marks status: Employees with lower status often share offices or have workstations without doors. In cultures where individuality is a less pronounced value, people are less territorial. For instance, Brazilians routinely stand close in shops, buses, and elevators, and when they bump into each other they don't apologize or draw back.

SUCHENG

In United States, each person has so much room. Every individual has a separate room in which to sleep and sometimes another separate room in which to work. Also, I see that each family here lives in a separate house. People have much less space in China. Families live together with sons bringing their families into their parents' home and all sharing the same space. At first when I came here it felt strange to have so much space, but now I sometimes feel very crowded when I go home.

Norms for touching also reflect cultural values. In one study, Americans, who are relatively reserved, were observed engaging in an average of only two touches an hour. The emotionally restrained British averaged zero touches per hour. Parisians, long known for emotional expressiveness, touched 110 times per hour. Puerto Ricans touched most, averaging 180 touches an hour (Knapp, 1972, p. 109).

Patterns of eye contact also reflect cultural values. In the United States, frankness and assertion are valued, so meeting another's eyes is considered appropriate and a demonstration of personal honesty. Yet in many Asian and northern European countries, direct eye contact is considered abrasive and disrespectful (Hall, 1969). In Brazil, eye contact is often so intense that people from the United States consider it rude staring. As the example with Mr. Watanabe and Mr. Thompson suggests, this cultural difference can cause misunderstandings in intercultural business negotiations.

Four principles provide a foundation for understanding nonverbal communication. First, nonverbal behavior can supplement or replace verbal communication. Second, nonverbal behaviors regulate interaction. Third, nonverbal communication is often especially powerful in establishing and expressing relational meanings. Finally, nonverbal behaviors reflect cultural values and are learned rather than instinctive. We're now ready to explore the many types of behavior in the intricate nonverbal communication system.

TYPES OF NONVERBAL COMMUNICATION

Because so much of our interaction is nonverbal, this system includes many kinds of communication. In this section, we will consider nine forms of nonverbal behavior, noticing how we use each to establish relationships, convey relational messages, and express personal identity and cultural values.

Look at the man at the left. What do his facial expression and body posture tell you about how he relates to the homeless man at the right? (© Serge Attal/Sygma)

Face and Body Motion

Kinesics is a technical term that refers to body position and body motions, including those of the face. Our bodies communicate a great deal about how we see ourselves. A speaker who stands erectly and appears confident announces self-assurance, whereas someone who slouches and shuffles may seem to say, "I'm not very sure of myself." We also communicate moods with body posture and motion. For example, someone who is walking quickly with a resolute facial expression appears more determined than someone who saunters along with an unfocused gaze. We sit rigidly when we are nervous and adopt a relaxed posture when we feel at ease. Audiences and members of groups indicate attentiveness and interest by body posture.

Body postures and gestures may signal whether we are open to interaction. Someone who sits with arms crossed and looks downward seems to say, "Don't bother me." That's also a nonverbal strategy students sometimes use to dissuade teachers from calling on them in classes. To signal that we'd like to interact, we look at others and sometimes smile. We also use gestures to express how we feel about others. We use a hand gesture to say okay and a different one to communicate contempt. In the 1968 Olympics held in Mexico City a group of African American athletes raised clenched hands to symbolize black power—a politically radical gesture in that country. The athletes were punished for their communication by having their medals taken away.

Our faces are intricate communication messengers. The face alone is capable of over 1,000 distinct expressions that result from variations in tilt of head and movements of eyebrows, eyes, and mouth (Eckman, Friesen, & Ellsworth, 1971). Our eyes can shoot daggers of anger, issue challenges, express skepticism, or radiate feelings of love. With our faces we can indicate disapproval (scowls), doubt (raised eyebrows), admiration (warm eye gazes), and resistance (stares). The face is particularly powerful in conveying responsiveness and liking (Keeley & Hart, 1994; Patterson, 1992). Speakers often use facial expressions to suggest they are open and confident.

How we position ourselves relative to others may express our feelings toward them. On work teams, friends and allies often sit together and competitors typically maintain distance. Couples communicate dissatisfaction by increasing distance and by decreasing smiles and eye gazes (Miller & Parks, 1982). We also use nonverbal behaviors, such as smiles and warm gazes, to signal we like others and are happy with them (Walker & Trimboli, 1989).

CLEVER HANS

In the 1900s, Herr von Osten trained his horse Hans to count by tapping his front hoof. Hans learned quickly and was soon able to multiply, add, divide, subtract, and perform complex mathematical calculations. He could even count the number of people in a room or the number of people wearing eyeglasses. Herr von Osten took Hans on a promotional tour. At shows he would ask Hans to add 5 and 8, divide 100 by 10, and do other computations. In every case Hans performed flawlessly, leading others to call him "Clever Hans." Because some doubters thought Clever Hans's feats involved deceit, proof of his mathematical abilities was demanded.

The first test involved computing numbers that were stated on stage by people other than von Osten. Using his hoof, Hans pounded out the correct answers. However, he didn't fare so well on the second test in which one person whispered a number into Hans's left ear and a different person whis-pered a number into his right ear. Hans was told to add the two numbers and pound out the sum, an answer not known by anyone present. Hans couldn't solve the problem. On further investigation, it was deduced that Hans could solve problems only if someone he could see knew the answer. When Hans was given numbers and asked to compute them, viewers leaned forward and tensed their bodies as Hans began tapping his hoof. When Hans tapped the correct number, onlookers relaxed their body postures and nodded their heads, which was Hans's signal to stop tapping. Hans was clever, not because he could calculate, but because he could read nonverbal communication.

Source: Sebeok, T. A., & Rosenthal, R. (Eds). (1981). *The Clever Hans phenomenon: Communication with horses, whales, apes and people.* New York: New York Academy of Sciences.

For good reason, poets call the eyes "the mirrors of the soul." Our eyes communicate some of the most important and complex messages about how we feel. If you watch infants, you'll notice that they focus on others' eyes. Babies become terrified if they can't see their mothers' eyes, but they aren't bothered when other parts of their mothers' faces are hidden (Spitz, 1965). As adults, we often look at eyes to judge emotions, honesty, interest, and self-confidence. This explains why strong eye contact tends to heighten the credibility of public speakers.

Haptics

Haptics, or touch, refers to nonverbal communication involving physical touch. Touch is the first of our five senses to develop (Leathers, 1976), and many communication scholars believe touching and being touched are essential to a healthy life. Research reveals that mothers in dysfunctional families touch babies less often and less affectionately than mothers in healthy families. In disturbed families, parents sometimes push children away and handle them harshly, nonverbally signaling rejection (Birdwhistell, 1970).

Everyday Application

COMMUNICATING CLOSENESS

What do your nonverbal behaviors say about how you feel toward others? To find out, observe yourself with someone you really like and feel comfortable with, a stranger, and someone you don't trust or like. How close do you sit or stand to each of the three people? How does your posture differ? What facial expressions and eye contact do you use with each person?

Touching also communicates power and status. People with high status touch others and invade others' spaces more than people with less status (Henley, 1977). Cultural views of women as more touchable than men are reflected in gendered patterns of touch. Parents touch sons less often and more roughly than they touch daughters (Condry, Condry, & Pogatshnik,

1983). These patterns early in life teach the sexes different rules for using touch and interpreting the touches of others. As adults, women tend to engage in touch to show liking and intimacy (Montgomery, 1988), while men more typically rely on touch to assert power and control (Henley, 1977; Leathers, 1986). Feminine socialization to be deferential and nice to others explains why some women don't voice objections to unwanted touching. These gendered patterns contribute to sexual harassment where women are often targets of unwelcome touch (Le Poire, Burgoon, & Parrott, 1992).

CELIA

The manager at the restaurant where I work is always touching me. He doesn't do anything that's really intimate or wrong, but his hand brushes mine or he touches my back and lets his hand linger. I don't like it, but I'm afraid to cause a scene or make him feel bad.

Physical Appearance

Western culture places an extremely high value on **physical appearance.** For this reason, most of us notice how others look, and we form initial evaluations based on their appearance, over which they have limited control. We first notice obvious physical qualities such as sex, skin color, and features. After interpreting these, we then form judgments of how attractive others are and make inferences about their personalities. In one study, researchers found that people associate plump, rounded bodies with laziness and weakness. Thin, angular physiques were thought to reflect youthful, hard-driven, nervous, stubborn personalities, and athletic body types were seen as indicating strong, adventurous, self-reliant personalities (Wells & Siegel, 1961). Although these associations may have no factual basis, they can affect decisions about hiring, placement, and promotion.

Cultures stipulate ideals for physical form. Currently in the West, the cultural ideals emphasize thinness and softness in women and muscularity and height in men (Wolf, 1991). This general cultural standard is qualified by ethnic identity. In traditional African societies, full-figured bodies are perceived as symbolizing health, prosperity, and wealth, which are all desirable (Villarosa, 1994). African Americans who embrace this value accept or prefer women who weigh more than the current ideal for European American women (Root, 1990; Thomas, 1989).

CASS

I found out how much appearance matters when I was in an auto accident. It messed up my face so that I had scars all over one side and my forehead. All of a sudden nobody was asking me out. All these guys who had been so crazy about me before the accident lost interest. Some of my girlfriends seemed uneasy about being seen with me. When I first had the wreck, I was so glad to be alive that I didn't even think about plastic surgery. After a couple of months of seeing how others treated me, however, I had the surgery.

Communication Highlight

A FIGURE THAT DOESN'T ADD UP

Barbie, the dream girl doll who made her first appearance in 1959, has a figure that isn't humanly possible. Barbie's measurements would be 40"–18"–32" in life-size terms. That's a bizarre ideal for women.

Source: Quindlen, A. (1994, September 13). The image of a modern girl. *Raleigh News & Observer,* p. A9.

Class membership further modifies ethnic values concerning weight. In 1994, *Essence* magazine reported that African American women who are either affluent or poor are likely to have strong black identities that allow them to resist Caucasian preoccupations with thinness. On the other hand, middle-class African American women who are upwardly mobile are more inclined to deemphasize their ethnic identities to get ahead, and they are more susceptible to obsessions with weight and eating disorders (Villarosa, 1994).

Artifacts

Artifacts are personal objects we use to announce our identities and personalize our environments. We craft our image by how we dress and what objects we carry and use. Nurses and doctors wear white and frequently drape stethoscopes around their necks; professors travel with briefcases, while students more often tote backpacks. White-collar professionals tend to wear tailored outfits and dress shoes, whereas blue-collar workers often dress in jeans or uniforms and boots. The military requires uniforms that define individuals as members of the group. In addition, stripes, medals, and insignia signify rank and accomplishments.

We also use artifacts to define settings and personal territories. When the president speaks, the setting is usually replete with symbols of national identity and pride such as the flag. At annual meetings of companies, the chair usually speaks from a podium that bears the company logo. In much the same manner, we claim our private spaces by filling them with objects that matter to us and that reflect our experiences and values. Lovers of art adorn their homes with paintings and sculptures that announce their interests and personalize their private space. Religious families often express their commitments by displaying pictures of holy scenes and the Bible, the Koran or another sacred text. Our artifacts also symbolize important relationships and experiences in our lives. For example, pictures of family members decorate many offices. On my writing desk, I have a photograph of my sister Carolyn; an item that belonged to my father; the first card my

partner, Robbie, ever gave me; and a jar of rocks from a beach where I retreat whenever possible. These artifacts personalize my desk with reminders of people and experiences I cherish.

JAGAT MAN LAMA

To make my home here I had to put out my statue of Buddha and make the small shrine that each of us keeps in our home in my country. Seeing it is important for me to feel comfortable. I really felt at home when the smell of incense became part of the apartment where I now live. I smell it faintly when I open the door each day, and that makes me feel at home.

In her book *Composing a Life,* Mary Catherine Bateson (1990) comments that we turn houses into homes by filling them with objects that matter to us. We make impersonal spaces familiar and comfortable with our artifacts. We use mugs given to us by special people, nurture plants to enliven indoor spaces, surround ourselves with books and magazines that announce our interests, and sprinkle our world with material reflections of what we care about.

Artifacts communicate important relational meanings. We use them to perform our identities and to express how we perceive and feel about others. Although clothing has been more unisex in recent years, once you venture beyond the campus context, gendered styles are evident. To perform gender, we dress to meet cultural expectations of men and women. Thus, women sometimes wear makeup, dresses that may have lace or other softening touches, skirts, high heel shoes, jewelry, and hose. Typically, men wear less jewelry, and their clothes and shoes are functional. Flat shoes allow a person to walk comfortably or run if necessary; high heels don't. Men's clothing is looser and less binding, and it includes pockets for wallets, change, keys, and so forth. In contrast, women's clothing tends to be more tailored and often doesn't include pockets, so women have to carry a purse to hold personal items.

We also use artifacts to perform racial identity. In recent years, marketers have offered more ethnic clothing and jewelry, so people of color can more easily acquire artifacts that express their distinctive cultural heritages. In addition, African Americans often dress more stylishly and dramatically than European Americans and may even engage in "styling," which is dressing to appear as if you are well off, especially if you aren't (Ribeau, Baldwin, & Hecht, 1994).

SHELBY

Whites don't understand styling. They think we are trying to put on airs or something, because that's what they'd be doing if they dressed like we sometimes do. But for me, styling is a way to show I personally have style, have flair, if you know what I mean. It's a way to say I'm somebody, which is important when you're black in a white society. If you don't say you're somebody, nobody else is going to say it for you.

Others also use artifacts to communicate how they see us. Many hospitals still swaddle newborns in blue and pink blankets to designate sex. Even though many parents today try to be nonsexist, they may still send gender messages through the toys they give children. In general, parents and especially fathers give sons toys that encourage rough play (trains) and competitiveness (baseball gloves, toy weapons), whereas they give daughters toys that cultivate nurturing (dolls, play stoves) and attention to appearance (makeup kits, frilly clothes) (Caldera, Huston, & O'Brien, 1989; Lytton & Romney, 1991). We give gifts to say "You matter to me." Some objects are invested with cultural meanings as well: Engagement rings and wedding bands signify commitment. We also symbolize that we're connected to others by wearing their clothes, as when women wear male partners' shirts.

Everyday Application

ARTIFACTUAL GENDER MESSAGES

What do your artifacts say about you? Are your clothes casual or formal? Are they traditional, the latest fad, or something uniquely your style? If you wear jewelry, what does it "say" about you? Does it suggest you are playful (novelty jewelry), rich (real gold and precious stones), or ethnically identified? What do the objects in your room convey about your values, interests, and the important people in your life?

ENVIRONMENTAL RACISM

The term *environmental racism* arose to describe a pattern whereby toxic waste dumps and hazardous [industrial] plants are located in low-income neighborhoods and communities of color. It's no coincidence that industries expose our most vulnerable communities to pollutants and carcinogens that are seldom imposed on middle- and upper-class people. The pattern is very clear: The space of minorities and poor people can be invaded and contaminated, but the territory of more affluent citizens cannot be.

Source: Robert Cox, President of the National Sierra Club, 1994–1996, personal communication.

Proxemics and Personal Space

Proxemics refers to space and how we use it (Hall, 1968). Every culture has norms for using space and for how close people should be to one another. In the United States, we interact with social acquaintances from a distance of 4 to 12 feet, but are comfortable with 18 inches or less between us and close friends and romantic partners (Hall, 1966). Confirming that space reflects intimacy, research shows that marital partners who are dissatisfied typically maintain greater distance than do happy partners (Miller & Parks, 1982). When we are angry with someone, we tend to move away from him or her and to resent it if he or she approaches us.

Space also announces status, with greater space being assumed by those with higher status (Henley, 1977). Substantial research shows that women and minorities generally have less space than Caucasian men in our society (Spain, 1992). The prerogative to invade someone else's personal space is also linked to power, with those having greater power being most likely to trespass into others' territory (Henley, 1977). Responses to invasions of space also reflect the cultural association between gender and power: Men are more likely to respond aggressively when their space is invaded, whereas women are more likely to yield space to the aggressor (Fisher & Byrne, 1975). This reflects gendered socialization that encourages women to accommodate others and men to vie for status and resist aggression.

How people arrange space reflects how close they are and whether they want interaction. In rigidly organized businesses, there may be private offices with closed doors and little common space. In contrast, more open businesses are likely to have fewer closed doors and a greater amount of common space to invite interaction among members. Couples who are very interdependent tend to have greater amounts of common space and

The way furniture is arranged in a room can either encourage or discourage communication and interaction. (© John Riley/Tony Stone Images, Inc.)

less individual space in their homes than do couples who are more independent (Fitzpatrick, 1988; Fitzpatrick & Best, 1979; Werner, Altman, & Oxley, 1985). Similarly, families that enjoy interaction arrange furniture to invite conversation and eye contact. In families that seek less interaction, chairs may be far apart and may face televisions instead of each other (Burgoon, Buller, & Woodhall, 1989; Keeley & Hart, 1994). People also invite or discourage interaction by how they arrange office spaces. Some professors and executives have desks that face the door and a chair beside the desk for open communication with individuals who come to their offices; other professionals turn desks away from the door and position chairs across from their desks to preserve status and distance.

Environmental Factors

Environmental factors are elements of settings that affect how we feel and act. For instance, we respond to architecture, colors, room design, temperature, sounds, smells, and lighting. Rooms with comfortable chairs invite relaxation, whereas rooms with stiff chairs prompt formality. Dimly lit rooms can enhance romantic feelings, although dark rooms can be depressing. We feel solemn in churches and synagogues with their somber colors and sacred symbols such as crosses and menorahs.

We tend to feel more lethargic on sultry, summer days and more alert on crisp fall ones. Delicious smells can make us feel hungry, even if we weren't previously interested in food. Our bodies synchronize themselves to patterns of light, so that we feel more alert during daylight than during the evening. In settings where people work during the night, extra lighting and even artificial skylights are sometimes installed to stimulate alertness.

Restaurants use environmental features to control how long people spend eating. For example, low lights, comfortable chairs or booths, and soft music are often part of the environment in upscale restaurants. On the other hand, fast-food eateries have hard plastic booths and bright lights, which encourage diners to eat and move on. To make a profit, restaurants have to get people in and out as quickly as possible. Studies indicate that faster music in the background speeds up the pace of eating (Bozzi, 1986).

ENVIRONMENTAL AWARENESS

Think of two places where you feel rushed and two where you linger. Describe the following about each place:

1. How is furniture arranged?
2. What kind of lighting is used?
3. What sort of music is played, and what other sounds are there in the place?
4. How comfortable is the furniture for sitting or lounging?
5. What colors and art are in the places?

Based on your observations, can you make generalizations about environmental features that promote relaxation and ones that do not?

A number of Asian cultures place special emphasis on environmental features that are thought to influence not only patterns of interaction, but also feelings and moods. The Asian practice aims to arrange furniture and walls to be "in harmony" with the earth. When an environment is in harmony with the earth, it is assumed that those in that environment will be similarly in harmony with the natural world.

Chronemics

Chronemics refers to how we perceive and use time to define identities and interaction. Nonverbal scholar Nancy Henley (1977) reports that we use time to negotiate and convey status. She has identified a cultural rule that stipulates important people with high status can keep others waiting. Conversely, people with low status are expected to be punctual in Western society. It is standard practice to have to wait, sometimes a long while, to see a doctor even if you have an appointment. This carries the message that the doctor's time is more valuable than ours. Professors can be late to class and students are expected to wait, but students are sometimes reprimanded if they appear after a class begins. Subordinates are expected to report punctually to meetings, but bosses are allowed to be tardy.

Chronemics express cultural attitudes toward time. In Western societies time is valuable, so speed is highly valued (Keyes, 1992; Schwartz, 1989). Thus, we want computers, not typewriters, and we replace our computers and modems as soon as faster models hit the market. We often try to do several things at once to get more done, rely on the microwave to cook faster, and take for granted speed systems such as instant copying,

ALL IN A DAY'S WORK

North Americans and Germans differ in the time they invest in work. The typical job in Germany requires 37 hours a week, and a minimum of 5 weeks paid leave annually is guaranteed by law. Stores close on weekends and on four of five week nights so that workers can have leisure time. In the United States, jobs typically require 44 to 80 hours a week, and many workers can't take more than a week's leave at a time. Further, many U.S. workers take second jobs even when their first jobs allow a comfortable standard of living. Germans can't understand this, remarking that "[f]ree time can't be paid for" (p. B1). Personal time is considered so precious in Germany that it's illegal to work more than one job during holidays, which are meant to allow people to restore themselves.

Source: Benjamin, D., & Horwitz, T. (1994, July 14). German view: "You Americans work too hard—and for what?" *Wall Street Journal*, pp. B1, B6.

photos, and so forth (McGee-Cooper, with Trammel, & Lau, 1992). Many other cultures have far more relaxed attitudes toward time and punctuality. It's not impolite in many South American countries to come late to meetings or classes, and it's not assumed people will leave when the scheduled time for ending arrives. Whether time is savored and treated casually or compulsively counted and hoarded reflects larger cultural attitudes toward living.

The duration of time we spend with different individuals reflects our interpersonal priorities. A manager spends more time with a new employee who seems to have executive potential than with one who seems less impressive. A speaker spends more time responding to a question from a high-status member of the audience and less time on a question from a person without high visibility. We try to spend more time with people we like than with those we don't like or who bore us. Researchers report that increasing contact is one of the most important ways college students intensify relationships, and reduced time together signals decreasing interest (Baxter, 1985; Dindia, 1994; Tolhuizen, 1989).

Chronemics also involve expectations of time, which are established by social norms. For example, you expect a class to last 50 to 75 minutes. Several minutes before the end of a class period, students often close notebooks and start gathering their belongings, signaling the teacher that time is up. A similar pattern is often evident in business meetings. Similarly, we expect religious services to last approximately an hour, and we might be upset if a rabbi or minister talked for 2 hours. These expectations reflect our culture's general orientation toward time, which is that it is a precious commodity to be hoarded and saved (Lakoff & Johnson, 1980, pp. 7–8). Many everyday expressions reflect the cultural view that time is like money—a valuable and limited resource to be used wisely: You're *wasting* my time. This will *save* some time. I don't *have* any time to *give* you. That mistake *cost* me 3 hours. I've *invested* a lot of time in this class, and now I'm *running out* of time.

Paralanguage

Paralanguage refers to communication that is vocal but does not involve words themselves. It includes sounds, such as murmurs and gasps, and vocal qualities, such as volume, rhythm, pitch, and inflection. Our voices are versatile instruments that tell others how to interpret us and what we say. Vocal cues signal others to interpret what we say as a joke, threat, statement of fact, question, and so forth. Effective public speakers know how to modulate inflection, volume, and rhythm to enhance their verbal messages.

Everyday Application

PRACTICING PARALANGUAGE

Say "Really" so that it means:

1. I don't believe you.
2. Wow! That's amazing.
3. That doesn't square with what I've heard.
4. I totally agree.

Say "Get lost" so that it means:

1. I want you out of here.
2. That's a dumb idea.
3. I'm crazy about you.

We use our voices to communicate feelings to friends and romantic partners. Whispering, for instance, signals secrecy and intimacy, while shouting conveys anger. Depending on the context, sighing may communicate empathy, boredom, or contentment. Research indicates that tone of voice is a powerful clue to feelings between marital partners. Negative vocal tones are among the most important symbols of marital dissatisfaction (Gottman, Markman, & Notarius, 1977; Noller, 1987). Negative intonation may also signal dissatisfaction or disapproval in work settings. A derisive or sarcastic tone communicates scorn or dislike more emphatically than words. The reverse is also true: A warm voice conveys liking, and a playful lilt suggests friendliness.

Whispered secrets reflect special intimacy between people.
(© E. Williamson/The Picture Cube)

Our voices affect how others perceive us. To some extent we control vocal cues that influence image. For instance, we can deliberately sound firm and sure of ourselves in job interviews or when explaining why we deserve a raise. The president adopts a serious and strong voice when announcing military actions. We also know how to make ourselves sound apologetic, seductive, or angry when those images suit our purposes. In addition to the ways we intentionally use our voices to project an image, vocal qualities we don't deliberately manipulate affect how others perceive us. For instance, individuals with accents are often stereotyped. Someone with a pronounced Bronx accent may be perceived as brash, and someone with a southern drawl may be stereotyped as lazy. People with foreign accents are often falsely perceived as less intelligent than native speakers.

RAYNA

When I first moved to the United States, I didn't understand many words and idioms. I did not understand that "A bird in the hand is worth two in the bush" meant it is smart to hold on to what is sure. I did not understand that "Hang a right" meant to turn right. So when I did not understand, I would ask people to explain. Most times they would say the very same thing over, just louder and more slowly, like I was deaf or stupid. I felt like saying to them in a very loud, slow voice, "I am Indian, not stupid. You are stupid."

We modulate our voices to reflect our cultural heritage and to announce we are members of specific cultures. For example, African American speech has more vocal range, inflection, and tonal quality than European American speech (Garner, 1994). In addition, among themselves African Americans often engage in highly rhythmical rappin' and "high talk" to create desired identities (Ribeau, Baldwin, & Hecht, 1994). We also use paralanguage to perform gender. To perform masculinity, men use strong volume, low pitch, and limited inflection, all of which conform to cultural prescriptions for men to be assertive and emotionally controlled. To perform femininity, women tend to use higher pitch, softer volume, and more inflection; these vocal features reflect cultural views of women as deferential and nice. We also perform class by our pronunciation of words, our accents, and the complexity of our sentences.

Silence

A final type of nonverbal behavior is **silence,** which can communicate powerful messages. The assertion "I'm not speaking to you" actually speaks volumes. We use silence to communicate different meanings. For instance, it can symbolize contentment when intimates are so comfortable they don't need to talk. Silence can also communicate awkwardness, as you know if you've ever had trouble keeping conversation going with a new acquaintance. We feel pressured to fill the void.

Silence can also disconfirm others. In some families, children are disciplined by being ignored. No matter what the child says or does, parents refuse to acknowledge his or her existence. In later life, the silencing strategy may also surface. You know how disconfirming silence can be if you've ever said hello to someone and gotten no reply. Even if the other person didn't deliberately ignore you, you felt slighted. We sometimes deliberately freeze out others when we're angry with them. In some military academies, such as West Point, silencing is a recognized method of stripping a cadet of personhood if the cadet is perceived as having broken the academy code. "Whistleblowers" and union-busters are often ostracized by peers. Similarly, the Catholic church excommunicates people who violate its canons.

Everyday Application

OBSERVING NONVERBAL COMMUNICATION

To find out whether research findings about nonverbal communication apply in real life, observe any of the contexts listed below. Describe environmental features and artifacts in the settings. Also, identify patterns of proxemics, kinesics, chronemics, haptics, and paralanguage. Do your observations concur with research findings discussed in this chapter?

1. Expensive retail stores and discount stores
2. Executive and secretarial offices
3. Faculty clubs and student cafeterias
4. Library and student union
5. College administrative buildings and classroom buildings on campus

Describe how nonverbal factors reflect the different identities of these contexts and the kinds of activities and interactions each context invites and discourages.

In this section, we've discussed nine types of nonverbal behavior. The complex system of nonverbal communication includes kinesics, haptics, physical appearance, artifacts, proxemics, environmental features, chronemics, paralanguage, and silence. We use these nonverbal behaviors to announce our identities and to communicate how we feel about relationships with others. In the final section of this chapter, we consider guidelines for improving the effectiveness of our nonverbal communication.

IMPROVING NONVERBAL COMMUNICATION

Nonverbal communication, like its verbal cousin, can be misinterpreted. Following two guidelines should reduce nonverbal misunderstandings in your interactions.

Monitor Your Nonverbal Communication

The monitoring skills we have stressed in other chapters are also important for competent nonverbal communication. Self-reflection allows you to take responsibility for how you present yourself and your nonverbal messages. Think about the foregoing discussion of ways we use nonverbal behaviors to announce our identities. Are you projecting the image you desire? Do your facial and body movements represent how you see yourself and how you want others to perceive you? Do friends ever tell you that you seem uninterested or far away when they are talking to you? If so, you can monitor your nonverbal actions so that you more clearly communicate your involvement and interest in conversations. To reduce the chance that work associates will think you're uninterested in meetings, use nonverbal behaviors that convey responsiveness and attention.

Have you set up your spaces so that they invite the kind of interaction you prefer, or are they arranged to interfere with good communication? Paying attention to nonverbal dimensions of your world can empower you to use them more effectively to achieve your interpersonal goals.

Be Tentative When Interpreting Others' Nonverbal Communication

Although stores are filled with popular advice books that promise to show you how to read nonverbal behaviors, there really isn't a sure-fire formula. It's naive to think we can decode something as complex and ambiguous as nonverbal communication. People who believe that may misjudge others.

In this chapter, we've discussed findings about the meanings people attach to nonverbal behaviors. It's important to realize these are only generalizations about conclusions people draw. We have not and cannot state what any particular behavior means to specific individuals in a given context. For instance, we've said that satisfied couples tend to sit closer together than unhappy couples. As a general rule, this is true. However, sometimes very contented couples prefer autonomy and like to distance themselves at times. In addition, someone may maintain distance because she or he has a cold and doesn't want a partner to catch it. It's also possible that people socialized in non-Western cultures learned different rules for proxemics. Because nonverbal communication is ambiguous and personal, we should not assume we can interpret it with absolute precision. An ethical perspective on communication suggests we should qualify interpretations of nonverbal behavior with awareness of personal and contextual considerations.

Personal Qualifications Generalizations about nonverbal behavior by definition state what is generally the case. They do not tell us about the exceptions to the rule. Nonverbal patterns that accurately describe most people may not apply to particular individuals. Although eye contact generally indicates responsiveness, some individuals close their eyes to concentrate when listening. In such cases, it would be inaccurate to conclude that a person who doesn't look at us isn't listening. Similarly, people who cross their arms and condense into a tight posture are often expressing hostility or lack of interest in interaction. However, the same behaviors might mean a person is cold and trying to conserve body heat. Most people use less inflection, fewer gestures, and a slack posture when they're not really interested in what they're talking about. The same behaviors, however, may mean only that they're tired.

DERRICK

I'd like to tell off those jerks who write the popular books on reading nonverbal behavior. One of the things they say is that crossing your legs a certain way means you're closed. Well, I have a bum knee from football, and there's only one way I can cross my legs. It doesn't mean anything about whether I'm open or closed. It means my knee doesn't work.

Because nonverbal behaviors are ambiguous and vary among people, we need to be cautious about how we interpret others. A key principle to keep in mind is that nonverbal behaviors, like other symbols, have no intrinsic meaning. Meaning is something we construct and assign to behaviors. A good way to keep this distinction in mind is to check perceptions and to rely on I-language, not you-language, which we discussed in Chapter 5. You can check perceptions to find out if the way you interpret another's nonverbal behavior is what that other person means: "I feel that you're not really involved in this conversation; is that how you feel?" In addition, you can rely on I-language. You-language might lead us to inaccurately say of someone who doesn't look at us, "You're communicating lack of interest." A more responsible statement would use I-language to say, "When you don't look at me, I feel you're not interested in what I'm saying." Using I-language reminds us to take responsibility for our judgments and feelings. In addition, it reduces the likelihood we will make others defensive by inaccurately interpreting their nonverbal behavior.

Contextual Qualifications Like the meaning of verbal communication, the significance of nonverbal behaviors depends on the contexts in which they occur. How we act doesn't reflect only how we see ourselves and how we feel. In addition, our actions reflect the various settings we inhabit. We are more or less formal, relaxed, and open depending on context. Most people are more at ease on their own turf than someone else's, so we tend to be more friendly and outgoing in our homes than in business meetings and public spaces. We also dress according to context. When I am on campus or in business meetings, I dress professionally, but at home I'm usually in jeans or running clothes. My students sometimes express surprise at my dress when they come by my home. Like all of us, I select clothes to suit various occasions and contexts.

Immediate, physical settings are not the only context that affects nonverbal communication. As we have seen, all communication reflects the values and understandings of particular cultures. We are likely to misinterpret people from other cultures when we impose the norms and rules of our culture on them. An Arabic man who stands practically on top of others to talk with them is not being rude according to his culture's standards, although Westerners might interpret him as pushy. A Tibetan woman who makes little eye contact is showing respect by the norms in her country, although an American might view her as evasive.

E L E N I

I have been misinterpreted very much in this country. My first semester here, a professor told me he wanted me to be more assertive and to speak up in class. I could not do that, I tell him. He said I should put myself forward, but I have been brought up not to do that. In Taiwan, that is very rude and ugly, and we are taught not to speak up to teachers. Now that I have been here for 3 years, I sometimes speak in classes, but I am still more quiet than Americans. I know my professors think I am not so smart because I am quiet, but that is the teaching of my country.

Even within our own country we have diverse communication cultures, and each has its own rules for nonverbal behavior. We run the risk of misinterpreting men if we judge them by the norms of feminine communication culture. A man who doesn't make "listening noises" may well be listening intently according to the rules of masculine culture. Similarly, when women nod and make listening noises while another is talking, men may misperceive them as agreeing. According to the rules of feminine communication cultures, ongoing feedback is a way of signaling interest, not necessarily approval. Within the understandings of African American culture, styling is not arrogant egotism as the same behaviors might be according to Caucasian norms. We have to adopt dual perspective when interpreting others, especially when they and we belong to different cultures. To enhance your awareness of cultural influences on communication, the next chapter deals with that topic in detail.

We can become more effective nonverbal communicators if we monitor our own nonverbal behaviors and qualify our interpretation of others by keeping personal and contextual considerations in mind. Using I-language is one way to help us avoid the danger of misreading others.

SUMMARY

In this chapter, we've explored many facets of the world beyond words. We learned that nonverbal communication functions to supplement or replace verbal messages, to regulate interaction, to reflect and establish relational level meanings, and to express cultural membership. These four principles of nonverbal behavior help us understand the complex ways in which nonverbal communication operates and what it may mean.

We discussed nine types of nonverbal communication. These are kinesics (face and body motion), haptics (touch), physical appearance, artifacts, proxemics (use of space), environmental features, chronemics (use of time), paralanguage, and silence. Each form of nonverbal communication reflects cultural understandings and values and also expresses our personal identities and feelings toward others. We use nonverbal behaviors to announce and perform identities, using actions, artifacts, and contextual features to embody the rules we associate with gender, race, class, sexuality, and ethnicity. In this sense, nonverbal communication has a theatrical dimension, because it is a primary way we create and present images of ourselves.

Because nonverbal communication, like its verbal cousin, is symbolic, it has no inherent meaning that is fixed for all time. Instead, its meaning is something we construct as we notice, organize, and interpret nonverbal behaviors that we and others enact. Effectiveness requires that we learn to monitor our own nonverbal communication and to exercise caution in interpreting that of others.

FOR FURTHER REFLECTION AND DISCUSSION

1. Attend a gathering of people from a culture different from yours. It might be a Jewish temple if you're Christian, a black church if you're Caucasian, or a meeting of Asian students if you are Western. Observe nonverbal behaviors of the people there: How do they greet one another, how much eye contact accompanies interaction, how close to one another do people sit?

2. Make a survey of restaurants near campus. Describe the kinds of seats, lighting, music (if any), and distance between tables. Do you find any connections between nonverbal patterns and expensiveness of restaurants?

3. Describe the spatial arrangements in the home of your family of origin. Was there a room in which family members interacted a good deal? How was furniture arranged in that room? Who had separate space and personal chairs in your family? What do the nonverbal patterns reflect about your family's communication style?

4. Discuss current gender prescriptions in the United States. How are men and women "supposed" to look? How are these cultural expectations communicated? Now think about how you might resist or even alter unhealthy cultural gender prescriptions.

5. Is it unethical to interpret others' nonverbal communication from our perspectives?

KEY TERMS

nonverbal communication	proxemics
kinesics	environmental factors
haptics	chronemics
physical appearance	paralanguage
artifacts	silence

Focus Questions

1 Does communication shape culture or does culture shape communication?

2 How does understanding cultures enhance communication effectiveness?

3 Is there an ethical responsibility to learn to communicate effectively in a culturally diverse world?

4 What is the role of language in instigating changes in societies?

CHAPTER 7

Communication and Cultures

oncha cradles his daughter in his arms and sings her to sleep while his village wife plows the small field of vegetables outside their cottage. Later today she will repair the walls on the cottage for the harsh winter ahead. Tomorrow Concha begins the 2-day walk to Kathmandu where he will live with his city wife and children. That will be his home for the next 6 months while he leads treks in the Himalayas. Halfway across the globe, John returns home after a long day at his law office. He parks his Buick in the garage and walks in the kitchen where his wife, Ginny, is nursing their son, Daniel. After dinner he will mow the lawn and repair a leaky faucet, then pack a bag for tomorrow's flight to a conference 2,000 miles away. He'll be gone a week, and the au pair will help Ginny with Daniel.

More than distance separates these two families. They have different understandings of what family means and how it operates. In Nepal, gender roles are not as rigidly divided as they are in the

(Carmen Lomas Garza, *Tamalada* (1987). Gouache, 20 × 27". © 1987 Carmen Lomas Garza. Photo © Wolfgang Dietze. Collection of Leonila Ramirez, Don Ramon's Restaurant, San Francisco, Calif.)

United States—both women and men, as well as extended families, care for children. Both sexes engage in the hard labor of farming and maintaining homes. The strong value attached to family in Nepal explains why it is common for men to have more than one family. Having both a village family and a city family ensures a continuous home life for the many Nepalese men who often spend half of each year based in Kathmandu from which mountain treks and expeditions originate. Having two families is acceptable in Nepal, but no Nepalese would hire an au pair, since family and neighbors should care for children. What Concha and Ginny consider normal and good reflects their respective cultures.

For each of us, the culture in which we are raised shapes how we think, behave, communicate, and make sense of the world and ourselves. The process of socialization, which we discussed in Chapter 3, teaches us what our culture considers normal, what it values, who we are, what family means, how people interact, and a host of other things. In other words, culture provides a structure for our lives and gives us a set of rules for how to think, act, communicate, feel, and live.

You'll recall that when we defined communication in Chapter 1, we noted that it is a systemic process. This means that forms of communication can be understood only within their particular systems, or contexts. Culture is one of the most important systems within which communication occurs. Communication is closely linked to culture, because communication expresses, sustains, and alters cultures. Your culture directly shapes how you communicate, teaching you whether interrupting is appropriate, how much eye contact is polite, and whether argument and conflict are desirable in groups and personal relationships. We are not born knowing how, when, and to whom to speak, just as we are not born with attitudes about different races, religions, sexual orientations, and other aspects of identity. We learn these as we interact with others, and we then reflect cultural teachings in our own communication.

In this chapter, we explore relationships between communication and culture. In previous chapters, we've already seen a number of ways in which communication reflects and expresses cultural values. Now we're ready to focus more closely on this topic. We'll define culture and discuss the intricate ways it is entwined with communication. Then we'll focus on guidelines for increasing the effectiveness of communication between people of different cultures.

UNDERSTANDING CULTURE

Although the word **culture** is part of our everyday vocabulary, it's difficult to define. Culture is part of everything we think, do, feel, and believe, yet we can't point to a thing that is culture. In other words, culture is a very abstract concept that has no one concrete referent and no single meaning. Most simply defined, culture is a way of life. It is a system of ideas, values, beliefs, and customs that is communicated by one generation to the next and that sustains a particular way of life (Spencer, 1982, p. 562). To better understand cultures we'll now consider two premises about them.

Multiple Cultures May Coexist in a Single Society

When we speak of different cultures, we often think of societies that are geographically distinct. For instance, India, South America, Africa, and Arabia are separate cultures. Yet geographic separation isn't what defines a culture. Instead, a culture exists when a distinct way of life shapes what a group of people believes, values, and does. Groups with distinct ways of life can coexist in a single society or physical territory.

In most societies there is a dominant, or mainstream, way of life. Although many groups may exist within a single society, not all of them identify equally and exclusively with the dominant culture. Mainstream Western culture was created by Western, heterosexual, land-owning, able-bodied males who were Christian at least in heritage, if not in actual practice. Yet Western society includes many groups outside of the cultural mainstream. Gays, lesbians, and bisexuals experience difficulty in a society that defines them as marginal and refuses to grant them social recognition or legal rights (Wood, 1995b). Mainstream customs often ignore the traditions of people who follow religions such as Judaism and Buddhism.

Everyday Application

COMMUNICATING CULTURE

Locate a standard calendar and also an academic calendar used on your campus. Check each calendar to determine which of the following holidays of different cultural groups are recognized and which are declared as holidays on the calendar by suspension of normal operations in communities and campuses:

Christmas	Hanukkah	Easter	Martin Luther King Day
Yom Kippur	Elderly Day	Passover	

What do calendars communicate in recognizing or not recognizing traditions of various cultures?

The dominance of groups in the cultural mainstream is often evident in nonverbal communication. For example, Western culture often conveys the message that people without disabilities are normal and people with disabilities are not. Notice how many buildings have no ramps and how many public presentations don't include signers for people with hearing limitations. Most campus and business buildings include portraits that are predominantly of white men, leaving people of color and women unrepresented as important figures. Groups outside of the mainstream are distinct cultures that communicate in ways consistent with the values and norms of their communities. As Sabrina notes in her commentary, tension and misunderstanding can erupt when values and communication practices of different cultures clash.

SABRINA

I get hassled by a lot of girls on campus about being dependent on my family. They say I should grow up and leave the nest. They say I'm too close to my folks and my grandparents, aunts, uncles, and cousins. But what they mean by "too close" is that I'm closer with my family than most whites are. It's a white standard they're using, and it doesn't fit most African Americans. Strong ties with family and the black community have always been our way.

Co-cultures are groups of people who live within a dominant culture, yet also are members of another culture that is not dominant in a particular society. For many years, social groups that lived in a dominant culture yet simultaneously belonged to a second culture were called subcultures. However, the prefix *sub* connotes inferiority as if subcultures are somehow less complete than "regular" cultures. The term *co-culture* was coined to describe groups of people who hold dual membership in the dominant culture and a second one (Samovar & Porter, 1994). This is an example of using language to shape perceptions and attitudes.

One of the best indicators that a culture or co-culture exists is communication. Although all of us communicate, we don't all do it in the same way. Because we learn to communicate in the process of interacting with others, people from different cultures use communication in different ways and attach different meanings to particular communicative acts. For example, many Asian cultures emphasize harmonious and cooperative communication, whereas Western culture encourages greater degrees of conflict and competition. When Westerners and Easterners work together in groups, their different ways of communicating may cause misunderstandings. Members of cultures share perspectives on communication that outsiders do not have, which is why cross-cultural communication is sometimes difficult.

TABLE 7.1 Rules of Gender Communication Cultures

Feminine Communication Rules	Masculine Communication Rules
1. Include others. Use talk to show interest in others, and respond to their needs.	1. Assert yourself. Use talk to establish your identity, expertise, knowledge, etc.
2. Use talk cooperatively. Communication is a joint activity, so people have to work together. It's important to invite others into conversation, wait your turn to speak, and respond to what others say.	2. Use talk competitively. Communication is an arena for proving yourself. Use talk to gain and hold attention, to wrest the talk stage from others; interrupt and reroute topics to keep you and your ideas spotlighted.
3. Use talk expressively. Talk should deal with feelings, personal ideas, and problems, and should be used to build relationships with others.	3. Use talk instrumentally. Talk should accomplish something such as solving a problem, giving advice, or taking a stand on issues.

Gender as a Co-Culture   Of the many co-cultures that exist, gender has received particularly intense study. Because we know more about it than other co-cultures, we'll explore gender as an extended example of a co-culture. Researchers have investigated both how women and men are socialized in separate co-cultures and how their communication differs in practice. One of the earliest studies showed that children's games are a primary agent of gender socialization (Maltz & Borker, 1982). Typically, children's play is sex-segregated, and there are differences between the games the sexes tend to play.

Games girls favor, such as house and school, involve few players; require talk to negotiate how to play, since there aren't clear-cut guidelines; and depend on cooperation and sensitivity between players. Baseball, soccer, and war, which are typical boys' games, require more players and have clear goals and rules, so less talk is needed to play. Most boys' games are highly competitive both between teams and for individual status within teams. Interaction in games teaches boys and girls distinct understandings of why, when, and how to use talk. Table 7.1 summarizes rules of feminine and masculine communication cultures.

Research on adult women's and men's communication reveals that the rules taught through child play remain with many of us as we grow older. For instance, women's talk is generally more expressive and focused on feelings and relationships, whereas men's talk tends to be more instrumental and competitive (Aries, 1987; Beck, 1988; Johnson, 1989, 1996; Wood, 1994c,d). These differences are often evident in professional contexts. Women leaders tend to engage in more personal communication with subordinates and peers than do men (Helgesen, 1990; Natalle, 1996). In group discussions, women's communication often includes attention to group climate and relationships between members, while men's communication may focus more on task issues.

(© 1992 by Jennifer Berman. Reprinted by permission.)

Another general difference is what each sex regards as the primary basis of relationships. For men, activities tend to be a key foundation of close friendships and romantic relationships (Inman, 1996; Swain, 1989; Wood & Inman, 1993). Thus, men typically cement friendships through doing things together (playing soccer, working on cars, watching sports) and through doing things for one another (trading favors, washing a car, doing laundry). Many women see communication as the crux of relationships. It is not only a means to instrumental ends, but an end in itself. Thus women often regard talking about feelings, personal issues, and daily life as the way to build and continuously enrich relationships.

Given the differences between how women and men, in general, use communication, it's hardly surprising that the sexes often misunderstand one another. One clash between gender communication cultures occurs when women and men discuss problems. When women talk about something that is troubling them, they are often looking first for communication that expresses empathy and connection. Yet masculine socialization teaches men to use communication instrumentally, so they tend to offer advice or solutions (Tannen, 1990; Wood, 1994d, 1996b). Thus, women sometimes interpret men's advice as communicating lack of personal concern. On the other hand, men may feel frustrated when women offer empathy and support instead of advice for solving problems. In general, men also make fewer personal disclosures, whereas women regard sharing confidences as an important way to enhance closeness (Aries, 1987; Johnson, 1996).

Men and women, in general, also have different styles of listening. Socialized to be responsive and expressive, women tend to make listening noises such as "um hm," "yeah," and "I know what you mean" when others are talking (Tannen, 1990; Wood, 1996b). This is how they show they are following and interested. Masculine culture, however, doesn't emphasize affirming others vocally or verbally, so men tend to make fewer listening noises than women. Thus, women sometimes feel men aren't listening to them because men don't symbolize their attention in the ways women have learned to expect. Men may also misinterpret women's listening noises as indicating agreement (versus attention) and be surprised if women later disagree with their ideas.

Perhaps the most common complication in communication between the genders occurs when a woman says "Let's talk about us." To men this often means trouble, because they interpret the request as implying there is a problem in a relationship. For women, however, this is not the only—

or even the main—reason to talk about a relationship. Feminine communication cultures regard talking as a primary way to celebrate and increase closeness (Riessman, 1990). Socialized to use communication instrumentally, however, men tend to think talking about a relationship is useful only if there is some problem to be resolved (Acitelli, 1988, 1993). For men, the preferred way to build closeness is to do things together. Larry's commentary illustrates this gender difference.

LARRY

Finally I see what happens between my girlfriend and me. She always wants to talk about us, which I think is stupid unless we have a problem. I like to go to a concert or do something together, but then she says that I don't want to be with her. We speak totally different languages.

Other Co-Cultures   Gender isn't the only co-culture, and communication between men and women is not the only kind of interaction that may be plagued by cross-cultural misunderstandings. Research indicates that communication patterns vary among social classes. For example, working-class people tend to use shorter, simpler sentences; less elaborate explanations; and more conventional grammar than members of the middle class (Bernstein, 1973).

Race and ethnicity are also communication cultures that involve distinct communication patterns. Communication scholar Mark Orbe (1994) describes the United States as two separate societies—one African American and one European American. We might amend Orbe's observation to note that there are more than two co-cultures in the United States. A recent report indicates African Americans generally communicate more assertively than European Americans (Ribeau, Baldwin, & Hecht, 1994). What African Americans consider authentic, powerful exchanges may be perceived as antagonistic by individuals from different communication cultures. The rapping and styling of African Americans is not practiced (or understood) by most European Americans (Houston & Wood, 1996).

Another feature of African American speech is extensive verbal artistry in which members play the dozens (a game of exchanging insults), speak indirectly (sometimes called signifying), and use highly dramatic language. These forms of communication allow historically oppressed social groups to express aggression and creativity indirectly when it would be unsafe to express them explicitly (Garner, 1994). African American communication reflects greater commitment to collective interests such as family or race, whereas European American communication tends to be more individualistic (Gaines, 1995). As a rule, African Americans also communicate more interactively than European Americans (Weber, 1994). This explains why African Americans call out responses such as "Tell it," "All right," and "Keep talking," during speeches, church sermons, and classes. What Caucasians regard as interruptions of a speaker, African Americans perceive as complimentary participation in communication. Table 7.2 illustrates the differences between European American and African American communication.

TABLE 7.2 A Translation Guide

Term	European American Meaning	African American Meaning
Sister	Female sibling	Black woman
Brother	Male sibling	Black man
I'm going to buy you a watch.	I am going to buy you a watch.	You're late. (signifying)
You call that dancing? My kid can dance better.	You are a poor dancer. (an insult)	Want to engage in "slammin' " or "jonin' "? (a game of reciprocal insults)
I'm so good at my job they ought to make me president.	Arrogant bragging	Verbal wit, not intended seriously (braggadocio)

Although members of a society share a common language, we don't all use it the same way. The United States includes a variety of co-cultures that teach distinct rules about how, when, why, and with whom to talk. Respecting the communication styles of different co-cultures increases our ability to participate competently in a diverse society. The remainder of this chapter considers both geographically separate cultures and co-cultures in a single society.

Cultures Are Systems

A culture is not a random collection of ideas, beliefs, values, and customs; instead, it is a coherent system of understandings, traditions, values, communication practices, and ways of living. As anthropologist Edward T. Hall noted, "You touch a culture in one place and everything else is affected" (1977, p. 14).

As you'll recall from our earlier discussion of systems, the parts of a system interact and affect one another. Thus, aspects of culture are interrelated and work together to create a whole. For example, one of the major changes in Western society was the Industrial Revolution. Prior to the mid-1800s, most families lived and worked together in one place. In agricultural regions, women, men, and children worked together to plant, tend, harvest, and store crops and to take care of livestock. In cities, family businesses were common. This preindustrial way of life promoted cooperative relationships and family togetherness.

The invention of fuel-powered machines led to mass production in factories where workers spent 8 or more hours each day. In turn, this provoked competition among workers to produce and earn more, and on-the-job communication became more competitive and individualistic. As men were hired for industrial jobs, their roles in family life diminished, and father–child relationships became generally less close and intense. These changes gave birth to the belief that women belong in the home nurturing families and men belong in the public sphere earning a living and having civic influence (Cancian, 1989). Thus, a change in work life produced reverberations throughout the culture.

The technological revolution that began in the 1970s and continues today has also had multiple and far-reaching repercussions. New communication technologies, such as the Internet and the World Wide Web, allow individuals to maintain regular communication over great distances. Computer networking allows many people to do their jobs in their own homes. Personal relationships, too, are affected by changes in communication. Today, many people sustain and even form friendships and romantic relationships over the Internet (Lea & Spears, 1995). New technologies change how, where, and with whom we communicate, just as they change the boundaries we use to define work and personal life. Because cultures are holistic, no change is ever isolated from the overall system.

We have seen that culture is a way of life that involves many interrelated dimensions. Both cultures and co-cultures are ways of life shared by members and not shared by people outside the culture or co-culture. To build on this basic definition, we'll now highlight relationships between communication and cultures.

COMMUNICATION AND CULTURE

Intercultural communication scholars Larry Samovar and Richard Porter (1995) claim that communication and culture cannot be separated from one another, because each influences the other. Culture is reflected in communication practices, and at the same time, communication practices shape cultural life. We'll discuss five principles that apply to co-cultures within a single geographic area as well as to cultures separated by physical distance.

Communication Expresses and Sustains Cultures

As we will see throughout this chapter, patterns of communication reflect cultural values and perspectives. Consider, for example, that many Asian languages include numerous words to describe particular relationships: my grandmother's brother, my father's uncle, my youngest son, my oldest daughter. This linguistic focus reflects the cultural emphasis on family relationships (Ferrante, 1995). There are far fewer English words to describe specific kinship bonds, which suggests that Western culture places less emphasis on ties beyond those in the nuclear family.

Asian cultures also revere the elderly, and this too is reflected in language. "I will be 60 tomorrow" is an Asian saying that means I have enough years to deserve respect. In contrast, Western cultures tend to prize youth and to have many positive words for youthfulness (young in spirit, fresh) and negative words for seniority (has been, outdated, old fashioned). The Western preoccupation with time and efficiency is evident in the abundance of words that refer to time (hours, minutes, seconds, days, weeks) and in common phrases such as "Let's not waste time." Among

PROVERBS EXPRESS CULTURAL VALUES

"No need to know the person, only the family." This Chinese axiom reflects the belief that individuals are less important than family units.

"A zebra does not despise its stripes." Among the African Masai, this saying encourages acceptance of things and oneself as they are.

"The child has no owner." "It takes a whole village to raise a child." These African adages express the cultural belief that children belong to whole communities, not just to their biological parents.

Source: Adapted from Samovar, L., & Porter, R. (1991). *Communication between cultures*. Belmont, CA: Wadsworth.

Buddhists, the adage "Something cannot become nothing" expresses belief that life continues in new forms after what Westerners call death. In the United States, "The early bird gets the worm" implies that initiative is valuable, and "Nice guys finish last" suggests that winning is important and that it's more important to be aggressive than nice.

Everyday Application

YOUR CULTURE'S SAYINGS

What do common sayings and proverbs in the United States tell us about cultural values? What cultural values are expressed by other sayings such as "You can't be too rich or too thin," "A stitch in time saves later nine," "A watched pot never boils," "You can't take it with you," and "You've made your bed, now you have to lie in it"? What other sayings can you think of that express key Western values?

Nonverbal communication also expresses cultural values. For example, "styling" is an African American manner of dressing very stylishly in order to project a good image. In the African American co-culture, dress is an important way of stating who you are. Similarly, African Americans tend to judge each other by how much wit, personal style, and humor are displayed in communication. Thus, rapping and witty exchanges are common communication patterns (Hecht, Collier, & Ribeau, 1993). The more

*Communication styles reflect
cultural membership.*
(© Goldberg/Monkmeyer)

restrained style of communication typical of European Americans may seem cold and impersonal to African Americans (Kochman, 1981). Reflecting a cultural value not to intrude on others, the Hopi and Navajo Native Americans regard direct eye contact as offensive, as do many Asians (Samovar & Porter, 1994). Both Asian and Asian American cultures value personal restraint and discipline, so they use fewer and less dramatic gestures and facial expressions than European Americans (Klopf, 1991).

INTAN

Eye contact is the hardest part of learning American culture. In my home we do not look at others. It would be very rude to do that. Instead, we look away or down when talking so as not to insult other persons. In America if I look down, it is thought I am hiding something or am dishonest. So I am learning to look at others when we talk, but it still feels very disrespectful to me.

Communication simultaneously reflects and sustains cultural values. Each time we express cultural values, we also perpetuate them. When Asian Americans veil emotions in interaction, they fortify and express the value of self-restraint and the priority of reason over emotion. The smiling and deferential postures encouraged in feminine speech communities perpetuate the Western idea that women are subordinate to men (Wood, 1994d). When Caucasians argue, push their own ideas, and compete in conversations, they uphold the values of individuality and assertiveness. Communication, then, is a mirror of a culture's values and a primary means of keeping them woven into the fabric of everyday life.

Cultures Consist of Material and Nonmaterial Components

Cultures include both material and nonmaterial elements. Material components are tangible objects and physical substances that have been altered by human intervention. For instance, material objects common in Western cultures include cars, phones, computers, shovels, and hammers. Each of these objects began with natural raw materials, such as metals, trees, and minerals, that were shaped into new forms for new uses.

The objects a culture invents reflect its values, needs, goals, and preoccupations. For example, cultures invent weapons, which tells us they value self-protection. A culture that creates an abundance of offensive weapons is likely to have goals of conquest as well. The numerous inventions to enhance speed and output in the United States suggest this country esteems efficiency and productivity (Wood, 1995b).

RAUL

In Mexico we spend much more time doing things than people do in America. To fix food we use only our hands and maybe knives and pots, but here kitchens have so many fancy tools. In Piste, my hometown, few people have phones, and even those who do often wait many hours to get a call through. Here everyone has a phone—sometimes more than one—and people expect to make instant connections anywhere in the world. Most Mexicans walk or take buses; if a bus is full, we wait for the next one or the one after that. Here everybody has his or her own car and people do not like to wait.

Raul realizes that the differences between the material objects common in Mexico and those in the United States are more than physical. They also reflect different cultural perspectives on time. Western cultures value speed—the more the better (Wood, 1995b). Mexican culture has a more leisurely view of time.

Everyday Application

IT'S A MATERIAL WORLD

Analyze the material symbols of your campus culture. What do statues, buildings, and landscaping say about what is valued on your campus? What do computers in most offices tell you about your campus's regard for information and efficiency? Which are the newest, largest, and nicest buildings on campus? How do the quality and aesthetics of classrooms compare with those of administrators' offices? What can you conclude about the values of your campus culture?

Cultures also include nonmaterial components. These are intangible creations that reflect a culture's values and that influence personal and social behavior. Four of the most important nonmaterial aspects of a culture are beliefs, values, norms, and language.

Beliefs Beliefs are conceptions of what is true, factual, or valid. Beliefs may be rooted in faith (God said that we live forever if we accept Him; you are reincarnated after "death"), experience (storing grain in elevated

The value placed on family life differs from culture to culture.
(© Keren Su/Stock, Boston)

places keeps it dry during the monsoons), or science (penicillin cures infections). Cultural beliefs are regarded as truths, even though they are sometimes false. In the 1600s, people in the United States believed in witches and drowned or burned at the stake anyone they considered a witch. At one point it was widely believed that the earth was flat, so sailors did not venture beyond what they believed to be the edge of the earth. Even after that, people thought that the earth was the center of the universe around which the sun revolved. We now know that the earth is round and that it revolves around the sun, rather than vice versa. Cultural beliefs even if not accurate, influence personal and social conduct.

Values Values are generally shared views of what is good, right, worthwhile, and important with regard to conduct and existence. Whereas beliefs have to do with what people think is true, values are concerned with what should be, or what is worthy in life. For example, cultures that value families create laws and social policies to support family life. The United States' commitment to individuals may explain why it is the only developed country without guaranteed family leave for all workers.

Different cultures have different values toward the natural world. Native Americans saw themselves as living in harmony with nature, with other creatures, and with the earth. Thus, they adjusted their lives to the natural rhythms of seasons, created communication rituals to celebrate changes in the seasons, worked with the land, and hunted to meet needs for food and clothing, but not for sport. On killing an animal, Native Americans had rituals to honor the dead animal's spirit and to express thanks to it for its life. Adopting a much different value, the Europeans who settled in the United States saw nature as something to be conquered, suppressed, and bent to serve humans. Thus, they attacked and subdued the wilderness in the name of progress. Land was, and often still is, clear cut for lumber or mining; the air is polluted by chemicals from factories and vehicles; toxins are dumped in seas and communities; animals are raised for slaughter and killed for sport. Each culture develops its own values about nature, moral conduct, and other matters. The values endorsed by a culture, in turn, are expressed in the communication of its members.

Norms Norms are informal rules that guide how members of a culture act, as well as how they think and feel. Norms define what is normal, or appropriate, in various situations. Although norms may be written down formally, they are usually informal rules that specify what is appropriate in specific circumstances. For instance, in the United States, salads are usually served before a main course, but they follow it in France and much of Europe. In China, defendants are presumed guilty, whereas in the United States, they are presumed innocent until proven guilty. In America, children are expected to grow up and leave their families of origin in order to start their own families. In some Asian societies, however, children are expected to live with or near their parents and to operate as a single large family. What we view as normal reflects the teachings of our particular culture, not absolute truths. The values endorsed by a culture are woven into communication, so that how people talk and interact nonverbally both reflect and perpetuate particular cultural values.

Norms are often rooted in cultural traditions. For example, in the United States and some other countries, women have assumed their husbands' names because of the tradition that a man is the head of a household. Although some couples now choose not to use the man's name for their identities, the tradition of regarding men as heads of families still prevails and, with it, the normative practice of women's symbolically becoming one with their husbands. Norms of communication may also reflect cultural values. In the United States, for instance, there are many norms that respect the values of individuals' privacy, property, and autonomy: knocking on closed doors, asking permission to borrow others' property, having separate utensils for eating and serving food and individual places for meals, and moving without consulting any authorities. In countries with collectivist values, however, different communicative norms prevail. Koreans do not set individual places, and they use the same utensils for serving and eating. In China, no citizen would change jobs or move without first getting approval from the local unit of the Communist Party (Ferrante, 1995).

Language   Language shapes how we think about the world and ourselves. As we saw in Chapter 5, language is packed with values. Consequently, in the process of learning language, we learn our culture's values, beliefs, and norms. The value that most Asian cultures attach to age is structured into Asian languages. For instance, the Korean language makes fine distinctions among different ages, and any remark to another person must acknowledge the other's age (Ferrante, 1995). To say "I am going to school" in Korean, a teenager would say "hakkyo-eh gahndah" to a peer of the same age, "hakkyo-eh gah" to a parent, and "hakkyo-eh gahneh" to a grandparent (Park, 1979).

Language also reflects cultural views of personal identity. Western cultures tend to emphasize individuals, whereas many Eastern cultures place greater emphasis on family and community than on individuals. It's unlikely that an Eastern textbook on human communication would even include a chapter on self, which is standard in Western textbooks. If I were a Korean, I would introduce myself as Wood Julia to communicate the greater value placed on familial than personal identity.

Language, norms, beliefs, and values are cultural couriers that carry a way of life forward from day to day and generation to generation. These nonmaterial components, in combination with material ones, are the cornerstones of a culture. They both reflect and perpetuate its character.

Cultures Are Shaped by Historical and Geographic Forces

The values and activities of cultures are not random or arbitrary. Many of them grow out of the history and geographic location of a society as those influences are named and carried forward in language. Much of what is done and believed in a culture depends on its physical environment, especially natural resources. The southern region of the United States has historically been more agrarian than the northern region because southern soil and climate are conducive to farming. Water is used freely in the United States, but very sparingly in the hill country of Nepal where it must be hand carried into villages. The scarcity of oil, wood, and coal in Korea influences Koreans to use fuels conservatively. Similarly, the lack of grazing land in Korea means there are few sheep and cows for meat and dairy products. To meet needs for food, Koreans rely on resources that are available in their country—rice and other grains, vegetables, and dogs, snakes, and soy products as sources of protein. Swampy lands are ideal for growing rice, but not for cultivating wheat. Many South American societies have siestas so that people are not drained by the fierce midday heat. Cities and towns on seaboards develop maritime industries and have more heavily seafood diets than inland areas.

A I K A U

Americans say they like oriental food, but really they do not know what it is. At home we use meat only to flavor. We have slivers of meat or chicken in a meal, but we do not have big pieces like in America. When my parents came here and opened a restaurant, they had to learn how to fix Asian food for American tastes, not like we fix it at home.

Just as our personal histories shape who we are, the traditions and history of a culture shape its character. Many Native Americans distrust Caucasian Americans because of a history of exploitation and betrayal. Similarly, African Americans have good reason to distrust Caucasians, since their ancestors were enslaved and exploited by whites. Jewish people have a painful legacy of persecution that explains why many are wary of non-Jews even today. In 1939, a ship transporting Jews from Nazi Germany docked in Miami, Florida, and was turned back. That incident is part of the history of Jewish people and helps us understand why they often distrust non-Jews and preserve their own culture.

Historical influences also shape the communication patterns of social groups. For instance, many African Americans are fluent in both mainstream communication patterns and ones more specialized in the black community. They know how to "play the part" and say they "definitely talk white" (Orbe, 1994, p. 292) in order to fit into the dominant culture. Other co-cultures, such as Jewish and gay groups, also become bilingual in order to be effective in both mainstream culture and their personal communities.

Many traditions that originally developed for functional reasons persist simply because "that's how we've always done things." An example of this is the gendered division of life in Western societies. Originally, women probably stayed near their homes because they had to nurse babies, and men did the majority of hunting because they could leave the home and because they had greater muscles and physical strength. Today brains are more important than brawn for providing for a family, and infants can be fed with formula or expressed and stored breast milk, so the mother's full-time presence is not essential. Although the original reasons for assigning women to homemaking and men to breadwinning are no longer valid, a traditionally gendered division of labor persists.

Cultural traditions shape daily activities and social life. For example, members of Buddhist societies tend to be very compassionate and gentle in keeping with Buddhist spiritual values. Hindus believe that what a person is and does in this life reflects past lives and determines one's fate in the next one. Thus, present behaviors are chosen with an eye toward what they are likely to bring about in the next incarnation. Cultures steeped in violence and warring may regard death and battle as unremarkable parts of normal life. In cultures less accustomed to war and violence, elaborate communication rituals convey the extraordinariness of war and violent death.

The traditions of a culture also regulate and order life. Cultures develop traditions that dictate who does what kinds of work, where and how long people work, how much status various jobs have, and how work fits into overall life. These traditions are communicated through cultural institutions (schools, churches, synagogues) and practices (different dress for blue- and white-collar jobs, individual or team structures on the job). In the United States, for instance, people are encouraged to work a lot and to identify themselves and their worth in terms of the work they do. The cultural value attached to work in the United States encourages Americans to put in longer hours at the workplace than members of many cultures. Many Americans even have more than one job. In a number of European countries, workers are required to take generous vacations, and extra jobs are discouraged. Consequently, in the United States, we communicate approval and admiration to individuals who work excessive hours (raises, advancement), whereas in some other societies disapproval would be expressed toward people who work more than 40 or so hours a week. Hendrick, an exchange student from Germany, notes differences between U.S. and German views of work.

Both verbal and nonverbal communication reflect cultural teachings. Here an elder and a young boy wear traditional yarmulkes and partake of unleavened bread and wine as part of a Passover seder.
(© Bill Aron/PhotoEdit)

HENDRICK

Americans are obsessed with work. Most students here work jobs too—sometimes 30 or 40 hours a week. I ask my American friends why they work so hard, and they tell me they need the money for their car or clothes or going out. But it seems to me that they need a car and nice clothes and to go out because they work. If they did not work, they would not need so much of the money that they work to get.

Calendars also reflect cultural traditions by designating days that have significance. In the United States the Fourth of July commemorates America's independence from Britain; in France, Bastille Day celebrates the storming of the Bastille; Eastern societies have a day each year to honor the elderly. National holidays symbolize important moments in a culture's life and remind members of what the culture values. On a less obvious level, cultural norms indicate who has power (more vacation time, larger offices), and cultural calendars define who is in the mainstream of a given society and who is not. Rachael, a young woman who took several of my classes, explains this point.

RACHAEL

It is hard to be Jewish in a Christian society, especially in terms of holidays. For me, Rosh Hashanah and Yom Kippur are high holy days, but they are not holidays on the calendar. Some of my teachers give me grief for missing classes on holy days, and my friends don't accept that I can't go out on Saturday, which is our sacred day. At my job they act like I'm being a slouch and skipping work because my holidays aren't their holidays. They get Christmas and New Year's Day off, but I celebrate Hanukkah, and Rosh Hashanah is the Jewish New Year. And I don't have to tell you why making Easter a national holiday offends Jewish people.

We Learn Culture in the Process of Communicating

We learn a culture's views and patterns in the process of communicating. As we interact with others, we come to understand the beliefs, values, norms, and language of our culture. By observing how others communicate, we learn language (dog) and what it means (a pet to love or a food to eat). This allows us to participate in a social world of shared meanings.

LEARNING TOGETHERNESS

Korean schools teach children to identify with a group. Bathroom breaks are a collective enterprise: All children in a class go to a large room and relieve themselves together (Ferrante, 1995). In the United States, that would be considered at least immodest and perhaps vulgar. The Asian view of personal identity as rooted in larger groups explains why Asians who lose face feel they have humiliated their entire families and communities.

As we know from our discussion of self in Chapter 3, each of us is talked into membership in a society. Newborn babies do not know whether to eat with forks and knives or chopsticks or fingers; they do not know how to dress and whether to decorate parts of their bodies with tattoos or jewelry; they do not know whether and when to smile. Yet, we learn our culture's rules about these and countless other matters in the process of human interaction.

We learn culture in a variety of communication contexts. We learn to respect our elders or not by how we see others communicate with older people and by what we hear others say about elders. We learn what body form is valued by what we see in media and how we hear others talk about people of various physical proportions. Children enter the world without strong gender scripts, but socialization teaches most boys to be masculine and most girls to be feminine (Wood, 1994b).

BOB

It's almost impossible to bring up children in a nonsexist way. My wife and I are really committed to that, so we gave dolls and trucks to both our son and our daughter, and we encouraged both of them at sports and required them both to do household chores. We never emphasized being thin to our daughter or developing muscles to our son, but they learned that anyway. Our 12-year-old came home from school the other day saying she was going on a diet. She's not fat, but she's learned to covet thinness. Every female movie star and singer is skinny, so she gets the culture's message despite what we try to teach her at home.

From the moment of birth, we begin to learn the beliefs, values, norms, and language of our society. Both conscious and unconscious learning are continuous processes through which we internalize the particular ways of life in our culture. By the time we are old enough to appreciate the idea that culture is learned, our cultural perspective and practices are already thoroughly woven into who we are.

Cultures Are Dynamic

The final principle about cultures is that they are **dynamic,** which means they evolve and change over time. Cultures must adapt to the natural world (for example, climate changes) and to human events (such as war), and they must evolve in order to progress. We'll discuss four sources of cultural change.

Invention **Invention** is the creation of tools, ideas, and practices (Samovar & Porter, 1991, p. 59). A frequently cited example of a tool is the wheel, which had far-reaching implications. Not only did invention of the wheel alter modes of transportation, but also it is the foundation for many machines and technologies. Other inventions that have changed cultural life are radio, television, computers, telephones, day-care centers, and automobiles.

Inventions include more than machines. Societies also invent, or create, medicines (antibiotics, polio vaccine, blood pressure medication) and methods of birth control that affect how people see themselves and what kind of lives they live. Medical inventions have dramatically extended the human life span and thereby altered our culture's views of age and of the timing of life events. For example, in the 1800s, when the average life span was around 40 years, people in the United States commonly married and had children while in their teens. Today, the average life span is around 70 years, and many people don't marry until their mid-twenties or early thirties and have children even later. Mid-twenties was middle age in 1900! As life spans lengthen, Western culture faces new challenges, including how to provide care for older citizens and how to enrich retirement. When the average life span was 60 to 65 years, someone who retired at 65 didn't have a long life expectancy. Today, a person who retires at 62 or 65 may have many more years of active life.

A L A N

I'm not working toward a degree, but just taking classes out of interest. I re-tired 5 years ago at 63, and at first it was nice not to have anything I had to do or anywhere I had to go. But then I got bored. After 40 years of being active, I didn't like just sitting around. A lot of my friends feel trapped in retirement. As a society, we haven't figured out how to make the later years satisfying.

Cultures also invent ideas that alter social life. For example, the concept of social diversity is a relatively recent addition to Western thinking. As we learn to recognize and appreciate a variety of cultures, diversity changes how we interact in educational, business, and social contexts. Another concept that has changed Western life is environmental responsibility. Information about our planet's fragility has been infused into cultural consciousness. Terms such as *environmental responsibility* and *environmental ethics* have entered our everyday vocabularies, and they reshape how we see our world and ourselves as stewards of the earth.

In 1991, Anita Hill testified at the hearings to determine whether Clarence Thomas would be allowed to serve on the Supreme Court. Hill's testimony was instrumental in raising public awareness about sexual harassment.
(© Paul Conklin/PhotoEdit)

Diffusion **Diffusion** is borrowing from another culture (Samovar & Porter, 1995). Obvious examples of diffusion are borrowing language and foods from other cultures. What we call English or the American language includes a number of words imported from other cultures. Everyday conversations among Westerners are punctuated with terms such as *brocade, touché,* and *yin-yang.* The Japanese have traditionally enjoyed sushi, which is raw fish. In recent years, many Westerners have tried and liked sushi. Taco Bells and Mandarin Palaces dot Western cities, and McDonalds has franchises throughout the world.

There are also more consequential forms of diffusion—ones that seriously alter a culture's way of life. Jagat Man Lama, a Nepalese leader, studied in India and took back what he learned to his native country. He has taught Nepalese villagers how to build water systems that provide unpolluted water and how to farm without harming the land. Many American businesses have adopted Japanese systems of management to improve working climates and productivity.

Cultural Calamity **Cultural calamity** is adversity that brings about change in a culture. For example, war may devastate a country, destroying land and people alike. Losing a war can alter a culture's self-image, reshaping it into one of conquered people, not victors. Cultural calamity may also involve disasters such as hurricanes, erupting volcanoes, and plagues. Any of these can wipe out countless lives and can alter patterns of life for the future.

The AIDS crisis is a recent example of a calamity that has transformed social activities. Communication that has heightened awareness of HIV/AIDS has altered how heterosexuals, gays, and lesbians think about and engage in romantic and sexual relationships. Traditionally, many gays were less monogamous than lesbians or straight women and men, but the AIDS threat has led to a rise in long-term commitments between gay men (Huston & Schwartz, 1996). The HIV/AIDS crisis also has altered dating and sexual practices among heterosexuals, especially college students (Bowen & Michal-Johnson, 1996).

Communication A fourth source of cultural change is communication. Co-cultures in the United States have used communication to resist the mainstream's efforts to define their identity. Anytime a group says "No, the way you describe Americans doesn't fit me," that group initiates change in the culture's views of itself and those who participate in it.

(© 1993 John Grimes. Reprinted by permission.)

A primary way in which communication propels change is by naming things in ways that shape how we understand them. For instance, the term *date rape* was coined in the late 1980s. Although historically many women had been forced to have sex by men they were dating, until recently there was no term that named what happened as a violent invasion and a criminal act (Wood, 1992b). Similarly, the term *sexual harassment* names a practice that is certainly not new, but only lately has been labeled and given social reality. Myra's commentary explains how important the label is.

MYRA

Fifteen years ago when I was just starting college, a professor sexually harassed me, only I didn't know to call it that then. I felt guilty, like maybe I'd done something to encourage him, or I felt maybe I was overreacting to his kissing me and touching me. But after the Thomas–Hill hearings in 1991, I had a name for what happened—a name that said he was wrong, not me. Only then could I let go of that whole business.

As a primary tool of social movements, communication impels significant changes in cultural life. Thirty years ago, the civil rights movement in the United States used communication to transform public laws and, gradually, public views of African Americans. Powerful speakers such as the Reverend Martin Luther King, Jr., and Malcolm X raised black Americans' pride in their identity and heritage and inspired them to demand their rights in Western culture. Simultaneously, African American leaders used communication to persuade the nonblack public to rethink its attitudes and practices. Language also reflects changes in cultural attitudes and practices. For example, the terms *boyfriend* and *girlfriend* are no longer the only ones people use to identify romantic interests; *partner, significant other,* and *special friend* are among the newer terms created to define romantic relations today.

In addition to bringing about change directly, communication also accompanies other sources of cultural change. Inventions such as antibiotics had to be explained to medical practitioners and to a general public that believed infections were caused by fate and accident, not viruses and bacteria. Ideas and practices borrowed from other cultures must similarly be translated into the language and culture of a particular society. Cultural calamities, too, must be defined and explained: Did the volcano erupt because of pressure in the earth or the anger of the gods? Did we lose the war because we had a weak military or because our cause was wrong? The ways a culture defines and communicates about calamities establish what these events mean and imply for future social practices and social life.

In sum, we've seen that cultures and co-cultures are distinct ways of life that order personal identity and social activities. Five principles about cultures capture the main points we've covered. First, communication is a primary way that cultures are expressed and sustained. Second, cultures consist of material and nonmaterial components, including beliefs, values, norms, and language. Third, all cultures are shaped by historical and geographic forces that are carried forward through oral traditions and other forms of communication among members of a culture. The fourth principle emphasizes that culture is learned in the process of communicating with others: We are talked into membership in a society. Finally, we saw that cultures continuously change in response to inventions, diffusion, calamities, and communication that challenges the status quo and argues for new ideas, roles, and patterns of life. We're now ready to consider guidelines for effective communication between members of cultures and co-cultures.

IMPROVING COMMUNICATION BETWEEN CULTURES

So far we've seen that a culture's beliefs, values, and norms are reflected in the content and style of its communication. Each of us acts, speaks, and interprets others from the distinct perspective of the cultures with which we identify. As long as we interact with others in our own culture we're likely to share understandings of how to communicate and interpret one another. When we encounter people from other cultures and co-cultures, however, we can't count on shared guidelines. Thus, misunderstandings often occur. Although we can't eliminate misunderstandings, we can minimize them and the damage they can cause. Let's consider two principles for effective communication between members of different cultures and co-cultures.

Resist the Ethnocentric Bias

Most of us unreflectively use our home culture as the standard for judging other cultures. European Americans may regard African American rapping and styling as noisy and theatrical, because those forms of communication are more dramatic than ones they typically use. On the other hand, African Americans may perceive European Americans as stodgy and cold because their communication is relatively restrained (Houston, 1994). Asians may regard European Americans as rude for maintaining direct eye contact, whereas European Americans may perceive Asians as evasive for averting their eyes. Westerners' habitual self-references may appear selfish and egocentric to Koreans, and Koreans may seem passive to Westerners. How we judge others depends more on the perspective we use to judge than on what others say and do.

Although it is natural to use our own culture as the standard for judging other cultures, this tendency interferes with understanding and communication. **Ethnocentrism** is the tendency to regard ourselves and our way of life as superior to other people and other ways of life. Literally, ethnocentrism means to put our own ethnicity (ethno) at the center (centrism) of the universe. Ethnocentrism encourages negative judgments of anything that differs from our own ways. In extreme form, ethnocentrism can lead one group of people to think it has the right to dominate and exploit other groups and to suppress other cultures. The most abhorrent example of extreme ethnocentrism was when the Nazi Germans declared themselves the "master race" and engaged in systematic genocide of Jewish people and others. Years later, the Chinese forced the Tibetans out of their homeland and into exile, where they remain today.

Yet we need not look to dramatic examples like Nazi Germany to find ethnocentrism. Sadly, it is a part of everyday experience. It occurs anytime we judge someone from a different culture as less sensitive, ambitious, good, or civilized than people from our culture. It is ethnocentric for Caucasians to judge African Americans as "putting on airs" when they engage in styling, since in their co-culture styling is a way of defining a powerful and positive self-image. Likewise, it is ethnocentric to look down on a Taiwanese for being unassertive, since deferential behaviors show politeness and respect in Taiwanese culture.

To reduce ethnocentrism, we should remember that culture is learned. What is considered normal and right varies among cultures. One way to acknowledge differences among cultures without judging them negatively is to adopt the perspective of **cultural relativism,** which recognizes that cultures vary in how they think, act, and behave, as well as in what they believe and value.

Cultural relativism is not the same as moral relativism. It is possible to acknowledge that a particular practice makes sense in its cultural context without approving of it. We may condemn clitoridectomies performed on young girls in some countries and also realize that genital surgery is rooted in long-standing traditions that have meaning in particular societies. Cultural relativism helps us remember that something that appears odd or even wrong to us may seem natural and right from the point of view of a different culture. That awareness facilitates understanding between people of different cultures and co-cultures.

Recognize That Responding to Diversity Is a Process

Developing skill in intercultural communication takes time. We don't move suddenly from being unaware of how people in other cultures interact to being totally comfortable and competent in talking with them. Dealing with diversity is a gradual process that requires time, experience with a variety of people, and a genuine desire to be part of a society that includes a range of people and communication styles. Five distinct responses to diversity range from total rejection to complete acceptance:

The Process of Responding to Multiple Cultures

Resistance
Tolerance
Understanding
Respect
Participation

At particular times in our lives, we may find ourselves adopting different responses to diversity or to specific forms of diversity. That's natural in the overall process of recognizing and responding to diversity in life.

Resistance   A common response to diversity is **resistance,** which occurs when we attack the cultural practices of others or proclaim that our own cultural traditions are superior. Resistance defies the value and validity of anything that differs from what is familiar (Berger, 1969). Without education or reflection, many people deal with diversity by making ethnocentric evaluations of others based on the standards of their own culture. Some individuals think their judgments reflect universal truths about what is normal and right. They aren't aware that they are imposing the arbitrary yardstick of their own particular culture and ignoring the yardsticks of other cultures. Judgment leads us to devalue whatever differs from our own ways. Thus, it limits human experience and understanding.

Resistance may be expressed in many ways. Hate crimes pollute campuses and the broader society. Defiance of other cultures fuels racial slurs, anti-Semitic messages, and homophobic threats. Resistance may also motivate members of a culture or co-culture to associate only with each other and to resist recognizing any commonalities with people from other cultures or co-cultures. Insulation within a single culture occurs in members of both majority and minority groups.

Members of minority groups may also resist and defy their native culture in order to fit into the mainstream. **Assimilation** occurs when people give up their own ways and take on the ways of the dominant culture. Philosopher Peter Berger (1969) calls this surrendering, since it involves giving up an original cultural identity for a new one. For many years, assimilation was the dominant response of immigrants to the United States. The idea of America as a "melting pot" encouraged newcomers to melt into the mainstream by surrendering any ways that made them different from native-born Americans. More recently, the melting pot metaphor has been criticized as undesirable because it robs individuals of their unique heritages. The Reverend Jesse Jackson proposed the alternative metaphor of "the family quilt." This metaphor portrays the United States as a country in which people's unique values and customs are visible, as are the individual squares in a quilt; at the same time, each group contributes to a larger whole, just as each square in a quilt contributes to its overall beauty.

Tolerance   A second response to diversity is **tolerance** in which a person accepts differences, although she or he may not approve of or even understand them. Toleration involves respecting others' rights to their own ways even though you may think their ways are wrong, bad, or offensive. Judgment still exists, but it's not actively imposed on others. Tolerance is open-minded in accepting the existence of differences, yet it is less open-minded in perceiving the value of alternative lifestyles and values. Although tolerance is less actively divisive than resistance, it is insufficient to foster a community in which people appreciate diversity and learn to grow from encountering differences.

CHUCK

Until I came to college I didn't know anyone who was gay. My parents taught me it was immoral, and I'd never questioned that. In my freshman year, I was good friends with Jim until he told me he was gay. I dropped him flat. Later I found out that a guy on my floor was gay, and this year two of my brothers at the house came out. I still don't really approve, but it doesn't bother me so much now.

Understanding   A third response to diversity involves **understanding** that differences are rooted in cultural teachings and that no customs, traditions, or behaviors are intrinsically better than any others. This response builds on the idea of cultural relativism, which we discussed earlier. Rather than assuming whatever differs from our ways is a deviation from a universal standard (ours), a person who understands realizes that diverse values, beliefs, norms, and communication styles are rooted in distinct cultural perspectives. A person who responds to diversity with understanding might notice that a Japanese person doesn't hold eye contact, but he or she wouldn't assume that the Japanese person was devious. Instead, she or he would try to learn what eye contact means in Japanese society in order to understand the behavior in its native cultural context. Curiosity, rather than judgment, dominates in this stage as we make active efforts to understand others in terms of the values and traditions of their cultures.

Respect   Once we move beyond judgment and begin to understand the cultural basis for ways that diverge from our own, we may come to **respect** differences. We can appreciate the distinct validity and value of styling, placing family above self, arranged marriage, and feminine and masculine communication styles. We don't have to adopt others' ways for ourselves in order to respect them on their own terms. Respect allows us to acknowledge genuine differences among groups, yet remain anchored

Communicating with people who differ from us fosters personal growth. (© Bob Daemmrich/Tony Stone Images, Inc.)

in the values and customs of our own culture (Simons, Vázquez, & Harris, 1993). Learning about people who differ from us increases our understanding of them and, thus, our ability to communicate effectively with them. Respect for others requires the ability to see them and what they do on their own terms, not ours. In other words, respect avoids ethnocentrism.

Participation   A final response to diversity is **participation** in which we incorporate some of the practices and values of other groups into our own lives. More than other responses, participation encourages us to develop skills for taking part in a multicultural world in which all of us can share in some of each other's customs. Henry Louis Gates (1992), a Harvard professor, believes that the ideal is a society in which we build a common civic culture that celebrates both differences and commonalities.

Participation calls for us to be **multilingual,** which means we are able to speak and think in more than one language. Members of co-cultures already are at least bilingual: African Americans know how to operate in mainstream Caucasian society and in their own, distinct ethnic communities (Orbe, 1994). Most women know how to communicate in both feminine and masculine ways, and they adapt their style to the people with whom they interact (Henley, 1977). Bilingualism is also practiced by many Asian Americans, Mexican Americans, lesbians and gays, and members of other groups that are simultaneously part of a dominant and minority culture (Gaines, 1995).

My partner, Robbie, and I have learned how to communicate in both feminine and masculine styles. He was socialized to be assertive, competitive, instrumental, and analytical in conversation, while I learned to be more deferential, cooperative, relational, and creative. When we were first married, we often frustrated each other with our different ways of talking. I perceived him as domineering, sometimes insensitive to feelings, and overly analytical in his conversational style. He perceived me as being too focused on relationship issues and inefficient in moving from problems to solutions. Gradually, each of us learned to understand the other's ways of communicating and to respect our differences without judging them by our own standards. Still later we came to appreciate and participate in each other's style so that now both of us are fluent in both languages. This not only has improved communication between us, but also has made each of us more competent communicators in general.

Not everyone will go through the entire process of developing skills for participating in a multicultural world. Some of us will become proficient at understanding, but will not move to respect or participation. Also, we may reach different stages in our ability to respond to particular cultures. For example, I haven't developed real skill in African American rapping, but I have learned to use masculine modes of communicating. The different responses to cultural diversity that we've discussed represent parts of a process of learning to interact with cultural groups other than our own. In the course of our lives, many of us will move in and out of various responses as we interact with people from multiple cultures. At specific times we may find we are tolerant of one cultural group and respectful of another, and those responses may change over time.

SUMMARY

In this chapter, we've learned about the close connections between communication and cultures. Cultures and co-cultures are ways of life that are expressed, altered, and sometimes changed by communication. The ways that we speak and behave nonverbally reflect our culture's values and norms and, at the same time, our communication sustains those values and norms and the perception that they are natural and right. In elaborating this view of culture, we saw that cultures consist of both material and nonmaterial components, they are shaped by historical and geographic forces, they are learned through socialization, and they are dynamic—always evolving and changing. The final section of the chapter emphasized the importance of learning to communicate effectively in a multicultural society in which no one way is shared by all. Ethnocentrism and judgment are the twin dangers to effective cross-cultural communication. Moving beyond narrow judgments based on our own culture allows us to understand, respect, and sometimes participate in a diverse world and to enlarge ourselves in the process.

In this chapter, we've focused on differences between cultures and people in them. We need to understand how we differ from one another if we are to communicate effectively and if we are to live and work together in a diverse social world. Yet, it would be a mistake to be so aware of differences that we overlook our commonalities. No matter what culture we belong to, we all have feelings, dreams, ideas, hopes, fears, and values. Our common humanness transcends many of our differences, an idea beautifully expressed in a poem by Maya Angelou (1990, p. 5).

Human Family

I note the obvious differences
between each sort and type,
but we are more alike, my friends
than we are unalike.
We are more alike my friends
than we are unalike.

FOR FURTHER REFLECTION AND DISCUSSION

1. Some scholars claim that there are many co-cultures in the United States. Examples are deaf people, persons with disabilities, and elderly people. Do you agree that these groups qualify as distinct co-cultures? What is required for a group to be considered a co-culture?

2. Continue the exercise started on page 186 by listing common sayings or adages in your culture. For each saying, decide what it reflects about the beliefs, values, and concerns of your culture.

3. Attend a meeting of a cultural or co-cultural group different from your own. Notice patterns of verbal and nonverbal communication, and describe what they suggest about the culture or co-culture's character.

4. Consider metaphors for U.S. society. For many years, it was described as "the melting pot," a metaphor that suggested all of the differences among people from various cultures would be melted down and merged into a uniform culture. In recent years,

however, the idea of a melting pot has been criticized for trying to obliterate differences, rather than respect them. The Reverend Jesse Jackson refers to the United States as a "family quilt," while others say it's a collage or a rainbow in which differences exist and are noted as parts of the overall, diverse society. Flora Davis (1991) calls the United States a "salad bowl." What do you think she means by the metaphor of salad bowl? What metaphor would you recommend?

5. As a class, discuss the tension between recognizing individuality and noting patterns common in specific social groups. Is it possible simultaneously to realize that people have standpoints in social groups and that members of any group vary? You might recall the concept of totalizing from Chapter 5 to assist your consideration of this issue.

KEY TERMS

culture	ethnocentrism
co-cultures	cultural relativism
beliefs	resistance
values	assimilation
norms	tolerance
dynamic	understanding
invention	respect
diffusion	participation
cultural calamity	multilingual

PART TWO

Contexts
of Communication

Focus Questions

1 How does communication create interpersonal climates in relationships?

2 Is conflict healthy in relationships?

3 How can we assert ourselves while respecting others?

4 Is self-disclosure always constructive?

CHAPTER 8

Foundations of Interpersonal Communication

You have scheduled a performance review with your co-worker, Jenette. You need to call her attention to some problems in her work while also communicating that you support her and value her in the company.

You know your neighbor Steve is worried about losing his job because his company has announced it will make substantial layoffs. You want to let him know it's safe for him to open up to you.

You're concerned about reports of drugs at the school your 13-year-old son attends. You want to warn him about the dangers of drugs without making him feel you're judging him. Also, you want to establish open lines of communication between the two of you so that he can talk to you about drugs and other issues.

Disclosing private thoughts and feelings tends to enhance close-ness. (© Mark Antman/The Image Works)

In each of these scenarios, achieving your goals depends on your ability to create an effective context for communication. Offering criticism in a supportive manner, encouraging others to disclose private feelings, and establishing open lines of communication are likely only if you first cultivate a climate that fosters openness and trust between people.

Communication climate is the overall feeling between people. Perhaps you feel foggy-headed or down when the sky is overcast and upbeat when it's sunny. Does your mood ever shift as the weather changes? Do you respond differently to the different seasons? Most of us are affected by aspects of the physical climate. In much the same way external climates influence how we feel, interpersonal climates affect how we communicate with others. We feel on guard when a supervisor is angry, when a co-worker is in a stormy mood, and when a friend seems to attack us. In each case, the communication climate is clouded over.

Interpersonal climate is an important foundation of effective communication in all contexts. On the job we need to know how to create supportive, productive climates that foster good work relationships and outcomes. In social relationships, we hope to build climates that allow us and others to feel at ease. In personal relationships, we try to develop climates that allow us to disclose private feelings and thoughts without fear of criticism or ridicule. Thus, interpersonal climate is important in a range of communication contexts.

This chapter focuses on climate as a cornerstone of effective communication in all relationships. We'll begin by discussing self-disclosure, a form of communication that can promote an open climate of communication if it is used appropriately. Next, we'll discuss various climates and the specific kinds of communication that foster each one. Third, we'll consider the role of conflict in relationships, and we'll see that creating healthy climates and using communication skills help us manage conflict constructively. The final section of the chapter identifies guidelines for creating and sustaining healthy interpersonal climates. To extend this chapter's discussion of foundations for interpersonal communication, Chapter 9 will explore communication in two particularly important relationships—close friendships and romantic intimacy.

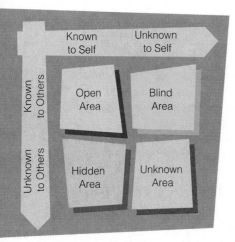

FIGURE 8.1
The Johari Window

SELF-DISCLOSURE

Self-disclosure is revealing personal information about ourselves that others are unlikely to discover in other ways. We self-disclose when we express private hopes and fears, reveal personal feelings, and share experiences, perceptions, and events that are private. Although we don't reveal our private selves to everyone and don't do it a great deal of the time even with intimates, self-disclosure is an important kind of communication.

Self-disclosure has notable values. First, sharing personal feelings, thoughts, and experiences often enhances closeness between people. By extension, when others understand our private selves, they may be more sensitive in responding to us as unique individuals. Self-disclosing also tends to invite others to self-disclose, so we may learn more about them. Finally, self-disclosure can affect what we know about ourselves and how we feel about who we are. For example, if we reveal a weakness or an incident of which we're ashamed and another person accepts the disclosure without judging us negatively, we may find it easier to accept ourselves.

Self-Disclosure and Personal Growth

A number of years ago, Joseph Luft and Harry Ingham created a model that describes different kinds of knowledge related to individual growth as the development of relationships with others (Luft, 1969). They called the model the Johari Window (Figure 8.1), which is a combination of their first names, Joe and Harry.

Four types of information are relevant to the self. Open, or public, information is known to both us and others. Your name, height, major, and tastes in music are probably free information that you share easily with others. Our co-workers and casual acquaintances often know information about us that is in our open area.

The blind area contains information that others know about us, but we don't know about ourselves. For example, others may see that we are insecure even though we think we've concealed that well. Others may also recognize needs or feelings that we haven't acknowledged to ourselves. Co-workers and supervisors may recognize strengths, weaknesses, and potentials in us of which we are unaware.

The third area in the Johari Window includes hidden information, which we know about ourselves but choose not to reveal to most others. You might not tell many people about your vulnerabilities or about traumas in your past because you consider this private information. You might not reveal blemishes in your work history to employers.

The unknown area is made up of information about ourselves that neither we nor others know. This consists of your untapped resources, untried talents, and unknown reactions to experiences you've never had. You don't know how you will manage a crisis until you've been in one; you can't tell what kind of parent you would be unless you've had a child; you don't know whether you have managerial aptitudes until you are in a management role.

Because a healthy self-concept requires knowledge of yourself, it's important to gain access to information in your blind and unknown areas. One way to do this is to expand your experiences by entering unfamiliar situations, trying novel things, and experimenting with new kinds of communication. Another way to increase self-knowledge is to share self-perceptions with others and learn how they see you. We can gain insight into ourselves by reflecting on others' perceptions. Self-disclosure, then, is one means to learn about ourselves and to enhance personal growth.

Self-Disclosure and Closeness

According to researchers, self-disclosure is a key gauge of closeness, especially among Westerners (Derlega & Berg, 1987; Hansen & Schuldt, 1984). Self-disclosure should take place gradually and with appropriate caution. It's unwise to tell anyone too much about ourselves too quickly, especially if revelations could be used against us. We begin by disclosing relatively superficial information ("I haven't had any experience in this kind of assignment," "I'm from a small town," "I'm afraid of heights"). If a person responds with acceptance to early and limited disclosures, we're likely to reveal progressively intimate information ("My father served time in prison," "I'm not very skillful at reprimanding people for poor work," "I'm having marital difficulties right now"). If these disclosures are also met with understanding and confidentiality, trust and interest in further communication continue to grow.

(John Ahearn, *Janel and Audrey* (1983). Acrylic on plaster, 32 × 32 × 9". Photograph © D. James Dee. Courtesy Alexander and Bonin, N.Y.)

JAN

Josh and I have been married for 15 years. At first we shared a lot of personal information and private thoughts with each other, but we don't do that much now. Yet, I feel so close to Josh because he knows me in ways no one else does. All the experiences and feelings we shared earlier help us understand the significance of things that happen now. We don't even have to talk because we know layers and layers of each other.

In the early stages of relationship development, reciprocity of disclosures seems important. If you mention a personal weakness to a new acquaintance, you'll be more comfortable if the other person responds by describing some weakness she or he has. Most of us are willing to keep disclosing to a person we don't know well only if the other person also reveals personal information (Cunningham, Strassberg, & Haan, 1986). The need to match disclosures recedes in importance once trust is established. Partners in stable relationships don't feel the need to reciprocate

DIFFERENT MODES OF CLOSENESS

Research indicates that women generally disclose more frequently and more deeply than men. Until recently, this difference was interpreted to mean that men are less interested in or comfortable with intimacy. Recent work suggests, however, that the sexes may not differ in how much they value closeness, but they create it in different ways.

Feminine communication cultures emphasize using personal talk to create and sustain closeness. Thus, in general, women learn to disclose personal thoughts and feelings as a primary way of enhancing intimacy. This is called *closeness in dialogue*.

Because masculine communication cultures place less emphasis on personal talk, men typically don't regard intimate conversation and self-disclosure as primary paths to closeness. Instead, they usually learn to bond with others through doing things together. Their mode is called *closeness in the doing*.

The two ways of expressing and experiencing closeness are equally valid, yet different modes of intimacy.

Source: Wood, J. T., & Inman, C. C. (1993). In a different mode: Masculine styles of communicating closeness. *Journal of Applied Communication Research, 21,* 279–295.

disclosures immediately. Unlike beginning acquaintances, they have the time to reciprocate on a more leisurely schedule. Thus, disclosure between established friends or work associates is more likely to be greeted with a response to what has been revealed than with an equivalent disclosure. Of course, there are exceptions to these general patterns. People vary in how much they want to self-disclose, so an absolute amount of disclosure is not a sure-fire measure of closeness. Also, people vary in their perceptions of the link between disclosure and intimacy, so we need to respect individual differences.

Although self-disclosing is important early in relationships, it is not a primary communication dynamic in most enduring relationships. When we're first getting to know a colleague, friend, or intimate partner, we have to reveal ourselves and learn about her or him, so disclosures are necessary and desirable. In relationships that endure over time, however, disclosures make up very little of the total communication between partners. Although disclosure wanes over time, partners continue to reap the benefits of the trust and depth of personal knowledge created by early disclosures. Also, partners do continue to disclose new experiences and insights to one another; it's just that there is less disclosure as a relationship matures.

When a friendship, romance, or close working relationship wanes, typically there are decreases in the depth of disclosures. Diminished self-disclosures may be regarded as an indication that intimacy is fading (Baxter, 1987). We are reluctant to entrust others with our secrets and personal emotions when we no longer want closeness or when we sense the other is pulling away.

Men often prefer a side-by-side style of friendship where closeness is expressed through doing things together, such as fishing.
(© IPA/The Image Works)

SID

For 3 years Tom and I worked together, and we were really close. We'd even talked about starting up our own company and being partners. Tom and I knew everything about each other, and it was easy to talk about anything, even problems or failures, with him. But last year he stopped talking about himself. At first I didn't notice and just kept telling him what was going on with me, but then I got to feel kind of awkward—like it was one way and I was more exposed than he was. I asked Tom if anything was wrong and he said no, but he didn't talk to me like he used to. Finally, I found out he was working with another guy to start a franchise. When he stopped talking openly with me, it was a signal that our relationship was over.

Appropriate self-disclosure is an important communication skill. It fosters closeness with others, insight into ourselves, and knowledge of others. Self-disclosure is one form of communication that cultivates openness and comfort between people. To understand more fully how we shape the contexts of interaction, we turn now to a discussion of communication climate.

COMMUNICATION CLIMATE

Communication climate is the overall feeling or emotional mood between individuals. Communication climate isn't something we can see or measure objectively, and it isn't just the sum of what people do together. Instead, climate is the dominant feeling between individuals. In interacting in some situations and with some people, we feel tense and on guard, and we are inclined to defend ourselves and criticize the other. In other interactions, we feel comfortable, at ease, and friendly.

Perhaps the greatest single influence on communication climate is the extent to which people feel confirmed. The philosopher Martin Buber (1957, 1970) believed that each of us needs confirmation to be healthy and to grow. Buber also emphasized that full humanness can develop only when people confirm others and are confirmed by them. The essence of confirmation is valuing. We all want to feel we are valued, especially by our intimates. When others confirm us, we feel cherished and respected. When they disconfirm us, we feel discounted and less good about ourselves.

FIGURE 8.2
Continuum of Interpersonal Climates

Interpersonal climates exist on a continuum from confirming to disconfirming (Figure 8.2). Of course, few relationships are purely confirming or disconfirming. In reality, most fall between the two end-points of the continuum. In these, some communication is confirming while other messages are disconfirming, or communication cycles between being basically confirming and basically disconfirming.

Levels of Confirmation and Disconfirmation

Communication scholars have extended insight into confirming and disconfirming climates (Cissna & Sieburg, 1986). They have identified specific kinds of communication that confirm or disconfirm others on three levels (see Table 8.1). The most basic form of confirmation is recognition that another person exists. We do this with nonverbal behaviors (offering a smile, hug, or handshake; maintaining eye contact when speaking in public; looking up when someone enters our office) and verbal communication ("Hello," "Good to meet you," "I see you're home"). We disconfirm others at a fundamental level when we don't acknowledge their existence. For example, you might not speak to or look at a person when you enter a room or might not look at a teammate who comes late to a meeting. Not responding to another's comments also disconfirms his or her presence. Parents who punish a child by refusing to speak to her or him disconfirm the child's existence. In Chapter 6, we discussed "the silent treatment" as a way to disconfirm another's existence.

REGGIE

Any African American knows what it means to have your existence denied. The law may forbid segregation now, but it still exists. When I go to an upscale restaurant, sometimes people just look away. They ignore me, like I'm not there. I've even been ignored by waits in restaurants. This is especially true in the South where a lot of whites still don't want us in their clubs and schools.

A second and more positive level of confirmation is **acknowledgment** of what another feels, thinks, or says. Nonverbally we acknowledge others by nodding our heads or by making strong eye contact to indicate we are listening. Verbal acknowledgments are direct responses to others' communication. If a friend says, "I'm really worried that I blew the LSAT exam," you could acknowledge that by responding, "So you're scared that you didn't test well on it, huh?" This is a paraphrasing response, which we discussed in Chapter 2. It acknowledges both the thoughts and the feelings of the other person. If a co-worker tells you, "I'm not sure I have the experience to handle this assignment," you could acknowledge that disclosure by saying, "Sounds as if you feel this is a real challenge."

TABLE 8.1 Levels of Confirmation and Disconfirmation

	Confirming Messages	Disconfirming Messages
Recognition	You exist. "Hello."	You don't exist. Silence
Acknowledgment	You matter to me. We have a relationship. "I'm sorry you're hurt."	You don't matter. We are not a team. "You'll get over it."
Endorsement	What you think is true. What you feel is okay. "I feel the same way."	You are wrong. You shouldn't feel what you do. "Your feeling doesn't make sense."

We disconfirm others when we don't acknowledge their feelings or thoughts. For instance, if you responded to your friend's statement about the LSAT by saying, "Want to go out and throw some darts tonight?" that would be an irrelevant response that ignores the friend's comment. It also disconfirms another when we deny the feelings she or he communicates: "You did fine on the LSAT" or "Oh, don't worry—you'll handle the assignment fine."

LISA

I'm amazed by how often people won't acknowledge what I tell them. A hundred times I've been walking across campus and someone's come up and offered to guide me. I tell them I know the way and don't need help, and they still put an arm under my elbow to guide me. I may be blind, but there's nothing wrong with my mind. I know if I need help. Why can't others acknowledge that?

Lisa makes an important point. We shouldn't assume we know more than others about what they want or need. To disregard another's statements is to disconfirm him or her. You may recall that in previous chapters we've cautioned against speaking for others. It is fundamentally disconfirming to have others deny us our own voices.

The final level of confirmation is **endorsement.** Endorsement involves accepting another's feelings or thoughts as valid. You could endorse the friend who is worried about the LSAT by saying, "It's natural to be worried about the LSAT when you have so much riding on it." We disconfirm others when we don't accept their thoughts and feelings. For example, it would be disconfirming to say, "How can you worry about whether you can do this assignment when so many people are being laid off? You should be glad to have a job." This response rejects the validity of the other person's expressed feelings and is likely to close the lines of communication between the two of you.

GUIDELINES FOR COMMUNICATING WITH PERSONS WITH DISABILITIES

1. When talking with someone who has a disability, speak directly to the person, not to a companion or an interpreter.

2. When introduced to a person with a disability, offer to shake hands. People who have limited hand use or who have artificial limbs can usually shake.

3. When meeting a person with a visual impairment, identify yourself and anyone who is with you. If a person with a visual impairment is part of a group, preface comments to him or her with a name.

4. You may offer assistance, but don't provide it unless your offer is accepted. Then ask the person how you can best assist (ask for instructions).

5. Treat adults as adults. Don't patronize people in wheelchairs by patting them on the shoulder or head; don't use childish language when speaking to individuals who have no mental disability.

6. Respect the personal space of persons with disabilities. It is rude to lean on a wheelchair, since that is part of a person's personal territory.

7. Listen mindfully when talking with someone who has difficulty speaking.

Don't interrupt or supply words to others. Just be patient and let them finish. Don't pretend to understand if you don't. Instead, explain what you understood and ask the person to respond.

8. When you talk with persons who use a wheelchair or crutches, try to position yourself at their eye level and in front of them to allow good eye contact.

9. It is appropriate to wave your hand or tap the shoulder of persons with hearing impairments as a way to get their attention. Look directly at the person and speak slowly, clearly, and expressively. Face those who lip read, face a good light source, and keep hands, cigarettes, and gum away from your mouth.

10. Relax. Don't be afraid to use common expressions such as "See you later" to someone with a visual impairment or "Did you hear the news?" to someone with hearing difficulty. They're unlikely to be offended and may turn the irony into a joke.

Source: Adapted from AXIS Center for Public Awareness of People with Disabilities, 4550 Indianola Avenue, Columbus, OH 43214.

As our discussion suggests, confirmation and disconfirmation occur on levels. The most essential confirmation we can give is to recognize that another exists. Conversely, the most basic kind of disconfirmation is to ignore another's existence. When we don't speak to others or look away when they approach us, we disconfirm their very presence. We say, "You aren't there." On the second level, we confirm others by acknowledging their ideas and feelings, which carries the relational level meaning that they matter to us. In essence, we say, "I am paying attention because your feelings and ideas matter to me." We disconfirm others on this level when we

Most people, including those with disabilities, like to communicate at eye level with others.
(© Peter L. Chapman)

communicate that they don't matter to us, that we don't care what they feel or think. The highest form of confirmation is acceptance of others and what they communicate. We feel validated when others accept us as we are and what we think and feel. Disconfirmation is not mere disagreement. Disagreements, after all, can be productive and healthy, and they imply that people matter enough to each other to argue. It is disconfirming to be told that we or our ideas are crazy, wrong, stupid, or deviant.

WAYNE

I've gotten a lot of disconfirmation since I came out. When I told my parents I was gay, Mom said, "No, you're not." I told her I was, and she and Dad both said I was just confused, but I wasn't gay. They refuse to acknowledge I'm gay, which means they reject me. My older brother isn't any better. His view is that being gay is a sin against God. Now what could be more disconfirming than that?

When we understand that confirmation is basic for all of us and that it is given or withheld on different levels, we gain insight into relationships. If you think about what we've discussed, you'll probably find that the relationships in which you feel most valued and comfortable are ones with a high degree of confirmation.

Everyday Application

ANALYZE YOUR RELATIONSHIPS

Think about two relationships in your life. One should be a relationship in which you feel good about yourself and accepted by the other person. The second relationship should be one in which you feel disregarded or not valued. Identify instances of each level of confirmation in the satisfying relationship, and instances of each level of disconfirmation in the unpleasant one. Recognizing confirming and disconfirming communication should give you insight into why these relationships are so different.

Confirming and disconfirming messages are one important influence on the climate of personal relationships. In addition, other kinds of communication contribute to the overall feeling of a relationship. We'll now consider specific forms of communication that shape the interpersonal atmosphere between friends and romantic partners.

(Reprinted by permission of United Feature Syndicate, Inc.)

DEFENSIVE AND SUPPORTIVE CLIMATES

Communication researcher Jack Gibb (1961, 1964, 1970) studied the relationship between communication and interpersonal climates. He began by noting that in some relationships we feel defensive and on guard while in others we feel safe and supported. To understand how communication contributes to these two interpersonal climates, Gibb identified six types of communication that promote defensive climates and six contrasting types of communication that foster supportive climates.

Evaluation Versus Description

We tend to become defensive when we believe others are evaluating us. Few of us feel what Gibb called "psychologically safe" when we are the targets of judgments. Other communication researchers report that evaluative communication evokes defensiveness (Eadie, 1982; Stephenson & D'Angelo, 1973). It's not surprising that Wayne in the last commentary felt judged by his family when he told them he was gay. His parents and brother made evaluations—very negative ones of him and of gayness. Even positive evaluations may provoke defensiveness, since they imply that another person feels entitled to judge us. Examples of evaluative statements are "You have no discipline," "It's dumb to feel that way," "I approve," "You shouldn't have done that," "You did the right thing," and "That's a stupid idea."

Descriptive communication doesn't evaluate others or what they think and feel. Instead, it describes behaviors without passing judgment. I-language, which we learned about in Chapter 2, describes what the person speaking feels or thinks, but it doesn't evaluate another (you-language does evaluate). For example, "I wish you hadn't done that" describes your feelings, whereas "You shouldn't have done that" evaluates another's behavior. Descriptive language may also refer to another, but it does so by describing, not evaluating, the other's behavior. For example: "You seem to be sleeping more lately" (versus "You're sleeping too much"). "You've shouted three times today" (versus "Quit flying off the handle"). "You are running late" (versus "You shouldn't have kept me waiting").

Everyday Application

USING DESCRIPTIVE LANGUAGE

To develop skill in supportive communication, translate the following evaluative statements into descriptive ones.

Evaluative	*Descriptive*
This report is poorly done.	This report doesn't include background information.
You're lazy.	_____
I hate the way you dominate conversations with me.	_____
Stop obsessing about the problem.	_____
You're too involved.	_____

Certainty Versus Provisionalism

Language characterized by certainty is absolute and often dogmatic. It suggests there is one and only one answer, valid point of view, or reasonable course of action. Because communication laced with certainty proclaims an absolutely correct position, it slams the door on further discussion. Leaders can stifle creativity and team cohesion if they express certainty about what the team should generate or which approaches to teamwork are best. There's no point in talking with people whose minds are made up and who demean any point of view other than their own. Certainty is also communicated when people restate their own positions in response to others' ideas.

One form of communication characterized by certainty is ethnocentrism, which we discussed in Chapter 7. Ethnocentrism is an attitude based on the assumption that our culture and its norms are THE only right ones. For instance, someone who says "It is just plain rude to call out during a sermon" doesn't understand the meaning of the call–response pattern in African culture. The speaker instead assumes that the European American communication style is the only correct one. Dogmatically asserting "It's disrespectful to be late" reveals a lack of awareness of cultures that

Closed-mindedness fosters defensiveness in others.
(© Anne Dowie)

are less obsessed with speed and efficiency than the United States. Certainty is also evident when we say "This is the only idea that makes sense." "My mind can't be changed because I'm right." "Only a fool would vote for that person." "There's no point in discussing it further."

MONIKA

My father is a classic case of closed-mindedness. He has his ideas and everything else is crazy. I told him I was majoring in communication studies, and he hit the roof. He said there was no future in learning to write speeches and told me I should go into business so that I could get a good job. He never asked me to describe communication studies. If he had, I would have told him it's a lot more than speech writing. He starts off sure that he knows everything about whatever is being discussed. He has no interest in exploring other points of view or learning something new. He just locks his mind and throws away the key. We've all learned just to keep our ideas to ourselves around him—there's no communication.

An alternative to certainty is provisionalism, which communicates openness to other points of view and criticism of an expressed view. When we speak provisionally, or tentatively, we suggest we have a point of view, yet our minds aren't sealed. We signal that we're willing to consider alternative positions, and this encourages others to voice their ideas. Provisional communication includes statements such as "The way I tend to see the issue is . . . " "One way to look at this is . . . " "It's possible that . . . " "Probably what I would do in that situation is . . . " Notice how each of these comments signals that the speaker realizes there could be other positions that are also reasonable. Tentative communication reflects an open mind, which is why it invites continued conversation.

Strategy Versus Spontaneity

Most of us feel on guard when we think others are manipulating us or being less than up-front about what's on their minds. Defensiveness is a natural response to feeling that others are using strategies in an effort to control us. As we have seen in previous chapters, effective communication requires thought, planning, and efforts to adapt to others so that we can share meaning. Strategic communication, in contrast, does not have the goal of sharing meaning with another. Quite the contrary: It aims to manipulate one person by keeping motives or intentions hidden (Eadie,

1982). An example of strategic communication is this: "Would you do something for me if I told you it really matters?" If the speaker doesn't tell us what we're expected to do, it feels like a setup.

We're also likely to feel that another is trying to manipulate us with a comment such as "Remember when I helped you with your math last term and when I did your chores last week because you were busy?" With a preamble like that, we suspect a trap of some sort is being set. We also get defensive when we suspect others of using openness to manipulate how we feel about them. For instance, people who disclose intimate personal information early in a relationship may be trying to win our trust and to trick us into revealing details of our own personal life. Nonverbal behaviors may also convey strategy, as when a person pauses a long time before answering or refuses to look at us when she or he speaks. A sense of deception pollutes the communication climate.

SANDY

This guy I dated last year was a real con artist, but it took me a while to figure that out. He would look me straight in the eye and tell me he really felt he could trust me. Then he'd say he was going to tell me something he'd never told anyone else in his life, and he'd tell me about fights with his father or how he didn't make the soccer team in high school. The stuff wasn't really that personal, but the way he said it made it seem that way. So I found myself telling him a lot more than I usually disclose and a lot more than I should have. He started using some of the information against me, which was when I started getting wise to him. Later on, I found out he ran through the same song and dance with every girl he dated. It was quite an act!

Spontaneity is the counterpoint to strategy. Spontaneous communication may well be thought out, yet it is also open, honest, and nonmanipulative. "I really need your help with this computer glitch" is a more spontaneous comment than "Would you do something for me if I told you it really matters?" Likewise, it is more spontaneous to ask for a favor in a straightforward way ("Would you help me?") than to preface a request with a recitation of all we've done for someone else. Whereas strategic communication comes across as contrived and devious, spontaneous interaction feels authentic and natural.

Control Versus Problem Orientation

Controlling communication is also likely to trigger defensiveness. Similar to strategic communication, controlling communication overtly attempts to manipulate others. A common instance of controlling communication is when a person insists her or his solution or preference should prevail. Whether the issue is trivial (what movie to see) or serious (where to locate after college), controllers try to impose their point of view on others. This disconfirms and disrespects others.

Defensiveness arises because the relational meaning is that the person exerting control thinks she or he has greater power, rights, or intelligence than others. It's disconfirming to be told our opinions are wrong, our preferences don't matter, or we aren't smart enough to have good ideas. Controlling communication is particularly objectionable when it is combined with strategies. For example, a wife who earns a higher salary than her husband might say to him, "Well, I like the Honda more than the Ford you want, and it's my money that's going to pay for it." The speaker not only pushes her preference, but also tells her husband that she has more power than he does because she makes more money.

Problem-oriented communication is less likely than control to generate defensiveness. Rather than imposing a preference, problem-oriented communication focuses on finding answers that satisfy everyone. The goal is to come up with a solution that all parties find acceptable. Here's an example of problem-oriented communication: "It seems that we have really different ideas about how to spend our vacation. Let's talk through what each of us wants and see if there's a way for both of us to have a good vacation." Notice how this statement invites collaboration and confirms the other and the relationship by expressing a desire to meet both people's needs. According to communication researchers, problem-oriented behaviors tend to reduce conflict and keep lines of communication open (Alexander, 1979; Civickly, Pace, & Krause, 1977). One of the strengths of focusing on problems is that the relational level of meaning emphasizes the importance of the relationship between communicators. In contrast, controlling behaviors aim for one person to triumph over the other, an outcome that undercuts interpersonal harmony.

Neutrality Versus Empathy

People tend to become defensive when others act in a neutral, or detached, manner. It's easy to understand why we might feel uneasy with people who seem uninvolved, especially if we are talking about personal matters. Research on interview climates indicates that defensiveness arises when an interviewer appears withdrawn and distant (Civickly et al., 1977). Neutral communication implies a lack of regard and caring for others. Consequently, it may be interpreted as disconfirming.

In contrast to neutrality, expressed empathy confirms the worth of others and our concern for their thoughts and feelings. Empathy is communicated when we say "I can understand why you feel that way," "It sounds like you really feel uncomfortable with your job," or "I don't blame you for being worried about the situation." Gibb (1964) stressed that empathy doesn't necessarily mean agreement; instead, it conveys recognition of and respect for others' perspectives. Especially when we don't agree with others, it's important to communicate that we respect them as persons. Doing so fosters a supportive communication climate, even if differences continue to exist.

Superiority Versus Equality

The final pair of behaviors affecting climate concerns the relationship between people that is communicated at the relational level of meaning. We feel understandably on guard when talking with people who act as if they are better than we are. Obviously, this disconfirms our worth by making us feel inadequate in their eyes. Consider several messages that convey superiority: "I know a lot more about this than you." "You just don't have my experience." "Is this the best you could do?" "You really should go to my hairdresser." Each of these messages says loud and clear, "You aren't as good (smart, savvy, competent, attractive) as I am." Predictably, the result is that we protect our self-esteem by defensively shutting out the people and messages that belittle us.

CARL

I am really uncomfortable with one of the guys on my team at work. He always acts like he knows best and all the rest of us aren't as smart or experienced or whatever. The other day, I suggested a way we might improve our team's productivity and he said, "I remember when I used to think that." What a putdown! I feel uneasy saying anything around him, because he always judges me.

We feel more relaxed and comfortable when communicating with people who treat us as equals. At the relational level of meaning, expressed equality communicates respect and equivalent status between people. This promotes an open, unguarded climate in which interaction flows freely. Communicating equality has less to do with actual skills and abilities, which may differ between people, than with interpersonal attitudes. We can have outstanding experience or ability in certain areas and still show regard for others and what they have to contribute to interaction. Creating a climate of equality allows everyone to be involved without fear of being judged inadequate.

Everyday Application

ASSESSING COMMUNICATION CLIMATE

Use the behaviors we've discussed as a checklist for assessing communication climates. The next time you feel defensive, ask whether others are communicating superiority, control, strategy, certainty, neutrality, or evaluation. Chances are one or more of these laces communication.

For a communication climate you find supportive and open, check to see whether the following behaviors are present: spontaneity, equality, provisionalism, problem orientation, empathy, and description.

To improve defensive climates, try modeling supportive communication. Resist the normal tendencies to respond defensively when a climate feels disconfirming. Instead, focus on being empathic, descriptive, and spontaneous; showing equality and tentativeness; and solving problems.

We've seen that confirmation, which may include recognizing, acknowledging, and endorsing others, is the basis of healthy communication climates. Our discussion of defensive and supportive communication enlightens us about specific kinds of communication that express confirmation or disconfirmation. With this foundation, we're ready to consider the role of conflict in human relationships and how communication allows us to manage it productively.

CONFLICT IN RELATIONSHIPS

Conflict exists when individuals who depend on each other have different views, interests, or goals and perceive their differences as incompatible. Conflict is a normal, inevitable part of all relationships. When people interact and affect each other, disagreements are unavoidable. You like meat, and your friend is a strict vegetarian. You believe money should be enjoyed, and your partner believes in saving for a rainy day. You favor one way of organizing a work team, and your colleague thinks another is better. You want to move where there's a great job for you, but the location has no career prospects for your partner. Again and again, we find ourselves seemingly at odds with people who matter to us. When this happens, we either part ways or resolve the differences, preferably in a way that doesn't harm the relationship.

YIH-TANG LIN

I had a very bad conflict with my ex-girlfriend. When we disagreed, she wanted to argue about problems, but I couldn't do that. I was brought up to see conflict as bad. I learned to smooth over problems. So I would avoid conflict and say everything was okay when it was not. I think this kept us from working out problems.

The presence of conflict doesn't indicate a relationship is in trouble, although how people manage conflict does influence relational health. Conflict is a sign that individuals are involved with each other. If they weren't, they wouldn't need to resolve differences. This is a good point to keep in mind when conflicts arise, because it reminds us that a strong connection underlies disagreement. Let's now explore what conflict is and how we can communicate effectively when conflicts arise.

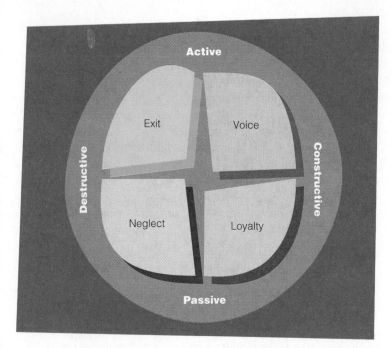

FIGURE 8.3
Responses to Relational
Distress

Conflict May Be Overt or Covert

Overt conflict exists when individuals express differences in a straightforward manner. They might discuss their disagreement, honestly identify their different points of view, argue about ideas, or engage in a shouting match. In each case, differences are out in the open.

Yet, much conflict isn't overt. **Covert conflict** exists when partners camouflage disagreements and express it indirectly. When angry, a person may deliberately do something to hurt or upset a partner. For instance, if you're annoyed that your roommate left the kitchen a mess, you might play the stereo when she or he is sleeping. A man who is angry with his wife might deliberately be half an hour late to meet her when he knows she hates to be kept waiting. Covert aggression sidesteps the real problems and issues, which makes it virtually impossible to resolve the problems. This implies that resolving tensions and differences between people is most likely when they communicate openly.

CARLOTTA

My roommate will never say when she's mad or hurt or whatever. Instead, she plays games that drive me crazy. Sometimes she'll just refuse to talk to me and deny anything is wrong. Other times she forgets some of my stuff when she gets our groceries and pretends it was an accident. I have to guess what is wrong because she won't just come out and tell me. It really strains our friendship.

Conflict Can Be Managed Well or Poorly

Since conflict is natural and inevitable, we need to learn to deal with it in ways that benefit us as individuals and our relationships. Depending on how we handle disagreements, conflict can strengthen a relationship or split it apart.

A series of studies identified four distinct ways Westerners respond to relational distress (Rusbult, 1987; Rusbult, Johnson, & Morrow, 1986; Rusbult & Zembrodt, 1983; Rusbult, Zembrodt, & Iwaniszek, 1986). These are represented in Figure 8.3. According to this model, responses to conflict can be either active or passive, depending on how emphatically they address problems. Responses can also be constructive or destructive in their capacity to resolve tension and to preserve relationships.

When conflict is managed well, it can enhance relationships.
(© Anne Dowie)

The exit response involves leaving a relationship either by walking out or by psychologically withdrawing. "I don't want to talk about it" is a vocal exit response. Because exit doesn't address problems, it is destructive. Because it is forceful, it is active. The neglect response occurs when an individual denies or minimizes problems. "You're making a mountain out of a mole hill" is a neglect response that denies a serious issue exists. The neglect response is also disconfirming because it fails to acknowledge and respect how another feels. Neglect is destructive because it evades difficulties, but it does so passively by avoiding discussion. The loyalty response is staying committed to a relationship despite differences. Loyalty might be expressed by responding to conflict by hoping or trusting that things will get better on their own. Loyalty is silent allegiance, so it is a passive response. Because it doesn't end a relationship and preserves the option of addressing tension later, loyalty is considered constructive. Finally, voice is an active, constructive strategy that responds to conflict by talking about problems and trying to resolve differences so that a relationship remains healthy. "I want to talk about the tension between us" exemplifies the voice response to conflict.

Although each of us has a preferred response, we can develop skill in other responses. Constructive strategies (voice and loyalty) are advisable for relationships that you want to maintain. Of those two, voice is stronger because it actively intervenes to resolve conflict. Loyalty may be useful as an interim strategy when partners need time to reflect or cool off before dealing with tension directly. Once you understand your current tendencies for responding to conflict, you can consider whether you want to develop skill in alternatives to them.

Conflict Can Be Good for Individuals and Relationships

Although we tend to think of conflict negatively, it can benefit us and our relationships in several ways. When managed constructively, conflict can help us grow as individuals and strengthen our relationships. We can enlarge our personal perspectives by engaging conflict as a trigger for personal growth and learning. We deepen insight into our ideas and feelings when we have to express them and consider critical responses from others. Differences prompt personal growth if they help us see when it's appropriate to change our minds. Conflict allows us to consider points of view different from our own. Based on what we learn, we may change our opinions, behaviors, or goals. Conflict can also increase insight into ourselves, relationships, and situations. This too spurs personal growth.

FAIR FIGHTING

Like cholesterol, conflict has good and bad forms. In their 1973 book, *The Intimate Enemy: How to Fight Fair in Love and Marriage,* George Bach and Peter Wyden state that verbal conflict between intimates can actually benefit relationships if it is managed well. One value of conflict is that it lets partners air problems, worries, or resentments before they fester. Conflict also has the potential to expand partners' understandings of each other. An argument about a specific issue often provides broader information about why partners feel as they do and what meanings they attach to the issue. These values can be realized if partners practice good communication skills.

Now that we understand how communication influences interpersonal climates and how communication skills allow us to realize the constructive values of conflict, we're ready to consider specific guidelines for communicating to create healthy, positive climates in social, professional, and personal relationships.

GUIDELINES FOR CREATING AND SUSTAINING HEALTHY CLIMATES

We've seen that communication plays a vital role in creating the climate of relationships in general and the climate for dealing with conflict in particular. To translate what we've learned into pragmatic information, we'll discuss five guidelines for building and sustaining healthy climates.

Actively Use Communication to Shape Climates

As we have seen, conflict is a natural and potentially productive part of healthy relationships. The goal is not to eliminate conflict, but rather to find ways to communicate effectively about tensions and differences. Several principles suggest themselves. First, we want to create interpersonal climates that are supportive, since those make it more likely conflict will be overt and also encourage open communication. What you've learned about defensive and supportive climates should allow you to monitor your communication to make sure it contributes to open, positive interaction. You can identify and avoid disconfirming patterns of talk such as evaluation and superiority. In addition, you can actively work to use supportive communication such as problem orientation and tentativeness.

Shaping climate with communication also draws on many of the skills we've discussed in previous chapters. For example, effective communication during conflict requires being mindful, engaging in dual perspective, confirming others, and paraphrasing. In addition, effective communication is fostered when we confirm others, check perceptions, and use I-language. In Chapter 11, we will return to the topic of conflict as it surfaces in small groups and teams.

Active management of communication climates also involves accepting and growing from the tension generated by conflicting needs that sometimes surface in relationships. For instance, you may want private time, but your partner wants to do something together. Although friction between contradictory needs can naturally make us uncomfortable, we should recognize its constructive potential. The discomfort of tension pushes us to transform our relationships by changing the dynamics in them.

Accept and Confirm Others

Throughout this chapter, we've seen that confirmation is a cornerstone of healthy climates and fulfilling communication. Although we can understand how important confirmation is, it isn't always easy to give it. Sometimes we disagree with others or don't like certain things they do. Being honest with others is important because it enhances trust between people. Communication research indicates that, in fact, people expect real friends to be sources of honest feedback, even if it isn't always pleasant to hear (Rawlins, 1994). This implies we should express honest misgivings about our friends' behaviors or other aspects of their identity. It is false friends who tell us only what we want to hear. Deceit, no matter how well intentioned, diminishes personal growth and trust between people. As Aaron's commentary explains, we can offer honest feedback within a context that assures others we value and respect them.

AARON

When I first came to school here, I got in with a crowd that drank a lot. At first I drank only on weekends, but then it got so I was drinking every night and drinking more and more. My classes were suffering, but I didn't seem able to stop on my own. Then my friend Betsy told me she was worried about me and wanted to help me stop drinking so much. I'd have been angry if most people had said that, but Betsy talked to me in a way that said she really cared about me. I saw that she was a better friend than all my drinking buddies, because Betsy cared enough not to stand by when I was hurting myself. All my other so-called friends just stood by and said nothing.

It can be difficult to accept and affirm others when we find their needs taxing or discover conflicts between our preferences and those of others. It's not unusual for one partner to desire more closeness than another or for partners to differ in the paths they travel to achieve closeness. These are common problems, and partners need to discuss them in order to work out mutually agreeable solutions.

(Reprinted with special permission of King Features Syndicate.)

For a relationship to work, both partners need to feel confirmed. This doesn't mean that you feel as another person does or that you defer your own needs. Instead, the point is to recognize and respect others' needs just as you wish them to respect yours. Dual perspective is a primary tool for accepting others because it calls on us to consider them on their own terms. Although personal talk may make you feel most close to another person, you should also realize that some people feel closer when they do things together. To meet both of your needs, you could take turns honoring each other's preferred paths to closeness. Alternatively, you might combine the two styles of intimacy by doing things together that invite conversation. For example, backpacking is an activity in which talking naturally occurs.

Affirm and Assert Yourself

It is just as important to affirm and accept yourself as to do that for others. You are no less valuable; your needs are no less important; your preferences are no less valid. It is a misunderstanding to think that interpersonal communication principles we've discussed concern only how we behave toward others. Equally, they pertain to how we should treat ourselves. Thus, the principle of confirming people's worth applies equally to others and to yourself. Likewise, we should respect and honor both our own and others' needs, preferences, and ways of creating intimacy.

Although we can't always meet the needs of all parties in relationships, it is possible and desirable to give voice to everyone, including yourself. If your partner favors greater autonomy than you, you need to recognize that preference and also assert your own. If you don't express your feelings, there's no way others can confirm you. Thus, we should assert our feelings and preferences while simultaneously honoring different ones in others.

LIZ

Ever since I was a kid, I have muffled my own needs and concentrated on pleasing others. I thought I was taking care of relationships, but actually I was hurting them, because I felt neglected. My resentment poisoned

TABLE 8.2 Aggression, Assertion, and Deference		
Aggressive	Assertive	Deferential
We are going to spend time together.	I'd like to create more time for us.	If you don't want to spend time with each other, I won't push.
Tell me what you're feeling; I insist.	I would like to understand more of how you feel.	If you don't want to talk about how you feel, okay.
I don't care what you want; I'm not going to a movie.	I'm really not up for a movie tonight.	It's fine with me to go to a movie if you want to.

relationships in subtle ways, so it was really destructive. I've been developing my skills in telling others what I want and need, and that's improving my relationships.

Unlike aggression, assertion doesn't involve putting your needs above those of others. But unlike deference, assertion doesn't subordinate your needs to those of others. Assertion is a matter of clearly and nonjudgmentally stating what you feel, need, or want. This should be done without disparaging others and what they want. You should simply make your feelings known in an open, descriptive manner. Table 8.2 illustrates aggressive, assertive, and deferential responses.

Because relationships include more than one person, they must involve acceptance and affirmation of more than one. Good relationships develop when partners understand and respect each other. The first requirement for this to happen is for each person to communicate honestly how she or he thinks and feels and what she or he wants and needs. A second requirement is for each person to communicate respect for the other's feelings and needs.

We should remember that the meaning of assertion varies among different cultures. For instance, openly asserting your own ideas is considered disrespectful in Korea and parts of China. Even if Koreans or Chinese don't want to do something, they seldom directly turn down another's request. Thus, people with diverse cultural backgrounds may have different ways of affirming and asserting themselves. To communicate effectively with others, we need to learn how they affirm themselves and how they express their feelings in direct or indirect ways.

We can tolerate sometimes not getting what we want without feeling personally devalued. However, it is far more disconfirming to have our needs go unacknowledged. Even when people disagree or have conflicting needs, each person can state his or her feelings and express awareness of the other's perspective. Usually there are ways to acknowledge both viewpoints, as Dan's comments illustrate.

DAN

My supervisor did an excellent job of letting me know I was valued even when I got passed over for a promotion last year. I'd worked hard and felt I had earned it. Jake, my supervisor, came to my office to talk to me before the promotion was announced. He told me that both I and the other guy were qualified, but that the other person had seniority and also field experience I didn't have. Then Jake told me he was assigning me to a field position for 6 months so that I could get the experience I needed to get promoted the next time a position opened up. Jake communicated that he understood how I felt and that he was supporting me, even if I didn't get the promotion. His talk made all the difference in how I felt about staying with the company.

Self-Disclose When Appropriate

As we noted earlier, self-disclosure allows people to know each other in greater depth. For this reason, it's an important communication skill, especially in the early stages of relationships. Research indicates that appropriate self-disclosure tends to increase trust and feelings of closeness (Cosby, 1973). In addition, self-disclosure can enhance self-esteem and security in relationships because we feel others accept our most private selves. Finally, self-disclosure is an important way to learn about ourselves. As we reveal our hopes, fears, dreams, and feelings, we get responses from others that give us new perspectives on who we are. In addition, we gain insight into ourselves by seeing how we interact with others in new situations.

Although self-disclosure has many potential values, it is not always advisable. As we have seen, self-disclosures necessarily involve risk—the risk that others will not accept what we reveal or that they might use it against us. Appropriate self-disclosure minimizes these risks by proceeding slowly and in climates where sufficient trust has been proven. It's wise to "test the waters" gradually before plunging into major self-disclosures. Begin by revealing information that is personal but not highly intimate or able to damage you if exploited. Before disclosing further, observe how the other person responds to your communication and what she or he does with it. You might also pay attention to whether the other person reciprocates by disclosing personal information to you. Because self-disclosures involve risk, we need to be cautious about when and to whom we reveal ourselves. When trust exists and we want to intensify a relationship, self-disclosure is one of many communication practices that can be healthy.

Respect Diversity in Relationships

Just as individuals differ, so do relationships. There is tremendous variety in what people find comfortable, affirming, and satisfying in interpersonal interaction. It's counterproductive to try to force all people and relationships to fit into a single mode. For example, you might have one friend who enjoys a lot of verbal disclosure and another who prefers less. There's no reason to try to persuade the first friend to disclose less or the second one to be more revealing. Similarly, you may be comfortable with greater closeness in some of your relationships and more autonomy in others. The differences between people create a rich diversity of relationships we can experience.

Because people and relationships are diverse, we should strive to respect a range of communicative choices and relationship patterns. In addition, we should be cautious about imposing our meaning on others' communication. People from various cultures, including distinct co-cultures in the United States, have learned different communication styles. What Westerners consider openness and healthy self-disclosure may feel offensively intrusive to people from some Asian societies. The dramatic, assertive speaking style of many African Americans can be misinterpreted as abrasive by European Americans. One effective communication technique for improving your understanding of others is to ask them what they mean by certain behaviors. This conveys the relational message that they matter to you, and it allows you to gain insight into the interesting diversity among us.

The guidelines we've discussed combine respect for self, others, and relationships. Using these guidelines should improve your ability to communicate in ways that foster healthy, affirming climates in your relationships.

SUMMARY

In this chapter, we've explored self-disclosure and communication climates as foundations of interaction with others. Self-disclosure allows us to share ourselves with others, gain additional insight into ourselves, and build closeness in relationships. Self-disclosure doesn't occur in a vacuum. Instead, it most likely happens when there is a communication climate that is affirming, accepting, and supportive.

A basic requirement for healthy communication climates is confirmation. Each of us wants to feel valued, especially by those for whom we care most deeply. When partners recognize, acknowledge, and endorse each other, they give the important gift of confirmation. They communicate, "You matter to me." We discussed particular kinds of communication that foster supportive and defensive climates in relationships. Defensiveness is bred by evaluation, certainty, superiority, strategies, control, and neutrality. More supportive climates arise from communication that is descriptive, provisional, equal, spontaneous, empathic, and problem oriented.

The communication skills that build supportive climates also help us manage conflict constructively so

that it enriches, rather than harms, relationships. By creating affirming, healthy climates, we establish foundations that allow us to deal with tensions openly and to communicate in ways that enhance the likelihood we can resolve differences or find ways of accepting them with grace.

To close the chapter, we considered five guidelines for building healthy communication climates. The first one is to assume responsibility for communicating in ways that actively enhance the mood of a relationship. Second, we should accept and confirm others, communicating that we respect them, even though we may not always agree with them or feel the same as they do. The third guideline is a companion to the second one: We should accept and confirm ourselves. Each of us is entitled to assert our own thoughts, feelings, and needs. Doing so allows us to honor ourselves and to help our partners understand us. A fourth guideline is to self-disclose when appropriate so that we increase our security in relationships and so that we add to the information we have about ourselves and others.

Finally, embracing diversity in relationships is a source of personal and interpersonal growth. People vary widely, as do the relationship patterns and forms they prefer. By respecting differences among us, we expand our insights into the fascinating array of ways that humans form and sustain relationships. In Chapter 9, we'll continue thinking about interpersonal communication by exploring how it influences friendships and romantic relationships.

FOR FURTHER REFLECTION AND DISCUSSION

1. Think about the most effective work climate you've ever experienced. Describe the communication in that climate. How does the communication in that situation reflect skills and principles discussed in this chapter?

2. When do you find it most difficult to confirm others? Is it hard for you to be confirming when you disagree with another person? After reading this chapter, can you distinguish between agreeing, or approving, and confirming another person?

3. Using the six categories for defensive and supportive styles of communication, describe communication in your classroom. Do the categories allow you to analyze why your classroom feels supportive or defensive?

4. Interview a professional in the field of work you plan to enter or return to after completing college. Ask your interviewee to describe the kind of climate that is most effective in that work situation. Ask your interviewee what specific kinds of communication foster and impede a good working climate. How do your interviewee's perceptions relate to material covered in this chapter?

5. Think about self-disclosure in a relationship in your life. Was self-disclosure more frequent and more immediately reciprocated early in the relationship than after it was established? Based on what you learned in this chapter, explain changes in patterns of disclosure.

6. How often do you rely on exit, voice, loyalty, and neglect styles when responding to conflict or tension in relationships? What does your response style achieve and prevent?

KEY TERMS

communication climate	endorsement
self-disclosure	conflict
recognition	overt conflict
acknowledgment	covert conflict

Focus Questions

1 Are there patterns in how friendships and romantic relationships develop?

2 How do couples handle tensions between wanting time together and wanting separate space?

3 Are there communication strategies for maintaining long-distance relationships?

4 Does abuse end when an abusive partner apologizes and acts lovingly?

CHAPTER 9

Communication in Personal Relationships

I t's been a rough semester. You're not doing well in your classes, and you're having trouble balancing work and school. You feel overwhelmed by all of it. Then you talk to your best friend about your problems. She tells you about a semester that was bad for her, and you feel less alone. Even though you haven't solved everything, you feel better because you shared your feelings with someone who cares about you.

Long-distance romance is so hard! Your partner graduated last term and took a job 500 miles away. You call and write a lot, but that's no substitute for seeing each other every day. After 8 weeks apart, you're finally together for a long weekend. Just being together makes you feel more complete and happy. You can't imagine not having this person in your life.

(Rufino Tamayo, *The Lovers* (1943). Oil on canvas, 34¼ × 44¼". San Francisco Museum of Modern Art. Purchased with the aid of funds from W. W. Crocker.)

As these examples indicate, personal relationships are important in our lives. Imagine that suddenly you have no friends and no romantic partner. How would your life be different? What would be missing? If you're like most people, a great deal would be missing. Friends and romantic partners provide growth, comfort, pleasure, and fulfillment. We need people we care about and who care about us.

Good communication skills are essential to forming and sustaining healthy personal relationships. In the previous chapter, we discussed self-disclosure, communication climate, and management of conflict as foundations of relationships. In this chapter, we focus on communication in the specific contexts of close friendships and romantic relationships. To launch the discussion, we'll define personal relationships. Next, we'll consider how communication guides the development of friendships and romances over time. Finally, we'll examine some of the special challenges for personal relationships in our era.

THE CHARACTER OF PERSONAL RELATIONSHIPS

Personal relationships are voluntary commitments between irreplaceable individuals who are influenced by rules, relational dialectics, and the surrounding contexts.

Personal relationships are unique—each one has its own special qualities and style. In addition to uniqueness, personal relationships are distinguished from other social connections by commitment, rules, embeddedness in contexts, and relational dialectics. We'll discuss each feature.

Uniqueness

The vast majority of our relationships are social, not personal. A **social relationship** is one in which participants interact within social roles, rather than as unique individuals. For instance, you might exchange assistance with a classmate, play racquetball each week with another person, and talk about politics with a neighbor. In each case, the person could be replaced by someone else in the same role. You could find other people for assistance, racquetball, and political conversations. In these relationships, the specific people are less important than the roles they fulfill. The value of social relationships lies more in what participants do than in who they are, since a variety of people could fulfill the same functions.

In personal relationships, partners invest themselves.
(© Tom & Dee Ann McCarthy/The Stock Market)

In personal relationships, however, the particular people and what they do define the connection. I'm not committed to marriage in the abstract, but to a particular man named Robbie and the unique ways in which we have fitted ourselves together. Intimate partners cannot be replaced by others (Blumstein & Kollock, 1988). When a partner leaves or dies, that relationship ends. We may later have other intimates, but a new spouse or best friend will not be a facsimile of the former one. Unlike social relationships, personal ones are unique and partners are irreplaceable.

Commitment

For most of us, passion is what first springs to mind when we think about intimacy. **Passion** involves intensely positive feelings and desires for another person. The sparks and emotional high of being in love or discovering a new friend stem from passion. It's why we feel "butterflies in the stomach" and fall "head over heels." As much fun as passion is, it isn't the primary foundation for enduring relationships.

Passion is a feeling based on rewards we get from being involved with a person. **Commitment,** in contrast, is a decision to remain with a relationship. The hallmark of commitment is the intention to share the future. Committed friends and romantic partners assume they will continue together. Because a committed relationship assumes future, partners are unlikely to bail out if the going gets rough. Instead, they weather bad times (Lund, 1985). Commitment is a decision to stay together *in spite of* trouble, disappointments, sporadic restlessness, and lulls in passion.

(Reprinted by permission of Johnny Hart and Creators Syndicate, Inc.)

Commitment grows out of **investments,** which are what we put into relationships that we could not retrieve if the relationship were to end. When we care about another person, we invest time, energy, thought, and feelings into interaction. In doing this, we invest *ourselves* in others. Investments are powerful because they are personal choices that can't be recovered. We can't get back the feelings and energy we invest in a relationship. We can't recover history shared with another. The only way to make good on investments is to stick with a relationship (Brehm, 1992). For good or ill, then, investments bind us to relationships.

Relationship Rules

All relationships have **rules** that guide how partners communicate and interpret each other's communication. As in other contexts, relationship rules define what is expected, what is not allowed, and when and how to do various things. Typically, relationship rules are unspoken understandings between partners. Although friends and romantic partners may never explicitly discuss rules, they discover how important rules are if one is violated!

As you may recall from our discussion in Chapter 5, there are two kinds of rules that guide our communication. Constitutive rules define what various communication means in personal relationships. For instance, women friends often count listening to problems as caring, whereas men tend to count hanging out and diversionary activities as ways of caring (Tavris, 1992; Wood, 1994d). Friends work out a number of constitutive rules to define communication that expresses loyalty, support, rudeness, love, joking, acceptance, and so forth.

Regulative rules influence interaction by specifying when and with whom to engage in various kinds of communication. For example, friends often have a regulative rule that says it's okay to criticize each other in private, but it's not acceptable to do so in front of others. Many men regard interrupting as a normal part of conversation between friends, whereas

RULES OF FRIENDSHIP

Researchers asked Westerners what it takes to maintain a good friendship. Here are the common rules identified:

1. Stand up for a friend when she or he isn't around.
2. Share your successes and how you feel about them.
3. Give emotional support.
4. Trust and confide in each other.
5. Help a friend when he or she needs it.
6. Respect a friend's privacy.
7. Try to make friends feel good.
8. Tolerate your friend's friends.
9. Don't criticize a friend in front of others.
10. Don't tell a friend's confidences to other people.
11. Don't nag or focus on a friend's faults.

Source: Based on Argyle, M., & Henderson, M. (1984). The rules of friendship. *Journal of Social and Personal Relationships, 1,* 211–237.

women sometimes interpret interruptions as rude (Tannen, 1990; Wood, 1994d). Romantic partners may regulate physical displays of affection to private settings.

Friends and romantic partners generate rules about what they want and expect of each other, such as support, time, and acceptance. Equally important are "shalt not" rules that define what won't be tolerated. For example, most Westerners would consider it a betrayal if a friend slept with their romantic partner. Rules regulate both trivial and important aspects of interaction. Not interrupting may be a rule, but breaking it probably won't destroy a good friendship. On the other hand, deceitful communication or verbal abuse sound the death knell of a friendship.

Embeddedness in Contexts

Personal relationships are not isolated from the social world. Instead, the surroundings of relationships influence interaction between partners. Friendships and romances are affected by neighborhoods, social circles, family units, and society as a whole. For instance, Western culture values heterosexual marriage, which means men and women who marry receive more social support than do cohabiting partners or gay and lesbian couples. Our families of origin shaped what we look for in intimates—how important is social status, income, intelligence, and so on? Our social circles establish norms for activities such as drinking, involvement with community groups, studying, and partying. In many ways, families, friends, and society affect what we expect of relationships and how we communicate in them.

WINSLOW

I never realized how much a social group influences other relationships until I had a summer job with a big accounting firm in New York. Everyone there went out to fancy restaurants and plays or concerts instead of fast-food places and movies. I started doing it too so that I could be part of the talk about the latest plays and stuff. I sure didn't save much money from my summer job!

Both particular others and the generalized other, which we discussed in Chapter 3, affect activities and expectations in personal relationships. Families may voice approval or disapproval about our choices of intimates or of the way we operate in our private relationships. Our society's technological advances and mobility make long-distance relationships more possible than in earlier times. The increasing number of people involved in dual-career relationships is revising traditional expectations about how much each partner participates in earning income, homemaking, and child care. As our society becomes more diverse, interracial and interethnic relationships are more common and socially accepted. Thus, both our social circles and the larger society are contexts that affect the kinds of relationships we form and the ways we communicate within them.

Relational Dialectics

A final quality of personal relationships is the presence of **relational dialectics.** These are opposing and continuous tensions in all relationships. Leslie Baxter, a scholar of interpersonal communication, identifies three relational dialectics (Baxter, 1990, 1993).

Autonomy/Connection   Intimates experience tension between wanting autonomy and wanting connection. Because we want to be deeply linked to others, we cherish time with our intimates, share experiences, and feel connected. At the same time, each of us needs an independent identity. We don't want our individuality to be swallowed up by relationships, so we seek distance, even from our intimates.

Relationship counselors agree that a continuous friction in most close relationships arises from the contradictory impulses for autonomy and connection (Beck, 1988; Scarf, 1987). Friends and romantic partners may vacation together and be with each other virtually all the time for a week or more. They're often surprised when they return home and crave time apart. Intense immersion in togetherness prompts us to reestablish independent identity. Both autonomy and closeness are natural human needs. The challenge is to preserve individuality while also creating intimacy.

Novelty/Predictability   The second dialectic is a tension between wanting familiar routines and wanting novelty. We like a certain amount of routine to provide security and predictability to our lives. Friends often have standard times to get together, and romantic couples settle on preferred times and places for going out. Yet too much routine is boring, so partners occasionally explore a new restaurant or do something spontaneous and different to introduce variety into their customary routine.

Openness/Closedness   The third dialectic is tension between the desire for openness and the desire for privacy. Although intimate relationships are sometimes idealized as totally open and honest, in reality complete openness would be intolerable (Baxter, 1993; Petronio, 1991). We want to share our inner selves with our intimates; yet, there may be times when we don't feel like sharing or topics that we don't want to talk about. All of us need some privacy, and our partners need to respect that. Wanting some privacy doesn't mean a relationship is in trouble. It means only that we need both openness and closedness in our lives.

Everyday Application

UNDERSTANDING YOUR DIALECTICS

Trace the presence of the three dialectics in a close relationship of yours. What are the ways you ensure enough of both autonomy and connection, openness and privacy, and novelty and routine? What happens when you feel too much or too little fulfillment for any of the six human needs?

Managing Dialectics   Baxter (1990) identifies four ways intimates deal with dialectical tensions. One response, called **neutralization**, negotiates a balance between the poles of a dialectic. This involves striking a compromise in which both needs are met to an extent, but neither is fully satisfied. A couple might agree to be generally open, but not highly disclosive. The **separation** response favors one need in a dialectic and ignores the other. For example, friends might agree to make novelty a priority and suppress their needs for routine. Separation also occurs when partners cycle between dialectical poles to favor each pole alternately. A couple could spend weekends together and have little contact during the week.

A third way to manage dialectics is **segmentation**, in which partners assign each need to certain spheres, issues, activities, or times. For instance, friends might be open about many topics, but respect each other's privacy and not pry in one or two areas. Romantic partners might be autonomous in their professional activities, yet very connected in their interaction in the home and their involvement with children.

The final method of dealing with dialectics is **reframing.** This is a complex strategy that redefines apparently contradictory needs as not really in opposition. My colleagues and I found examples of reframing in a recent study of intimate partners (Wood et al., 1994). Some of the couples said that their autonomy enhanced closeness because knowing they were separate in some ways allowed them to feel safer being connected. Instead of viewing autonomy and closeness as opposing, these partners transcended the apparent tension between the two to define the needs as mutually enhancing.

STANLEY

For a long time I've been stressed about my feelings. Sometimes I can't get enough of Annie, and then I feel crowded and don't want to see her at all. I never understood these switches, and I was afraid I was unstable or something. Now I see that I'm pretty normal after all.

Research suggests that separation by fulfilling one need and squelching the other is generally the least satisfying response (Baxter, 1990). Repressing any natural human impulse diminishes us. The challenge is to find ways to honor and satisfy the variety of needs that humans have. Understanding that dialectics are natural and constructive allows us to accept and grow from the tensions they generate.

THE EVOLUTIONARY COURSE OF PERSONAL RELATIONSHIPS

Every personal relationship develops at its own pace and in unique ways. Yet, there are commonalities in the evolutionary course of most friendships and romances.

Friendships

Although friendships sometimes jump to life quickly, usually they unfold through a series of stages. Bill Rawlins (1981, 1994), an interpersonal communication researcher, developed a six-stage model of how friendships develop (Figure 9.1).

Role-Limited Interaction   Friendships begin with an encounter. We might meet a new person at work, through membership on athletic teams or clubs, or by chance in an airport, store, or class. During initial encounters we tend to rely on standard social rules and roles. We are polite, and careful about what we disclose. Early interaction may be awkward and uncertain, since individuals haven't worked out their own patterns of relating to each other. One exception to this generalization is electronically conducted relationships in which people often venture into more personal, disclosive communication in the early stages of acquaintance (Lea & Spears, 1995).

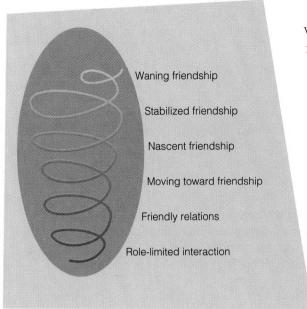

FIGURE 9.1
Stages of Friendship

Willingness to take some risks early in relationships may be greater when people aren't interacting face to face.

Friendly Relations The second stage of friendship is friendly relations, in which individuals check the other out to see whether common ground and interests exist. Riddick tells Jason that he really likes adventure movies. If Jason says he does too, then they've found a shared interest. A business person engages in small talk to see if an associate wants to get more personal. People who have formed friendly relations over the Internet often tell each other about experiences and recommend books, films, and recording artists. Although friendly exchanges are not dramatic, they allow us to explore the potential for a deeper relationship with another person.

Moving Toward Friendship Moving toward friendship involves stepping beyond social roles. To signal we'd like to personalize a relationship, we could introduce a more personal topic than those we have discussed so far in a relationship. We also move toward friendship when we arrange meetings. Maria might ask Raul to go to lunch after class. Sometimes we involve others to lessen the potential awkwardness of being with someone we don't yet know well. For instance, you might invite a new acquaintance to a party where others will be present. People who have gotten to know each other over the Internet or the World Wide Web sometimes develop enough interest to meet in person. As individuals interact more personally, they begin talking about feelings, values, goals, interests, and attitudes. This personal knowledge forms the initial foundation of friendship.

Nascent Friendship Nascent friendship is one that is in an early or embryonic stage. If initial interaction has been satisfying, individuals may begin to think of themselves as friends or as becoming friends. At this point, social norms and roles become less important, and friends begin to work out their own private ways of relating. When my friend Sue and I were in graduate school, we developed a ritual of calling each day between 5 and 6 to catch up. Some friends settle into patterns of getting together for specific things (watching games, shopping, playing racquetball, going to movies). Other friends share a wider range of times and activities. The milestones of this stage are that individuals begin to think of themselves as friends and to work out private roles and rules for interaction. Thus, interaction between nascent friends establishes basic patterns and climate for the friendship.

Stabilized Friendship   When friends feel established in each other's life, friendship stabilizes. The benchmark of this stage is the assumption of continuity. Whereas in earlier stages individuals didn't count on getting together unless they made a specific plan, stabilized friends assume they'll keep seeing each other. They no longer have to ask whether they'll get together, because they are committed to the relationship as continuous in their lives. Stabilized friends communicate their assumption of ongoing closeness. For example, stabilized friends might say, "What do you want to do this weekend?" rather than asking, "Do you want to get together this weekend?" The former question assumes they will see each other.

Another criterion of this stage is trust. Through disclosing private information and responding with acceptance, individuals earn each other's trust. In turn, they feel safe sharing even more intimate information and revealing vulnerabilities that are normally concealed from others. Stabilized friendships may continue indefinitely, in some cases lasting a lifetime.

Waning Friendship   Friendship withers when one or both people cease being committed to it. Sometimes friends drift apart because each is pulled in different directions by career demands or personal life. In other cases, friendships deteriorate because they've run their natural course and become boring. A third reason friendships end is violations of rules friends establish. Telling a friend's secrets to a third person violates an agreement to keep confidences. Being unsupportive in conversations may also violate rules of friendship. When friendships deteriorate, communication changes in predictable ways. Defensiveness and uncertainty rise, causing individuals to be more guarded and less open. Communication may also become more strategic as individuals try to protect themselves from further exposure and hurt.

Everyday Application

FADED FRIENDSHIPS

Remember three friendships that were once very close but have faded away. Describe the reasons they ended. How did boredom, differences, external circumstances, or violations contribute to decay of the friendships? How did communication patterns change as the friendships waned?

Even when serious violations occur between friends, relationships can sometimes be repaired. For this to happen, both friends must be committed to rebuilding trust and talking openly about their feelings and needs.

Romance

Like friendships, romances also have a typical evolutionary path. We perceive romantic relationships as escalating, navigating, or deteriorating. Within these three broad categories there are a number of more specific stages.

Escalating In moving toward romantic commitment, we recognize six stages of interaction. The first is individuals who aren't interacting. We are aware of ourselves as individuals with particular needs, goals, love styles, and qualities that affect what we look for in relationships. Prior to forming romantic relationships, we also have learned a number of constitutive and regulative communication rules that affect how we interact with others and how we interpret their communication.

The second stage is **invitational communication** in which individuals express interest in interacting. This stage involves both initiating to others and responding to invitations they make to us. "Want to dance?" "Where are you from?" "I love this kind of music," "Hi, my name's Shelby," "Did you just start working here?" are examples of invitations to interact. Invitational communication usually follows a conventional script for social conversation. The meaning of invitational communication is found on the relational level, not the content level. "I love this kind of music" literally means a person likes the music. On the relational level of meaning, however, the message is "I'm available and interested. Are you?"

Out of all the people we meet, we are romantically attracted to only a few. The three greatest influences on initial attraction are self-concept, proximity, and similarity. How we see ourselves affects the people we consider candidates for romance. How we define our sexual orientation, for example, is a primary influence on whom we consider potential romantic partners. Social class also influences whom we notice and consider appropriate for us. The myth that the United States is color-blind and classless is disproven by the fact that most people pair with others of their race and social class. In fact, social prestige influences dating patterns now more than it did in the 1950s (Whitbeck & Hoyt, 1994).

In addition to personal identity, proximity influences initial attraction. We can interact only with people we meet, whether in person or in cyberspace. Consequently, where we live, work, and socialize and the electronic networks in which we participate constrain the possibilities for relationships. This reminds us that communication is systemic, a principle we noted in Chapter 1. From that discussion, you may recall that the systemic character of communication means that contexts affect what happens when people transact. Some contexts, such as college campuses, promote meeting potential romantic partners, whereas other contexts are less conducive to meeting and dating. Specialized electronic networks and home pages are set up for people who want to talk about particular topics, develop friendships, or meet potential romantic partners.

Similarity is also important in romantic relationships. In the realm of romance, "birds of a feather" seems more true than "opposites attract." In general, we are attracted to people whose values, attitudes, and lifestyles are similar to ours. Similarity of personality is also linked to long-term marital happiness (Caspi & Harbener, 1990). In general, people tend to match themselves with others who are about as physically attractive as they are. We may fantasize about relationships with stunning people, but when reality settles in we're likely to pass them by for someone at our level of attractiveness. In general, we seek romantic partners who are similar to us in many respects. For similarities between people to enhance attractiveness, they must be recognized and communicated (Duck, 1994a,b). In other words, attraction grows when individuals discuss common feelings, experiences, values, beliefs, and goals.

Explorational communication is a stage in which individuals explore the possibilities for a relationship. We communicate to announce our identities and to learn about others. As in the early stages of friendship, potential romantic partners fish for common interests: Are you from the West? Do you like jazz? What's your family like? Do you follow politics? As we continue to interact with others, both breadth and depth of information increase. Because we perceive self-disclosure as a sign of trust, it tends to escalate intimacy (Berger & Bell, 1988). At this early stage of interaction, reciprocity of disclosure is expected so that neither person is more vulnerable than the other (Duck, 1992; Miell & Duck, 1986).

G I N D E R

Last year I went out with a guy for a couple of months. After we'd been seeing each other a while, I told him some private stuff about me. The problem was that he didn't tell me anything personal about himself. I felt really exposed with him knowing more about me than I did about him. Plus I felt like he must not trust me if he wouldn't reveal anything.

If early interaction increases attraction, then individuals may escalate the relationship. **Intensifying communication** increases the depth of a relationship by increasing the amount and intimacy of interaction. My students nicknamed this stage "euphoria" to emphasize the intensity and happiness it typically embodies. During this phase, partners spend more and more time together, and they rely less on external structures such as movies or parties. Instead, they immerse themselves in the budding relationship and may feel they can't be together enough. Further disclosures are exchanged, personal biographies are filled in, and partners increasingly learn how each other feels and thinks. Communication tends to be increasingly personal and intense during this phase of romance.

WHAT DRIVES RELATIONAL ESCALATION

According to researchers, some romantic relationships are driven by events and circumstances, which push a couple toward commitment. Timing, approval from friends and family, good jobs, and so forth are events that can drive relationships forward. Other relationships seem to be driven by relationship factors—feelings and fit between two particular individuals. Trust, compatibility, history, shared values, and self-disclosure are examples of relationship events that can drive romance forward. Long-term satisfaction with marriage is more positively associated with relationship-driven commitments than with event-driven ones. Here are examples.

Emeka and Fred started dating in their senior year. Both families supported the relationship, and Emeka and Fred felt it was time to settle down. They married a month after graduation, but separated a year later.

Tyrone and Ella dated for 3 years. By the time they walked down the aisle, they knew each other well and had learned how to be a very compatible couple. Three years later, they are very satisfied with the marriage.

Source: Surra, C., Arizzi, P., & Asmussen, L. (1988). The association between reasons for commitment and the development and outcome of marital relationships. *Journal of Social and Personal Relationships, 5,* 47–64.

The intensifying stage often involves idealizing and personalized communication. Idealizing occurs when we see a relationship and a partner as more wonderful, exciting, and perfect than they really are (Hendrick & Hendrick, 1988). During euphoria, partners often exaggerate each other's virtues, downplay or don't notice vices, and overlook problems in the relationship. It is also during euphoria that partners begin to develop relationship vocabularies that include nicknames and private codes. Sometimes Robbie and I greet each other by saying "namaste." This is a Nepali greeting that expresses good will. Saying it reminds us of our trek in the mountains of Nepal. Relationship vocabularies reflect and fuel intimacy.

PRIVATE LANGUAGE

What are the special words and nonverbal codes in a close relationship of yours? Do you have a way to signal each other when you're bored at a party and ready to leave? Do you use nicknames and private words? Would you feel any loss if you had no private language in your relationship?

Committed romantic partners create a relational culture that includes private understandings of meanings, rules, and patterns of interacting. (© Bob Daemmrich/The Image Works)

Private language heightens partners' sense of being a special couple. Partners make up words and nicknames for each other, and they develop ways to send private messages in public settings. Private language not only reflects intimacy, but also enhances it ("Public Pillow Talk," 1987).

Revising communication, although not part of escalation in all romantic relationships, occurs often enough to merit our consideration. During this stage, partners come down out of the clouds to talk about their relationship's strengths, problems, and potential for the future. With the rush of euphoria over, partners consider whether they want the relationship to last. If so, they work through problems and obstacles to long-term viability. In gay relationships, partners often have to resolve differences in openness about their sexual orientations. Heterosexual couples may need to work out differences in religions and conflicts in locations and career goals.

As you might expect, during this phase of romance, communication often involves negotiation and even conflict. This is natural, since during revising communication it's necessary to talk about negative features of a relationship and ways to improve them. These topics seldom arise in earlier stages of romance, since difficulties are not a serious problem until a long-term future is contemplated. Many couples are able to revise their relationships in ways that make them stronger and more able to endure. Other couples find they cannot resolve problems. Thus, it is not unusual for people to fall in love and move through the intensifying stage but then choose not to stay together. It is entirely possible to love a person with whom we don't want to share our life.

Commitment is a decision to stay with a relationship permanently. This decision transforms a romantic relationship from one based on past and present experiences and feelings into one with a future. Prior to making a commitment, partners don't view the relationship as continuing forever. With commitment, the relationship becomes a given, around which they arrange other aspects of their lives. This stage is analogous to stabilized friendship, since the basis of both is assumed continuity.

Navigating Navigating is the ongoing process of communicating to sustain intimacy over time and in the face of changes in individuals, the relationship, and surrounding contexts. Although navigating can be an extended stage in romantic intimacy, it is not stable, but rather is very

STYLES OF LOVING

Just as people differ in their tastes in food and ways of dressing, so do we differ in how we love. Researchers have identified six different styles of loving, each of which is valid in its own right, although not all styles are compatible with one another (Figure 9.2). See if you can identify your style of loving in the descriptions below.

Eros is a style of loving that is passionate, intense, and fast-moving. Not confined to sexual passion, eros may be expressed in spiritual, intellectual, or emotional ways.

Storge (pronounced store-gay) is a comfortable, best friends kind of love that grows gradually to create a stable and even-keeled companionship.

Ludus is a playful, sometimes manipulative, style of loving. For ludic lovers, love is a challenge, a puzzle, a game to be relished, but not to lead to commitment.

Mania is an unsettling style of loving marked by emotional extremes. Manic lovers are often insecure of their value and their partners' commitment.

Agape is a selfless kind of love in which a beloved's happiness is more important than one's own. Agapic lovers are generous, unselfish, and devoted.

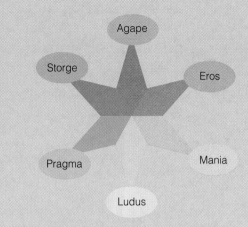

FIGURE 9.2 **The Colors of Love**

Pragma is a pragmatic and goal-oriented style of loving. Pragmas rely on reason and practical considerations to select people to love.

Sources: Hendrick, C., & Hendrick, S. (1996). Gender and the experience of heterosexual love. In J. T. Wood (Ed.), *Gendered relationships.* Mountain View, CA: Mayfield. Hendrick, C., Hendrick, S., Foote, F. H., & Slapion-Foote, M. J. (1984). Do men and women love differently? *Journal of Social and Personal Relationships, 2,* 177–196. Lee, J. A. (1973). *The colours of love: An exploration of the ways of loving.* Don Mills, Ontario: New Press. Lee, J. A. (1988). Love-styles. In R. J. Sternberg & M. L. Barnes (Eds.), *The psychology of love* (pp. 38–67). New Haven, CT: Yale University Press.

dynamic. Couples continuously work through new problems, revisit old ones, and accommodate to changes in their individual and joint lives. To use an automotive analogy, navigating involves both preventive maintenance and periodic repairs (Canary & Stafford, 1994). Navigating communication aims to keep intimacy satisfying and healthy and to deal with any problems and tensions that arise.

The nucleus of intimacy is **relational culture,** which is a private world of rules, understandings, meanings, and patterns of interacting that partners create for their relationship (Wood, 1982). Relational culture includes how a couple manages relational dialectics. Mei-Ling and Gregory may do a great many things together, whereas Lana and Kaya emphasize autonomy. Brent and Carmella may be open and expressive, while Marion and Senona prefer more privacy in their marriage. There aren't right and wrong ways to manage dialectics, since individuals and couples differ in what they need. The unique character of each relationship culture reflects how partners deal with tensions between autonomy and connection, openness and privacy, and novelty and routine (Fitzpatrick & Best, 1979; Wood, 1995b).

Relational culture also involves communication rules that partners work out. Couples develop agreements, usually unspoken, about how to signal anger, love, sexual interest, and so forth. They also develop routines for contact. Robbie and I catch up while we're fixing dinner each day. Other couples reserve weekends for staying in touch. Especially important in navigating is "small talk," through which partners weave together the fabric of their history and their current lives, experiences, and dreams.

Deterioration   Steve Duck (1992) proposed a five-phase model of relational decline. **Dyadic breakdown** is the first stage, and it involves degeneration of established patterns, understandings, and routines that make up a relational culture. Partners may stop talking after dinner, no longer bother to call when they are running late, and in other ways neglect the "little" things that tie them together. As the fabric of intimacy weakens, dissatisfaction mounts.

There are general gender differences in the causes of dyadic breakdown. For women, unhappiness with a relationship most often arises when communication declines in quality and/or quantity. Men are more likely to be dissatisfied by specific behaviors. For instance, men report being dissatisfied when their partners don't greet them at the door and make special meals (Riessman, 1990). For many men, dissatisfaction also arises if they have domestic responsibilities that they feel aren't a man's job (Gottman & Carrere, 1994). It seems that women feel a relationship is breaking down if "we don't really communicate with each other anymore," whereas men tend to feel dissatisfied if "we don't do fun things together any more." Another gender difference is in who notices problems in a relationship. As a rule, women are more likely than men to perceive declines in intimacy. Since many women are socialized to be sensitive to interpersonal nuances, they are likely to notice tensions and early symptoms of relational distress (Cancian, 1989; Tavris, 1992).

The **intrapsychic phase** involves brooding about problems in the relationship and dissatisfactions with a partner (Duck, 1992). Women's brooding about languishing relationships tends to focus on perceived declines in closeness and intimate communication, while men's reflections more often center on lapses in joint activities and concrete acts of consideration between partners. It's easy for the intrapsychic phase to become a self-fulfilling prophecy: As gloomy thoughts snowball and awareness of positive features of the relationship ebb, partners may actually bring about the failure of their relationship. During the intrapsychic phase, partners may begin to think about alternatives to the relationship.

Dyadic negotiation, the third phase in relational decline, doesn't always occur (Duck, 1992). When it does, the phase tends to involve conflict. Women are more likely to respond to conflict by initiating discussion of problems, and men often deny problems or exit rather than talk about them. Communication scholars report that many people avoid talking about problems, refuse to return calls from partners, and in other ways evade confronting difficulties (Baxter, 1984; Metts, Cupach, & Bejlovec, 1989). Although it is painful to talk about problems, avoiding discussion does nothing to resolve them and may, in fact, make them worse. What happens in the negotiation phase depends on how committed partners are, whether they perceive attractive alternatives to the relationship, and whether they have the communication skills to work through problems constructively.

If partners lack commitment and/or communication skills needed to resuscitate intimacy, they enter the **social phase** of disintegration, which involves figuring out how to tell outsiders they are parting. Either separately or in collaboration, partners decide how to explain their breakup to friends, children, in-laws, and social acquaintances. When partners don't cooperatively create a joint explanation for breaking up, friends may take sides, gossip, and disparage one or the other partner as the "bad guy" (La Gaipa, 1982).

Social support is a phase in which partners look to friends and family for support during the breakup. Others can provide support by being available and by listening. Partners may give self-serving accounts of the breakup in order to save face and secure sympathy and support from others. Thus, Vera may tell her friends all of the ways in which Frank was at fault and portray herself as the innocent party. During this phase, partners often criticize their exes and expect friends to take their side (Duck, 1992). Although self-serving explanations of breakups are common, they aren't necessarily constructive. We have an ethical responsibility to monitor communication during this period so that we don't say things we'll later regret.

Grave dressing is the final phase in relational decline, and it involves burying the relationship and accepting its end. During grave dressing, we work to make sense of the relationship—what it meant, why it failed, and how it affected us. Typically, we mourn a relationship that has died. Even the person who initiates a breakup is often sad about the failure to realize what seemed possible at one time. Grave dressing completes the process of relational dissolution by putting the relationship to rest so that partners can get on with their individual lives.

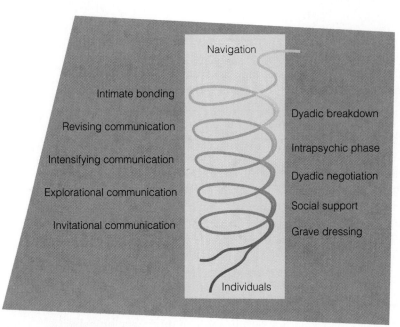

FIGURE 9.3
Stages of Romantic Relationships

Navigation

Intimate bonding

Revising communication

Intensifying communication

Explorational communication

Invitational communication

Dyadic breakdown

Intrapsychic phase

Dyadic negotiation

Social support

Grave dressing

Individuals

The stages we've discussed describe how most people experience the evolution of romance (see Figure 9.3). However, not all couples follow the standard pattern. Some partners skip one or more stages, and many of us cycle more than once through certain stages. For example, a couple might soar through euphoria, work out some tough issues in revising, then go through euphoria a second time. It's also normal for long-term partners to move out of navigation periodically as they experience both euphoric seasons and intervals of dyadic breakdown. In the ebb and flow of enduring romantic relationships, there is a great deal of movement. What remains constant as long as intimacy exists are partners' commitment to a future and investments in the relationship.

Everyday Application

YOUR RELATIONSHIP'S EVOLUTION

Recall a romantic relationship of yours that ended. Trace how it evolved from first meeting through final encounter. Do the stages we've discussed apply to the evolution of your romantic relationship? If not, how would you change or add to the stages we've described?

CHALLENGES IN PERSONAL RELATIONSHIPS

To sustain fulfilling personal relationships, partners rely on communication to deal with internal tensions between themselves and external pressures from other people and commitments. How skillfully we manage these challenges with effective communication is a major influence on the endurance and quality of personal relationships. We'll consider five specific challenges that many friends and romantic partners face.

Adapting to Diverse Communication Styles

Personal relationships may be strained when friends have different ways of communicating that reflect their different cultures. A range of communication styles is common in a diverse society such as ours. For instance, in many Asian societies, individuals are socialized to be unassuming and modest, while the United States encourages being assertive and celebrating ourselves. Thus, a native Japanese might perceive a friend from Milwaukee as arrogant for saying, "Let's go out to celebrate my job offer." A Thai woman might not get the support she wants from a friend from Brooklyn because she learned not to assert her needs and the Brooklyn friend was taught that people speak up for themselves.

Misunderstandings also arise from differences among co-cultures in the United States. Joe, who is white, might feel hurt if Markus, an African American friend, turns down going to a concert in order to go home to care for an ailing aunt. Joe might interpret this as a rejection by Markus, since he perceives that the aunt is an excuse, signifying that Markus really doesn't want to be with him. Joe would interpret Markus differently if he realized that, as a rule, African Americans are more communal than Caucasians, so taking care of extended family members is a priority (Gaines, 1995). Ellen may feel her friend Jed isn't being supportive when instead of listening to her problems, he offers advice or suggests they go out to take her mind off her troubles. Yet, he *is* showing support according to masculine rules of communication. Jed, on the other hand, may feel Ellen is intruding on his autonomy when she pushes him to talk about his feelings. According to feminine rules of communication, however, Ellen *is* showing interest and concern.

Differences themselves aren't usually the cause of problems between intimates. Instead, how we interpret and judge diverse communication styles is the root of much tension and hurt (remember the abstraction ladder we discussed in Chapter 2?). Jed interpreted Ellen according to his communication rules, not hers, and she interpreted Jed according to her communication rules, not his. The tension between them results from how they interpret each other's behaviors, not the behaviors themselves.

Dealing with Distance

Geographic separation can be difficult for friends and romantic couples. Many of us will be involved in long-distance romantic relationships, since they are increasingly common. Fully 70% of college students are or have been in long-distance romances (Rohlfing, 1995). The number of long-distance romantic relationships will increase further as more partners pursue independent careers.

Perhaps the two greatest problems for long-distance commitments are the lack of daily communication about small events and issues and unrealistic expectations about interaction when partners are physically together.

COPING WITH GEOGRAPHIC SEPARATION

Students report nine strategies for long-distance love.

1. Recognize that long-distance relationships are common; you're not alone.

2. Create more social support systems (friends) while separated from a romantic partner.

3. Communicate creatively—send video and audio tapes.

4. Before separating, work out ground rules for going out with friends, phoning, visiting, and writing.

5. Use time together "wisely" to be affectionate and have fun. Being serious all the time isn't smart.

6. Maintain honesty. Especially when partners live apart, they need to be straight with each other.

7. Build an open, supportive communication climate so that you can talk about issues and feelings.

8. Maintain trust by abiding by ground rules that were agreed on, phoning when you say you will, and keeping lines of communication open.

9. Focus on the positive aspects of separation, such as career advancement or ability to focus on work.

Source: Westefield, J.S., & Liddell, D. (1982). Coping with long-distance relationships. *Journal of College Student Personnel, 23,* 550–551.

The first problem—not being able to share small talk and daily routines—is a major loss, especially for partners who can't communicate over the Internet. As we have seen, communication about the ordinary comings and goings of days helps partners keep their lives woven together. The mundane conversations that romantic partners have form the basic fabric of their relationship. A second common problem is unrealistic expectations for time together. Because partners have so little time when they are physically together, they often believe every moment must be perfect. They may feel that there should be no conflict and that they should be with each other all of the time they have together. Yet, this is a very unrealistic expectation. Conflict and needs for autonomy are natural in all romantic relationships. They may be even more likely in long-distance couples, since partners are used to living alone and have established independent rhythms that may not mesh well.

The good news is that these problems don't necessarily sabotage long-distance romance. Most researchers report that partners can maintain satisfying commitments in spite of geographic separation (Rohlfing, 1995). To overcome the difficulties of long-distance love, many couples engage in creative communication to sustain intimacy. The Communication Highlight summarizes some of the ways intimates bridge the distance. Since the research that is the basis of the material was conducted, electronic communication has mushroomed, making it one of the primary ways many couples who are apart stay in touch.

Creating Equitable Relationships

Equity between partners affects satisfaction with relationships. Researchers report that the happiest dating and married couples believe both partners invest equally (Hecht, Marston, & Larkey, 1994). When we think we are investing more than a partner, we tend to be resentful. When it seems our partner is investing more than we are, we may feel guilty. Imbalance of either sort erodes satisfaction.

Although few partners demand moment-to-moment equality, most of us want our relationships to be equitable over time. Equity has multiple dimensions. We may evaluate the fairness of financial, emotional, physical, and other contributions to a relationship. One area that strongly affects satisfaction of spouses and cohabiting partners is equity in housework and child care. Inequitable division of domestic obligations fuels dissatisfaction and resentment, both of which harm intimacy (Gottman & Carrere, 1994). Marital stability is more closely linked to equitable divisions of child care and housework than to income or sex life (Fowers, 1991; Suitor, 1991).

More than four of five marriages today include two wage earners (Wilkie, 1991). Unfortunately, divisions of family and home responsibilities have not changed much in response to changing employment patterns. Even when both partners in heterosexual relationships work outside the home, in 80% of dual-worker families women do the vast majority of child care and homemaking (Nussbaum, 1992; Okin, 1989). In only 20% of dual-worker families do men assume equal domestic responsibilities (Hochschild with Machung, 1989).

How are domestic responsibilities managed when both partners are the same sex? Lesbian couples create more egalitarian relationships than either heterosexuals or gays. More than any other type of couple, lesbians are likely to communicate collaboratively to make decisions about domestic work and parenting (Huston & Schwartz, 1995). Consequently, lesbians are least likely to have negative feelings about inequity (Kurdek, 1993). Gay men, like their heterosexual brothers, use the power derived from income to authorize inequitable contributions to domestic life. In gay couples, the man who makes more money has and uses more power, both in making decisions that affect the relationship and in avoiding housework (Huston & Schwartz, 1995). This suggests that power is the basis of gendered divisions of labor and that men, more than women, seek the privileges of power, including evasion of domestic work.

Couples who share equitably in domestic responsibilities are happier than couples who don't.
(© Chuck Savage/The Stock Market)

Violence between intimates cuts across lines of class, race, and ethnicity. (© Thelma Shumsky/The Image Works)

As a rule, women assume **psychological responsibility,** which involves remembering, planning, and coordinating domestic activities. Parents may alternate who takes children to the doctor, but it is usually the mother who remembers when check-ups are needed, makes appointments, and reminds the father to take the child. Cards and gifts are signed by both partners, but women typically assume the burden of remembering birthdays and buying cards and gifts. Successful long-term relationships in our era require partners to communicate collaboratively to design equitable divisions of responsibility.

MOLLY

It really isn't fair when both spouses work outside of the home but only one of them takes care of the home and kids. For years, that was how Sean's and my marriage worked, no matter how much I tried to talk with him about a more fair arrangement. Finally, I had just had it, so I quit doing everything. Groceries didn't get bought, laundry piled up and he didn't have clean shirts, he didn't remember his mother's birthday (and for the first time ever, I didn't remind him), and bills didn't get paid. After a while he suggested we talk about a system we could both live with.

Resisting Violence and Abuse Between Intimates

Although we like to think of romantic relationships as loving, many are not. Unfortunately, violence and abuse are common between romantic partners, and they cut across lines of class, race, and ethnicity (French, 1992; West, 1995). Violence is high not only in heterosexual marriages, but also in dating relationships (French, 1992; Muehlenhardt & Linton, 1987; Stets, 1990; Thompson, 1991). It also appears that cohabiting couples have the highest incidence of violence of all couples—women who cohabit suffer one and a half to two times more physical violence than married women (Stets & Straus, 1989). In addition to physical abuse, verbal and emotional brutality poison all too many relationships.

The majority of detected violence and abuse in intimacy seems to be committed by men against women. Currently in the United States, a woman is beaten every 12 to 18 seconds by a husband or intimate, and four women are beaten to death each day in this country (Brock-Utne, 1989). Rape and date rape are escalating, especially when individuals

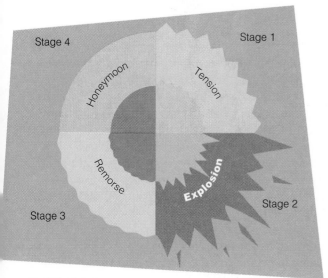

FIGURE 9.4
Cycle of Abuse

have been drinking ("What Teens Say," 1994). Too often, individuals don't leave abusive relationships because they feel trapped by economic pressures or by relatives and clergy who counsel them to stay (West, 1995).

Violence seldom stops without intervention. Instead it follows a predictable cycle: Tension mounts in the abuser, the abuser explodes by being violent, the abuser then is remorseful and loving, the victim feels loved and reassured that the relationship is working, and then tension mounts anew and the cycle begins again (see Figure 9.4). Relationships that are abusive are unhealthy for everyone involved. They violate the trust that is a foundation of intimacy. In addition, they jeopardize the comfort, health, and sometimes the life of victims of violence. Less obvious is the damage abusers do to themselves. Using physical force against others is a sign of weakness—an admission that a person must resort to the most crude and unimaginative methods of influence. Abusers can lower their self-esteem and destroy relationships that they want.

There is a twofold relationship between communication and violence between intimates. Most obviously, patterns of communication between couples and intrapersonal communication of abusers can fuel tendencies toward violence. Some partners deliberately annoy and taunt each other, a pattern that can lead to serious abuse. Also, the language abusers use to describe physical assaults on partners includes denial, trivializing the harm done, and blaming the partner or circumstances for "making me do it" (Stamp & Sabourin, 1995). These intrapersonal communication patterns allow abusers to deny their offenses, justify unjustifiable actions, and cast responsibility outside of themselves. None of these communication patterns is likely to diminish or end violence.

Violence between intimates is also promoted by cultural communication practices that normalize violence. Media are saturated with incidents of rape and physical violation of women. From magazines to films to MTV, violence against women is pervasive in media. News accounts that refer to "loving her too much" and "love that gets out of hand" camouflage the brutality and *un*lovingness of violence (Meyers, 1994).

Violent relationships are *not* the fault of victims. Contrary to the misperception that victims either are masochists or deserve what they get, there is no justification for physical violence against an intimate. A person cannot earn battering, nor do victims encourage it (Goodrich, Rampage, Ellman, & Halstead, 1988). If you know or suspect that someone you care about is a victim of abuse, don't ignore the situation and don't assume it's "none of my business." It is an act of friendship to notice and offer to help. Victims of violence must make the ultimate decisions about what to do, but the support and concern of friends can help them.

Negotiating Safer Sex

In the HIV/AIDS era, sexual activities pose serious, even deadly threats to romantic relationships. The World Health Organization estimates that 40 million people will be diagnosed as having HIV by the year 2000 ("Death Toll," 1991). Despite vigorous public education campaigns, a great many individuals still don't practice safer sex, which includes abstinence, restriction of sexual activity to a single partner who has been tested for HIV, and/or use of latex condoms (Reel & Thompson, 1994). In a recent nationwide survey, only 48% of men and 32% of women reported using condoms (Clements, 1994). Not practicing safer sex puts both partners at grave risk for early death.

Why don't people who know about HIV/AIDS consistently follow safer sex techniques? Communication scholars have discovered two primary reasons. First, ironically, many individuals find it more embarrassing to talk about sex than to engage in it. They find it awkward to ask direct questions of partners ("Have you been tested for HIV?" "Are you having sex with anyone else?") or to make direct requests of partners ("I want you to wear a condom," "I would like for you to be tested for HIV before we have sex"). Naturally, it's difficult to talk explicitly about sex and the dangers of HIV/AIDS. However, it is far more difficult to live with HIV or the knowledge you infected a lover.

A second reason people sometimes fail to practice safer sex is that their rational thought and control are debilitated by alcohol and other drugs. In a series of studies of college students' sexual activities, communication researchers Sheryl Bowen and Paula Michal-Johnson (1996) found that safer sex precautions are especially likely to be neglected when individuals drink heavily. The National Council on Alcoholism and Drug Dependence reports that sexually active teens are less likely to use condoms after drinking ("What Teens Say," 1994). Alcohol and other drugs loosen inhibitions, including appropriate concerns about personal safety.

Discussing and practicing safer sex may be awkward, but there is no sensible option. Good communication skills help ease the discomfort of negotiating safer sex. It is more constructive to say "I feel unsafe having unprotected sex" than "Without a condom, you could give me AIDS." (Notice that the first statement uses I-language, whereas the second one relies on you-language.) A positive communication climate is fostered by relational language, such as "we," "us," and "our relationship" to talk about sex (Reel & Thompson, 1994). Individuals who care about themselves and their partners are honest about their sexual histories and careful in their sex practices.

Sexual attraction or activities may also be part of friendships. Friendships between heterosexual men and women, gay men, or lesbians sometimes include sexual tensions. Because Western culture so strongly emphasizes gender and sex, it's difficult not to perceive people in sexual terms (Johnson, Stockdale, & Saal, 1991; Nardi & Sherrod, 1994; O'Meara, 1989). Even if sexual activity doesn't occur between heterosexual women and men, gays, or lesbians, sexual undertones may ripple beneath the surface of their friendships. Sexual attraction, tension, or invitations can be problems between friends who don't want to have a sexual relationship. Trust may be damaged if someone you consider a friend makes a pass at you. Once a friend transgresses the agreed-on boundaries of a friendship, it's hard to know how to act with each other and what to expect.

Personal relationships in our era face a number of challenges that require communication skill and sensitivity. Among these are dealing with cultural differences, maintaining long-distance intimacy, negotiating safer sex, ensuring equity, and avoiding violence.

SUMMARY

In this chapter, we've explored communication in personal relationships, which are defined by commitment, uniqueness, relational dialectics, relationship rules, and interaction with surrounding contexts. We traced the typical evolutionary paths of friendships and romances by noting how partners communicate during escalating, stabilizing, and declining stages of personal relationships. As we saw, communication is a primary dynamic in intimacy, influencing how we meet and get to know others, the patterns of interaction between friends and romantic partners, and the creation of relational cultures that, ideally, are healthy and affirming.

In the final section of the chapter, we considered five important challenges that friends and romantic partners face in the present era. The communication principles and skills we have discussed in this and previous chapters can help us meet the challenges of adapting to diverse communication styles, sustaining intimacy across geographic distance, creating equitable relationships, resisting violence, and negotiating safer sex. Good communication skills are essential to managing these challenges so that we, our intimates, and the relationships we co-create survive and thrive over time.

FOR FURTHER REFLECTION AND DISCUSSION

1.   Think about the distinction between love and commitment and the role each plays in personal relationships. Describe relationships in which commitment is present but love is not. Describe relationships in which love exists, but there's no commitment. What can you conclude about the values of each?

2.   Review the rules of friendship that researchers have identified. Do these match with your experiences in friendships? Do you have additional rules that are unique to your close friendships?

3.   Think about differences in the goals and rules for friendships and romantic relationships. Does comparing the two kinds of relationship give you any insight into the difficulties that commonly arise when two people who have been friends become romantically involved? What are the difficulties of trying to be friends with someone with whom you've been romantically involved?

4.   Are you now or have you been involved in a long-distance personal relationship, either friendship or romance? How did you communicate to bridge the distance? Do your experiences parallel the chapter's discussion of challenges in long-distance relationships?

5.   If others in your class are willing to talk openly about a difficult subject, discuss how couples can communicate about safer sex. Try to help each other understand any reservations, fears, or discomforts that surround talk about safer sex. Then try to generate communication strategies to make it easier for people to discuss health precautions and other topics important for sexual partners.

KEY TERMS

personal relationships
social relationships
passion
commitment
investments
rules
relational dialectics
neutralization
separation
segmentation
reframing
invitational communication
explorational communication
intensifying communication
revising communication
relational culture
dyadic breakdown
intrapsychic phase
dyadic negotiation
social phase
social support
grave dressing
psychological responsibility

Focus Questions

1 How are groups and teams different?

2 What are the limitations of groups and teams?

3 What are the strengths of groups and teams?

4 How do cultural values influence communication in groups and teams?

5 How does egocentric communication affect group cohesion and progress?

CHAPTER 10

Foundations of Group and Team Communication

eams take too much time to decide anything."
"Working in groups increases creativity and
commitment."
"Groups suppress individuality."
"Teams make better decisions than individuals do."

With which of these statements do you agree? People who enjoy
working in groups would tend to agree with the second and fourth
statements. The first and third claims are more likely to ring true
to people who find group work difficult or unrewarding. Actually,
there's some truth to each of the statements. Groups generally do
take more time to reach decisions than individuals, yet group decisions are often superior to those made by a single person. Although
group interaction stimulates creativity, it may also suppress
individuals.

Teams have become increasingly popular in today's business world. Team members must communicate continuously (and well!) to meet their shared goals. (© Robert Rathe/Stock, Boston)

Communication is one of the major influences on whether groups and teams are productive and enjoyable or inefficient and unpleasant. Communication in groups and teams calls for many of the skills and understandings we discussed in previous chapters. For example, constructive group communication requires that members express themselves clearly, check perceptions, support others, respect differences, build good climates, and listen effectively.

This chapter and the one that follows will help you discover how to communicate effectively when you work in groups and teams. Reading these two chapters will enlarge your appreciation of the ways in which communication shapes and is shaped by small group work. That insight will enhance your ability to participate and lead effectively in group and team situations.

In this chapter, we begin by noting the increasing popularity of groups and teams in modern life. Next we define *group* and *team* and point out similarities and differences between the two. In the third section of the chapter, we discuss potential weaknesses and strengths of group discussion. We then examine influences on interaction among members of groups and teams. Finally, we discuss various kinds of group communication and consider how each affects collective climate and productivity.

THE RISE OF GROUPS AND TEAMS

Whether your experiences in groups have been positive, negative, or a mix of the two, you probably have belonged to a number of groups during your life. Pick up any paper and you will see announcements and advertisements for social groups, volunteer service committees, personal support groups, health teams, focus groups sought by companies trying out new products, and political action coalitions. In the workplace, as well, collective units are increasingly prevalent as our businesses increasingly move away from reliance on individual workers and toward a preference for work teams. It is a rare person in the United States who doesn't have a wealth of group experiences.

The tendency toward teamwork is especially pronounced in the workplace. Whether you are an attorney working with a litigation team, a health care professional who participates in health delivery teams, or a factory worker on a team assigned to reduce production time, working with others probably will be part of your career. It's likely that your raises and advancement will depend significantly on how well you work in team situations. The reason for increasing reliance on teams is that they often do better work than individuals. As members of a team communicate, ideas are stimulated and creativity is stoked. Frequently, the results are better ideas and greater personal satisfaction with work.

In this chapter, we'll cover some of the foundations for participating in many types of groups and teams; in Chapter 11, we will focus in greater depth on work teams.

Everyday Application

GROUPS IN YOUR LIFE

To how many groups do you belong? Below list the groups in which you currently participate.

Social Groups: _____

_____

Personal Support Groups: _____

_____

Work Groups: _____

_____

Volunteer Service Committees: _____

_____

WHAT ARE SMALL GROUPS?

Let's start with a basic question: What is a small group? Are six people standing together on a street corner waiting to cross the street a group? Are five individuals studying in a library a group? Are four students in a class a group? The answer is no in each of these cases. These are situations in which we have a collection of individuals, but not a group. For a group to exist, there must be interaction and interdependence among individuals, a common goal, and shared rules of conduct. Thus, we can define a **group** as three or more individuals who interact over time, depend on each other,

TEAM EXCELLENCE AND EXCELLENCE IN TEAMS

Over a decade ago, the Xerox Corporation discovered the value of teamwork. CEO Paul Allaire says he's a firm believer in the power of teamwork. As a result, over 75% of Xerox employees at all levels are actively involved in work teams that are responsible for everything from reducing costs of delivery and improving customer satisfaction to designing new products.

Xerox recognizes excellence in team performance with its Team Excellence Award, which involves a formal ceremony and a monetary reward shared by all members of the winning team. One recent winner was the "Fly-by-Nites," a team that reduced the cost of overnight air shipments by a dramatic 1.9 million dollars and that improved speed of deliveries, which increased customer satisfaction.

Source: Bowles, J. G. (1990, September 24). The human side of quality. *Fortune*, n.p.

and follow shared rules of conduct in order to reach a common goal. To be a group, members must perceive themselves as interdependent—as somehow needing one another and counting on one another. Group interdependence and interaction generate cohesion, or a feeling of group identity. Later in this chapter, we'll discuss cohesion in greater detail.

A **team** is a special kind of group that is characterized by different and complementary resources of members and by a strong sense of collective identity. Like all groups, teams involve interaction, interdependence, shared rules, and common goals. Yet, teams are different from general groups in two respects. First, teams consist of people with diverse skills. Whereas a group may consist of several people, each of whom contributes to all aspects of group work, a team consists of people who bring specialized and different resources to a common project. Second, teams develop greater interdependence and a stronger sense of identity than standard groups. Teams see themselves as a unit much more than ordinary groups do (Lumsden & Lumsden, 1997). All teams are groups, but not all groups are teams.

All groups consist of individuals who are interdependent and who interact over time. People who are in one place but not interacting are not a group, nor does a group exist if people have only a fleeting exchange that is insufficient to generate cohesion. Groups and teams also develop rules that members understand and follow. You'll recall from earlier chapters that constitutive rules state what counts as what. For example, in some groups, disagreement counts as a positive sign of involvement, while other groups regard disagreement as negative. Regulative rules regulate how, when, and with whom we interact. For instance, a group might have regulative rules

"May I suggest that in today's group-therapy session we all work on our contact with reality."

(Reprinted by courtesy of *Omni* magazine. © 1979.)

stipulating that members don't interrupt each other and that it's okay to be a few minutes late, but more than 10 minutes is a sign of disregard for other group members. Groups generate rules over time in the process of interacting and figuring out what works for them.

MIEKO

When I first came here to go to school, I felt very alone. I met some other students from Japan, and we formed a group to help us feel at home in America. For the first year, that group was most important to me and the others because we felt uprooted. The second year it was good, but not so important because we'd all started finding ways to fit in here and we felt more at home. When we met the first time of the third year, we decided not to be a group anymore. The reason we wanted a group no longer existed.

Groups are also characterized by shared goals. Some common objective or objectives bring and hold members together. Citizens form groups to accomplish political goals, establish social and art programs, protest zoning decisions, and protect the security of neighborhoods. Workers form teams to develop and market products, evaluate and refine company programs, and improve productivity. Other groups form around goals such as promoting personal growth (therapy groups), sharing a life (families), socializing (singles clubs), having fun and fitting in (peer groups), or participating in sports (intramural teams). As Mieko explains in her commentary, without a common goal, a group doesn't exist. Groups end if the common objective has been achieved or if it ceases to matter to members. To better understand small groups, we'll now consider their potential values and limits, features that affect participation, and the influence of culture on communication in groups.

POTENTIAL LIMITATIONS AND STRENGTHS OF GROUPS

A great deal of research has compared individual and group decision making. As you might expect, the research identifies both potential weaknesses and strengths of groups relative to individuals.

(Horace Pippin, *Harmonizing* (1944). Oil on canvas. Allen Memorial Art Museum, Oberlin College, Ohio. Gift of Joseph and Enid Bissett, 1964.)

Limitations of Groups

The two most significant disadvantages of group discussion are the time required for group process and the potential of conformity pressures that can interfere with high-quality work from groups.

Time   If you've ever worked in a group—and who hasn't?—you know that it takes much longer for groups to decide something than it takes an individual. Operating solo, an individual can think through ideas efficiently and choose the one she or he considers best. In group discussion, however, all members must have an opportunity to voice their ideas and to respond to the ideas others put forward.

It takes substantial time for each person to describe ideas, clarify misunderstandings, and respond to questions or criticisms. In addition, groups require time to deliberate about alternative courses of action. Thus, group discussion is probably not a wise choice for routine policy making and emergency tasks. When creativity and thoroughness are important, however, the values of groups may outweigh the disadvantage of time they require.

Conformity Pressures   Groups also have the potential to suppress individuals and to encourage conformity. This can happen in two ways. Most obviously, conformity pressures may exist when a majority of members have an opinion different from that of a minority of members or a single member. It's hard to hold out for your point of view when most of your peers have a different one. In effective groups, however, all members understand

and resist conformity pressures. They realize that the majority is sometimes wrong and the minority, even a single person, is sometimes right. This implies that members should communicate in ways that encourage expression of diverse ideas and open debate about different viewpoints. Our earlier discussion of communication that creates an open climate (see Chapter 8) is relevant to effective group work.

Conformity pressures may also arise when there is one member who is extremely charismatic, has high prestige, or has greater power than other members. Even if that person is all alone in a point of view, he or she has the status to pressure others to go along. Sometimes a high-status member doesn't intend to influence others and may not overtly exert pressure. The status, however, is still there and influential. President Kennedy, for example, often tried not to shape views of his advisers, but they regarded him so highly that in some cases they suspended their individual critical thinking and agreed with whatever he said (Janis, 1977). As this example illustrates, often neither a high-status person nor others are consciously aware of pressures to conform. Effective discussion occurs when members guard against the potential to conform uncritically.

LANCE

I used to belong to a creative writing group where all of us helped each other improve our writing. We were all equally vocal, and we had a lot of good discussions and even disagreements when the group first started. But then one member of the group got a story of hers accepted by a big magazine, and all of a sudden we thought of her as a better writer than any of us. She didn't act any different, but we saw her as more accomplished, so when she said something everybody listened and nobody disagreed. It was like a wet blanket on our creativity because her opinion just carried too much weight once she got published.

Strengths of Groups

The primary potential strengths of groups in comparison to individuals are that groups generally have greater resources, are more thorough, are more creative, and generate greater commitment to decisions (Wood, 1992a).

Greater Resources   A group obviously exceeds any individuals in the number of ideas, perspectives, experiences, and expertise it can bring to bear on solving a problem. Especially in teams, the different resources of individual members are a key to effectiveness. One member may know the technical aspects of a product, another understands market psychology, a third is talented in advertising, and so forth. Health care teams consist of specialists who combine their knowledge to care for a patient. When my father was hospitalized after a series of strokes, we had a health care team that included a neurologist, a cardiologist, a physical therapist, a social worker, and a registered nurse. Each member of the team had a different expertise, and they coordinated their specific skills and knowledge to provide him with integrated care.

Interaction among team members often heightens commitment to collective goals.
(© Craig Aurness/Woodfin Camp & Associates, Inc.)

More Thorough Groups also tend to be more thorough than individuals, probably because members act as a "check and balance" system for each other. The parts of an issue one member doesn't understand, another person does; the details of a plan that bore one person interest another; the holes in a proposal that one member doesn't see will be recognized by others. Greater thoroughness by groups isn't the result simply of more people. It also reflects interaction among members. Discussion itself promotes more critical and careful analysis because members propel each other's thinking (Wood, 1992a). **Synergy** is a special kind of energy that combines and goes beyond the energies, talents, and strengths of individual members (Lumsden & Lumsden, 1997).

Greater Creativity A third value of groups is that they are generally more creative than individuals. Again, the reason seems to lie in the synergetic communication process in groups. When members know how to communicate effectively, they interact in ways that spark good ideas, integrative thinking, and creativity. Any individual eventually runs out of new ideas, but groups seem to have almost infinite generative ability. As members talk, they build on each other's ideas, refine proposals, see new possibilities in each other's comments, and so forth. The result is often a greater number of overall ideas and more creative final solutions.

LAURA

The first time I heard about brainstorming was on my job when the supervisor said all of us in my department were to meet and brainstorm ways to cut costs for the company. I thought it was silly to take time to discuss cost saving when each person could just submit suggestions individually. But I was wrong. When my group started, each of us had one or two ideas—only that many. But the six of us came up with more than 25 ideas after we'd talked for an hour.

Enlarged Commitment Finally, an important strength of groups is their ability to generate commitment to decisions. The greater commitment fostered by group discussion arises from two sources. First, participation in the decision-making process enhances commitment to decisions. Thus, groups build commitment among members, which is especially important if members will be involved in implementing the decision. Second, because groups have greater resources than an individual decision-maker, their decisions are more likely to take into account the points of view of various people whose cooperation is needed to implement a decision. This is critical, since a decision can be sabotaged if the people it affects dislike it or believe their perspectives weren't considered.

Greater resources, thoroughness, creativity, and commitment to group goals are powerful values of group decision making. To realize these values, however, members must be aware of the trade-off in time required for group discussion and must resist pressures to conform or induce others to conform without critical thought.

FEATURES OF SMALL GROUPS

The values of groups that we've identified are realized only if members participate effectively. This is most likely when members understand group features and when they have good communication skills. What happens in discussion results from how members communicate verbally and nonverbally to create understandings, meanings, and a group culture that foster high-quality work. If members don't participate, a group can't achieve its potential to be creative, to be thorough, to draw on many resources, and to develop commitment to decisions. Thus, we need to know what influences communication in small groups, and how communication itself influences the nature and quality of group work. We'll consider five features of small groups that directly affect participation.

Cohesion

Cohesion is the degree of closeness, or members' feelings of esprit de corps and group identity. In highly cohesive groups, members see themselves as linked tightly together and unified in goals. In turn, this results in greater satisfaction with being in a group than is felt by members of noncohesive units. High cohesion and the satisfaction with membership it generates tend to increase members' commitment to a group and to achieving common goals. Consequently, cohesiveness is important to effective and satisfying group communication.

Perhaps you wonder whether you can foster cohesion in groups. If so, you'll be pleased to know that cohesion can be encouraged in a number of ways. First, it's important to engage in communication that emphasizes the group or team and the common objectives of all members. Comments that stress pulling together and collective interests build cohesion by reinforcing group identity. Cohesion is also fostered by communication that highlights similarities among members—what interests, goals, experiences, and ways of thinking are common to different people in the group. A third way to enhance cohesion is by expressing affection, respect, and inclusion so that all members feel valued and part of the group (Gibb, 1961, 1964; Schutz, 1966).

COMMUNICATION AND COHESION

Select a group to which you belong and rate its level of cohesion as high, moderate, or low. Next, pay attention to the communication among members of the group during one meeting. Based on the discussion, answer the following five questions:

1. To what extent does communication focus on the group or team?
2. To what extent does talk among members emphasize collective goals?
3. To what degree do members talk about pulling together and collaborating?
4. To what extent do members comment on similarities among their goals, interests, experiences, and so on?
5. To what degree do members communicate affection and respect to one another?

Cohesion and participation influence each other reciprocally. Cohesion is promoted when all members are involved and participating in group communication. At the same time, because cohesiveness generates a feeling of identity and involvement, once established, it fosters participation. Thus, high levels of participation tend to build cohesion, and strong cohesion generally fosters vigorous participation. Encouraging all members to be involved in discussion and attending responsively to everyone's contributions generally foster cohesion and continued participation.

Although cohesion is important for effective group communication, too much cohesion can actually undermine sound group work. When members are extremely close, they may be less critical of each other's ideas and less willing to engage in analysis and arguments that are necessary to develop the best outcomes. When groups are too cohesive, they may experience **groupthink**, which exists when members cease to think critically and independently about ideas generated by a group. Groupthink has occurred in high-level groups such as presidential advisory boards and national decision-making bodies (Janis, 1977; Wood, Phillips, & Pedersen, 1986). What tends to happen is that members perceive their group so positively that they share an illusion it cannot make bad decisions. Consequently, they are less careful in screening and evaluating ideas generated in the group. The predictable result is inferior group outcomes.

Group Size

The sheer number of people in a group affects the amount of communication. Consider the difference between communication between two friends and communication in a group of five people. When friends talk, there are

Group members with high power are often the center of group communication and often have greater influence on group decisions. (© Anne Dowie)

two people sending and receiving messages. In a group of five, there are five people doing the same thing! Each idea that's expressed must be understood by four others who may also choose to respond. Consequently, the greater number of people in a group, the fewer contributions any individual may make. Since participation is linked to commitment, larger groups may generate less commitment to decisions than smaller ones. Large groups with eight or more members may also be less cohesive than smaller ones.

Because there are disadvantages to large groups, you might assume that small groups of three would be the most effective. However, groups can be too small as well as too large. With too few members, a group has limited resources, which eliminates a primary advantage of groups for decision making. Also, in very small groups, members may be unwilling to disagree or criticize each other's ideas, since alienating one person in a two- or three-person group would dramatically diminish the group. Most researchers agree that five to seven members is the ideal size for a small group (Wood, 1992a).

YOLANDA

The worst group I was ever on had three members. We were supposed to have five, but two dropped out after the first meeting, so there were three of us to come up with proposals for artistic programs for the campus. Nobody would say anything against anybody else's ideas, even if we thought they were bad. For myself, I know I held back from criticizing a lot of times because I didn't want to offend either of the other two. We came up with some really bad ideas because we were so small we couldn't risk arguing.

Power Structure

Power structure is a third feature that influences participation in small groups. **Power** is the ability to influence others (Wood et al., 1986). There are different kinds of power, or ways of influencing others. **Power over** is the ability to help or harm others. This form of power is usually expressed in ways that highlight the status and visibility of the person wielding influence. A group leader might exert positive power over a member by providing mentoring, positive reports to superiors, and visibility in the group. A leader could also exert negative power over a member by withholding these benefits, assigning unpleasant tasks, and responding negatively to the member's communication during group meetings.

GENDERED POWER PATTERNS

Men and women, as groups, differ in how they define and use power. Men tend to see power as finitely limited and as something to be guarded for oneself. Women, on the other hand, generally regard power as unlimited and, therefore, as something to be shared freely. Another difference lies in how the sexes see the ends of power. Men, more than women, see power as something a person has and uses to enhance individual status and to distinguish himself from "the pack." The tendency among women is to perceive power as a resource for empowering others so that more people are involved and the best decisions, policies, and so on are reached. These different orientations toward power are consistent with gendered communication cultures and the divergent rules of communication they impress on women and men.

Source: Helgesen, S. (1990). *The female advantage: Women's ways of leadership.* New York: Doubleday/Currency.

Power to is the ability to empower others to reach their goals (Boulding, 1990; Staley, 1988). Individuals who empower others do not broadcast their own influence. Instead, they act "behind the scenes" to enlarge others' influence and help others succeed. Power to is expressed in creating opportunities for others, recognizing achievements, and arranging circumstances to facilitate others in accomplishing their goals. In small groups, power to involves the capacity to create community, inspire loyalty, and build team spirit so that members of groups are productive and satisfied (Boulding, 1990). Group members who use power to help each other foster a win–win group climate in which each member's success is seen as advancing collective work. Members perceive themselves as a unit that benefits from the successes of each individual member.

The power structure of a group refers to how much power various members have. Power may result from position (CEO, president, professor, best friend of the boss) or it may be earned (demonstrated competence or expertise). If all members of a group have relatively equal power, the group has a distributed power structure. On the other hand, if one or more members have greater power than others, the group has a hierarchical power structure. Hierarchy may take the form of one person who is more powerful than all others, who are equal in power to each other. Alternatively, hierarchy may be more complicated with multiple levels of power. A leader might have the greatest power, three others might have equal power to each other but less than the leader, and four other members might have relatively little power.

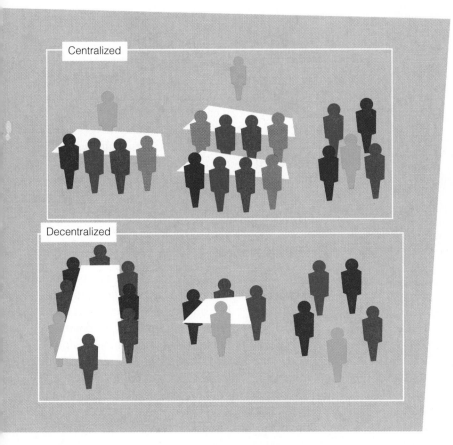

Centralized

Decentralized

FIGURE 10.1
Group Interaction Patterns

How are individual power and group power structure related to participation? First, members with high power tend to be the centers of group communication—they talk more and others talk more to them. **Social climbing** is the process of trying to increase personal status in a group by winning the approval of high-status members. If social climbing doesn't work to increase the status of those doing it, they often become marginal participants in groups. In addition, members with a great deal of power often have greater influence on group decisions. Not surprisingly, high-power members tend to find group discussion more satisfying than members with less power (Wood et al., 1986). This makes sense, since those with power get to participate more and get their way more often.

Power not only influences communication, but also is influenced by communication. In other words, how members communicate can affect the power they acquire. Individuals who know how to organize collective work tend to earn power quickly. This is an example of earned power that is conferred because a member provides skills valued by the group. Members who demonstrate they've done their homework and who contribute to the group likewise gain power.

Interaction Patterns

Another important influence on participation is the interaction patterns in a group. Some groups are centralized so that one or two people have key positions and most or all communication is funneled through them (see Figure 10.1). Other groups have decentralized patterns in which communication is more balanced and, thus, more satisfying to everyone. As you might suspect, the power of individual members and the power structure of the group often affect interaction patterns. If one or two members have greater power than others, a centralized pattern of interaction is likely to emerge. Decentralized patterns are more typical when members have relatively equal power.

"As the organizational chart shows, we have decided to merge our hunting and gathering divisions."

(Reprinted from *The Wall Street Journal* by permission of Cartoon Features Syndicate.)

One strategy for controlling communication in groups is to manage nonverbal influences on interaction. If you want a centralized communication structure (and hierarchical power), you might arrange chairs so that one person is more central than others. On the other hand, if you want a decentralized structure, chairs would be arranged so that no person was more central than any other. Equalized participation directly enhances satisfaction with belonging to a group and commitment to a group's decisions.

Group Norms

A final feature of small groups that affects communication is norms. Norms are standardized guidelines that regulate how members act, as well as how they interact with each other. Our definition of a small group, in fact, emphasizes that individuals must share understandings about their conduct in order to be a group. Like rules in relationships, a group's norms define what is allowed and not allowed and what kind of participation is rewarded. A group meets the first time and one member brings popcorn for everyone. A different member brings pretzels at the next meeting. By the third meeting, it's likely that members will expect some snack and that someone will bring it. A norm has developed for the group.

Group norms regulate everything from trivial to critical aspects of a group's life. Relatively inconsequential norms may regulate how members dress, whether they take breaks during meetings, and whether interruptions are allowed when members are speaking. More substantive norms govern how carefully members organize their work, how critically they analyze ideas, how well they listen to one another, how they respond to differences and conflict, and how strongly they identify as a group.

Norms grow directly out of interaction. For example, at a group's initial meeting, one person might dismiss another's idea as dumb and several members might not pay attention when others are speaking. If this continues for long, a norm for disrespect will develop and members will form a habit of not being responsive communicators. On the other hand, when one member says an idea is dumb, another person might counter by saying, "I don't think so. I think we ought to consider the point." If others then do consider the idea, a norm for respectful communication may develop.

Because norms become entrenched, it's important to pay attention to them from the outset of a group's existence. By noticing patterns and tendencies, you can exert influence over the rules that govern conduct in a group.

FIGURE 10.2
Ranking the Individualism of Various Cultures

Source: Based on Hofstede, G. (1980). *Cultural consequences: International differences in work-related values.* Beverly Hills, CA: Sage.

CULTURAL INFLUENCES ON GROUP DECISION MAKING

In Chapter 1 we noted that communication is systemic, which means it occurs within systems, or contexts, that influence the character of communication. Like other forms of communication, small group communication is embedded in larger social and cultural systems that affect how groups are perceived and how members interact in them. In Chapter 7, we noted that communication reflects culture, and that principle pertains to groups, as well as to individuals and relationships. Groups in the United States tend to reflect Western values and styles of communicating. For example, the democratic ideology of our society is reflected in the widespread tendency toward democratic leadership in groups. Let's consider several pronounced Western values that shape group communication.

Individualism

One of the most pronounced values of Western society is **individualism,** which holds that each person is unique and important and should be recognized for her or his personal activities (Hofstede, 1980; Triandis, 1990). This means individual achievement and personal freedom are strongly respected. In group discussions, individualism is evident in the extent to which Western groups acknowledge the individuals who make contributions and in the assumption that each individual has the right to express himself or herself freely and fully. In addition, an individualist orientation leads people to give their primary loyalty to themselves, rather than to a group or employer (Goleman, 1990). Contrast this with the greater emphasis on collectivism in countries such as Japan, Pakistan, Nepal, and Colombia. In those societies, groups are less likely to spotlight individual members and more likely to consider everything contributed to be part of the group (see Figure 10.2).

Assertiveness

Perhaps because Westerners place such high value on individualism, they also admire assertiveness. People are expected to speak up, assert their ideas, and stand up for their rights. Like other cultural values, this one is not universal. In Thailand, the Philippines, and Japan, assertiveness not only is not admired, but is considered offensive. Filipinos regard bluntness as extremely rude and disrespectful (Gochenour, 1990) and instead admire "pakikisma," which is harmonious interaction. Cultural differences in perceptions of assertiveness explain why intercultural discussions are sometimes frustrating. A person from Chicago argues forcefully for her position and offends a Japanese member of the group. The American regards the Japanese member as uninterested and uncommitted because he won't take a firm position.

BETSY

I think I really misjudged a guy in a class project group I was in last term. No matter what anyone said, Park Jin Kean nodded and praised the idea. When we asked him what he thought, he would say stuff like "I do not have an opinion to advance" or "I will support whatever others want." I just thought he was a real wimp, but now I see that he just had a different point of view on how to communicate as a good group member.

Equality

A second strong Western value is equality. The United States is founded on the belief that "all people are created equal." Even though there are clear status markers and much class division in the United States, the value of equality is strongly endorsed in Western society, and this value influences communication in small groups. In small groups, the value placed on equality is reflected in the assumption that every member has an equal right to speak and that no member is better than others. In a number of other cultures, hierarchies are used to order people according to particular criteria. Even in Western society, the ideal of equality is qualified in specific ways. For example, men are often more assertive and more likely to put themselves forward than women, so male members of groups may speak more and their comments may be given greater respect.

Progress and Change

Westerners also tend to value progress and change, especially in the area of technology. Communication scholars Larry Samovar and Richard Porter (1995) explain that the Western emphasis on progress is not a specific belief or activity, but a basic mind-set by which Westerners operate. Valuing change and progress leads Westerners to focus on the future and to believe they can (and should) control virtually all things. The mind-set favoring progress is obvious in the ways Western groups define problems and the kinds of solutions they seek. The typical Western decision-making committee would feel it had failed if it did not recommend changes in existing policies, even if no changes were necessary. The goal is to produce change and to progress forward. In societies such as Japan and China, history is more revered, and traditions are more likely to be sustained by group decisions.

Risk and Uncertainty

The importance Westerners place on progress also explains why they tend to be more tolerant of risk than members of many cultures. To embark on new paths, try bold innovations, and experiment with untested ideas require daring and willingness to take risks. Associated with risk is acceptance of uncertainty as a normal part of life and of moving forward. Countries such as the United States, Sweden, Ireland, and Finland accept uncertainty more easily than do countries such as Greece, Germany, Peru, and Japan (Samovar & Porter, 1995). One implication is that Western groups are more likely to accept new ideas if those promise to contribute to what they regard as progress. Ironically, valuing newness and change doesn't always translate into appreciating people or ideas that depart from Western cultural values. Westerners' generally high regard for change is in tension with resistance, sometimes quite strong, to people and ideas that challenge Western conventions.

Informality

Another cultural value in Western societies is informality. People generally treat each other directly and in a relaxed way. How often have you heard someone follow a formal introduction by saying, "Please call me by my first name"? College classes tend to feature informal interaction between professors and students. In contrast, classes in a number of cultures are rigidly organized with the teacher being at the center and perhaps on a stage, or raised platform. Sometimes the teacher's voice is virtually the only one to be heard. Once initial introductions have been made, Americans largely avoid titles and formal rituals of conduct that are followed in other countries such as Japan, Egypt, Turkey, and Germany (Javidi & Javidi, 1994).

Many workplaces allow or even encourage casual dress to create a communication climate that is friendly and open. Based on what these team members are wearing, what kind of communication climate do you think exists in their organization?
(© Mark Richards/PhotoEdit)

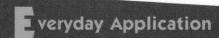

ASSESSING THE VALUES IN YOUR GROUP

Select one group to which you belong and which has existed for an extended period of time. Identify communication that reflects the values discussed in the foregoing pages:

Communication that reflects individuality: _____

_____

Communication that reflects assertiveness: _____

_____

Communication that values risk: _____

_____

Communication that expresses equality: _____

_____

Communication that fosters informality: _____

_____

In sum, we've seen that a small group is three or more individuals who interact over time, have a common purpose, and share understandings about their conduct. Teams are a special kind of group in which members have specific and different resources and in which cohesion and sense of collective identity exceed those typical of most groups. The advantages of groups and teams for problem solving are that they have greater resources and tend to be more thorough, creative, and powerful in generating commitment to decisions than individuals are. The amount of time discussion requires and the possibility of conformity pressure are potential weaknesses that should be curbed. We've also identified cohesion, size, power structure, interaction patterns, and norms as features of groups that affect participation. Finally, we've noted that small groups exist in particular cultural contexts that shape how members communicate and work together.

TABLE 10.1 Types of Communication in Groups

Task Communication

Initiates ideas
Seeks information
Gives information
Elaborates ideas
Evaluates, offers critical analysis

Procedural Communication

Establishes agenda
Provides orientation
Curbs digressions
Guides participation
Coordinates ideas

Summarizes others'
  contributions
Records group progress

Climate Communication

Establishes and maintains
  healthy climate
Energizes group process
Harmonizes ideas
Recognizes others
Reconciles conflicts
Builds enthusiasm for group

Egocentric Communication

Aggresses toward others
Blocks ideas
Seeks personal recognition
  (brags)
Dominates interaction
Pleads for special interests
Confesses, self-discloses, seeks
  personal help
Disrupts task
Devalues others
Trivializes group and its work

COMMUNICATION IN SMALL GROUPS

We've seen that effective small group discussion requires knowing when groups are likely to be superior to individuals and understanding how group features affect participation. We're now ready to consider the variety of ways in which members communicate in groups. We'll discuss ways members contribute in groups, decision-making methods, and communication responsibilities of leadership.

Forms of Group Communication

Because communication is the heart of all groups, the ways members communicate are extremely important to the effectiveness of group process. There are four kinds of communication in groups (see Table 10.1). The first three, task, procedural, and climate communication, are constructive because they foster good group process and outcomes. The fourth kind of communication is egocentric, or dysfunctional, communication. It tends to detract from group cohesion and from effective decision making.

Task Communication   **Task communication** focuses on the problem, issues, or information before a group. It provides ideas and information, ensures members' understanding, and uses reasoning to evaluate ideas and information. Task contributions may initiate ideas, respond to others' ideas, or provide critical evaluation of information before the group. Task contributions also include asking for ideas and evaluation from others. Task comments emphasize the content of a group's work.

Procedural Communication   If you've ever participated in a disorganized group, you understand the importance of **procedural communication,** which helps a group get organized and stay on track in its decision making. Procedural contributions establish an agenda, coordinate the comments of different members, and record group progress. In addition, procedural contributions may curb digressions and tangents, summarize progress, and regulate participation so that everyone has opportunities to speak and nobody dominates.

Climate Communication   A group is more than a task unit. It also includes people who are involved in a relationship that can be more or less pleasant and open. **Climate communication** focuses on creating and maintaining a constructive climate that encourages members to contribute freely and to evaluate ideas critically. Climate comments emphasize a group's strengths and progress, recognize others' contributions, reconcile conflicts, and build enthusiasm for the group and its work.

Egocentric Communication   The final kind of group communication is not recommended, but does sometimes surface in groups. **Egocentric communication,** or dysfunctional communication, is used to block others or to call attention to oneself. It detracts from group progress because it is self-centered, rather than group-centered. Examples of egocentric talk are devaluing another member's ideas, trivializing the group's efforts, aggressing toward other members, bragging about one's own accomplishments, dominating, disrupting group work, and pleading for special causes that aren't in a group's interest.

Everyday Application

YOUR COMMUNICATION IN GROUPS

1. How do you contribute to small group discussions?
2. Do you specialize in task, procedural, or climate communication?
3. Observe yourself in a small group setting and record the focus of your comments. Which kinds of group communication do you do well? In which areas do you want to develop greater skill?

Task, procedural, and climate communication work together to foster productive, organized, and comfortable group discussion. Most of us are particularly skilled in one or two kinds of communication. For instance, some people have a gift for reconciling conflicts and using humor to break tension. Other people are very organized and become procedural leaders. Still others are especially skillful in task matters, knowing how to evaluate data and how to determine what information is needed to make decisions. All three communication emphases contribute to effective groups. The kinds of communication that you associate with yourself reflect your self-

The most effective work teams spend a good deal of time on task communication; however, they also find time to share a good laugh. (© J. Wilson/Woodfin Camp & Associates)

concept, which we discussed in Chapter 3. Interacting in groups and making a commitment to enlarge your current communication skills should allow you to broaden your repertoire for contributing to group work.

Egocentric communication, on the other hand, does not contribute to enjoyable group interaction of high-quality outcomes. Egocentric participation can sabotage a group's climate and hinder its progress in achieving its goals. If it occurs, others in the group should intervene to discourage it. Communicating clearly that egocentric behavior will not be tolerated in your group fosters norms for effective interaction. In the following dialogue, an excerpt from a student discussion is coded into the types of communication we have identified.

Ed: We might start by discussing what we see as the goal of this group. *[procedural]*

Jan: That's a good idea. *[climate]*

Bob: I think our goal is to come up with a better meal plan for students on campus. *[task]*

Ed: What do you mean by "better"? Do you mean cheaper or more varied or more tasteful? *[task]*

Ann: I think we need to consider all three. *[task]*

Ed: Well, we probably do care about all three, but maybe we should talk about one at a time so that we can keep our discussion focused. *[procedural]*

Bob: Okay, I vote we focus first on taste—like it would be good if there were some taste to the food on campus! *[task and climate (humor)]*

Jan: Do you mean taste itself or quality of food, which might also consider nutrition? *[task]*

Bob: Pure taste! When I'm hungry, I don't think about what's good for me, just what tastes good. *[task]*

Jan: Well, maybe that's a reason why we might want the food service to think about nutrition—because we don't. *[task]*

Bob: If you're a health food nut, that's your problem. I don't think nutrition is something that's important in the food service on campus. *[task; possibly also egocentric if his tone toward Jan was snide]*

Ed: Let's do this: Let's talk first about what we would like in terms of taste itself. *[procedural]* Before we meet next time, it might be a good idea for one of us to talk with the manager of the cafeteria to see whether they have to meet any nutritional guidelines in what they serve. *[task]*

Ann: I'll volunteer to do that. *[task]*

Ed: Great. Thanks, Ann. *[climate]*

Bob: I'll volunteer to do taste testing! *[climate (humor)]*

Jan: With your weight, you'd better not. *[egocentric]*

Bob: Yeah, like you have a right to criticize me. *[egocentric]*

Ann: Look, none of us is here to criticize anyone else. We're here because we want to improve the food service on campus. *[climate]* We've decided we want to focus first on taste *[procedural],* so who has an idea of how we go about studying that? *[task]*

This dialogue includes all four kinds of communication that we have discussed. It's particularly noteworthy to recognize how skillfully Ann communicates to defuse tension between Bob and Jan before it disrupts the group. You might also notice that Ed provides the primary procedural leadership for the group, and Bob is effective in interjecting humor. Several members recognize contributions to the discussion.

In effective group discussion, communication meets the task, procedural, and climate demands of teamwork and avoids egocentrism that detracts from group progress and cohesion. By understanding how varied types of communication affect collective work, you can decide when to employ each type of communication in your own participation in groups. Although you may not currently be proficient in all three valuable kinds of group communication, with commitment and practice you can develop skill.

SUMMARY

In this chapter, we've considered what small groups are and how they operate. We defined groups as three or more individuals who meet over time, share understandings of how to interact, and have a common goal. The potential weaknesses of group discussion, notably conformity pressures and time, must be recognized and managed in order to realize the important advantages of group decision making.

Communication in groups and teams is influenced by many factors, including cohesion, size, power, rules, interaction patterns, and cultural values. Each of these features shapes the small group system within which communication transpires. Effective communication in groups and teams requires that members be aware of and exert control over features that make up the group system. By managing these influences, you should be able to enhance the content and climate of communication, the outcomes of group deliberation, and members' feelings about participation.

The final section of the chapter focused on the kinds of communication that occur in small groups.

There we saw that effective group interaction requires task, climate, and procedural contributions and is hindered by egocentric communication. Developing skill in the three constructive types of communication and avoiding egocentric comments will make you a valuable member of any group.

In Chapter 11, we will build on what we have learned in this chapter. There we will identify the kinds of task teams that dot the contemporary landscape, and we will discuss leadership, organization of group discussion, and ways of managing conflict so that it benefits group work.

FOR FURTHER REFLECTION AND DISCUSSION

1. Recall the last group in which you participated. Did you find it effective in achieving its task goals? Was the climate comfortable? Now describe your group according to key features discussed in this chapter:

size, interaction patterns, cohesion, power, rules, and cultural influences. Do these features explain the climate and task effectiveness of your group?

2. Observe a group discussion on your campus or in your town. Record members' contributions by classifying them as task, climate, procedural, or egocentric. Do the communication patterns you observe explain the effectiveness or ineffectiveness of the group?

3. Talk with several people who have lived in non-Western cultures. Ask them whether the cultural values that affect group communication in the United States are present in the countries where they lived. In your conversation, explore differences in cultural values and how these affect small group interaction.

4. Experiment with the different group structures described in this chapter. Agree on a topic that class groups will discuss for 20 minutes. Have half of the class members work in groups that are organized centrally and the other half in groups that are organized decentrally. Discuss the influence of the different seating patterns on interaction, productivity, and members' satisfaction.

KEY TERMS

group
team
synergy
cohesion
groupthink
power
power over
power to
social climbing
individualism
task communication
procedural communication
climate communication
egocentric communication

Focus Questions

1 When is brainstorming useful in groups?

2 Can several people lead a group effectively?

3 What style of leadership is best?

4 Is there a standard way to organize task groups?

5 How does conflict affect group discussion?

CHAPTER 11

Effective Communication in Task Groups

There are many kinds of groups, and each type has distinctive goals and communication patterns. Social groups provide us with recreation and the stimulation of conversation with people we enjoy. Communication in social groups tends to be relaxed, informal, and more focused on interpersonal climate than on task goals. Personal growth groups enable individuals to deal with significant issues and worries in a context in which there is interpersonal support. In personal growth groups, communication is generally personal in topic and tone and its goals are to support members and to help them clarify issues in their lives. Although groups differ in their primary purposes and focus, most groups include interaction that is beyond their basic purpose. For example, social groups often move into task discussion, as when one friend asks another for advice in solving a problem. Groups that exist to accomplish a task typically include some social communication, and therapy groups usually involve both task and social dimensions that contribute to the primary goal of personal growth.

One of the most prominent types of group in modern life is the task group, which pursues goals other than recreation or personal growth. Task groups aim to accomplish some defined objective, such as creating a policy, making a decision, solving a problem, advising others, or generating ideas. Because task groups are extensively relied on in professional and civic life, this chapter concentrates on communication that allows task teams to manage projects, develop ideas, and make decisions. Of course, much of this information is relevant to other types of groups as well. We'll begin by identifying types of task groups. Next, we'll discuss leadership communication in task groups. We'll then consider a method of organizing efficient and productive discussion. In the fourth section of this chapter we'll consider alternative methods of making decisions in groups. Finally, we'll return to the topic of conflict, which we first discussed in Chapter 8. Our examination of conflict will concentrate on both the constructive potential of conflict and ways to manage it effectively.

(Diego Rivera, *The Making of a Fresco Showing the Building of a City* (1931). True fresco, 22' 7" × 29' 9". Courtesy San Francisco Art Institute. Photograph © D. Wakely.)

TASK GROUPS

The task group, which is often a team, has emerged as a major feature of modern life. Earlier in this century, the majority of people worked relatively independently. Each person had his or her individual job responsibilities and coordinated with others only when necessary. Recognition of the values of group communication, however, has led to increasing reliance on groups in preference to individuals for much of the work in business and civic life (Sher & Gottlieb, 1989). There are several types of task groups, each with a specific purpose and value. We'll discuss six common types of task teams.

Project Teams

Project teams are increasingly popular in business and professional life. Project teams consist of a number of individuals who have special expertise in relation to some project and who work together over a period of time to combine their knowledge and skills to accomplish a common goal. A task

In focus groups, facilitators encourage participants to express and elaborate on their ideas, feelings, and impressions. In this focus group, participants are offering their observations about different formulations of a new beverage. (© Anne Dowie)

might be establishing a training system for a company, creating a public relations campaign for a new product, or determining the public image of a corporation in a community.

Communication in the project team allows each member to draw on the resources of other members and to coordinate their different areas of experience and talent. To launch a new product, pharmaceutical companies often compose product teams that include scientists who understand the technical character of the new drug, personnel in marketing, product design, advertising, and customer relations. Working together, these individuals develop a coherent plan for testing, packaging, advertising, and marketing the new product to the public. If the individuals worked separately in their specific areas, they would generate a less coordinated and effective plan: Marketing wouldn't know what advertising was planned, advertising wouldn't understand the overall image for the product, and customer relations wouldn't have informed advertising and marketing of salient issues in the target market for the product.

A project team is valuable when many individuals will work on a single project, and what each person does has implications for other members of the team. Wadsworth Publishing Company put together a project team for this book. Members of the team included a communication editor, who oversaw all aspects of development and production; a production editor, who coordinated with team members in charge of copy editing, selecting art, and obtaining permissions for cartoons and photos; a copy editor, who refined my writing; a marketing manager, who matched information about this book with interests of faculty and students; a designer, who created page layout and visual features used in this book; and sales representatives who were involved from the early stages to provide feedback on faculty needs and student concerns. The team was able to develop a holistic vision of the book and to then infuse that vision into each and every aspect of its development and marketing.

Focus Groups

Another popular work team is the focus group, which is used to find out what people think about a specific idea, product, issue, or person. Focus groups are a mainstay of advertisers who want to understand attitudes, preferences, and responses of people they want to buy their product: What do 18- to 25-year-olds think of a new light beer? How do retirees respond

Brainstorming stimulates creative thinking and encourages participation among group members. Every idea, no matter how "off the wall," should be recorded. (© Paula Lerner/ Woodfin Camp & Associates)

to a planned advertising campaign for cruises? Focus groups are also popular in political life: What do middle-class women and men think of a politician's record on social issues? How do young voters feel about economic issues? Is a candidate regarded as trustworthy by African Americans?

Focus groups are guided by a leader or facilitator who encourages members to communicate their ideas, beliefs, feelings, and perceptions relevant to the topic. The contributions group members make serve as the foundation for later decisions, such as how to refine the recipe for the light beer, increase perceptions of Incumbent Y's trustworthiness, and tailor the advertising for the cruises. The facilitator doesn't offer personal judgments and opinions, but guides group members to express themselves, respond to each other's communication, and analyze the reasons for their thoughts, feelings, and responses. To prepare for leading a focus group, a facilitator usually develops a list of major questions and probes that can be used to encourage participants to elaborate responses (Lederman, 1990).

Brainstorming Groups

Group discussion is especially effective in stimulating creative ideas. Interaction seems to spark imagination and innovation, so groups are often superior to individuals when the goal is to generate ideas. These groups are called idea-generation or brainstorming groups.

In **brainstorming,** the goal is to come up with as many ideas as possible. Since criticism tends to stifle creativity, no criticism is allowed during this phase (see Table 11.1). Creativity and even wild thinking are encouraged in order to come up with the most imaginative ideas possible. When group members start to run dry of ideas, a leader or leaders can prompt further brainstorming by suggesting extensions of ideas that have been generated and new dimensions of the topic.

Perhaps you're concerned that brainstorming might produce unrealistic ideas or ones that haven't been well analyzed. That's not really a problem, since brainstorming is followed by evaluative discussion. During evaluation, members work together to appraise all of the ideas that were generated through brainstorming. Criticism is now appropriate and constructive, since the group must decide which idea or ideas merit more focused attention. During this stage, infeasible ideas are discarded, weak or undeveloped ideas are improved, related ones are consolidated, and promising ones are discussed further.

TABLE 11.1 Rules for Brainstorming

1. Do not make any evaluations of ideas that are volunteered. Both verbal and nonverbal criticism are inappropriate.

2. Record ideas on a board or newsprint so that all members of the group can see them.

3. Go for quantity: The more ideas, the better.

4. Build on ideas. An idea presented by one member of the group may stimulate an extension by another member. This is desirable.

5. Encourage creativity. Wild and even preposterous ideas should be welcomed. An idea that seems wacky may lead to other ideas that are more workable.

The leader or facilitator of a brainstorming group should set a tone for creative communication. To do this, leaders should demonstrate energy, respond enthusiastically to members' ideas, and communicate excitement. Leaders may also need to stoke members' creativity if they hit a dry spell prematurely. This can be done by making encouraging comments, such as "Who can add to the list of ideas?" "Let's think about extending and combining some of the ideas we already have." "We're being too restrained— let's come up with some wild proposals." "Let's generate about five more ideas before we move on."

Everyday Application

BRAINSTORMING

To discover the value of brainstorming, try this: First, write down as many ideas as you individually can think of to one of the questions below. Then join four to six other students in your class, and as a group, spend 10 minutes generating responses to the same question. Be sure to follow the rules for brainstorming that appear in Table 11.1 above.

1. List ways in which computer technology could be incorporated into teaching on your campus.
2. What would improve the school newspaper?
3. Develop ideas for your class's graduation gift to the university or college.

What do you conclude about the value of brainstorming as a method of promoting creative communication in groups?

Advisory Groups

As their name suggests, advisory groups provide information and advice to others. They are probably the most common type of task group. Advisory groups do not actually make policies or decisions. Instead, they inform others who make the actual decisions. Advisory groups are constituted when an individual wants to be briefed by experts on a topic about which she or he must make a decision. For example, at my university, the chancellor established the Chancellor's Sexual Harassment Advisory Committee, to which he appointed the chair of Women's Studies, the university's Human Resources director, the president of the Graduate Student Forum, two undergraduates, and several faculty members. Our committee was asked to inform the chancellor about sexual harassment on our campus and about policies concerning sexual harassment that were in place at other campuses. The Chancellor also asked our committee to advise him on a sexual harassment policy for our campus. Our committee gathered and analyzed information and deliberated about the goals of policy and ways to achieve them. The Chancellor made the final decision after being advised by our group.

In 1995, Vice President Al Gore worked with an advisory group consisting of leaders of major environmental organizations in the United States. Bringing together a handful of key players to discuss national environmental policy accomplished two objectives. First, it informed the vice president by allowing him to learn about environmental issues that national policies should address. Second, the interaction among members of the advisory group generated understandings and ideas that none of the individuals had prior to group communication.

Advisory groups may also consist of peers who advise each other. In a *Wall Street Journal* column addressed to small-business owners, management consultant Howard Upton (1995) described a system of peer-advisory groups developed by chief executives of the Petroleum Equipment Institute. The executives created groups of 10 to 12 presidents of the 700 distributorships in the United States and Canada. By conferring regularly with peers, these presidents were able to advise each other on common problems, practices, and goals. The members found that by pooling experience and reports on methods of problem solving, they were able to inform each other in ways that enhanced everyone's effectiveness.

In business and civic affairs, executives are seldom experts on the range of issues relevant to decisions they must make. According to Howard Upton, "It is impossible for the head of any company, large or small, to succeed without benefit of outside advice" (1995, p. A14). The solitary manager, president, or CEO who relies only on his or her own ideas is not functional in modern life. Advisory groups allow individuals to benefit from other experts' information and advice pertinent to developing effective policies and making informed decisions.

Quality Circles

A **quality circle** is three or more individuals who are employed in different areas of an organization and who work together to improve quality in an organization (Lumsden & Lumsden, 1997). Originally, quality circles were part of total quality management (Deming, 1982), in which intensive team-work and highly participative work structures are used to maximize the quality of an organization's output. Quality circles are now used in a variety of organizations, whether or not they embrace total quality management as an overall organizational philosophy. Typically, quality circles mix not just people with differing areas of expertise, but also people at different levels in an organization's hierarchy. Thus, a secretary may contribute as much as someone in senior management to discussion of ways to improve office productivity.

The first few meetings of a quality circle typically involve a lot of complaining about problems ("Quality Circles," 1991). This is natural and has the beneficial effect of helping members become comfortable with one another because they create common ground over shared frustrations. In addition, this opening talk generally alerts the group to special concerns and areas of knowledge that each member can contribute. After initial venting of frustrations, quality circles focus discussion on solving problems. Communication concentrates on identifying needs that exist, areas in which organizational functioning could be improved, and areas of stress or discontent for employees.

To be effective, quality circles must be given the power to solve problems. Nothing is more frustrating than to be asked to work on a problem but be denied the authority to implement changes or assurance that others will implement them. This means that quality circles should be formed if and only if organizational leaders are receptive to implementing solutions the groups devise. When given appropriate authority, quality circles often generate impressive and creative solutions to organizational concerns such as lowering expenses, improving safety, and acknowledging accomplishments. Quality groups usually make reports on a regular basis (once a week or once a month) to keep management informed of the group's insights, progress, and intentions.

Decision-Making Groups

A fifth kind of task group exists to solve problems or make decisions. In some cases, decision-making groups are formed to render a specific decision or policy: What should be Corporation X's policy on medical leave? How should we determine raises for employees? What operations and personnel should we reduce or eliminate to achieve a 15% decrease in annual expenses?

In other cases, ongoing groups are charged to deal with decisions and problems in specific areas. Many organizations have standing committees that assume responsibility for budget, public relations, external communication, and other matters. In my department, we have standing committees that are in charge of decisions related to curricula, teaching quality, hiring and promotion, and advising. Because these are ongoing committees, members have acquired expertise in the particular issues within the groups' purview.

Leaders of decision-making groups are responsible for creating a supportive communication climate for group work, organizing discussions productively, and ensuring constructive communication among members. Later in this chapter, we will discuss a method for organizing decision making, and we will also discuss leadership in more detail.

More and more, task groups are becoming prominent in professional and civic life. Project teams, focus groups, brainstorming groups, advisory groups, and decision-making groups are common forms of task groups. When members and leaders know how to communicate effectively, these task groups maximize the strengths of group communication that we discussed in Chapter 10. They allow diverse individuals with varying experience, expertise, interests, and talents to interact and generate ideas, understandings, plans, and decisions that are more creative and better informed than those an individual could devise.

COMMUNICATION RESPONSIBILITIES OF LEADERSHIP

What makes a leader? For decades it was assumed that leaders are born, not made. In following this assumption, researchers attempted to identify the traits of effective leaders. Personal qualities ranging from intelligence to emotional balance and physical energy were studied in an effort to understand the traits of born leaders. This line of study was unsuccessful in discovering any consistent traits that mark leaders. It was, however, effective in shifting our understanding of leadership. The lack of identifiable leader traits led researchers to realize that leadership is not a person or a set of personal qualities. Instead, leadership is a set of functions that assist groups in accomplishing tasks and maintaining a good climate.

Leadership, Not Leader

Leadership may be provided either by one individual or by several members who contribute to guiding the process and ensuring effective communication within the group. Leadership exists when one or more members communicate to establish a good working climate, organize group process, and focus discussion productively on the task at hand. Recalling our discussion in Chapter 10, you may realize that the functions of leadership we just identified parallel the three types of constructive communication that group members make in discussions. A fourth function of leadership is to control disruptive members, which addresses the egocentric communication we discussed in Chapter 10.

When a single person provides leadership, one person performs the functions necessary for effective group discussion. When leadership is not vested in a single person, several members share responsibilities. Whether there is one leader or shared leadership, the primary responsibilities are to organize discussion, ensure sound research and reasoning, create a productive working climate, build group morale, promote effective communication among members, and discourage egocentric communication that detracts from group efforts.

KRYSTAL

The most effective group I've ever been in had three leaders. I was the person who understood our task best, so I contributed the most to critical thinking about the issues. But Belinda was the one who kept us organized. She really knew how to see tangents and get us off of them, and she knew when it was time to move on from one stage of work to the next. She also pulled ideas together to coordinate our thinking. Kevin was the climate leader. He could always tell a joke if things got tense, and he was the best person I ever saw for recognizing others' contributions. I couldn't point to any one leader in that group, but we sure did have good leadership.

When we realize that leadership is a series of functions that move groups along, it becomes clear that more than one person may engage in leadership in a specific group or team. Sometimes one member communicates to provide guidance on tasks and procedures, and another member communicates to build a healthy group climate. A group needs both climate and task leadership to be maximally effective. It is also possible for various people to provide leadership at different times in a group's life. The individual who guides the group at the outset may not be the one who advances the group's work in later phases. Depending on what a group needs at a specific time, different leadership functions are appropriate and may come from different members. Even when an official leader exists, other members may contribute much of the communication that provides leadership to a group. Although the official leader has the responsibility for a group's decision (and gets the credit or blame!), others may supply a substantial amount of leadership.

Styles of Leadership

Think about the groups in which you've participated. Some of them probably operated casually and were even unfocused at times, others were productive and participative, and still others were regimented and controlled by one person who had and exerted power. If these three portraits of groups seem familiar, then you already have an experiential understanding of different styles of leadership.

A laissez-faire, or hands-off, leadership style can be effective with motivated and mature group members. (© Anne Dowie)

Although leadership can't be reduced to a set of traits, it can be understood as an overall style of communication. Different styles of leadership have a specific impact on group productivity and climate (Lewin, Lippitt, & White, 1939). Again, these may be enacted by a single person who is a group leader or by a group of members who provide leadership. Researchers have identified three primary styles of leadership, each of which involves distinctive forms of communication and each of which has a unique impact on group climate and productivity. Many groups cannot be neatly classified into one of the three styles of leadership. Instead, groups often are blends of the styles, and the blends may change over time.

Laissez-Faire Leadership *Laissez-faire* is a French phrase that roughly translates as "do nothing." **Laissez-faire leadership** is laid-back and nondirective. Laissez-faire leaders don't provide guidance or suggest directions in which groups should move. Laissez-faire leaders also don't exert their authority, preferring to let the group set its own goals and at its own speed. If problems develop in a group, laissez-faire leaders feel no need to intervene, since they don't assume responsibility for what the group does.

Laissez-faire leadership is not always undesirable. When a group consists of members who are mature, experienced, and self-directed, there may be little need for control by one or more leaders. Yet, this is more the exception than the rule. Most groups need guidance, at least at times, in order to develop and sustain a good climate and to be productive. For this reason, laissez-faire leadership generally is not recommended. It tends to cultivate unfocused discussion and inefficient work. Thus, laissez-faire leadership may hinder high productivity or quality decisions (Bass, 1990). In addition, laissez-faire leadership typically fosters an unproductive climate, since lack of direction generates frustration among members. Inefficiency is perhaps the most common characteristic of laissez-faire leadership (White & Lippitt, 1960).

Authoritarian Leadership As the name suggests, **authoritarian leadership** is directive and dictatorial. This style of leadership tends to be used by a single leader, rather than several members who share leadership. Authoritarian leaders may announce directions for discussion, assign specific tasks to members, make decisions without consulting others in the group, and otherwise exert control over the group process. As you might suspect, groups that have authoritarian leadership are often very efficient, but members' morale and quality of work may not be optimal.

Authoritarian leadership generally discourages interaction among members and fosters a centralized pattern of leader-to-member, member-to-leader communication. The lack of communication among members interferes with the development of group morale and a sense of cohesive identity. Although groups with authoritarian leaders sometimes produce good decisions, this style of leadership seldom promotes satisfaction and esprit de corps among members. Further, authoritarian leadership doesn't cultivate initiative and commitment among members, so group climate and morale are not ideal. Dependence, apathy, low cohesion, and resentment are common responses to authoritarian leadership (Gibb, 1969; Lewin et al., 1939).

DOUG

It took me a while to learn that my boss doesn't want any of us to take initiative or state our ideas unless we agree with him. He is a classic authoritarian leader, who tells us what to do, as well as what answers and decisions he wants us to produce. He blasts anyone who doesn't play "yes man" to him. By now, none of us cares what happens in our project group. We don't even try to think of ways to improve our work. He's taught us not to take any initiative by penalizing us anytime we depart from his agenda and his prejudgments.

Democratic Leadership   **Democratic leadership** provides direction and guidance, but does not impose rigid authority. Democratic leadership—whether provided by one individual or by several members—fosters the development of members by encouraging them to formulate their own goals and procedures and to take initiative within a group. Democratic leadership tends to generate high and generally balanced communication among members. In turn, high participation fuels group cohesion and members' satisfaction with belonging to a group (Gibb, 1969). Finally, democratic leadership tends to yield high-quality task outcomes that are generally more original and creative than those produced by groups with authoritarian or laissez-faire leadership (White & Lippitt, 1960).

Before concluding this discussion, we should emphasize that effective leadership cannot be reduced to a one-size-fits-all formula. Although researchers have found that the democratic style of leadership is linked to good group climate and productivity, that research has been conducted in societies committed to democratic values. In societies that place higher value on authoritarian structures, an autocratic style of leadership might well be more acceptable and effective. Further, authoritarian leadership may be effective in certain contexts in democratic societies—for instance, when it is nearing 5 o'clock and a group hasn't finished its work. Laissez-faire leadership, too, can be effective when groups have the expertise, commitment, and self-direction they need to perform a task. Like other forms of communication, good leadership is responsive to particular members, situations, circumstances, and cultures.

We should also note that effective leadership may change over time. What a group needs to be productive varies at different points in a group's life cycle and in relation to the maturity of members (Hershey & Blanchard, 1993). When a group first begins working, direction in framing the issues and determining the group's objectives is vital, and the person who supplies this is performing the critical leadership at that time. As a group continues working, however, it often matures and no longer needs strong task guidance. At that point, the most effective leadership communication may focus on consideration, or climate contributions. Recognizing the group's progress and the efforts of individual members heightens morale and motivates further commitment to the task. As members invest in group work, the person who initially provided leadership may delegate more and more responsibility to individuals. This acknowledges their abilities, increases satisfaction, and heightens their loyalty to the group and its decisions (Johnson & Johnson, 1991).

In sum, leadership is a dynamic process of meeting the changing and various needs for effective communication in small groups. Whether provided by one or several members, effective leadership involves communication that advances a group's task, organizes deliberations, builds group morale, controls disruptions, and fosters a constructive climate.

DECISION-MAKING METHODS

Task groups make decisions: They develop plans for new products, advise others on decisions, develop policies, and solve problems. To accomplish these objectives, task groups must have methods of making decisions. Four common methods of group decision making have been identified. Each one involves distinct communication styles and has particular strengths and disadvantages (Wood & Phillips, 1990). We'll describe each method and consider when it is likely to be most constructive and appropriate.

Consensus

Perhaps the most popular decision-making method in Western societies is **consensus,** which occurs when all members of a group manage to agree on a decision. Members may differ in how enthusiastically they support a decision, but everyone agrees to accept a consensus decision. Communication to achieve consensus involves wide participation and often very prolonged discussion among members. For everyone to support the decision, everyone must be involved in crafting it.

The strength of the consensus method is that it involves all members; thus, consensus decisions tend to have strong support. In addition, consensus tends to increase cohesion and satisfaction with a group, since the method has generated commitment to both the process and its outcome. As you probably realize, the greatest disadvantage of the consensus method is the time required to hear all members and to secure everyone's commitment to a single decision. This makes consensus inappropriate for trivial

These citizens at a New Hampshire town meeting vote on issues that are important to their community. Reaching consensus on each issue would be difficult and extremely time consuming with a group this large. (© Paula Lerner/Woodfin Camp & Associates)

decisions, emergency issues, or decisions on which members cannot come to agreement, even after extended discussion (Wood & Phillips, 1990).

Voting

A second method of making decisions is **voting**; that is, a decision is made based on the support of a certain number of group members. Some groups have simple majority rule, while others require two-thirds or three-fourths support before a decision can be accepted. The obvious drawback of voting is that it can lead to a decision that doesn't have widespread support. For instance, the majority rule method allows 51% of members to win a vote, leaving 49% dissatisfied. Voting has the potential to foster dissatisfaction and reduced group cohesion. Also, voting may abbreviate the thoroughness of analysis, clarification of issues, and evaluation of different possibilities. Yet, voting also has advantages, notably its efficiency and resolution. Thus, when time is short, when a decision is not major, or when a group needs to move on, voting may be advisable.

Compromise

A third method of decision making is **compromise,** in which members work out a solution that satisfies each person's minimum criteria, but that may not fully satisfy all members. When decisions are made by compromise, the purposes of communication are to clarify what each member or subgroup of members needs in order to accept a decision and to identify issues on which members are willing to bend. Compromise decisions often involve trading and bargaining—I'll give on this point if you'll give on that one (Wood & Phillips, 1990). What tends to happen is that members hammer out a decision that meets each person's bottom line, but may not generate great enthusiasm from anyone.

The shortcomings of the compromise method are obvious. One is that decisions are often less coherent than decisions made by consensus. This is due to the fact that compromises may involve a series of separate considerations designed to satisfy particular members. Thus, the parts of a decision may not come together into an integrated whole. Also, as we've noted, compromise decisions often don't have enthusiastic support from those who agree to them. So why would any group resort to compromise? The answer is that sometimes it seems the only way to make a decision. If members are deadlocked even after extensive discussion, they may be unable to find enough common ground for consensus. Also, if members represent outside constituencies as in labor–management negotiations, they have conflicting interests and goals that make consensus unlikely.

Authority Rule/Group Ratification

A final method of group decision making actually doesn't involve a decision made by a group. Instead, **authority rule** occurs when some individual or group with authority tells a group what to do and the group ratifies the authority's decision. In some cases, the authority is a member of the group who has high status—the group leader, for example. In other cases, the authority is someone outside the group who appoints the group to give the appearance of a democratic method and to distribute responsibility for what may be an unpopular decision. In reality, an autocratic process is used, but that may be hidden for public relation reasons. Sometimes this method involves discussion first, after which the authority announces the decision. Authority rule can also be implemented without prior discussion when a person informs a group what it will decide.

You probably can guess the drawbacks of this decision-making method. It can incur resentment in members who may dislike being forced to ratify a decision of which they don't approve or being used to camouflage an autocratic process. Equally important, this method short-circuits the potential of group discussion to generate outcomes superior to those of individuals. Control by one person doesn't make use of the increased resources, creativity, and thoroughness of groups, so authority-rule decisions may be less good than ones reached through other methods. Finally, authority rule can dampen participation in the long run if members think their ideas make no difference in decisions made.

On the other hand, authority rule has advantages in some situations. Obviously, this method is very efficient, so it has the virtue of saving time. Also, it may be useful for routine decisions that could take up more time to discuss than their importance justifies.

CEDRIC

I wish someone would teach my work group about authority rule. There are eight of us who meet as a group to decide everything that affects our department. Each of us likes to have our say and to talk things through, and that makes a lot of sense for big decisions like how to assign projects or evaluate subordinates or design new policies. But we talk just as long about trivial decisions. Last week we had a 40-minute discussion about whether to give our secretary individual gifts or pool our money to buy one large gift for the holidays. Forty minutes! We talked just as long about new carpeting for our office. Everyone had a different color preference, and we never did agree. We should let one person make a decision on these things.

There is no single best method of making group decisions. Instead, what is appropriate varies according to factors such as the nature of the decision, preferences of group members, and time available for reaching decisions. Many ongoing groups rely on multiple methods of decision making and attempt to use the method that is most appropriate in each particular situation.

ORGANIZING GROUP DISCUSSION

Perhaps the biggest complaint about group work is that it often seems disorganized. The reason is that groups often *are* disorganized, primarily because members don't know how to move efficiently through a decision-making process. Individuals vary greatly in how they approach issues and make decisions, so it's unlikely that a group of individuals will share procedural tendencies. The goal of group organization is to provide a common procedure that allows members to move efficiently and effectively through systematic problem solving.

Communication scholars have developed a number of ways to organize discussion. Of these, **standard agenda** is the one that enjoys greatest support and has endured the longest time (Wood et al., 1986). Standard agenda is a logical seven-step method for making decisions. In our discussion, we'll focus on the kinds of communication that occur during each of the stages in standard agenda. Figure 11.1 summarizes the stages.

FIGURE 11.1
Stages in Standard Agenda

I. Define the Problem
   A. Define terms
   B. Phrase a question to guide deliberation
II. Analyze the Issues
   A. Gather information on history, how issues have been addressed elsewhere, and so on
   B. Analyze causes of problem or need
   C. Discuss desired outcomes of decision
III. Establish Criteria
IV. Generate Possible Solutions
   A. Review research
   B. Brainstorm
V. Evaluate Possible Solutions
VI. Select and Implement Solution
VII. Develop an Action Plan to Monitor Solution

Stage One: Define the Problem

One of the most common errors groups make is to assume all members agree on the problem or issue to be resolved and turn immediately to discussing possible solutions. This is a mistake, because in reality people often don't agree on what the problem is or what decision they must make. For instance, I once served on a group that was instructed to review the undergraduate curriculum in my department. I assumed this meant we were to consider whether the courses we offered reflected national trends in the communication field. Another member thought our job was to decide what the requirements for a major should be. A third person believed we were to evaluate whether we offered a broad enough scope of courses and whether we offered them frequently enough. Each of these views of the task makes sense, but they aren't equivalent. Our first task as a group was to define exactly what it was we were to do.

Decision-making groups often find it useful to decide whether they are dealing with issues of fact, value, or policy. Each type of issue requires a different sort of analysis and decision, so groups need to agree on their focus. Factual tasks involve finding the answers to some questions. Usually, factual group reports are descriptive. For instance, the group I mentioned previously could address the factual question "What are the undergraduate courses taught in our department, and how frequently are they offered?" Answering this question requires only that the group consult records on departmental offerings and count the number of times each course has been offered.

A value question concerns what ought to be or what should be the case. Often, value questions entail asking which group or interest to consider most important. For example, "Are faculty or student interests more important in curricular design?" Another value question is "Which courses offer the most valuable educational experiences to undergraduates?" Answering the first question involves deciding whether faculty or student interests and preferences take priority. Discussing the second question would require members to consider alternative values education can serve—broadening the mind, developing skills, increasing understanding.

What are the standards for judging educational value—national trends, student judgments of courses, faculty competencies, or the overall mission of a particular college (liberal arts, for example)? Deciding how to define valuable educational experiences allows a group to proceed with common understandings.

A policy focus requires a group to decide what should be done and who should do it. For example, my group might have concentrated on deciding what courses our committee should recommend be offered each term and which ones should be offered only yearly. Alternatively, we might have focused on recommending what requirements the dean or college should make about undergraduate courses in our department. Policy issues revolve around questions of viability, feasibility, need, and responsibility for implementation. Groups must identify the needs at stake, evaluate the viability of different ways to meet needs, and determine who can most effectively implement recommendations (Wood et al., 1986).

CLARIFYING QUESTIONS

Phrase a question of fact, value, and policy for each of the following topics:

Class Attendance

Fact _____

Value _____

Policy _____

Graduation Requirements at Your School

Fact _____

Value _____

Policy _____

Affirmative Action at Your School

Fact _____

Value _____

Policy _____

Although groups should decide whether their basic purpose is to make a factual, value, or policy decision, most task deliberations involve all three types of questions. We often need facts to design policy (for example, how many students currently enroll in each class we offer?), and values are at stake in virtually every decision, no matter how objective or factual it may appear.

Whether a group is dealing with facts, values, or policies, part of the work in stage one is to define all terms in the group's question. As we learned in Chapter 5, language is ambiguous. Because meanings vary among people, it's unwise to assume key words in a group's mission mean the same thing to all members. We've already seen that a word such as *should* needs to be clarified by identifying the standards for what ought to be the case. Other ambiguous words also need to be defined in the initial meetings of a group. For example, "What is the most meaningful way to structure a curriculum?" cannot be answered until the word *meaningful* is defined clearly.

In clarifying its focus, a group should also attempt to minimize bias. Asking "How can we give students the classes they want?" is obviously biased toward only students' perspectives. Likewise, "How can we let faculty teach the courses they want?" is biased toward only faculty interests. Once members have decided whether they are dealing with issues of fact, value, or policy and have clarified key terms, the group is ready to move to stage two.

Members of a zoning board analyze information pertinent to reaching a sound decision about future growth in their community. What can you tell from the members' nonverbal communication? Do they look involved in the task and responsive to one another?
(© Michael Heron/Woodfin Camp & Associates)

Stage Two: Analyze the Issues

The focus of this stage is gathering and analyzing information about the issues confronting a group. Initially, members need to decide what information they need: reports from prior groups dealing with this issue, existing records, opinion polls, interviews with experts, information about how others handle the problem, and library research are all valuable sources of information that may shed light on issues before the group. (Chapter 13 discusses ways of conducting and evaluating research.)

During this phase, communication among members tends to be highly task focused as people present information to the group and as members evaluate it. Members want to be critical of information so that they screen out any that isn't accurate or helpful. Asking about the credentials and bias of any interviewees is important, as is questioning the methods used for conducting opinion polls. To do a good job of analyzing information, members may wish to consult books that cover principles of logic and reasoning.

Stage Three: Establish Criteria

What would a good decision look like? That's the question members deal with during stage three of the standard agenda. **Criteria** are standards members use to evaluate alternative solutions or decisions. Without clear criteria, it's easy for groups to make decisions that don't meet needs or that create new problems. Establishing clear criteria before considering solutions helps a group avoid these pitfalls. The curriculum group on which I served established four criteria: The recommended curriculum (1) must allow all majors to meet requirements for the major; (2) cannot include courses that our faculty are not qualified to teach; (3) must offer courses that have high student demands most frequently; and (4) must conform to the university's requirements for undergraduate major and for faculty teaching loads. These criteria provided us with a blueprint for evaluating possible decisions in the next phase of our work.

Stage Four: Generate Solutions

Once a group understands the issues surrounding its topic and has agreed on criteria for assessing resolutions, the group's focus turns to generating possible decisions. There are two primary sources of solutions (Wood, 1992a). First, the research conducted during stage two of standard agenda often uncovers a number of possible solutions. My curriculum group's research revealed how curricula are designed in communication departments around the country, so all of those methods were options for us. We also learned about prior curricular reforms in the department and why they hadn't worked, so we were spared the embarrassment of repeating poor decisions.

A second source of alternative solutions is brainstorming, which we mentioned earlier. Brainstorming encourages ideas to flow freely without immediate criticism. In brainstorming, the goal is to generate as many and as creative answers as possible. Members should volunteer any ideas that occur to them, even ones that seem iffy or far out. Also, they should prompt each other to think imaginatively. For brainstorming to work, members must refrain from criticizing ideas when they are contributed. Evaluation is appropriate later, but at this point it can inhibit participation, and good ideas might not be voiced. One member records each idea so that the group has a complete list of possibilities.

Stage Five: Evaluate Solutions

Once members have a good list of solutions based on research and brainstorming, the goal is to evaluate each one against the criteria established in stage three of standard agenda. Any solutions that don't meet all criteria are discarded. Remaining are those that satisfy all of the standards members consider important for a good decision. Sometimes only a single solution meets all criteria. In other cases, members must decide which one of several solutions most fully meets the criteria.

Ideally, by this point members will be able to arrive at a consensus on the best decision. Sometimes consensus doesn't develop, however, and members must rely on other methods of decision making. If there is sufficient time, it's worthwhile to keep talking in the hope of reaching a consensus that has everyone's support. If time is limited or extensive discussion indicates consensus is not possible, then voting or compromise are viable options. Occasionally, rule by authority is exercised, although usually this method is enacted much earlier in a group's life.

"Okay, Williams, we'll vote . . . how many here say the heart has four chambers?"

Stage Six: Choose and Implement the Best Decision

In stage six, the group implements its decision. Implementation may involve writing a formal report to the individual or group that initially charged the group. This is the way advisory groups implement their decisions, since the goal is to generate advice for another person or group.

Many groups who work effectively through the first five stages of standard agenda stumble in the final stage by saying "We recommend that such and such decision be implemented." A vague recommendation like this does not specify what is necessary to ensure that a decision will be implemented effectively. Since group members are the experts on the issues, they need to make very specific recommendations regarding who is to do what at what time and by what means. Should the decision be implemented by the CEO, the department chair, the group itself, or some other person or group? Is the decision to be implemented by forwarding it to some governing body, circulating it for comment, announcing it to others, adding it to a handbook of policies? When should the decision take effect, and how should those affected be notified of the decision? Addressing logistical questions involved in implementation is an important group responsibility.

Stage Seven: Develop an Action Plan to Monitor the Solution

The final responsibility of decision-making groups is to develop an action plan for monitoring the effectiveness of their solution and, if necessary, modifying the solution. This involves generating methods to assess the impact of a decision and to determine whether the decision achieves the intended result while not creating any new problems. The point here is to check back on the effectiveness of the solution once it has been put into effect. Even with very careful group work, decisions usually need some fine-tuning to make them ideally effective. That's why it's a good idea to develop ways to evaluate the impact of your decision and to check on whether its implementation is smooth.

Members should specify how they will measure the success of its decision. My curricular group recommended that it conduct a poll of majors and faculty one year after the new curriculum was implemented to find out if students were able to get the courses they needed and if faculty thought teaching assignments were fair. Without monitoring, even a sound decision can run amiss or can produce side effects nobody envisioned. By specifying monitoring provisions and who is to implement them, a group ensures that what seems like a good decision in theory actually works in practice. If it doesn't work, modifications must be made to achieve the desired goal. Thus, the action plan should identify a person or group to make modifications, if any are needed.

SIBBY

A student group I was in came up with a great plan for printing student evaluations of all courses so that students could decide which ones to take. We got funding for the project, collected the data, and printed up the booklets. It wasn't until a year later that we figured out most students weren't reading the booklets because we weren't distributing them to the places students are likely to be when they sign up for courses—advisers' offices, for instance. If we had monitored our solution from the start, it would have worked better.

Standard agenda is a tested method for making sound decisions. It guides members through the various stages and issues that need to be considered in order to develop, implement, and assess its decision. Many groups use the standard agenda to schedule meetings. One or more meetings are devoted to each stage, a process that allows members to think ahead and to keep discussion focused.

UNDERSTANDING AND MANAGING CONFLICT IN GROUPS

Conflict exists when individuals who are interdependent have different views, interests, or goals that seem incompatible. In Chapter 8, we learned that conflict is a natural and productive part of relationships. Likewise, conflict is normal and can be productive in group discussion. Conflict stimulates thinking, ensures that different perspectives are considered, and enlarges members' understanding of issues involved in making decisions and developing policies. To achieve these goals, however, conflict must be managed carefully. In this section, we build on the discussion of conflict (see Chapter 8) to consider how it can be managed in the specific context of group discussion. We want to identify ways groups can deal with conflict so that they achieve their potential to enrich the process and outcomes of collective endeavors.

TABLE 11.2 Characteristics of Group Conflict	
Disruptive Conflict	Constructive Conflict
Competitive	Cooperative
Self-interested	Collective focus
Win–lose approach	Win–win approach
Closed climate	Open climate
Defensive communication	Supportive communication
Personal attacks	Issue-focused

TREY

I used to think conflict was terrible and hurt groups, but last year I was a member of a group that had no—I mean, zero—conflict. A couple of times I tried to bring up an idea different from what had been suggested, but my idea wouldn't even get a hearing. The whole goal was not to disagree. As a result, we didn't do a very thorough job of analyzing the issues, and we didn't subject the solution we developed to critical scrutiny. When our recommendation was put into practice, it bombed. We could have foreseen and avoided the failure if we had been willing to argue and disagree in order to test our idea before we put it forward.

Trey's commentary is instructive. Although many of us may not enjoy conflict, we can nonetheless recognize its value—even its necessity—to effective group work. Just as conflict in relationships can enlarge perspectives and increase understanding, conflict in groups has the potential to foster critical, thorough, and insightful deliberations.

Types of Conflict

The issue isn't whether to allow or avoid conflict, but how to handle it so that it enhances group work, rather than hinders it. Depending on how it is handled, conflict may be disruptive or constructive. Effective leadership helps groups to communicate in ways that allow conflict to be constructive and helpful in reaching good decisions and to avoid communication that fosters disruptive conflict. Table 11.2 summarizes the differences between these two basic forms of group conflict.

Disruptive Conflict   Disruptive conflict exists when disagreements interfere with effective work and the healthy communication climate in groups. Typically, disruptive conflict is marked by communication that is competitive as members vie with each other to wield influence and get their way. Accompanying the competitive tone of communication is a self-interested focus in which members talk only about their ideas, their solutions, their points of view. The competitive and self-centered communication in

(Reprinted by permission of United Feature Syndicate, Inc.)

disruptive conflict fosters a win–lose orientation to conflict. Members express the belief that only one or some members can win, typically by having others accept their views.

As a result of disruptive conflict, group climate deteriorates. A closed atmosphere develops in which members feel defensive and apprehensive. Members may feel it's unsafe to volunteer ideas because they might be harshly evaluated or scorned by others. Personal attacks may occur as members criticize one another's motives or attack one another personally.

Disruptive conflict results from communication that produces defensiveness and that detracts members' attention from a focus on collective concerns and goals. In Chapter 8, we saw that defensive climates are promoted by communication that expresses evaluation, superiority, control orientation, neutrality, certainty, and closed-mindedness. Just as these forms of communication undermine personal relationships, so too do they interfere with group climate and productivity.

Constructive Conflict   Constructive conflict occurs when members understand that disagreements are natural and can help them achieve their shared goals. This attitude is reflected in communication that is cooperative: Each person listens respectfully to others' opinions and voices her or his own ideas. Members also use communication to emphasize shared interests and collective goals that bind them together. The cooperative, collective focus of communication encourages a win–win orientation. Discussion is open and supportive of differences, and disagreements are focused on issues, not personalities.

To encourage constructive conflict, communication should demonstrate interest in hearing differing ideas, openness to others' points of view, willingness to alter opinions, and respect for the integrity of other members and the views they express. As we learned in Chapter 8, these forms of communication are ones that build supportive communication climates in which individuals feel it is safe to speak.

Constructive conflict benefits task teams. It allows members to broaden their understandings, generate a range of possible decisions or solutions, and subject all ideas to careful, cooperative analysis. Constructive conflict is most likely to occur when the appropriate groundwork has been established by creating a supportive, open climate of communication in the group. Group climate is built throughout the life of a group, beginning with the first meeting among members. Thus, it's important to communicate in ways that build a strong climate from the start so that it is established when conflict arises.

SUMMARY

In this chapter, we focused on task teams, groups that communicate to provide responses to ideas, people, and products; to inform and advise; to generate ideas; and to make decisions. Task teams are increasingly popular in modern professional life because they are often more effective than individuals in producing creative and high-quality decisions.

To be effective, task teams require leadership. As we have seen, leadership may be provided either by a single person or by a group of members. What matters is that one or more members communicate to organize discussion, ensure careful work on the task, and build cohesion, morale, and an effective climate for collective work. Meeting the task and climate responsibilities of leadership may be achieved by different styles of leadership. After discussing laissez-faire, authoritarian, and democratic styles of leading, we noted that effective leadership style depends on the particular circumstances of a group, including the values of the culture and organization in which it exists.

We also examined the advantages and limitations of consensus, voting, negotiation, and authority rule as methods of making decisions. No one decision-making method is best for all situations, since what will be effective varies according to particular group circumstances, tasks, and members. Thus, groups should consider their situations and needs in order to choose the most effective decision-making methods.

In this chapter, we also discussed standard agenda, which is a well-tested and effective way of organizing discussion so that it is thorough, efficient, and effective. Standard agenda also allows groups to break decision making down into units that can be managed in a series of separate meetings. What we covered

in this chapter should give you a good general understanding of how task teams work and how you can be an effective member of groups in which you choose to participate. Finally, we considered the role of conflict in enhancing group work, and we identified communication that fosters constructive conflict that improves the quality of group decision making. Constructive conflict in groups, as we have seen, grows out of a supportive communication climate that is built over the course of a group's life.

FOR FURTHER REFLECTION AND DISCUSSION

1. Interview a professional in the field you hope to enter after college. Ask her or him to identify ways in which the various task groups and teams discussed in this chapter are used on the job. What can you conclude about the prevalence of task teams in modern professional life?

2. Think about different leadership styles that you've experienced in small groups in which you've participated. Are your responses to different leadership styles consistent with research findings about the effects of democratic, authoritarian, and laissez-faire leadership on group productivity and climate?

3. Form groups of five to seven members in your class to work on a problem using standard agenda. You might address the question "What is the best method of testing knowledge in this course?" or another question that you and your instructor select. Move through standard agenda, and record your key ideas

and conclusions for each stage. For example, in stage one you would need to define *best* and *knowledge* if you addressed the question suggested in this item. After the process is completed, as a class discuss the value of standard agenda as a problem-solving method.

4.   Draw on your experiences in groups to identify situations in which each decision-making method was effective or appropriate.

KEY TERMS

brainstorming
quality circle
laissez-faire leadership
authoritarian leadership
democratic leadership
consensus
voting
compromise
authority rule
standard agenda
criteria

Focus Questions

1 How can speaking anxiety actually enhance a speaker's effectiveness?

2 How can I pick a good topic for a speech?

3 How can I find out about my audience so that I can adapt my speech effectively?

4 Do people who aren't professional performers ever give speeches designed to entertain others?

CHAPTER 12

Planning Public Speaking

H ank is a commercial artist at a public relations firm. On Thursday, Hank's supervisor asks him to prepare a 10-minute presentation on the firm for a client whose million-dollar account the firm hopes to get.

Bonnie belongs to a student group that brings major personalities to campus to talk with students about current issues. She is asked to introduce the keynote speaker, who is a nationally prominent individual.

Miranda volunteers as a peer counselor at a rape crisis center. The person who agreed to deliver an outreach program to a local high school calls in sick the day of the program and Miranda is asked to fill in.

Juan is a skilled software designer who has created a number of innovative programs for computer users. Although he usually works alone or with other programmers, today he has to give a 20-minute talk explaining a new program to people who have little experience with new technologies.

THE FIRST AMENDMENT: FREEDOM OF RELIGION, OF SPEECH, AND OF THE PRESS

Congress shall make no law respecting an establishment of religion, or prohibiting the free exercise thereof; or abridging the freedom of speech, or of the press; or the right of people peaceably to assemble, and to petition the Government for a redress of grievances.

While at a public hearing on the location of a toxic waste dump, a representative of a chemical company claims that chemicals stored in the dump are safer than they really are. Kelly feels compelled to speak up so that listeners know the truth about the danger of the chemicals.

Although these people aren't professional speakers, each of them is called on to make oral presentations. Public speaking is a natural part of most people's lives. It is a form of communication that advances professional effectiveness and personal influence on communities and society. Freedom to express our ideas in public is so basic to a free and democratic society that it is guaranteed by the First Amendment in the Bill of Rights.

The role of public speaking in professional life is more obvious for some careers than others. If you plan to be an attorney, a politician, or an educator, it's easy to see that speaking in public will be a routine part of your life. The importance of public speaking is less obvious, yet also present, in other careers. If you intend to be an accountant, a city planner, a counselor, a doctor, or a business person, you will have many opportunities to speak to small and large groups. Whatever profession you enter, public speaking skills will be important. The ability to present ideas effectively in public situations will also enhance your influence in civic, social, and political contexts. In other words, public speaking is not an activity reserved for the few. It is a basic communication skill that we all need if we wish to have a voice in what happens in our work, personal lives, and society.

Like other communication skills, effectiveness in public speaking can be developed with commitment and practice. Although some people may have more experience and perhaps even more aptitude than others, everyone can learn to make effective presentations. As we will see, many of the skills we've already studied pertain to public speaking.

This chapter and the two that follow lead you through the process of planning, developing, and presenting public speeches. We'll begin by considering communication apprehension, which is a common and often mis-

In most professions, the ability to make effective presentations is critical for advancement.
(© Charles Gupton/The Stock Market)

understood issue. Next we'll discuss similarities between public speaking and other kinds of communication we've studied. The third focus of this chapter is foundations of effective public speaking: selecting and limiting topics, defining purpose, and developing a thesis statement. In the final portion of the chapter, we discuss adapting speeches to particular listeners whose knowledge, concerns, and attitudes should fundamentally influence the design of public presentations.

The following two chapters extend the material in this one. Chapter 13 identifies types of support for public speeches and discusses methods of conducting research. In Chapter 14, we focus on organizing and presenting public speeches. After reading these three chapters, you should be prepared to plan, develop, and present an effective speech.

COMMUNICATION APPREHENSION: NATURAL AND OFTEN HELPFUL

If the above heading seems odd to you, then you'll be interested to learn that communication apprehension (sometimes called stage fright) is very common and can actually enhance speaking effectiveness. Most of us have felt nervous about speaking at various times and in particular situations. Some of us are comfortable interacting with one or two people, but we feel uneasy speaking to large groups. For other individuals, public speaking seems easier than carrying on an interpersonal conversation. The communication situations that prompt apprehension vary among people, as Tomoko and Trish illustrate.

TOMOKO

Talking to a big group of people is no problem for me. I like being able to prepare what I want to say in advance and to control what happens. But I get very nervous about one-on-one talking. It's too personal and spontaneous for me to feel secure about what will happen.

TRISH

I can talk all day with one friend or a few of them and be totally at ease, but put me in front of a group of people and I just freeze. I feel I'm on display or something; everything I say has to be perfect, and it all depends on me. It's just a huge pressure.

(David Park, *Audience* (c. 1953). Oil on canvas, 20 × 16". Collection of the Oakland Museum of California. Gift of Mrs. Roy Moore.)

Both Tomoko and Trish are normal in feeling some anxiety about specific communication situations. There are very few individuals who don't sometimes feel apprehensive about talking with others (Richmond & McCroskey, 1992). What many people don't realize is that a degree of anxiety is natural and may actually improve communication. When we're anxious, we're more alert and energetic, largely because our bodies produce adrenalin and extra blood sugar to enhance our vigilance and strength (Bostrom, 1988). The burst of adrenalin increases vitality, which can make speakers more dynamic and compelling (Bradley, 1978). You can channel the extra energy into gestures and movement when you are speaking. Effective gestures can enhance the impact of a presentation.

You should also realize that both novice and seasoned speakers experience anxiety. Many politicians feel nervous before and during a presentation, even though they make hundreds of speeches. Likewise, teachers who have taught for years usually feel tension before meeting a class, and seasoned journalists such as Mike Wallace claim they get butterflies when conducting interviews. The energy that is produced in response to communication anxiety allows politicians, teachers, and journalists to be more dynamic and interesting. Thus, some anxiety about speaking is both normal and useful.

Although a degree of anxiety about speaking is natural, too much can interfere with effectiveness. When anxiety is sufficient to hinder our ability to interact with others, communication apprehension exists. **Communication apprehension** is anxiety associated with real or anticipated communication encounters (McCroskey, 1977; Richmond & McCroskey, 1992). Communication apprehension exists in degrees. It isn't something that we either experience totally or don't experience at all. Communication apprehension can also occur at times other than when we're actually speaking. In fact, many people experience anxiety primarily in advance of communication situations—they worry, imagine difficulties, dread the occasion, and otherwise experience discomfort long before the real or possible communication situation arises. We can also feel apprehensive in the process of talking.

COMMUNICATION ANXIETY AMONG DEAF COMMUNICATORS

Is communication anxiety experienced only by people who communicate orally? To find out, Melanie and Steve Booth-Butterfield, two communication researchers, studied 89 students in three publicly funded residential schools for the deaf. They discovered that deaf individuals, like ones who use oral communication, were affected by communication apprehension. Their signing was less clear, less effective, weaker, smaller, and less intense as deaf individuals' communication anxiety increased. The Booth-Butterfields also found that the deaf students had lower overall communication apprehension levels than students who hear and speak.

Source: Booth-Butterfield, M., & Booth-Butterfield, S. (1994). Communication anxiety and signing effectiveness: Testing an interference model among deaf communicators. *Journal of Applied Communication Research, 22,* 273–286.

Deaf communicators experience some of the same challenges that face people who communicate orally, including communication apprehension. (© Vanessa Vick/Photo Researchers, Inc.)

Causes of Communication Apprehension

Researchers who have studied communication apprehension believe it stems from two major sources. In some cases, communication apprehension is a response to specific situational factors. In other instances, apprehension is more general and its source lies in personal history.

Situational Causes of Apprehension   For many of us, certain contexts or features of contexts spark anxiety. Sometimes anxiety is legitimate. For instance, if you find a burglar when you enter your home, anxiety is a natural and appropriate response! In other cases, we feel apprehensive because features of a situation or features we imagine worry us. Before a performance review, it's natural to be a little anxious about what your supervisor might say regarding areas in which you need to improve. Even if that topic doesn't come up, you may experience apprehension from imagining that it might. It doesn't matter whether stress is related to actual aspects of a situation or not, since we act according to what we believe is the case.

(THE WIZARD OF ID by permission of John Hart and Creators Syndicate, Inc.)

Research indicates that five situational factors often generate apprehension. First, we tend to be more anxious when communicating with people who are unfamiliar to us or who we think are different from us. It's easy to understand why we might be more anxious, since there is greater uncertainty with unfamiliar people than with individuals we know and with whom we have a history of interaction. Uncertainty is also present in unusual situations, which may increase apprehension. If you've never interviewed for a job, your first few interviews will be novel experiences that are impossible to predict and, thus, anxiety producing.

A third situational cause of apprehension is being in the spotlight. When we are the center of attention, we tend to feel self-conscious and anxious that we might embarrass ourselves by acting inappropriately. Public speaking triggers anxiety in individuals who are uneasy when attention is focused on them.

Evaluation is another cause of apprehension. We are often uneasy when we're being evaluated (Motley & Molloy, 1994). If your boss or professor is present when you speak, you may feel under scrutiny and anxious. Similarly, we may feel apprehensive when we have to communicate with someone who has higher status or social power than we do. For example, people sometimes feel apprehensive about talking with professors, socializing with supervisors, or meeting parents of the person they intend to marry. In such cases, we may feel we're inadequate and don't measure up to others, and that stimulates anxiety.

TIM

The CEO at my company wants us to be like a family, so he drops into our offices to be friendly and has parties at his home. We all know he means well, but to tell the truth, it makes us uncomfortable. We're not equals; he decides our salaries, so we can't relax and communicate naturally when he's around.

A final situational reason for apprehension is a past failure or failures in a particular speaking situation. If you've had bad experiences leading groups on a number of occasions, chances are you will have anxiety about leading another group. We can also be apprehensive if we had one particularly dramatic failure. For example, my doctor called me one day to ask me if I would coach her for a speech she had to give to a medical society. I was surprised, since Eleanor is very effective in interacting with patients. When I asked why she thought she needed special assistance, Eleanor told me that the last speech she had given was 8 years ago in medical school. She was an intern and it was her turn to present a case to the other interns and the physician who supervised her. Just before the speech, she lost her first patient to a heart attack and she was badly shaken. All of her work preparing the case and rehearsing her presentation was eclipsed by the shock of losing a patient. As a result, she was disorganized, easily flustered, and generally ineffective. That single incident, which followed a history of successful speaking, was so traumatic that Eleanor developed acute speaking anxiety.

Everyday Application

PERSONAL REPORT OF COMMUNICATION APPREHENSION

Instructions Following are 24 statements that ask how you feel about communicating. Don't worry if some of the following statements seem similar to other statements. In the space to the left of each item, indicate the extent to which you agree that this statement describes you. Please record your *first* impressions without analyzing statements closely. Use the following scale:

1 = strongly agree it describes me

2 = agree it describes me

3 = undecided how well this describes me

4 = disagree that this describes me

5 = strongly disagree that this describes me

_____ 1. I dislike participating in group discussions.

_____ 2. Generally, I am comfortable while participating in group discussions.

_____ 3. I am tense and nervous while participating in group discussions.

_____ 4. I like to get involved in group discussions.

_____ 5. Engaging in group discussions with new people makes me tense and nervous.

_____ 6. I am calm and relaxed while participating in group discussions.

_____ 7. Generally, I am nervous when I have to participate in a meeting.

_____ 8. Usually, I am calm and relaxed while participating in meetings.

_____ 9. I am very calm and relaxed when I am called on to express an opinion at a meeting.

_____ 10. I am afraid to express myself at meetings.

_____ 11. Communicating at meetings usually makes me uncomfortable.

_____ 12. I am very relaxed when answering questions at a meeting.

_____ 13. While participating in a conversation with a new acquaintance, I feel very nervous.

_____ 14. I have no fear of speaking up in conversation.

_____ 15. Ordinarily, I am very tense and nervous in conversations.

_____ 16. Ordinarily, I am very calm and relaxed in conversations.

_____ 17. While conversing with a new acquaintance, I feel very relaxed.

_____ 18. I'm afraid to speak up in conversations.

_____ 19. I have no fear of giving a speech.

_____ 20. Certain parts of my body feel very tense and rigid while giving a speech.

_____ 21. I feel relaxed while giving a speech.

_____ 22. My thoughts become confused and jumbled when I am giving a speech.

_____ 23. I face the prospect of giving a speech with confidence.

_____ 24. While giving a speech, I get so nervous I forget facts I really know.

Computing Your Score This test allows you to calculate your overall communication apprehension score and your communication apprehension scores for particular speaking situations.

Group Score	Add scores for items 2, 4, and 6
	Subtract scores for items 1, 3, and 5
	Add 18 = _____

Meeting Score	Add scores for items 8, 9, 12
	Subtract scores for items 7, 10, 11
	Add 18 = _____

Dyad Score	Add scores for items 14, 16, 17
	Subtract scores for items 13, 15, 18
	Add 18 = _____
Public Speaking Score	Add scores for items 19, 21, and 23
	Subtract scores for items 20, 22, 24
	Add 18 = _____
Total Score	Add the four subscores together
	Total Communication Apprehension Score = _____

The overall scores may range from 24 to 120. (If your score is over 120 or less than 24, you calculated incorrectly.)

Scores of 83 or more indicate relatively high communication apprehension. People who score in this range tend to talk little, be shy, and be somewhat withdrawn and nervous in speaking situations.

Scores of 55 or less indicate relatively low communication apprehension. People who score in this range tend to enjoy being with others, like talking, and feel confident of their communication ability.

Source: McCroskey, J. C. (1982). *Introduction to rehetorical communication* (4th ed.). Englewood Cliffs, NJ: Prentice-Hall.

Chronic Communication Apprehension   Communication apprehension is more difficult to manage when it is stable and enduring. Rather than feeling anxious, often appropriately, about specific contexts, some individuals are generally apprehensive about communicating. Current knowledge suggests that chronic anxiety is learned. In other words, we can learn to fear communication, just as some of us learn to fear hospitals, animals, or lightning (DeFleur & Ball-Rokeach, 1989).

One source of learned communication apprehension is observation of other people who are anxious about communicating. A child whose parents are afraid of speaking in public and who talk about the risks and failures that accompany speaking may develop a personal fear of communicating. If we see friends perspiring heavily and being stressed about making presentations, we may internalize their anxiety as an appropriate response to speaking situations.

Observing anxious communicators doesn't fully explain enduring communication apprehension, since some people who have anxious models aren't apprehensive themselves. Reinforcement may make the difference between developing enduring anxiety and not doing so (Beatty, Plax, & Kearney, 1985). A child might become generally apprehensive if she or he is reprimanded for speaking in class, told repeatedly to be quiet during dinner, and punished for talking when adults are conversing. Because the child gets consistently negative responses to efforts to communicate, it's understandable if he or she learns to avoid communicating and to fear situations that require it.

MICHAEL

To this day, I have vivid memories of my father being sick, I mean throwing up sick, anytime he had to make a presentation to his work team. He would start getting edgy weeks before the presentation, then he'd get nervous, then he'd be unable to hold food down. By the day of a presentation, he was a basket case. That's probably why I was so fearful of speaking until I got help.

Reducing Communication Apprehension

Michael's last sentence is important. If communication apprehension is learned, it can also be unlearned—at least in many cases. Communication scholars have developed several methods of reducing communication apprehension that have made major differences in many individuals' lives. Although we can't discuss each method in depth here, we will briefly review all three. If you do not have significant communication apprehension, reading this section will help you understand people who do experience anxiety. If you have more communication apprehension than you would like, reading this section should help you reduce your anxiety.

Systematic Desensitization   One method, systematic desensitization, has an impressive rate of success (Daly & McCroskey, 1984). **Systematic desensitization** is a complex name for a method of treating many fears from fear of flying to fear of spiders and fear of speaking. It focuses on reducing the tension that surrounds the feared event, speaking for instance. When we're apprehensive, our heart rate quickens, muscles tighten, and breathing becomes more shallow (Beatty & Behnke, 1991). Systematic desensitization teaches individuals how to relax and thereby reduce the physiological features of anxiety. Once individuals learn to control breathing and muscle tension, they are asked to think systematically about speaking situations of progressive difficulty. The goal is to learn to associate feeling relaxed with images of themselves in communication situations.

Cognitive Restructuring   A second method of reducing communication apprehension is called **cognitive restructuring**, which is a process of revising how individuals think about speaking situations. According to this method, speaking is not the problem; rather, the problem is how we use irrational beliefs to interpret speaking situations. If we hold irrational beliefs about speaking, then it's not surprising that we might feel anxious. For example, if you think you must be perfect, totally engaging, and liked by everyone who hears you, then you've set yourself up for failure. You've created expectations that are impossible to meet, which might be why you feel emotionally uneasy about communicating. A key part of cognitive restructuring is teaching apprehensive individuals to identify and challenge

Imagining yourself communicating effectively can reduce anxiety and enhance effectiveness.
(© Anne Dowie)

negative self-statements. You may recall that we discussed vultures and downers when we explored self-concept in Chapter 3. The concepts pertain here also, since negative statements we make to ourselves can undermine our effectiveness. Thus, individuals are taught to find the errors in their irrational and negative self-statements. The statement "My topic won't interest everyone," for instance, would be criticized for assuming others won't be interested and for assuming any speaker can and should hold the attention of everyone.

An extension of cognitive restructuring was recently developed by Michael Motley and Jennifer Molloy (1994), who have studied communication apprehension for years. They tested a new therapy for individuals who have anxiety about public speaking. This approach has apprehensive individuals read a short booklet that encourages them to develop new and less debilitating perspectives on communication situations. The heart of this method is to change individuals' perspective on public speaking so that they view it not as a unique kind of communication, but as quite similar to normal conversations that they have every day. Preliminary findings indicate that this approach has substantial promise.

Positive Visualization   The rationale for cognitive restructuring also informs a third technique for reducing communication apprehension. **Positive visualization** aims to reduce speaking anxiety by guiding apprehensive speakers through imagined positive speaking experiences. This technique allows individuals to form a mental picture of themselves as effective speakers and to then enact that mental picture when in actual speaking situations (Hamilton, 1996). Researchers report that positive visualization is especially effective in reducing chronic communication apprehension (Ayres & Hopf, 1990; Bourhis & Allen, 1992).

The goal of positive visualization is to create detailed, positive images of yourself in progressively challenging speaking situations. Instead of thinking about all of the things you might do wrong and negative responses listeners might have, create a vivid and detailed mental image of yourself speaking successfully. You can do this by recalling our discussion of self-sabotaging communication in Chapter 3. Self-sabotaging communication would be making disparaging comments about your communication or your general merit. In positive visualization, the goal is to create a positive self-fulfilling prophecy by using only positive language and allowing only positive thoughts about your communication. By visualizing yourself communicating effectively, it is possible to create positive associations for public communication and for yourself as a communicator.

IN YOUR MIND'S EYE

Positive visualization can enhance success in a variety of situations. In professional life, managers are coached to visualize successful negotiations and meetings. In the world of sports, athletes are taught to imagine playing well, and those who engage in positive visualization improve as much as athletes who physically practice their sport.

According to psychologists, we act like the person we see ourselves as being. Applying this to athletics, business, or speaking, it seems that successful people are ones who see themselves as successful in their mind's eye.

Sources: Lau, B. (1989). Imagining your path to success. *Management Quarterly, 30,* 30–41. Porter, K., & Foster, J. (1986). *The mental athlete: Inner training for peak performance.* New York: Ballantine.

Skills Training   **Skills training** is a fourth method of reducing communication apprehension. Unlike the other approaches that assume anxiety causes communication problems, skills training assumes that lack of speaking skills causes us to be apprehensive about speaking. This method focuses on teaching individuals skills such as how to start conversations, organize ideas, and respond effectively to others (Phillips, 1991).

After reading about these methods of reducing communication apprehension, you may be thinking each of them seems useful. If so, your thinking coincides research that indicates a combination of all three methods is more likely to relieve speaking anxiety than any single method (Allen, Hunter, & Donahue, 1989). The major conclusion to draw is that communication apprehension isn't necessarily irremediable. There are ways to reduce it. Eliminating all communication anxiety isn't desirable, since as we've seen, it can enhance a speaker's dynamism and alertness. If you experience serious communication apprehension that interferes with your ability to express your ideas, ask your instructor to direct you to professionals who can work with you.

POSITIVE VISUALIZATION

First imagine yourself speaking to three of your friends on a topic about which you care. Now visualize your friends nodding and asking questions that indicate they are interested in what you say. Notice that they are looking intently at you and their postures are attentive.

The most engaging public presentations are often conversational in style. (© Bob Daemmrich/Stock, Boston)

Now imagine that someone you don't know joins your friends and you continue speaking. It's okay if you feel a little anxious, but visualize the stranger becoming very attentive to your communication. Notice how the new person looks at you with admiration.

Next, imagine that you are asked to speak on the same topic to a student group and you agree. Visualize the room in which you speak—it is a small conference room in the campus student union. The room seems warm and comfortable. When you enter there are 20 people there to hear you. Notice that they smile when you walk to the front of the room. See how they look at you expectantly because they are interested in your topic.

Visualize yourself starting your talk: You begin by telling the listeners that, like them, you are a student. Notice that they nod and acknowledge the connection between you and them. Feel yourself becoming relaxed and confident. Then you tell them what you will cover in your talk. Notice how your words flow easily and smoothly. See the nods and smiles of your listeners. As you speak, they stay engaged with you—interested, following your ideas, impressed by your knowledge. When you are through, the listeners break into spontaneous applause.

PUBLIC SPEAKING AS ENLARGED CONVERSATION

Years ago, James Winans (1938), a professor of communication, remarked that effective public speaking is really enlarged conversation. Winans meant that the skills of successful public speaking are not so different from those we use in everyday conversations. As Motley and Molloy (1994, p. 52) recently stated, "Except for preparation time and turn-taking delay, public speaking has fundamental parallels to everyday conversation." Whether we are talking with a couple of friends or speaking to an audience of 100 people, we need to consider others' perspectives, create a good climate for communication, be clear on what our point is, state it clearly, organize what we say so that others can follow our thinking, explain and support our ideas, and present our thoughts in an engaging and convincing manner. In public speaking, as in everyday conversation, these are the skills of effective communication.

PUBLIC SPEAKING AS EVERYDAY CONVERSATION

Communication scholar Michael Motley contends that public speaking is more like than unlike everyday interaction. He writes:

> The assumption is that the audience is focused with curiosity upon the speaker's message, and that success is measured by the extent to which the audience understands the message and its point of view. Thus, minor "mistakes" are as tolerable as in everyday communication, and appropriate delivery techniques—being those of everyday communication—are well within the range of the speaker's existing repertoire. . . . The audience is more focused on understanding the message than on evaluating the speaker. (p. 90)

Source: Motley, M. (1990). Public speaking anxiety qua performance anxiety: A revised model and an alternative therapy. *Journal of Social Behavior and Personality, 5,* 85–104.

Thinking of public speaking as enlarged conversation reminds us that good public speaking is not usually stiff or exceedingly formal. In fact, the most effective public speakers tend to use an informal, personal style that invites listeners to feel they are talking with someone, not being lectured to. In other words, public speaking doesn't require an entirely new and different set of communication skills. Instead, good public communication requires and builds on skills and principles we've discussed in earlier chapters.

I learned that effective public speaking is much like conversation when I first taught a large lecture course. For the first 10 years of my career, I had taught classes that enrolled 20 to 35 students, and I relied on an interactive communication style that involved all of us in the class. When I decided to teach a class with over 100 students, I worried that I couldn't develop an effective style of teaching a large class. For half of that semester, I lectured in a fairly formal style because I thought that was appropriate with over 100 students. One day a student asked a question that I answered by asking a question in return. He replied, then another student added her ideas, and an open discussion was launched. Both the students and I were more engaged with each other and the course material than we had been when I lectured formally. That's when I realized that effective teaching in large classes was enlarged conversation. Now, even when I am lecturing in large classes, I adopt a conversational style that fosters interaction and involvement.

So far we've seen that most people, whether experienced or beginning communicators, feel some anxiety about speaking. Some nervousness is actually helpful in making us more alert and dynamic in our interactions with others. We've also noted that effective public speaking is not unlike other forms of everyday communication. At its best, public speaking is enlarged conversation in which personal engagement between listeners and speakers is high. With this background, we're now ready to consider the first step in designing effective public presentation.

FIRST FOUNDATIONS OF PUBLIC SPEAKING

A well-crafted speech begins with a topic that is limited, a clear purpose for speaking, and a concise thesis statement that listeners can grasp quickly and retain.

Choosing Your Topic

The first step in preparing a public speech is to select a topic. Often students ask their instructors to designate a topic, but this would deprive them of the opportunity to speak on a topic that matters to them. The most important guideline for choosing a topic is to select one that you know and care about. Your expertise and commitment to the topic will enhance your speaking effectiveness. To stimulate your thinking about possible topics, you might consult sources such as *The Readers' Guide to Periodical Literature,* newspapers and news magazines, and current events programs on TV.

ALL RIGHT, CLASS. MY JOB IS TO TALK TO YOU AND YOUR JOB IS TO LISTEN — IF YOU FINISH FIRST PLEASE LET ME KNOW —

BRICKMAN

(Reprinted with special permission of King Features Syndicate.)

Select a Topic That Matters to You When you are asked to speak, seize the chance to have a voice on an issue that matters to you. Invariably, the most effective speeches involve topics about which speakers feel deeply. When we care about a topic, we have a head start in that we already know a fair amount about it. In addition, personal interest in the subject will enliven speaking. Perhaps you are a vegetarian and want to inform others of the moral, health, and economic reasons for vegetarianism. If you are committed to strong environmental policies on campus, you might want to persuade your classmates to be more environmentally conscious. Maybe you have strong beliefs about abortion, the death penalty, product testing on animals, inner-city crime, or other issues of current social consequence. A speech is the ideal opportunity to influence how others feel and think about important issues.

Select a Topic Appropriate to Your Situation Personal knowledge and interest aren't the only criteria for selecting a topic. We must also consider the expectations, demands, and constraints of particular speaking situations. Some contexts virtually dictate speaking content. For example, a rally for a political candidate demands speeches that praise the candidate; a ceremony honoring an individual requires speakers to pay tribute to the person; a keynote speech at a professional conference should address the concerns of that profession. Effective speakers consider what the context demands and invites in the way of content.

Select a Topic Appropriate to Your Audience Adapting to the speaking situation also requires us to consider our listeners when we choose and develop a topic. Speakers who don't demonstrate consideration of listeners' backgrounds and interests appear egotistical, and they are seldom effective. In selecting a topic, ask what issues interest your listeners, what knowledge they have, and what experiences and concerns they share with you. We'll have more to say about considering listeners later in this chapter. For now, just realize that you should take listeners into account when choosing a topic.

Narrow Your Topic   Once a civic group asked me to speak on "interpersonal communication." There are hundreds of books and courses on interpersonal communication. Clearly, "interpersonal communication" is too broad a topic for a single speech.

Effective speakers limit their speeches to a manageable focus (McGuire, 1989). A speech about "interpersonal communication" could focus on managing conflict or listening effectively or creating supportive climates. Any of these topics could be discussed in a 10- to 20-minute speech. If you're interested in the general topic of health reform, you might narrow that to reducing the costs of drugs, or enhancing support for research and development of orphan drugs, or increasing preventive medicine (wellness). You can't competently discuss the broad topic of health reform in a single speech, but you can cover a particular aspect of that topic.

Everyday Application

SELECTING YOUR TOPIC

Identify three topics that you know and care about.

Topic 1: _____

Topic 2: _____

Topic 3: _____

Now list three subtopics for each one. The subtopics should be narrow enough to be covered well in a short speech.

Topic 1: 1. _____

2. _____

3. _____

Topic 2: 1. _____

2. _____

3. _____

Topic 3: 1. _____

　　　　　 2. _____

　　　　　 3. _____

Select one of the nine subtopics for your upcoming speech.

Another way to narrow your speaking purpose is by using a **mind map** (Jaffe, 1995; Wycoff, 1991). A mind map is a holistic record of information on a topic. You create a mind map by free associating ideas in relation to a broad area of interest. For example, perhaps you wish to speak on the general topic of the environment. To narrow that broad topic to a manageable focus for a single speech, you could brainstorm issues related to the topic. Figure 12.1 shows many specific issues that might occur to someone who creates a mind map on the topic of environment.

Defining Your Purpose in Speaking

The second step in designing an effective speech is to define your purpose in speaking. This involves two tasks. First, you should decide whether your goal is to persuade, entertain, or inform listeners. Second, you should refine your narrowed topic into a single clear thesis statement.

Traditionally, three speaking purposes have been recognized: entertaining, informing, and persuading. You probably realize that these purposes often overlap. For example, informative speeches routinely include humor or interesting comments to entertain listeners. Persuasive speeches typically contain considerable information about issues and solutions. Speeches intended to inform may also persuade listeners toward new beliefs, attitudes, or actions. Although speeches often involve more than one purpose, usually there is a primary purpose.

One speaking goal is to entertain. In **speeches to entertain,** the primary objective is to engage, interest, and please listeners. You might think that speeches to entertain are presented only by accomplished comics and performers. Actually, many of us will be involved in speaking to entertain during our lives. You might be asked to give an after-dinner speech, present a toast at a friend's wedding, or make remarks at a retirement party for a colleague. In each of these cases, the primary goal is to entertain, although the entertainment might include information about the occasion, the couple being married, or the achievements of the colleague who is retiring. Even when your primary purpose in speaking is not to entertain, it's likely that you'll want to amuse and interest listeners whom you intend to inform or persuade. If you wish to include entertainment elements in your speech, it's a good idea to test your jokes or amusing comments on others. Don't assume that others will find humor in something you think is funny, and don't rely exclusively on close friends' judgment—after all, friends often think alike and have similar senses of humor. It's also a good idea to

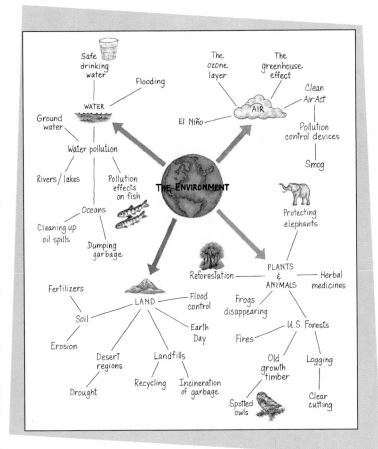

FIGURE 12.1
A Mind Map

Source: Jaffe, C. (1995). *Public speaking: A cultural perspective* (p. 30). Belmont, CA: Wadsworth.

avoid jokes and remarks that might offend some people. Even if you find them funny, they could alienate listeners, as Joanna's commentary illustrates.

JOANNA

I am so angry about a lecture I went to last week. The speaker was trying to sound like he was with it or something, so right at the start of his talk he tried to tell a joke. He asked, "How many State co-eds does it take to change a tire?" You should have heard the groan from all the women in the audience. He lost us right there.

Humor doesn't dominate in all speeches that have the goal of entertaining. We also seek to entertain when we tell stories. **Narrative speaking** involves rendering a story to share experiences, build community, pass on history, or teach a lesson. Narrative speaking often occurs in families as parents share stories of their courtship with children, discuss friends and relatives, and keep family memories alive. You probably heard a great many family stories as you were growing up. Narrative speaking is also very important in cultures that emphasize oral communication more than written. In some other countries and in many co-cultures in the United States, individual and collective histories are kept alive through storytelling. African Americans and Southerners have particularly strong oral history traditions; they weave families and communities together by telling stories that create common knowledge and understandings.

Speaking to inform is a common presentational goal. **Speeches to inform** have the primary goal of increasing listeners' understanding, awareness, or knowledge about some topic. For example, a speaker might want listeners to understand what activities do and don't spread HIV. Another focus for an informative speech would be to inform listeners about existing programs for recycling. In both cases, the primary purpose is to enrich listeners' knowledge. Speeches to inform may also take the form of demonstrations in which the speaker shows how to do something while giving a verbal explanation. For instance, a demonstration speech might show listeners how to use a new computer program or how to distinguish between poisonous and nonpoisonous mushrooms. Speeches to inform may also

Storytelling is a powerful way to pass on history and strengthen familial and community bonds. It plays a central role in oral cultures. (© Mark Richards/PhotoEdit)

aim to teach listeners something entirely new. Sasha, a student in one of my classes, gave a speech on arranged marriages, which are still the practice in her native country. Her goal was for students to understand the history of arranged marriages and the reasons why they work for many people.

Speeches to persuade have the purpose of changing people's attitudes, beliefs, or behaviors and/or motivating them to action. Persuasive goals are to influence attitudes, change practices, and alter beliefs. Rather than being primarily an entertainer or teacher, the persuasive speaker is an advocate who argues for a cause, issue, policy, attitude, or action. In one of my classes, a student named Chris gave a speech designed to persuade other students to contribute to the current Red Cross blood drive. He began by telling us that he was a hemophiliac and that his life depended on blood donations. He then informed listeners about the procedures for donating blood (a subordinate informational purpose) so that they would not be deterred by fear of the unknown. Next, he described several cases of people who had died or become critically ill because adequate supplies of blood weren't available. In the 2 weeks after his speech, more than one-third of the students donated blood!

Everyday Application

DEFINING YOUR PURPOSE

Write out the primary purpose of your speech.

I want my speech to _____

_____ .

Define the purpose of your speech by specifying the observable response that will indicate you have succeeded: At the end of my speech,

I want listeners to _____

_____ .

Does your primary purpose require you to meet subordinate goals such as including information in a persuasive speech?

To achieve my goal I need to entertain _____

inform _____

persuade _____

To further clarify your speaking goal, it's advisable to define a **specific purpose,** which is a behavioral objective or observable response that will indicate you have been effective in achieving your communication goal. For example: I want 25% of listeners to sign up to donate blood. I want people to laugh at my jokes. I want listeners to be able to give correct answers to questions about how HIV is and is not spread.

Developing a Thesis Statement

Once you have selected and narrowed your speaking topic and defined your purpose, then you're ready to develop the thesis statement for your speech. A **thesis statement** is the main idea of an entire speech. It should capture the key message in a short and precise sentence that listeners can remember easily (Table 12.1). "Donating blood is a good idea" is too general to provide listeners with a handle on what's to follow.

A good thesis statement is one listeners can grasp at the beginning of your talk and remember after you have finished. They may forget specific details and evidence you present, but you want them to remember the main idea. They are most likely to retain it if you create a concise thesis statement and repeat it several times during your talk.

TABLE 12.1 Sample Thesis Statements	
Ineffective	Effective
Think twice before you decide against affirmative action.	Affirmative action is still needed in the United States.
Vegetarianism is a way of life.	Vegetarian diets are healthy and delicious.
Big businesses should get breaks on taxes.	Tax breaks for businesses are good for the economy and for individuals.

A thesis statement refines what you've already done in limiting your topic and defining your purpose. Chris's thesis statement for his speech was this: Donating blood is painless, quick, and lifesaving for others. Although Chris's listeners may have forgotten many of the specific points in his speech, they remembered his main idea, which is the purpose of a thesis statement.

The foundation of effective public speaking is choosing and clarifying the focus of communication. As we've seen, this requires you to select and narrow a topic, define a primary purpose, and develop a clear, concise thesis statement. We're now ready to consider how listeners shape the goals, content, and style of public speaking.

ANALYZING YOUR AUDIENCE

In one of my classes, a student named Odell gave a persuasive speech designed to convince listeners to support affirmative action. He was personally compelling and dynamic in his delivery, and his ideas were well organized. The only problem was that his audience had little background on affirmative action, and he didn't explain exactly what the policy involves. He assumed listeners understood how affirmative action works, and he focused on its positive effects. His listeners weren't persuaded because Odell failed to give them information necessary to their support. Odell's speech also illustrates our earlier point that speeches often combine more than one speaking purpose—in this case giving information was essential to Odell's larger goal of persuading listeners.

In another class, a student named Christie spoke passionately about the morality of vegetarianism. She provided dramatic evidence of the cruelty animals suffer as they are raised and slaughtered. When we polled students after her speech, only two had been persuaded to consider vegetarianism. Why was Christie ineffective? She didn't recognize and address listeners' beliefs that vegetarianism wasn't healthy and that vegetarian foods are unappetizing. Christie mistakenly assumed that listeners would know it's easy to get sufficient protein, vitamins, and minerals without consuming meat, and she assumed they would understand vegetarian foods can be delicious. However, her listeners *didn't* know that, and they weren't about to consider a diet that they thought wasn't nutritious or palatable.

The mistake that Christie and Odell made was not adapting to their audiences. It's impossible to entertain, inform, or persuade people if we don't consider their perspectives on our topics. Speakers need to understand what listeners already know and believe and what reservations they might have about what we say (McGuire, 1989). To paraphrase the advice of an ancient Greek rhetorician, "The fool persuades me with his or her reasons, the wise person with my own." That is, effective speakers understand and work with listeners' reasons, values, knowledge, and concerns. This advice is as wise today as it was over 2,000 years ago.

All communication, including public speaking, involves interaction between people. The perspectives of listeners must be taken into account if you want them to consider your views. We consider the views of our friends when we talk with them. We think about others' perspectives when we engage in business negotiations. We use dual perspective when communicating with children, dates, and neighbors. Thus, audience analysis is important to effectiveness in all communication encounters. This implies that we should adapt our communication to the ideas, concerns, existing knowledge, and communication styles of those to whom we speak. To do this, we must understand who our listeners are and what is most likely to inform, entertain, or persuade them. We'll discuss two methods of analyzing audiences.

Demographic Analysis

You've heard the word *demographics* used to refer to common characteristics of people in a community or nation. **Demographic analysis** focuses on general features that are common to a group of listeners. Demographic characteristics include age, sex, religion, cultural heritage, race, occupation, political allegiances, and educational level. Knowing about the demographic commonalities in listeners tells a speaker two things. First, demographics provide direct information that can be used to prepare a speech. For example, if you know the age or age range of listeners, you know what experiences are likely to be part of their history. You could assume that 45-year-old listeners know a fair amount about the Vietnam War, but 20-year-olds might not.

Other demographic information can also guide speakers in preparing presentations that will interest and involve particular listeners. If speaking to an African American audience, for instance, a speaker should anticipate and invite "call out" responses from listeners. As we've noted in earlier chapters, more than European Americans, African Americans tend to participate actively by interjecting comments such as "Yeah," "Tell us more," and "You're saying it right, now" during a speech. Another demographic factor is age, which research indicates is an influence on persuadability. In general, as people age they are less likely to change their attitudes, perhaps because they've held their attitudes longer than younger individuals (Meyers, 1993). Thus, it's generally reasonable to expect to move older listeners less toward what you advocate than you might move younger listeners.

Knowing the educational background of listeners suggests what kinds of language may be appropriate. Once, when I was serving as an expert witness in a trial, I was asked about an instrument that had been used to measure an employee's effectiveness. I had reviewed the instrument in advance and determined that it was invalid and unreliable. I stated that as my opinion in court. One of the attorneys then asked me what validity and reliability were. The judge and jury didn't have statistical training, so I couldn't explain the technical meaning of convergent, predictive, internal, and external validity, and I couldn't explain the specialized indexes of reliability. After a few moments of thought, I answered that validity is a matter of whether an instrument measures what it claims to and reliability is a matter of whether the instrument consistently measures what it claims to measure over time. Had I been speaking to a group of researchers, I would have offered a different answer tailored to their greater statistical expertise.

We also know that people who have cognitively complex thinking styles want to understand things. For them, it's not enough to know that something *is* the case. They also need to know *why* it's the case—what makes it so (Meyers, 1993). Cognitive complexity tends to increase with age and education, so we can make predictions about listeners' cognitive complexity based on these other factors. When preparing a speech for cognitively complex listeners, we should provide more detailed evidence and explanations for our assertions than might be appropriate for a less cognitively complex group of listeners.

Speakers also use demographic information to make inferences about what listeners are likely to believe and what values and attitudes they are likely to have. For example, assume you plan to give a speech on the general topic of health reform. If your listeners' average age is 68, they are likely to be more interested in containment of drug costs and in reasonable options for long-term care of elderly people than in preventive care and vaccines for children. However, listeners in their twenties might find preventive health care more immediately relevant than ensuring reasonable options for long-term care of elderly citizens.

Knowing something about the general characteristics of listeners may also suggest what type of evidence and which authorities will be effective. Statistics bore many listeners, especially if they are presented in a dull manner, but they might interest an audience of economists or mathematicians. A quotation from Bill Clinton is more likely to be effective with a Democratic audience than with a Republican one. Citing Sandra Day O'Connor or Ruth Ginsberg might impress a group of women attorneys more than citing Clarence Thomas.

Demographic information provides general insights into what and whom listeners may find credible. Yet, it's important to remember that demographic information can provide only a general profile of a group. As we noted when we discussed stereotypes in Chapters 2 and 5, not all members of a particular social group conform to all features of that group. Although demographic analysis can give you some general information about groups of people, it doesn't offer precise insight into any particular individual.

LAMONT

A big filmmaker came to talk to our class, and I figured he was in a world totally different from ours. I mean the man makes multimillion-dollar movies and knows all the big stars. But he started his talk by telling us about when he was in college, and he talked about his favorite classes, about a bar he went to on Fridays, and about the special friends he'd made at college. I felt like he understood what my life is about, like he wasn't so different from me after all.

Speakers may also draw on demographic information to create connections with their listeners. Speakers who build common ground with listeners foster good will and openness to their ideas. Politicians create points of identification with voters in diverse regions. In the South, a candidate might tell stories about growing up in southern towns; in New England, the candidate might reminisce about college years at Harvard or Dartmouth; in the Midwest, the candidate might speak about friends and family who live there. A speaker might emphasize education to academics, a strong economy to economists, and the need for business-friendly policies to business people. Obviously, speakers shouldn't disguise or distort their ideas and positions in order to build common ground with listeners. However, understanding the demographic characteristics of listeners helps a speaker decide which aspects of her or his life and topic to emphasize in a particular situation.

Everyday Application

DEMOGRAPHIC ANALYSIS

Answer the following questions (or research the answers) about the listeners to whom you plan to speak:

1. How many women and men are in your audience?
2. What is the average age and the age range of your listeners?
3. How many of your listeners are*
    A. atheist
    B. Catholic
    C. Jewish
    D. Protestant
    E. other
4. How many of your listeners are
    A. African Americans
    B. Asian Americans
    C. European Americans
    D. Hispanic American
    E. Native Americans
    F. other ethnic identity

*Notice that categories for questions 3 and 4 are arranged alphabetically to minimize perceptions of bias.

5. What is the average educational level of listeners?
6. How many of your listeners are married, single, or divorced?
7. How many of your listeners live
    A. in dormitories
    B. in apartments
    C. with their families of origin
    D. with a spouse and/or children
    E. in fraternities or sororities
8. How many of your listeners have
    A. a high school diploma
    B. some college
    C. college degree
    D. some graduate work
    E. technical or professional training
9. What is the average income of your listeners' families?
    A. below $10,000
    B. between $10,001 and $30,000
    C. between $30,001 and $50,000
    D. between $50,001 and $100,000
    E. over $100,000

Demographic analysis can provide useful general information about listeners. It's important, however, to guard against stereotypes of groups of people. Although many college students are between 18 and 22 years old, an increasing number are older than 22. Thus, it would be inadvisable to design a speech to students for an exclusively 18- to 22-year-old audience. Although many women work outside of the home, not all do, and an audience of women should not be addressed as if no homemakers are present. Similarly, speakers shouldn't stereotype an audience of men as being uninterested in child care, since many men are very involved parents.

Goal-Focused Analysis

A second method of audience analysis is **goal-focused analysis,** which seeks information about listeners that relates directly to the speaker's topic and purpose. Using this method, speakers ask questions such as, What do my listeners already know about the topic? What attitudes and beliefs do they have relevant to the topic? Answers to key questions such as these provide a speaker with important information for creating an effective speech.

Although politicians and corporations can afford to conduct sophisticated polls to discover what people know, want, think, and believe, most of us don't have the resources to do that. So how do ordinary people engage in goal-focused analysis? One answer is to be observant. Usually, a speaker has some experience interacting with listeners or people similar to listeners. Drawing on past interactions, a speaker may be able to discern a great deal about the knowledge, attitudes, and beliefs of listeners.

It's also appropriate to gather information about listeners through conversations or surveys. For example, once I was asked to speak on women leaders at a Governor's Leadership Conference. To prepare my presentation, I asked the conference planners to send me information on the occupations and ages of people attending the conference. In addition, I asked the planners to survey conferees on their experiences acting as leaders and working with women leaders. The information I received informed me about the level of experience and the attitudes and biases in my listeners. Then I could adapt my speech to what they knew and believed.

Using demographic and goal-oriented analysis provides you with direct knowledge of listeners and information from which you can draw additional inferences. By taking listeners into consideration, you build a presentation that is interactive in which both you and they are respected.

SUMMARY

In this chapter, we considered the nature of public speaking and the foundations of designing effective presentations. We began by noting that almost everyone has some degree of anxiety about communicating. That is both natural and potentially useful, since it increases a speaker's dynamism. We also discussed communication apprehension that is sufficient to interfere with speaking. Communication apprehension may be either situational or enduring, and we considered common sources of each type of communication apprehension as well as ways of reducing it.

Rather than being an extraordinary activity that is different from other kinds of communication, public speaking is enlarged conversation in which a speaker interacts personally with listeners. To do this effectively, it's important to select and limit the speaking topic, choose a purpose, and develop a clear thesis statement. In addition, designing an effective presentation requires consideration of listeners. Good speeches take into account what listeners know, believe, value, think, and feel. When a speaker does adapt to listeners, they are likely to be more receptive to the speaker's ideas.

In the next chapter, we'll discuss ways to conduct research and use research in public speaking. Building good arguments increases a speaker's credibility and enhances the power of ideas presented. Before proceeding to Chapter 13, complete the checklist at the end of this chapter to make sure you've done the preliminary work to create a strong foundation for your speech.

FOR FURTHER REFLECTION AND DISCUSSION

1.   What was your overall score on the Personal Report of Communication Apprehension? Which of your subscores was the highest? Are the results of your test congruent with your perceptions of your comfort in talking with others? Are you concerned about your anxiety in any communication situations? If so, what might you do to reduce it?

2. Think about presentations that you hear—lectures by professors, talks at campus groups. How much does each speaker seem to take the audience into consideration in what she or he says? Does this make a difference in how effective the speakers are?

3. Notice examples of narrative speaking in everyday life. Preachers, rabbis, and priests use stories, or parables, to make points in their sermons. Teachers rely on stories to bring conceptual material to life. How much is storytelling part of communication in your community?

4. Reflect on the single best and worst public speech you've ever heard. What were the speaking goals of each presentation? How clear were the thesis statements in each? How fully did each speaker seem to consider the listeners?

5. What leads you to think that speakers understand who you are and adapt their remarks to your interest, knowledge, and concerns? What do they say and do to demonstrate that they have taken you and your circumstances into account?

KEY TERMS

communication apprehension
systematic desensitization
cognitive restructuring
positive visualization
skills training
mind map
speeches to entertain
narrative speaking
speeches to inform
speeches to persuade
specific purpose
thesis statement
demographic analysis
goal-focused analysis

CHECKLIST FOR PLANNING A PUBLIC SPEECH

My speech topic is _____

_____

My speaking goal is to _____

_____

My specific purpose is _____

_____

My thesis statement is _____

_____

1. I know the following demographic information about the people who
   will listen to my presentation:

   Age: _____

   Education: _____

   Political position: _____

   Sex ratio: _____

   Ethnicities: _____

   Other: _____

2. I know the following information about my audience that pertains
   directly to the purpose of my speech:

   Listeners' knowledge about the topic: _____

   _____

   Listeners' personal experience with the topic: _____

   _____

   Listeners' beliefs about the topic: _____

   _____

   Listeners' attitudes about my thesis: _____

   _____

   Listeners' interest in the topic: _____

   _____

Focus Questions

1 How do I support the claims in my speech?

2 What are the ethical guidelines for selecting and using evidence?

3 How can speakers make statistics interesting?

4 How do speakers "footnote" sources in a speech?

CHAPTER 13

Researching and Developing Support for Public Speeches

Every 12 seconds a woman is battered, and each day four women are battered to death by their intimates. This isn't a hearing; it's a public lynching designed to persecute a black man.

Chief Seattle said human life is a web in which we are all inter-related. He said, "Whatever we do to the web, we do to ourselves. All things are bound together."

A lot of women are battered in this country.

This hearing isn't fair.

People are connected to one another.

The first three sentences have impact. They pack a punch and catch our attention. In contrast, the second three sentences are flat and unmemorable. One difference between the sentences is that the first three include evidence to support ideas, whereas the second three simply advance claims without backing them up with any proof. Critical listeners will not accept unsupported claims, so speakers must develop evidence to fortify the ideas they advance.

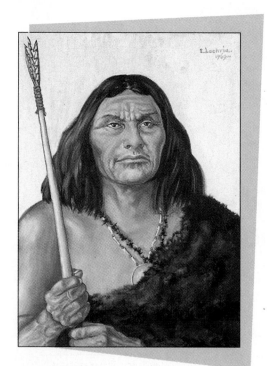

Chief Seattle provided an eloquent public voice for Native Americans. (© E. Lochrie/The Museum of the Rockies)

In the first statement, statistical evidence supports the claim that violence between intimates is a major problem in the United States. The second statement was made by Clarence Thomas in the 1991 Supreme Court confirmation hearings regarding Anita Hill's charges that he had sexually harassed her. By using a metaphor to compare the hearings to a lynching, Thomas induced some individuals to perceive the hearings not as an orderly, judicial process, but as a racist vendetta. The third statement draws on the credibility of a widely admired Native American to argue that humans are deeply interconnected. The first statement relies on statistics, the second on a figurative analogy, and the third on a quotation. Each of these is a form of support.

Supporting materials, such as statistics, analogies, and quotations, enhance the impact of a speaker's ideas. To inform or persuade others, we need to provide evidence, reasons, and facts. Supporting materials serve two important functions: They increase the impact of a speech by invigorating and fortifying ideas, and they increase speakers' personal credibility.

In this chapter, we will consider how to conduct research to develop speech topics and how to weave support into a presentation. Throughout the process of researching and building support for a speech, it's important to keep listeners firmly in mind. A speaker's success is tied directly to whether listeners understand, believe, and accept what she or he says. Stay aware of those with whom you will communicate, so that you can engage in research and develop support that will be effective in their minds.

CONDUCTING RESEARCH

Effective speeches require research. At the outset of developing a speech, you may already have a definite point of view and know a good deal about your topic. Mining your own knowledge and conducting further research will help you find additional information to enlarge your effectiveness. Research continues throughout the process of developing a speech. You begin by reading, thinking, and talking with others to discover the range of information available on your topic. Then you evaluate all the evidence you've found and decide which materials are most effective in supporting the specific claims in your speech. During the early stages of research, you may unearth information that convinces you to modify your original thesis statement. That's natural and desirable in the process of developing a speech.

We'll discuss four types of research that speakers should consider to develop informative and persuasive presentations: personal knowledge, interviews, library and on-line research, and surveys.

Personal Knowledge

The first source of information to consult is yourself. What do you already know about your topic? How are you involved with it? What experiences have you had that qualify you to speak on and care about the topic? Why does this topic matter to you? All of these are important questions to ask as you begin researching your speech. Accessing your personal knowledge is useful because you will probably be comfortable and engaging when you talk about experiences you have had and knowledge that you gained through personal involvement with a topic.

A second reason to include personal content in a speech is that it tends to enhance the credibility listeners confer on speakers (Bradley, 1978; Ostermeier, 1967). **Credibility** refers to willingness to believe in a person or to trust what a person says and does. This means that a speaker's credibility doesn't reside in the speaker, but is conferred by listeners—or not conferred if they find a speaker untrustworthy. Credibility is not a single thing, but a process that can change in the course of communication. Some speakers have high **initial credibility,** which is the expertise and trustworthiness listeners grant a speaker before a presentation begins. Initial credibility is based on titles, positions, experiences, or achievements that are known to listeners before they hear a speech. For example, Ralph Nader has high initial credibility in the area of public safety. In addition to initial credibility, speakers may also gain **derived credibility,** which is the expertise and trustworthiness that listeners grant as a result of how speakers communicate during presentations. Derived credibility may be earned when speakers organize ideas clearly, include convincing evidence, and have an engaging style of delivery. **Terminal credibility** is the cumulative expertise and trustworthiness listeners confer on a speaker as a result of initial and derived credibility. Terminal credibility may be greater or less than initial credibility, depending on how effectively a speaker communicates.

In recent years, we've heard a lot about credibility gaps and lack of credibility of national figures. This means that many people have lost confidence in many politicians and they no longer find many politicians credible, or believable. It's easy to understand why citizens don't find some national leaders credible. When a senator campaigns on a promise to restrict illegal aliens and then she or he is found to employ an undocumented alien, credibility withers. Likewise, when congressional representatives proclaim the importance of fiscal responsibility while simultaneously bouncing checks themselves, they lose credibility as advocates of governmental financial responsibility. We believe in people who practice what they preach, and we grant credibility to people who seem to have personal experience with what they talk about.

SOYANA

The greatest teacher I ever had taught a class in government policies and practices. Before coming to campus, he had been an adviser to three presidents. He had held a lot of different offices in government, so what he was teaching us was backed up by personal experience. Everything he said had so much more weight than what I hear from professors who've never had any practical experience.

In developing your speech, draw on your own experiences and knowledge to let listeners know that you are personally involved with the topic.

Everyday Application

USING YOUR EXPERTISE

List three experiences that directly involve you with the topic of your speech:

1. _____

2. _____

3. _____

Explain why these experiences qualify you to speak on the topic:

_____

_____

_____

_____

Interviews

To research your topic, you may want to conduct interviews with people who have expert knowledge. Interviews allow you to gather information, check the accuracy of ideas you have, and understand the perspective of people who are experts or who have special experience with your topic. Many community organizations have experts who can provide you with a wealth of information on specific topics. For example, the American Lung Association has chapters in most communities, and a staff person could furnish very recent information on the causes and frequency of lung disease, as well as ways to reduce the toll on health and life. Other organizations such as the Animal Protection Society, Sierra Club, Parent-Teacher Association, Habitat for Humanity, and Alcoholics Anonymous can provide up-to-date information, as well as background, in their respective areas of expertise.

Effective interviewers listen carefully and responsively.
(© Elizabeth Crews/Stock, Boston)

You need to plan interviews in advance, since experts often have busy schedules. When you call to request an interview, explain who you are and the purpose of the interview. Prepare a list of questions in advance to increase the productivity of an interview and ensure that you don't forget important questions. You should include both direct, or closed-ended, questions, which ask for specific information (How long have you held this position? How much does this program cost on an annual basis? When was the last study done?) and open-ended questions, which allow interviewees to give more elaborate responses (What do you think would improve the system here? Can you describe how your organization identifies priorities? Do you have anything else you wish to add?).

In addition to questions you prepare in advance, invite interviewees to initiate ideas. As experts, they may be aware of information and dimensions of a topic that haven't occurred to you. If an interviewee gives permission, it's acceptable to take notes during interviews. You should be careful, however, to keep your primary attention on the interviewee. Audiotaping of interviews is appropriate only if the interviewee agrees.

Everyday Application

POSSIBLE INTERVIEWEES

List four people you might interview to gain expert perspective and information on your topic. For each person, list the name, the title or position, and his or her relevance to the topic.

	Name	*Position/Title*	*Relevance to Topic*
1.			
2.			
3.			
4.			

Call two of the people on your list for an interview.

(© 1995 Dan Piraro. Dist. by Universal Press Syndicate.
Reprinted by permission.)

Sometimes it's also useful to interview people who don't have particular expertise but may represent the views of ordinary citizens. Talking with individuals who don't have special knowledge can help a speaker grasp general perspectives on a topic. This can be useful in adapting the speech to listeners who also may not be experts. Speakers who refer to interviews they conducted tend to be seen as credible by listeners. Quoting interviewees shows a speaker has invested personal initiative and effort in researching a topic. In addition, listeners often find experts' opinions persuasive (Olson & Cal, 1984). To maximize the impact of testimony, speakers should identify the source's credentials and explain why the individual qualifies as an expert. It's naive to assume listeners will know a source's credentials, experience, and other bases of expertise.

ANDY

I was super impressed when Michelle talked about her interviews with women who have been battered. She talked with several victims, and I admired that and thought it made her stronger as an authority on the topic. If she had talked only about articles and facts others have gathered, I don't think her presentation would have been nearly as effective.

Library and On-Line Research

Libraries and on-line services hold a wealth of information that can help you develop and support the ideas in your speech. There are a variety of on-line service companies that provide information in specific areas. If you don't know of these, you might check with your campus computer assistance center or a reference librarian. It's a good idea to begin library research by conducting a computer search to discover what information on your topic is available. Most college libraries have programs that can quickly identify all of the articles and books related to your topic. In addition to the computer search, three specific library resources can help you locate useful information: reference works, indexes, and databases.

Reference Works   There are many specialized references that can save you hours of work by directing you specifically to materials on your topic. *The Reader's Guide to Periodical Literature* summarizes articles published in 125 popular magazines, including *Newsweek, Ebony, Working Woman,* and *Fortune.* The *Public Affairs Information Service Bulletin* indexes books, pamphlets, and other materials pertinent to public affairs. *American Demographics* provides an amazing reservoir of information on Americans' patterns, behaviors, possessions, and so forth. It's the resource to check if you want to know how many televisions the average household has, how much sugar the average person consumes in a year, or how often most individuals eat out. *Facts on File* is a weekly publication that provides factual information and background on world news.

Indexes   Libraries also have indexes that summarize publications and backgrounds of individuals. Indexes of articles published in academic journals are important resources. *Psychological Abstracts,* for example, surveys articles published on psychological topics. If you want to know what research has been done on self-concept, you would simply need to look up self-concept in *Psychological Abstracts* and you would find a list (probably a very long one) of published research on the topic. There are also indexes of government documents that summarize laws, policies, and regulations related to many topics.

Everyday Application

CHECKING INDEXES

Go to your campus library and consult at least one index for information published on your topic.

The index I consulted is: _____

I found _____ publications on my topic.

I learned the following from three of the cited publications that I looked up and read in full:

1. _____

2. _____

3. _____

There are several good sources of background information on experts you may cite in your speech. Some of the more popular ones are *Who's Who in America, Who's Who in American Women, Biography Index,* and *Directory of American Scholars.* You enhance your own credibility and that of sources you cite when you provide detailed information about their qualifications and accomplishments.

BACKGROUND ON EXPERTS

Research the credentials of three authorities you plan to cite in your speech. Below write important information that contributes to their credibility.

1. _____ holds the following titles: _____

_____ and has the following

experiences and qualifications: _____

_____.

2. _____ holds the following titles: _____

_____ and has the following

experiences and qualifications: _____

_____.

3. _____ holds the following titles: _____

_____ and has the following

experiences and qualifications: _____

_____.

Databases   Today we no longer have to search in stacks and on bookshelves for library information. Databases stored in computers allow us to search a library's holdings from a terminal. One widely used database is Dialog Information Retrieval Service (DIRS), which includes nearly 1 million records from popular and academic publications and news services. There are also academic and medical databases. A librarian can tell you which databases are available in your library.

Not only can you search the collections of your library from a computer terminal, but you can use the Internet and on-line services to research holdings in other places. Technologies available in most modern libraries allow you to search for data all over the world. Computer terminals with telephone links give you access to massive databases that can provide excellent information for your speech.

CHARLENE

I'd never used a database before. I just know how to write on a computer, not do anything fancy. When we were assigned to do a computer search for our speech, I was pretty intimidated at first. But it wasn't hard to learn how, and I couldn't believe the information I got. I found over 100 pieces of research, and there were short summaries so I could figure out which ones to read. It was amazing!

Surveys

A final method of research is conducting surveys. **Survey research** involves asking a number of people about their opinions, preferences, actions, or beliefs. Surveys are useful in two situations. First, sometimes there isn't any published research on something important to your speech. Yumiko, a student taking his first speaking course, was concerned that many of his peers at the university had misperceptions about Japanese people and their traditions. He decided to use his speech as an opportunity to correct misperceptions. After 2 weeks of research, he was discouraged because he couldn't find any studies of American college students' views of Japanese. We developed a short questionnaire on views of Japanese that he handed out to 100 people on campus and in town. This gave Yumiko some information about prevailing stereotypes of Japanese. A survey such as the one Yumiko conducted is useful, but it has limits. Because casual surveys generally aren't random and don't meet other criteria for sound research, they need to be fortified with other forms of research.

For a speech on junk foods, one student surveyed 75 faculty, staff, and students to find out how often they ate various products. Another student surveyed her peers to find out how often they attended women's and men's basketball games. For a speech about the dangers of drinking, a young man surveyed his peers to find out how often and how much they drank each week. By gauging the attitudes and patterns of behavior of people like your listeners, you gain valuable insight into ways to adapt your presentation to your listeners' views, beliefs, and habits. The more directly your speech relates to your listeners and their lives, the more effective you will be.

A second use of surveys is to learn about your particular audience's knowledge and attitudes regarding your topic. Clearly, it isn't always feasible to survey listeners. Sometimes speakers don't have access to listeners prior to speaking; in other cases, the time and expense of a survey are prohibitive. When surveying listeners is feasible, however, it helps you find out what listeners know so that you can include information they don't have and not spend your time informing them about what they already know. It's also useful to discover what personal experience your listeners have pertinent to your topic, since attitudes based on direct experience are more difficult to change (Wu & Shaffer, 1988).

CONSTRUCTING A SURVEY

Prepare a list of 5 to 10 questions to discover general attitudes and behaviors relevant to your speech topic.

1. _____

2. _____

3. _____

4. _____

5. _____

6. _____

7. _____

8. _____

9. _____

10. _____

Decide where you will hand out the survey. Try to avoid any obvious bias based on location. For example, administering the survey at local bars and at the campus library might involve very different kinds of respondents. Handing it out at a church would exclude Jewish respondents as well members of other religions.

If you plan to speak on gun control, you might want to know whether your listeners are aware of existing legislation such as the Brady Bill, whether they hunt for sport, and whether they or members of their families own firearms for protection. For a speech on family leave practices, it would be helpful to find out whether listeners understand the limits of the 1993 Family Medical Leave Act and whether they are aware that the United States is the only industrialized nation that doesn't have guaranteed family leave.

Audience surveys can also help you learn what attitudes your listeners hold. At a minimum, you'll want to know whether your listeners agree or disagree with your position and how strongly they feel about it. If you want to argue for stronger sentencing of convicted felons and your listeners are strongly against that, then you might choose to limit your persuasive goal to reducing the strength of listeners' resistance to stronger sentencing.

(Jacob Lawrence, *The Library* (1960).
Tempera on fiberboard, 24 × 29 ⁷/₈".
National Museum of American Art,
Washington, D.C./Art Resource, N.Y.)

On the other hand, if they already agree with your position, you might try to move them toward action by asking them to write letters to senators or to vote for candidates who share their attitudes. What you can achieve in a given speech depends to a large extent on the starting beliefs and knowledge of your listeners (Wu & Shaffer, 1988).

In sum, researching a speech begins with yourself and your knowledge and experience relevant to your topic. Other sources to supplement your personal experience include library and computer-assisted research, interviews with experts, and surveys of both people in general and your specific audience. Now that we have explored ways to find information for a speech, we're ready to consider how it can be used to support ideas.

SUPPORTING IDEAS

Evidence is material used to support claims a speaker makes. Supporting your ideas may involve clarifying, proving, and demonstrating claims. In addition, support may enhance interest and emotional response to ideas. Evidence serves a number of important functions in speeches. First, it can be used to make ideas more clear, compelling, and dramatic. Second, evidence fortifies a speaker's opinions, which are seldom sufficient to persuade intelligent listeners. Finally, evidence heightens a speaker's credibility. A speaker who supports ideas well demonstrates that he or she is informed and prepared. Thus, including strong evidence allows speakers to gain derived credibility during a presentation.

The effectiveness of evidence depends directly on whether listeners understand and accept it. This reinforces the importance of audience analysis, which we discussed in detail in Chapter 12. Remember that even if you quote the world's leading authority in support of your ideas, the evidence won't be effective if your listeners don't find the authority credible (Olson & Cal, 1984). No matter how "true" your facts and statistics are, they have influence only if listeners believe them. Consequently, your choices of evidence for your speech should take listeners' perspectives into account. You want to include support that they find credible, interesting, and convincing, while also making sure your evidence is valid.

HARIHAR

Last week at the meeting of Nepalese Americans, a speaker talked to us about principles of ethical conduct. He quoted Jesus for principles such as loving your neighbors and being kind to others. But all of us in the group are Buddhist, and there are Buddhist precepts that say the same thing. For us, Buddha would have been a better person than Jesus to use for moral principles.

To decide when to use evidence in a speech, ask yourself "Will my listeners understand this point and believe this claim on my say-so alone?" If not, then you'll want to include evidence. The next decision you need to make is what type of evidence to use. Five forms of support are widely recognized and respected, and each tends to be effective in specific situations and for particular goals. Before including any form of evidence in a speech, the speaker should check the accuracy of her or his material and the credibility of the source. When presenting evidence to listeners, speakers have an ethical responsibility to give credit to the source (an oral footnote) and tell listeners the date of the evidence.

Statistics

Statistics are numbers that summarize a great many individual cases or that demonstrate relationships among phenomena. Statistics allow us to state quickly a great amount of information. For example, a speaker could demonstrate the prevalence of rape by stating "One in four college women today will be raped during her lifetime" and explaining the source of that number. Statistics can also be used to document connections between two or more things. For instance, a speaker could inform listeners that "You are 50% more likely to have an accident if you drink before driving." This draws listeners' attention to the link between drinking and automobile accidents.

If used unimaginatively, statistics bore many listeners. We've all been lulled to sleep by speakers who rattle off number after number. To avoid this fate for your speech, you may follow guidelines for using statistics effectively. First, limit the number of statistics you use in a speech. A few well-chosen numbers that are mixed with other kinds of support can be dramatic and persuasive, whereas a laundry list of statistics can be monotonous and ineffective. Second, round off numbers so that listeners can understand and retain them. We're more likely to remember that "approximately 1 million Americans are homeless" than that "987,422,118 Americans are homeless." Third, select statistics that aren't dated. Occasionally, a very old statistic is still useful. For example, the number of people who died in the Great Plague is not likely to change over the years.

(Cartoon by Signe Wilkerson. Reprinted by permission of Cartoonists & Writers Syndicate.)

In most cases, however, the most accurate statistics are recent. Remember that statistics are a numerical picture of how something was at a specific time. But things change, and speakers should get new snapshots when they do.

Effective use of statistics also requires you to translate them into information that is meaningful to listeners. A National Geographic program (National Geographic, 1994) on environmental responsibility forcefully made the point that Americans overconsume natural resources: It was stated that "North Americans make up only 6% of the world's population, yet they consume 40% to 60% of the planet's resources." To describe a million homeless people in terms listeners will immediately understand, a student speaker said, "That's 50 times the number of students on our campus." Another student speaker translated the statistic that 1 in 4 college-age women will be raped in her lifetime by saying "Of the 17 women students in this room today, 4 will probably be raped during their lives." Statistics aren't boring, but they can be poorly presented. With imagination and effort, you can make statistics interesting and powerful.

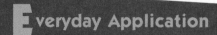

BRINGING STATISTICS ALIVE

Practice translating statistics into interesting and meaningful information. Here's an example.

Statistic	*Translation*
Americans annually spend 14 billion dollars on alcohol, 9 billion on tobacco, 2 billion on pets, and 200 million on juvenile reform.	For $1 spent on juvenile reform in America, $70 is spent on alcohol, $45 on tobacco, and $10 on pets.
Children under 10 watch television an average of 50 hours each week.	_____ _____ _____
The stealth bomber program cost $40 billion and produced a total of 20 aircraft.	_____ _____ _____
The number of working poor, people who make $13,000 or less a year, rose from 12% of the work force in 1979 to 18% in 1992.	_____ _____ _____

Now apply what you've learned to your own speech. Select three statistics you could use in your speech and translate them into meaningful, interesting terms.

Statistic 1 _____

_____

can be translated this way: _____

_____

Statistic 2 _____

_____

can be translated this way: _____

_____

Statistic 3 _____

_____

can be translated this way: _____

_____

_____

Examples

Examples are single instances used to make a point, dramatize an idea, or personalize information. There are four types of examples: undetailed, detailed, hypothetical, and anecdotes or stories.

Undetailed Examples   When speakers don't wish to spend a lot of time making a point, undetailed examples are useful. These are brief references that quickly provide specific instances of something. In this chapter, I've used a number of undetailed examples of student speeches to give you a concrete idea of conceptual points we're discussing. Undetailed examples may also be used to remind listeners of information with which they're already familiar. One student opened a speech on the costs of textbooks by saying, "Remember standing in the long lines at the bookstore and paying more than your tuition at the start of this term?" His listeners immediately identified with the topic of the speech.

Detailed Examples   As the name implies, detailed examples provide more elaborate information than undetailed ones. These can be valuable when listeners aren't familiar with an idea. A student included this detailed example in her speech on environmental justice: "Most of you haven't lived by a toxic waste dump, so you may not understand what's involved. In one community there is an incidence of cancer 150% higher than in the country as a whole. The skin on one man's hands was eaten away when he touched the outside of a canister that stored toxic waste." Detailed examples create vivid pictures that can be moving and memorable. However, they require time to develop, so they should be used sparingly.

Hypothetical Examples   Sometimes speakers don't have a real example that adequately makes a point. In such cases, speakers can create a hypothetical example, which is not factual but can add clarity and depth to a speech. To be effective, hypothetical examples must be plausible to listeners. They should be realistic illustrations of what it is you wish to exemplify. Hypothetical examples are often used to portray average cases, rather than to represent a single person or event. If you use a hypothetical example, you have an ethical responsibility to inform listeners that it is not a factual, real example.

THE TYPICAL AMERICAN FAMILY

On May 19, 1962, President John Kennedy used the following hypothetical example in his speech at Madison Square Garden at the rally for the National Council of Senior Citizens:

Let's consider the case of a typical American family—a family which might be found in any part of the United States. The husband has worked hard all of his life, and now he has retired. He might have been a clerk or a salesman or worked in a factory. He always insisted on paying his own way. This man, like most Americans, wants to care for himself. He has raised his own family, educated his children, and he and his wife are drawing social security now. Then his wife gets sick, not just for a week, but for a very long time. First the savings go. Next he mortgages his home. Finally he goes to his children who are themselves heavily burdened. Then their savings begin to go. What is he to do now? Here is a typical American who has nowhere to turn, so he finally will have to sign a petition saying he's broke and needs welfare assistance.

John F. Kennedy was a powerful public speaker. He wove many kinds of support into his speeches to strengthen his credibility and increase the impact of his ideas. (© Arthur Rickerby/Black Star)

Stories   A final kind of example is the story, or anecdote. Stories included in speeches are often based on personal experiences. President Ronald Reagan routinely included several personal stories in his speeches to personalize his ideas and create identification with listeners. Attorneys, too, rely on stories to persuade judges and jurors. They take all of the known facts in a case and weave them together in a way that makes sense and supports their client's position. The attorneys with whom I consult tell me that the key challenge in trial court is to create a story that covers all the facts and is more believable that the story created by the opposing council.

Stories may also be about people other than ourselves. Speakers often tell a story to put a human face on abstract issues. To help middle-class listeners understand the personal meaning of poverty, a student told this story in his speech:

To start her day, Annie pours half a glass of milk and mixes it half and half with water so that the quart she buys each week will last. If she finds day-old bread on sale at the market, she has toast, but she can't afford margarine. Annie coughs harshly and wishes this throat infection would pass. She can't afford to go to a doctor; even if she could, the cost of drugs is beyond her budget. She shivers, thinking that winter is coming. That means long days in the malls so that she can be in heated places. It's hard on her and the kids, but the cost of heat is more than she can pay. Annie is only 28 years old, just a few years older than we are, but she looks well into her forties. Like you, Annie grew up expecting a pretty good life, but then her husband left her. He doesn't pay child support, and she can't afford a detective to trace him. Her children, both under 4, are too young to be left alone, so she can't work.

This story translates the abstract idea of poverty into a three-dimensional personal picture. Annie's story puts a human face on poverty. A story that has depth requires time, so speakers have to consider whether the point they wish to make justifies the time a story will take. This suggests that stories, like detailed examples, should be used sparingly. Nonetheless, they are a valuable and often overlooked form of support.

Comparisons

Comparisons are associations between two things that are similar in some important way or ways. **Similes** are direct comparisons that typically use either *like* or *as* to link two things: A teacher is like a guide. A politician is like an orchestra conductor. Smoking is the same thing as giving away years of life. **Analogies** are metaphors that less directly assert likeness between two things: Life is a grand adventure. Voting is being a good neighbor. Gambling is an addiction. A student speaker used this analogy in her speech on what the college experience is: "College is a journey from the known to the unknown. Each step in the process takes us farther from what we knew before and leads us closer to new understandings."

Comparisons can be powerful rhetorical devices because they invite listeners to see something familiar in a new light. In 1963, the Reverend Martin Luther King, Jr., delivered his eloquent "I Have a Dream" speech to over 200,000 listeners. In it he compared the United States' unfulfilled promises to African American citizens to a check for which funds must now be provided. This was a compelling analogy that used the familiar idea of a check to explain civil rights promises that had been made but not yet kept by the country. The Communication Highlight on the next page allows you to appreciate the power of the analogy that Dr. King used in his speech.

Quotations

Quotations, or testimony, are exact citations of statements made by others. Speakers often use quotations to clarify ideas or to make them more memorable. If someone has stated a point you wish to make in an especially effective manner, then you may wish to quote his or her words. In a speech

Communication Highlight

I HAVE A DREAM
The Reverend Martin Luther King, Jr.

We've come to our nation's capital to cash a check. When the architects of our republic wrote the magnificent words of the Constitution and the Declaration of Independence, they were signing a promissory note to which every American was to fall heir. The note was a promise that all men—yes, black men as well as white men—would be guaranteed the unalienable rights of life, liberty and the pursuit of happiness.

It is obvious today that America has defaulted on this promissory note insofar as her citizens of color are concerned. . . . America has given the Negro people a bad check; a check which has come back marked 'insufficient funds.' But we refuse to believe that there are insufficient funds in the great vaults of opportunity of this nation. So we've come to cash this check—a check that will give us upon demand the riches of freedom and security of justice.

Martin Luther King, Jr., was a dynamic and eloquent public speaker, who skillfully used sophisticated rhetorical techniques to shape his message.
(© UPI/Bettmann)

Reprinted by arrangement with The Heirs to the Estate of Martin Luther King, Jr., c/o Joan Daves Agency as agent for the proprietor. © 1963 Martin Luther King, Jr., © renewed 1991 by Coretta Scott King.

on homeless citizens, a student quoted a metaphor used by a social worker: "Homelessness is a cancer that eats away at the vitality and decency of our society." To explain why many women of color reject the term *feminist* to describe themselves, a student named Juanita quoted her grandmother as saying, "White women aren't interested in the problems we face. They don't know our lives and they don't represent our needs." Notice that in this case, the woman quoted was both a layperson and an expert on the topic—her experience as a Latina qualified her to speak.

Quotations may also be used to substantiate ideas. Using an expert's testimony may be persuasive to listeners, but only if they respect the expert who is quoted. Thus, it's important to provide "oral footnotes" in which you identify the name, position, and qualifications of anyone whom you quote, as well as the date for the quoted statement. For example, in discussing preservation of wilderness, you might say, "Speaking in 1997, Tim Worth, former Colorado senator and current undersecretary of state

THE DECLARATION OF SENTIMENTS

Elizabeth Cady Stanton

The Seneca Falls Convention in 1848 formally launched the women's rights movement in the United States. In delivering a speech she co-authored with other women's rights advocates, Elizabeth Cady Stanton cleverly quoted the Declaration of Independence—with a few modifications in the original wording. Here's an excerpt:

We hold these truths to be self-evident: that all men and all women are created equal; that they are endowed by their Creator with certain inalienable rights, that among these are life, liberty, and the pursuit of happiness.

Source: Campbell, K. (1989). *Man cannot speak for her.* New York: Prager, p. 34.

for global affairs, warned that stronger environmental policies are needed if we want to preserve any wilderness land for the next generation." Whenever you quote another person, you are ethically required to give credit to that individual, just as you give credit for all other forms of evidence. This can be done by changing your tone of voice after stating an authority's name or by telling listeners, "This authority stated that . . ." It is also acceptable to say "quote" at the beginning of a quotation and "end quote" at the end of it, although this method of citing sources becomes boring if it is used repeatedly in a speech.

To be effective with intelligent listeners, quotations must meet four criteria. First, as we've already noted, sources should be people who listeners know and respect. You won't convince socially liberal listeners of anything by quoting Rush Limbaugh, and you'll never convince politically conservative listeners by quoting Gloria Steinem. Maya Angelou or bell hooks may be better known and respected by people of color than Ellen Goodman or Betty Friedan. This point reinforces our previous discussion of the importance of keeping your listeners in mind at each step in the process of designing and delivering a speech.

The second criterion for testimony is that it should come from someone who is qualified to speak on the issue (Olson & Cal, 1984). Wall Street whiz Elaine Garazelli is qualified to offer informed opinions on investments. However, she exceeded her area of expertise when she testified to the quality of a certain brand of panty hose. Garazelli is not more qualified to judge this product than any other woman who wears pantyhose. The hosiery company was counting on the **halo effect,** which involves assuming that an expert in one area is also an expert in other areas. The halo effect is also behind the use of athletic stars to advertise cereals (such as Wheaties) and other products for which they have no special qualifications (for example, Bill Cosby for Jello or Gladys Knight for Aunt Jemima). Although some people may fall prey to the halo effect, discerning listeners will not. Ethical and effective speakers rely on authorities who are qualified in the area for which their expertise is cited. In addition, effective speakers identify authorities' qualifications to enhance credibility in listeners' minds.

Everyday Application

SOURCES LISTENERS WILL ACCEPT

Below list six individuals whom you could cite in your speech. These should be people whom you have interviewed or have encountered in other research on your topic.

1. _____

2. _____

3. _____

4. _____

5. _____

6. _____

Now consider which of these individuals are most likely to be known and respected by the particular people who will listen to your speech. Put an asterisk (*) by the three you think would have the greatest credibility with your listeners.

Ethical use of quotations must also meet the criterion of accuracy. For instance, you should respect the context in which comments are made. It is unethical to take a statement out of context in order to make it more supportive of your ideas. Also, it's unethical to alter a direct quotation by adding or deleting words an individual used. Sometimes writers omit words and indicate this with ellipses: "Noted authority William West stated that 'there is no greater priority . . . than our children.' " In oral presentations, however, it is difficult to indicate omitted words in a smooth manner. When you use quotations, you are responsible for being accurate and fair in how you represent others and their ideas.

Finally, quotations should come from unbiased sources. It's hardly convincing when scientists paid by the tobacco industry tell us cigarettes don't cause cancer. For the same reason, it's not persuasive when spokespeople for chemical companies claim that their waste products are not harmful. These two sources are biased, since they have a vested interest in a particular viewpoint. Their bias injures their credibility as believable authorities

This speaker maintains eye contact with listeners while projecting visual aids from her laptop computer. (© InFocus Systems. Used by permission.)

on tobacco and chemical waste products, respectively. Testimony is an effective form of support if it relies on individuals who are qualified to speak on the topic, are not evidently biased, are quoted fairly and accurately, and are credible to a particular group of listeners.

Visual Aids

Support also is provided by **visual aids,** such as charts, graphs, photographs, transparencies, computer graphics, and physical objects. Visual aids can increase listeners' understanding and retention of ideas presented in a speech (Hamilton, 1996). People are more likely to remember material that is presented both orally and visually. Visual aids also tend to increase listeners' interest in a presentation, because they add variety to the message (Hamilton, 1996). Another value of visual aids is that they provide content cues to speakers, which reduces reliance on notes.

By using widely available computer technologies, it's often possible to prepare very sharp, effective visual aids. You may have software programs that allow you to design charts, graphs, and other visuals. Computer-generated visual aids can be easily transformed into transparencies, which are the most commonly used visual aid in most professional presentations (Hamilton, 1996). If you don't know how to design visuals on a computer, you might find it useful to check with your campus computer assistance office. The staff there probably will be able to prepare visual aids to enhance your speech or—better yet—to teach you how to prepare them yourself.

Visual aids may be used either to reinforce ideas presented verbally or to provide information in their own right. For example, a bar graph could effectively strengthen the statistics on juvenile reform we discussed earlier (see Figure 13.1).

The bar graph in Figure 13.1 dramatically reinforces the contrast among Americans' expenditures. Pie graphs, too, can forcefully emphasize contrasts and proportions (see Figure 13.2). Many software programs now allow you to generate attractive and informative graphs, charts, and other visual aids.

Diagrams or models are useful when a speaker is explaining a complex concept or a topic with which listeners may not be familiar. Especially in speeches of demonstration, a model or physical diagram can be very useful. One of my students prepared a diagram to show listeners how a nuclear reactor works. Maps help listeners understand geographic relations and issues.

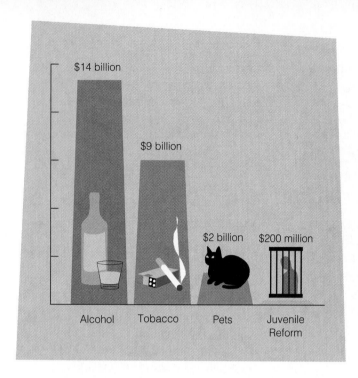

FIGURE 13.1
Bar Graphs Dramatize Statistics

FIGURE 13.2
Pie Charts Clarify Proportions

Photographs can be used to reinforce verbal messages or to be a primary source of evidence in their own right. To fortify her argument that development is eroding coastal land, a student showed enlarged pictures of an island community before development when healthy sand dunes existed and after development when the dunes had eroded. In a speech urging listeners to contribute to an organization that provides food to starving people in Third World countries, a student showed pictures of women, men, and children who were so starved they looked like skeletons. The old adage "A picture is worth a thousand words" was true in this case, because the student's picture spoke more compellingly about hunger than any words ever could have

Handouts are also very useful visual aids. Because listeners can take handouts with them, they are particularly valuable when a speaker wants information to remain with listeners. After a speech encouraging students to vote for a bill currently under consideration by the state legislature, a student gave every listener a handout with the names, addresses, and phone numbers of their representatives. Another student, who spoke on the topic of violence against women, concluded her speech by handing out a list of agencies and phone numbers that could be called by victims or other individuals who were aware of violence. In both cases, the handouts ensured that listeners would have critical information long after the speech was over.

You may have noticed that in both examples of students who used handouts, the written materials were passed to listeners at the end of the speeches. This was an effective choice on the speakers' parts, since it avoided the problems of breaking up a speech to pass out paper and of having listeners read the handout while the speaker was talking. Because handouts may distract listeners, it's wise to save them until you have finished speaking.

Everyday Application

FINDING VISUAL AIDS

Think about the possibilities for visual aids to enhance your speech. Below write out visual aids of each type that you could use. Don't worry that you might not actually include all of these. The point for now is to brainstorm possibilities for visually supporting your ideas.

Bar graph of: _____

Pie chart of: _____

Photographs of: _____

Diagram of: _____

Map of: _____

Handout on: _____

For visual aids to be effective, speakers should observe several guidelines (Williams, 1994). First, a visual aid should be large enough and clear enough to be seen clearly by all listeners. As obvious as this advice is, speakers routinely violate it by showing photographs or graphs that can be seen only by listeners toward the front of a room. Make sure any numbers, words, or emblems can be seen clearly by listeners in the back of a room. Make sure that letters in major headings are at least 3 inches high and letters in subpoints are a minimum of 2 inches high. Using an overhead projector allows speakers to present transparencies and other material in enlarged form. A second guideline is to keep visual aids simple and uncluttered. Detailed visuals with a great deal of information are more likely to confuse than clarify. A good basic rule for visual aids is to use them to highlight key information and ideas, not to summarize a speech.

WHEN DRAMA IS TOO DRAMATIC

In an effort to add drama to presentations, speakers sometimes make unwise and even dangerous choices. Some visual aids are *not* appropriate for use in any circumstances. For example, a real, functional firearm is dangerous in public situations. In addition to the fact that "there's no such thing as an unloaded gun," firearms may frighten listeners, and that's unlikely to enhance effectiveness.

Other visual aids that are risky and should be avoided include live animals, illegal substances, and chemicals that could react to one another. It's also unwise to use visual aids that might seriously upset or disgust listeners. For instance, showing pictures of aborted fetuses is likely to alienate a number of listeners. The purpose of visuals is to enhance your speech, not to be sensational for the sake of sensationalism.

Many visual aids are verbal texts—main ideas of a speech, major points in a policy, steps to action. When visual texts are used, certain guidelines apply. As a general rule, a visual text should have no more than six lines of words, should use phrases more than sentences, and should use a simple typeface. Color and variations in type size can be used to add emphasis to visual texts. This applies to handouts, overhead transparencies, and large visuals displayed at the front of a room.

Although visual aids can be very effective, it's possible to have too much of a good thing. When speakers use too many visuals, listeners may experience visual overload. As a guideline for deciding how many visuals to use in a speech, Cheryl Hamilton (1996) suggests this formula:

$$\frac{\text{Length of speech}}{2} + 1 = \text{maximum number of visuals}$$

If you are preparing a 10-minute speech, you would want to include no more than 6 visual aids (10/2 + 1 = 6).

Visual aids should enhance your speech. Unfortunately, many speakers use visuals ineffectively so that they do more harm than good. To avoid this fate yourself, remove or cover visual aids before and after you use them. A visual aid that's strong enough to be effective in supporting ideas will distract listeners' attention from what a speaker is saying if it is left in view when not being used. Also, speakers should maintain visual contact with listeners when using visual aids. Novice speakers often make the mistake of facing their charts or pictures when discussing them. This breaks the connection between a speaker and listeners. When carefully prepared and thoughtfully used, visual aids can add considerable clarity and impact to a presentation.

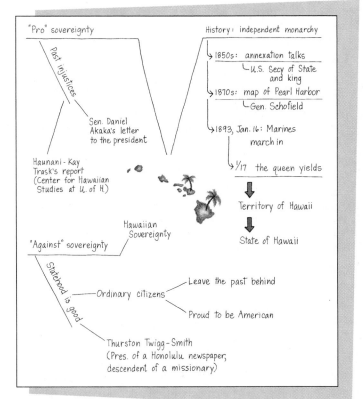

FIGURE 13.3
Mind Map of Evidence

Source: Jaffe, C. (1995). *Public speaking: A cultural perspective* (p. 153). Belmont, CA: Wadsworth.

It's a good idea to keep an ongoing record of evidence you discover during the research process. There are two ways to do this. The traditional method is to write out each piece of evidence, preferably on separate note cards. By the end of researching your speech, you should have a deck of cards that contain evidence you might use in the final speech.

A mind map is an alternative method of keeping track of information that you find while you are researching a speech. In Chapter 12, we discussed mind maps as a way to narrow a broad topic into more specific foci for speeches. The same method can also help you record information. A mind map is a more holistic, less linear way to record information than the conventional note card system. To construct a mind map for your speech, begin by writing the subject of your presentation in the center of a blank page. Then, draw a line from the center to each piece of evidence that you discover as you conduct your research. At this stage, you shouldn't try to determine which evidence you will use; for now, write down all the information you find. Once you have a complete record of information you've gathered, you can decide which evidence to include in your presentation. Figure 13.3 shows a mind map record of information related to a speech on Hawaiian sovereignty.

As you develop your presentation, keep in mind all five forms of evidence that you can use to enhance your ideas. Statistics, examples, analogies, quotations, and visual aids support your claims in varied ways. Whereas evidence such as statistics, examples, and quotations can provide strong logical support, visual aids and analogies are often more powerful in adding clarity, interest, and emotional appeal to a speech. All forms of evidence, when carefully chosen and ethically used, tend to increase the credibility listeners confer on a speaker and the extent to which they retain the speaker's ideas.

SUMMARY

This chapter extended the previous one by considering ways to research speeches and support ideas to be presented. Just as when you are first planning a speech, your listeners should influence how you research and support it. Thus, you need to ask yourself what kinds of research and what forms of support your particular listeners are most likely to find interesting and credible.

The process of researching a speech includes reviewing your personal experiences and knowledge relevant to your topics, interviewing experts who can expand your insight into the subject, scouting libraries for evidence, and conducting surveys to find out about others' beliefs, practices, and knowledge that are relevant to your topic. It isn't unusual for speakers to revise the focus of a speech in the course of conducting research. This is appropriate when information that you discover modifies or alters your knowledge or even your position.

Research for a speech provides speakers with different kinds of evidence that may be used to clarify, dramatize, and energize a speech. The five types of evidence we discussed are statistics, examples, analogies, quotations, and visual aids. These are effective forms of support when they are used thoughtfully and are adapted sensitively to the attitudes, values, and knowledge of listeners.

Now that you've gone through the phases of planning, researching, and finding support for public speaking, we're ready to consider the final steps in designing effective presentations. Chapter 14 explains how to organize and present public speeches. Before you move on to Chapter 14, take a moment to fill in the checklist on the next page for researching and supporting your speech.

FOR FURTHER REFLECTION AND DISCUSSION

1. After you've interviewed two experts on your topic, reflect on what you learned. What did they explain, reveal, or show you that added to your knowledge of the topic? What did you learn from lines of talk that they initiated?

2. With others in your class, discuss how the process of researching your speech affected your understandings, beliefs, and speaking goal. Explain what changed and why it did.

3. Construct a mind map to record evidence you discover while researching your speech. Does this method seem more holistic and helpful than a traditional listing of evidence?

4. During the next week, pay attention to evidence that others cite in public presentations. You might notice what evidence is used on news programs, by professors in classes, and by special speakers on your campus. Evaluate the effectiveness of evidence that others use. Are visuals clear and uncluttered? Do speakers explain the qualifications of sources they cite, and are those sources adequately unbiased? What examples and analogies are presented, and how effective are they?

5. Notice the use of stories to add to interest and impact to public presentations. Describe a speaker who uses a story effectively and one who uses a story ineffectively. What are the differences between the two cases? What conclusions can you draw about the effective use of stories in public presentations?

KEY TERMS

credibility
initial credibility
derived credibility
terminal credibility
survey research
evidence
statistics
examples
comparisons
similes
analogies
quotations
halo effect
visual aids

CHECKLIST FOR RESEARCHING AND SUPPORTING A SPEECH

1. I conducted the following research:

   A. Review of my personal experience showed that _____

   _____

   B. I interviewed (name/title): _____

   (name/title): _____

   (name/title): _____

   C. I checked these three indexes: _____

   _____

   _____

   D. I checked these three on-line sources: _____

   _____

   _____

   E. I surveyed _____ on the

   following issues: _____

   _____

2. I found the following key evidence for my speech:

   A. Statistics: _____

   _____

   B. Authorities I will quote: _____

   _____

   C. Examples: _____

   _____

   D. Analogies: _____

   _____

   E. Visual aids: _____

   _____

3. I have all of the information to identify my sources appropriately and to explain why they are qualified and relevant to the ideas I will present.

If you have not completed all items on this checklist, do so now before moving on to Chapter 14.

Focus Questions

1 What is oral style?

2 In a persuasive speech, is it more effective to present only your side of an issue or to present both sides?

3 How many major ideas can you cover in a 7- to 10-minute speech?

4 Should speakers memorize speeches?

5 Does the organization of a speech affect its impact on listeners?

Organizing and Presenting Public Speeches

Millions of people have back problems in this country. It's hard to recover from back problems, particularly ruptures of discs. A lot of problems are caused by strains caused by lifting heavy objects. It's important to take care of your back, since a disc rupture can immobilize you for up to 2 weeks. Another way discs rupture is from unhealthy everyday habits such as sitting too long in one position or not using chairs that provide good support.

Millions of people who suffer from back problems in this country could save themselves a lot of pain by avoiding the two primary causes of serious back injury. One major cause is excessive strain such as lifting heavy objects. A second cause is unhealthy everyday habits such as sitting too long in one position or using chairs without good back support. It's important to take care of your back, since a ruptured disc can immobilize you for up to 2 weeks.

Which of these paragraphs was easier for you to understand and follow? Which one made the most sense to you? If you're like most people, the second paragraph seemed more logical and coherent. The content of the two paragraphs is the same. What differs is how they are organized. In the first paragraph, the speaker wanders from discussing one cause (strain) of back problems, to noting the length of recuperation time, then back to discussing a second cause (unhealthy habits) of back problems. By contrast, in the second paragraph, the speaker tells us that there are two primary causes of back problems, so we're prepared at the outset to learn about two causes. The speaker then explains both causes, and only then does the speaker discuss the recuperation time we're in for if we don't take care of our backs. The organization of the second paragraph makes it easier to follow and retain the information that was presented.

This chapter guides you through the final stages in designing a public speech. Now that you've refined your purpose and thesis statement and discovered evidence to support your claims, you're ready to put your ideas in order and prepare to deliver your speech. In the pages that follow, we'll consider alternative ways to organize ideas, styles of presenting public speeches, and the character of oral language.

ORGANIZING SPEECHES

We've all sat through speeches in which speakers seemed disorganized. They rambled or moved from one idea to the next in a way that was hard to follow. Perhaps they didn't tell us in advance what to expect, so we couldn't follow their thinking. Perhaps they submerged main ideas instead of making them stand out so that we'd retain them.

It's impossible to overstate the importance of good organization for public speaking. If a speech is not well organized, it will be ineffective no matter how good the ideas are and no matter how thoroughly it is researched and supported. If listeners cannot follow a presentation, they won't be informed, persuaded, or impressed. They probably won't even retain the ideas in the speech.

Organization increases speaking effectiveness (Darnell, 1963; Spicer & Bassett, 1976). It does so for several reasons. First, people like structure, and they expect ideas to come to them in some ordered way, rather than in a jumble. Organization also influences comprehension of ideas. Listeners can understand and follow a speech that is well planned and ordered. Consequently, they're likely to remember what was covered in an organized speech. Listeners are less likely to retain the key ideas in a poorly organized speech. Further, experimental evidence indicates that listeners are more persuaded by an organized speech than a disorganized one (McCroskey & Mehrley, 1969). Finally, organization enhances speakers' credibility, probably

A SHIP WITHOUT A HELM

An ancient rhetorician named Quintilian had this to say about the value of organization:

Speech, if deficient in that quality arrangement [organization], must necessarily be confused, and float like a ship without a helm; it can have no coherence . . . just as it is not sufficient for those who are erecting a building merely to collect some stone and timber and other building materials, but

skilled masons are required to arrange and place them, so in speaking, however abundant the matter may be, it will merely form a confused heap unless arrangement be employed to reduce it to order and to give it connection and a firmness of structure.

Source: Taken from Butler, H. E. (Trans.). (1950). *The institutio oratoria of Quintilian* (Vol. 3, book 7, pp. 2–3). Cambridge, MA: Harvard University Press.

because a carefully structured speech reflects well on a speaker's preparation and respect for listeners (Baker, 1965). When someone gives a disorganized speech, listeners may regard the person as incompetent or unprepared. This lessens derived and terminal credibility.

Organizing an effective speech is not the same as organizing a good written paper, although the two forms of communication benefit by some similar structural principles. Oral communication requires more explicit organization, greater redundancy within the message, and less complex sentence structures. Unlike readers, listeners can't refer back to a previous passage if they become confused or forget an earlier point. Providing signposts to highlight organization and repeating key ideas increase listeners' retention of a message (Woolfolk, 1987). Consequently, speakers must organize clearly and use ample repetition to help listeners follow and retain important ideas in a presentation.

Consistent with the need for redundancy in oral communication, good speeches follow the form of telling listeners what you're going to tell them, presenting your message, then reminding them of your main points. This translates into preparing an introduction, a body, and a conclusion for an oral presentation. Our discussion of organization begins with the body, since that is the substance of a presentation. After considering various methods of structuring the primary material for a presentation, we'll discuss how to build an introduction and conclusion and how to weave in transitions to move listeners from one point to another.

(Detail from *Freedom Quilt Mural*, Atlanta, Ga. Photograph © Andre Jenny/ Uniphoto.)

Organizing the Body of a Speech

The body of a speech develops and supports the central idea, or thesis statement, by organizing it into several points that are distinct, yet also related. In short speeches of 5 to 10 minutes, no more than three points can be developed well and two are often adequate. In longer speeches of 11 to 20 minutes, more points can be developed. If you constructed a mind map to record the evidence you found while researching your speech, you might refer to it to select the major points for your speech.

Although speeches can be organized in many ways, we'll limit our discussion to seven patterns that are generally effective. As we discuss each pattern, you'll have the opportunity to think about how you might use it in your speech. Experiment with each structure for your presentation so that you see how the different patterns affect the substance and rhetorical impact of your ideas.

Time Patterns Time patterns (also called temporal and chronological patterns) organize ideas on the basis of temporal relationships. Listeners find it easy to follow a time pattern, since we think in terms of temporal order—what follows what. Because time patterns emphasize progression, development, or change, they encourage listeners to perceive topics as a process in which one thing leads to another.

Good visual aids increase understanding and retention of ideas. They can visually reinforce the organization of a presentation. (© Paula Lerner/Woodfin Camp & Associates, Inc.)

Time patterns are useful for describing processes that take place over time, for explaining historical events, and for informing listeners of how something works. Time patterns are also effective for presentations that create suspense and build to a climax. A student speaker led his listeners through the detective work of pharmaceutical research and development to the climactic discovery of a new drug for treating mood disorders. Another student traced changes in domestic roles in the United States prior to and after the Industrial Revolution. Relying on a time pattern, a third student explained the past and present of electronic communication and predicted what the future holds. In a persuasive speech opposing strip mining, a student described the progressive damage strip mining causes to land.

Everyday Application

USING THE TIME PATTERN

Think about how you might organize a speech using the time pattern. Below write two or three main points that would follow a temporal sequence.

1. _____

2. _____

3. _____

Spatial Patterns   Spatial patterns organize ideas according to physical relationships. This structure is especially appropriate for speeches that aim to describe or explain layouts, geographic relationships, or connections among objects or parts of a system. Because people have learned to think in terms of spatial relationships, this pattern is one that listeners generally follow with ease. We find it natural to think in terms of left to right, top to bottom, north to south, and back to front.

CREATING A SENSE OF TIME

The Reverend Martin Luther King, Jr., relied on a time pattern in his "I Have a Dream" speech. He opened with a reference to "today," then traced the history of African Americans in the United States. Next he returned to the present to argue that the government's promises to African Americans should be kept. He concluded by quoting a Negro spiritual that envisioned a future when all people of all races would be free. Throughout the speech, he wove in temporal references by using words such as *now, today,* and *urgency* and by repeating the key phrase *"Now is the time."* Read the following excerpts from his speech to appreciate how King crafted his speech around a temporal theme.

I am happy to join with you today in what will go down in history as the greatest demonstration in the history of our nation. . . .

Five score years ago, a great American, in whose symbolic shadow we stand today, signed the Emancipation Proclamation. . . .

But one hundred years later, the Negro is still not free. One hundred years later, the life of the Negro is still sadly crippled by the manacles of segregation and the chains of discrimination. . . .

We have come to this hallowed spot to remind Americans of the fierce urgency of now. . . . Now is the time to make real the promises of Democracy. Now is the time to rise from the dark and desolate valley of segregation to the sunlight of racial justice. Now is the time to lift our nation from the quicksands of racial injustice to the solid rock of brotherhood. Now is the time to make justice a reality for all of God's children. . . .

Nineteen-sixty-three is not an end, but a beginning. . . .

And as we walk we must make a pledge that we shall always march ahead. We cannot turn back. . . .

I say to you today, my friends, so even though we face the difficulties of today and tomorrow, I still have a dream. . . . I have a dream that one day this nation will rise up and live out the true meaning of its creed: "We hold these truths to be self-evident; that all men are created equal."

This will be the day. . . . This will be the day when all of God's children will be able to sing with new meaning "My country 'tis of thee, sweet land of liberty, of thee I sing.". . .

When we allow freedom to ring, when we let it ring from every village and every hamlet, from every state and every city, we will be able to speed up that day when all of God's children, black men and white men, Jews and Gentiles, Protestants and Catholics, will be able to join hands and sing in the words of the old Negro spiritual, "Free at last! Free at last! Thank God almighty, we are free at last!"

Sources: Text of speech and insights into the use of temporality to organize ideas based on Cox, J. R. (1989). The fulfillment of time: King's "I have a dream" speech (August 28, 1963). In M. C. Leff & F. J. Kaufeld (Eds.), *Texts in context: Critical dialogues on significant episodes in American rhetoric* (pp. 181–204). Davis, CA: Hermagoras Press.

Space patterns can be used to structure both informative and persuasive speeches. Student speakers have successfully used spatial patterns to inform listeners about the workings of nuclear reactors, the layout of a new library, and the four levels of forest vegetation. In persuasive speeches, students have relied on spatial patterns to argue that solar energy is sufficient to heat homes, that chlorofluorocarbons and other chemicals progressively destroy the three layers of atmosphere, and that Buddhism has spread from its origins in Eastern cultures to Western societies. Spatial presentations move listeners through two or more physical areas or locations.

Everyday Application

USING THE SPATIAL PATTERN

Think about how you might organize a speech using the space pattern. Below write two or three main points that would follow a spatial sequence.

1. _____

2. _____

3. _____

_____

Topical Patterns   A third way to structure speeches is the topical, or classification, pattern. Topical patterns order a presentation into several categories, classes, or areas of discussion. The classification pattern is appropriate when your topic breaks down into two or three areas that aren't related temporally, spatially, causally, or otherwise. Although topical patterns don't have the organic power of structures that highlight relationships, they are sometimes a good method of ordering points in a speech.

Using topical patterns, speakers have given informative speeches on the three branches of government, the social and academic activities funded by student fees, and the contributions of students, faculty, and staff to campus life. Notice how each of these informative topics can be logically divided into two or three subtopics that serve as the main points of a speech.

Topical patterns can also be effective for persuasive speeches. One student gave a convincing speech in favor of a candidate for local office. Her advocacy was based on the candidate's experience in public service, personal integrity, and commitment to the community. Another student designed a very creative persuasive presentation that extolled the value of studying the humanities, the natural sciences, and the social sciences.

Everyday Application

USING THE TOPICAL PATTERN

Think about how you might organize a speech using the topical pattern. Below write two or three main points that would follow a topical sequence.

1. _____

2. _____

3. _____

Comparative Patterns   As the name suggests, comparative patterns compare two or more objects, people, situations, events, or other phenomena. This presentational form is also called comparison/contrast and analogical structure. It encourages listeners to be aware of similarities or differences between two or more things. It is particularly effective in helping listeners understand a new idea, process, or event in terms of one with which they're already familiar. Appropriate for both informative and persuasive presentations, the comparative pattern highlights likeness or difference.

MAYUMI

I selected comparative organization for my informative speech about American and Japanese marriages, because I wanted the class to understand how people from my country think differently about marriage than Americans do. I divided my speech into courtship, division of household work, and meaning of divorce to show the difference between Americans and Japanese in each area.

Informative speeches using the comparative structure might explain how computers are like human brains, how research for new drugs is like a detective mission, or how fission and fusion are different sources of energy. I've heard persuasive student speeches that use the comparative pattern to argue that socialized medicine is inferior to or superior to private practice, that rape victims are treated differently than victims of any other crime, and that undergraduate education is different than career preparation. In each case, the comparative structure invites listeners to perceive how two or more phenomena are alike or different.

USING THE COMPARATIVE PATTERN

Think about how you might organize a speech using the comparative pattern. Below write two or three main points that would follow a comparative structure.

1. _____

2. _____

3. _____

Problem–Solution Patterns   This pattern divides a topic into two major areas: a problem and a solution. Usually a speaker begins by describing a problem and its severity and then proposes a solution. Occasionally, this sequence is inverted when a speaker begins by discussing a solution and then explains the problem it solves. The problem–solution structure can be used for informative presentations with thesis statements such as "Affirmative action (solution) is designed to rectify historical discrimination (problem)," or "The increased cost of running a university (problem) explains the rise in tuition costs (solution)."

More often, we see the problem–solution pattern used in persuasive speeches, since it lends itself naturally to advocating policies, answers, and practices. Students have used this pattern effectively to persuade others that vegetarianism (solution) can reduce cruelty to animals and world hunger (problems); that thousands of injuries and deaths on the highway could be prevented by mandatory air bags in all cars; that many people who are severely ill or dying could be helped if more people were organ donors (solution); and that the overcrowding of jails and the backlog of court cases (problems) could be decreased if we made all victimless crimes misdemeanors (solution).

The persuasive power of this pattern derives from the sequential involvement it invites from listeners. If they accept a speaker's description of a problem and believe it is serious, then they hunger for a solution. The speaker who presents one that meets the problem they've already acknowledged has a good chance of convincing listeners to endorse the recommended proposal.

USING THE PROBLEM–SOLUTION PATTERN

Think about how you might organize a speech using the problem–solution pattern. Below write two main points that would focus on a problem and a solution.

1. _____

2. _____

Cause–Effect and Effect–Cause Patterns   This pattern is used to argue a direct relationship between two things—a cause and an effect. In some instances, speakers wish to inform people that a situation, policy, or practice (effect) results from certain previous choices or events (causes). In other cases, speakers may argue that a specific action (cause) will lead to a desired or undesired effect. As these examples suggest, the cause–effect or effect–cause patterns are appropriate for both informative and persuasive speeches. We use them for informative presentations when our goal is to explain why something is the case (this effect is due to this cause(s)). The cause–effect structure is effective for persuasive speeches when the goal is to advocate some course of action, either personal or collective.

You should be aware that it is extremely difficult to *prove* direct causation. Even scientific researchers who are convinced that smoking causes cancer, emphysema, and other serious conditions cannot conclusively verify that smoking is *the* cause. What they can prove is that smoking is related to higher mortality and particular debilitating medical conditions. There is ample evidence to establish a relationship between smoking (or chewing tobacco) and the likelihood of developing cancer and other diseases. Although other factors, such as lifestyle and heredity, may increase or decrease the likelihood of developing dread diseases, smoking is one factor that is strongly related. The relationship between smoking and disease, however, does not definitively prove that smoking causes diseases. Thus, although speakers can seldom, if ever, prove direct causation, they can demonstrate relationships between causes and effects, and this is often persuasive to listeners.

USING THE CAUSE–EFFECT PATTERN

Think about how you might organize your speech using the cause–effect pattern. Below write two main points that highlight a cause or causes and an effect or effects.

1. _____

2. _____

Now think about how you might organize a speech using an effect–cause structure. Below write two main points that identify one or more effects and one or more causes of the effect.

1. _____

2. _____

Motivated Sequence Patterns   In the 1930s, a scholar of public speaking named Alan Monroe developed the motivated sequence pattern for organizing speeches (Monroe, 1935). Since then, it has been widely used in diverse communication situations, and it has proven quite effective (Gronbeck, McKerrow, Ehninger, & Monroe, 1994; Jaffe, 1995). The primary reason for the distinct effectiveness of the motivated sequence pattern is that it follows a natural pattern of human thought by gaining listeners' attention, demonstrating a need, offering a solution, and then helping them visualize and act on the solution. This pattern progressively increases listeners' motivation and personal involvement with a problem and its solution.

The motivated sequence pattern includes five sequential steps: Attention, Need, Satisfaction, Visualization, and Action. Step one is Attention, which is used to focus listeners' attention on the subject. Here a speaker makes a dramatic opening statement ("Imagine this campus with no trees whatsoever"), shows the personal relevance of the topic ("The air you are breathing right now exists only because we have trees"), or otherwise catches listeners' attention. Later in this chapter, we'll discuss additional ways to do this.

Step two establishes Need by showing that a real and serious problem exists ("Acid rain is slowly but surely destroying the trees of this planet"). Next is the Satisfaction step in which a speaker recommends a solution ("Stronger environmental regulations and individual efforts to use environmentally safe products can protect trees and, thus, the oxygen we breathe"). The fourth step is Visualization, which increases listeners' commitment to the solution identified in the Satisfaction step by helping them imagine the results that would follow from adopting the recommended solution ("You will have ample air to breathe and so will your grandchildren. Moreover, we'll all have the beauty of trees to enrich our lives"). Finally, speakers move to the Action step, which involves a direct appeal for concrete action on the part of listeners ("Refuse to buy or use any aerosol products," "Sign this petition that I am sending to our senators in Washington, D.C."). The Action step calls on listeners to take action to bring about the solution a speaker helped them visualize.

VELMA

I've heard a lot of speeches on discrimination, but the most effective I ever heard was Cindy's in class last week. Other speeches I've heard focused on the idea that discrimination is wrong, but that's something I already believe, so they weren't helpful. Cindy, on the other hand, told me how to do something about discrimination. She showed me how I could act on what I believe.

The motivated sequence pattern is especially persuasive because it goes beyond identifying a problem and recommending a solution. In addition, it intensifies listeners' desire for a solution by helping them visualize what it would mean and gains their active commitment to being part of the solution. When listeners become personally involved with an idea and with taking action, they are more enduringly committed.

Everyday Application

USING THE MOTIVATED SEQUENCE PATTERN

Think about how you might organize a speech using the motivated sequence pattern. Below write five main points for a motivated sequence appeal.

1. (Attention) _____

2. (Need) _____

3. (Satisfaction) _____

4. (Visualization) _____

5. (Action) _____

The seven patterns we've discussed represent different ways to organize public presentations. No one pattern is inherently superior to any other. Each one can be effective for certain speaking goals and with particular listeners. To structure your speech effectively, you should consider how each of the seven patterns might shape the content and impact of your presentation. For example, a temporal pattern allowed Martin Luther King, Jr., to emphasize progress and change by highlighting past, present, and an imagined future of race relations in the United States. Had he selected a problem–solution pattern, he might have focused on problems of racial inequity and ways that governmental policies could address those. Using a topical pattern, he might have drawn listeners' attention to personal, community, and social effects of discrimination. Each pattern affects the overall meaning of a speech. In creating your own presentation, think about the meaning invited by various patterns and select one that emphasizes your intent.

Everyday Application

EXPERIMENTING WITH ORGANIZATION

It's impossible to tell which organizational pattern will be most effective for a speech until all of the alternatives are considered. Here's an example of how one student considered the alternatives by composing a thesis statement appropriate for each pattern.

Time: Immigration has been part of our culture since Europeans first came to the United States.

Space: Different regions of the United States reflect the immigration of particular ethnic groups.

Topical: Immigration involves physical moves, psychological adjustments, and changes in work life.

Comparative: Countries with large populations of immigrants are more innovative and vigorous than countries with few immigrants.

Cause–Effect: Immigration has affected America's social programs, cultural life, and productivity.

Effect–Cause: Immigration to the United States in recent years is caused by the lack of education and opportunities in many other countries.

Problem–Solution: The fears of many Americans about increasing immigration could be lessened by interacting with people from other cultures.

Motivated Sequence: For immigration to be good for our country, we need to ensure strong educational and health programs, and that requires your support of pending legislation.

Now follow this exercise for your own topic. Write a thesis statement for each organizational pattern:

Time: _____

_____

Space: _____

_____

Topical: _____

_____

Comparative: _____

_____

Cause–Effect: _____

_____

Effect–Cause: _____

_____

Problem–Solution: _____

_____

Motivated Sequence: _____

_____

Which of the thesis statements best captures the central idea you want to communicate in your speech?

_____

One-Sided or Two-Sided Presentations

Perhaps you are wondering whether it's more effective to present only your point of view or both sides of an issue in a persuasive speech (the question isn't relevant to informational speeches). That's an important question, and it's one that communication scholars have studied in depth. The research conducted to discover whether one-sided or two-sided presentations are more effective suggests that the answer is "it depends." More specifically, it depends on the particular people a speaker will address, which reminds us again that good audience analysis is essential to effective public speaking. Decisions of whether to present one or more than one side of an issue depend on the particular listeners for whom a speech is intended.

Listeners' Expectations   Speakers always should try to learn what listeners expect so that they don't disappoint listeners by failing to meet expectations. In educational settings, listeners are likely to expect speakers to discuss more than one side of an issue. Expectations may also be shaped by prespeech publicity. Once I agreed to make a presentation on the need for a stronger campus policy on family leaves to allow parents time off from work when new children were born or adopted or when family members had medical crises. However, a flyer for my presentation (produced by someone else) included this promise: "Learn about the pros and cons of family leave policies." Because I knew that members of my audience who had seen the flyer would expect me to discuss disadvantages as well as values of family leave, I revised my presentation to provide both sides. I also prepared a visual aid that listed key pros and cons of family leave policies.

Audience Attitudes   It makes a difference whether listeners are likely to be disposed toward your ideas (Griffin, 1991). If they already favor your position, then you may not need to discuss alternative positions in depth. However, if listeners favor a position different from yours, then it's essential to acknowledge and deal with their views. If your listeners oppose what you propose, it's unlikely you will persuade them to abandon their position and adopt yours. With an audience hostile to your views, it's more reasonable to try to lessen their hostility to your ideas and/or the strength of their commitment to their present position (Trenholm, 1991).

When preparing a persuasive speech, learn as much as you can about your listeners' expectations, attitudes, and knowledge. (© Donna Binder/Impact Visuals)

PUBLIC SPEAKING AS INTERACTION

Public speaking is not one-way communication. Effective speakers don't try to impose their views on listeners without also entertaining the ideas of their listeners. The interactive quality of effective public speaking is well emphasized by this insight:

> *Arguments are not won by shouting down opponents. They are won by changing opponents' minds—something that can happen only if we give opposing arguments a respectful hearing.*

Source: Lasch, C. (1990, Spring). Journalism, publicity and the lost art of argument. *Gannett Center Journal*, pp. 1–11.

Failure to consider opposing ideas listeners hold diminishes a speaker's credibility, since listeners may assume that the speaker either is unaware of another side or is aware of their reservations but chooses to ignore them. Either conclusion lessens credibility and the potential for impact on listeners. Speakers have an ethical responsibility to give respectful consideration to listeners' ideas and positions. Doing so encourages reciprocal respect from listeners for the ideas you wish to present. R. J.'s commentary illustrates this.

R. J.

In my ROTC unit there's a lot of bad will toward the idea of gays in the military. Some of the guys have really strong feelings against it, so I was interested in what would happen at a required seminar last week with a guest speaker who was arguing that gays should be allowed in the services. He was really good! He spent the first 10 minutes talking about all of the concerns, fears, and reasons why officers and enlisted personnel disapprove of having gays in the military, and he showed a lot of respect for those reasons. Then he presented his own ideas and showed how they answered most of the concerns people had. I won't say everyone was persuaded 100% that gays should be allowed in, but I will say he managed to get a full hearing with a group that I thought would just turn him off from the word go. Since he talked to us, I've heard some of the guys saying that maybe gays wouldn't be a problem.

Audience Knowledge   What an audience already knows or believes about a topic should influence decisions of whether to present one or more sides of an issue. Listeners who are well informed about a topic are likely to be aware of more than one side, so your credibility will be enhanced if you include all sides in your presentation (Jackson & Allen,

1990). Also, highly educated listeners tend to realize that all issues have more than one side, so they may be suspicious of speakers who present only one point of view. As we will see in the next section, if your audience is likely to hear the other side later, it's wise for you to discuss it and refute it in your presentation.

Inoculation   In some instances, speakers know that listeners will later be exposed to counterarguments. In such cases, it's advisable to inoculate listeners. **Inoculation** in persuasion is similar to inoculation in medicine. We have vaccines to protect us from diseases to which we haven't yet been exposed. Similarly, persuasive inoculation immunizes listeners in advance against opposing ideas and arguments they may encounter in the future. When listeners later hear the other side, they have some immunity to arguments that oppose your position (Kiesler & Kiesler, 1971). For example, in political campaigns, candidates often make statements such as this: "Now my opponent will tell you that we don't need to raise taxes, but I want to show you why that's wrong." By identifying and dispelling the opposing candidate's ideas in advance, the speaker improves the chance that listeners will vote for her or him.

Listeners are more likely to be persuaded by counterproposals if you haven't inoculated them against the other side of the argument. In fact, research indicates that of the three options—one sided only, two sided, or two sided with refutation of the other side—generally the most persuasive strategy is to present both sides and refute arguments for the other side (Allen et al., 1990).

There is no quick and easy formula for deciding whether to present one-sided or two-sided discussions of a topic. Like most aspects of public speaking, this decision involves personal judgment on a speaker's part. That judgment should be informed by ethical considerations of what listeners have a right to know and what content is necessary to represent fairly the issues about which you speak. In addition, judgments of whether to present more than one side should take into account listeners' expectations, attitudes, and knowledge and the likelihood that listeners have been or will be exposed to counterarguments.

Now that you understand options for organizing the body of a speech, we're ready to discuss building introductions and conclusions and weaving transitions into speeches.

Designing the Introduction

The introduction to a speech is the first thing listeners hear. Thus, it's important for the introduction to gain listeners' attention and explain to them what the speech is about and how ideas will be developed.

Attention   The first objective of a good introduction is to gain listeners' interest and attention. There are many methods of doing this. You might begin with a dramatic piece of evidence—a quotation, striking visual aid,

(*Animal Crackers* reprinted by permission of Tribune Media Services.)

strong example, or startling statistic that compels interest: "One in 4 girls is sexually assaulted by a parent and 1 in 10 boys is." Alternatively, you might open with a question that invites listeners to become involved with the topic. Rhetorical questions are ones that do not require a response from listeners: "Do you know the biggest cause of death among college students?" Action questions do require listeners to respond in some fashion, perhaps by nodding their heads or raising their hands: "How many of you wear seat belts when you drive?" "How many of you went home over fall break?" Both rhetorical and action questions engage listeners personally at the outset of a speech.

There are other ways to capture listeners' attention. For example, speakers sometimes refer to current events or experiences of listeners that are related to the topic of a speech. A student who spoke on homelessness immediately after fall break opened this way: "If you're like me, you went home over the break and enjoyed the comforts of good food, a clean bed, and shelter—comforts that a home provides. But not everyone has those comforts." Speakers may also begin by mentioning their personal experience with a topic to establish initial credibility: "I've spent the last three summers working with inmates in a prison." Another effective way to capture listeners' attention is to provide them with direct experience, which is a highly effective foundation for persuasion (Baron & Berne, 1994). For example, in a speech advocating low-fat eating, a speaker began his presentation by passing out samples of low-fat cookies he had baked. All of his listeners then had an immediate experience with delicious and healthy food.

When appropriate to speaking situations, humor can also be an effective way to open a speech, but only if it succeeds in amusing listeners. A joke that fails diminishes credibility and may arouse negative responses from listeners. Unless you're sure a joke will be funny to listeners, it's better to avoid using humor to open a speech. Thus, it's a good idea to try jokes out on people who are similar to your listeners.

Statement of Purpose   The second function of an introduction is to state the main message of your speech, which is the thesis statement that you developed in Chapter 12. Your thesis should be a short, clear sentence that

ATTENTION DEVICES IN STUDENT SPEECHES

Students have used the following methods to capture initial audience attention:

Question to create suspense: Have you ever wondered what life would be like if there were no deadly diseases?

Startling evidence: Nearly two-thirds of people over 60 who are poor are women.

Personal involvement: Many of you have to work extra hours to make the money for your textbooks so that the student store can make its 35% profit—that's right, 35% profit just for selling you a book.

Inviting listeners' participation: Imagine that you could design the undergraduate curriculum at this university. What would you recommend for all students who attend?

Quotation: "One earth, one chance" is the motto of the Sierra Club.

captures the overall theme of your presentation. Remember that the thesis should only announce the key idea of your speech so that listeners have a clear understanding of your topic: "Today, I want to inform you about one of the last remaining wilderness areas in our country, the Arctic National Wildlife Refuge." "In the next few minutes, I will describe the problem of drugs on our campus and ask your help in solving it." "I want to inform you about your legal rights when interviewing for a job."

Preview of Body   The final purpose of an introduction is to tell listeners about coming attractions. You want to preview your major points so that they understand how you will develop ideas and can follow you. The preview provides a brief elaboration of your thesis statement by announcing the main points of your speech. Typically, a preview enumerates, or lists, the main points: "In discussing the Arctic National Wildlife Refuge, I will describe the Coastal Plain, which is the biological heart of the refuge, and then tell you about the Porcupine Caribou, who come there each year to calve." "I will demonstrate that there has been a marked increase in students' use of illegal drugs in recent years and ask you to sign a petition in support of a policy to educate students about the dangers of drugs." "To inform you about your legal rights in an interview, I will first discuss the laws that protect your privacy and prohibit discrimination. Then I will explain what you can do if an interviewer violates these laws." Because a good preview directs listeners to think along the lines you will follow in developing your speech, it increases their understanding and retention of information (Baird, 1974).

An effective introduction gains listeners' attention and tells them what you will speak about and how you will develop ideas. Since the average introduction takes up less than 10% of speaking time, speakers need to think carefully about how best to achieve the three goals of introductions.

Crafting the Conclusion

The next step in organizing a speech is to craft a strong conclusion. As you may recall, we noted that effective public speaking includes deliberate redundancy to enhance listeners' retention of key ideas. The conclusion is a speaker's last chance to drive home the main points of a presentation. An effective conclusion summarizes content and provides a memorable final thought. As you may realize, these two functions are similar to the attention and preview in introductions. In repeating key ideas and leaving the audience with a compelling final thought, a speaker provides psychological closure on the speech. As is the case for introductions, conclusions are short, generally taking less than 5% of total speaking time. Thus, it's important to accomplish the two objectives of a conclusion very concisely (Miller, 1974).

To summarize the content of your speech, it's generally a good idea to restate your thesis and each major point. You can do this in a sentence or two. Here are three examples: "Today I've suggested that our country is richer and better because of the many different peoples who have immigrated here. The diversity makes us stronger and more innovative than homogeneous cultures." "If you believe, as I do, that our planet is in trouble, then please evaluate candidates for the upcoming election according to their stands on environmental issues and policies." "I hope my speech has informed you of your legal rights in interviews and what you can do if an interviewer violates them." Each of these summaries restates the thesis and reminds listeners of the key points that support it.

Following the summary of content, a conclusion should offer listeners a final idea, ideally something particularly memorable or strong or an ending that returns to the opening idea to provide satisfying closure. In a speech on environmental activism, the speaker began with "One earth, one chance is the Sierra Club motto" and ended with "We have one chance to keep our one earth. Let's not throw it away." This was effective because the ending returned to the opening words, but gave them a slightly different twist. A student who presented an informative speech on changes in the work force closed his presentation this way: "I began this speech by telling you that current statistics estimate at least 50% of the jobs today will not exist in 20 years. The information I gave you about coming shifts in the marketplace should allow you to prepare for a job that will exist." A third example, again from a student speaker, is this memorable closing: "I've given you logical reasons to be a blood donor, but let me close with something more personal: I am alive today because there was blood available for a massive transfusion when I had my automobile accident. Any one of us could need it tomorrow."

Effective conclusions are short and focused. They highlight central ideas one last time and offer listeners a powerful or compelling concluding thought.

Building in Transitions

The final organizational issue is **transitions,** which are words and sentences that connect ideas and main points in a speech so that listeners can follow a speaker. Transitions signal listeners that you are through talking about one idea and ready to move to the next one. Thus, they tie ideas together. Good transitions are like signposts for listeners. They tell listeners where you have been, where you are, and where you are heading (Wilson & Arnold, 1974).

Transitions may be words, phrases, or entire sentences. Within the development of a single point, it's effective to use transitional words such as *therefore, and so, for this reason, as this evidence suggests,* and *consequently.* To make transitions from one point to another in a speech, phrases can be used to signal listeners that you are starting to discuss a new idea: "My second point is . . . ," "Now that we have seen how many people immigrate to America, let's consider what they bring to us," and "In addition to the point I just discussed, we need to think about . . . " To move from one to another of the three major parts of a speech (introduction, body, and conclusion), you can signal your audience with statements that summarize what you've said in one part and point the way to the next. For example, here's an internal summary and transition: "I've now explained in some detail why we need stronger educational and health programs for new immigrants, so let me close by reminding you of what's at stake." This statement cues listeners that the speaker has finished developing the body of the speech and will now summarize it.

Transitions may also be made using nonverbal communication. Speakers often rely on gestures to signal transitions or to supplement verbal transition statements. For example, you might hold up one, two, and three fingers to reinforce your movement from the first to the second to the third main point in the body of your speech. Changes in vocal intensity, eye contact, and inflection can effectively mark movement from one idea to the next. For instance, you could conclude the final point of the body of your speech with strong volume and then drop the volume to begin the conclusion. Silence is also effective in marking transitions. A pause after the introduction signals listeners that a speaker is going to a new place. Visual aids, too, help listeners follow development of a speech. A chart that lists major points in a speech can be used and pointed to as you begin discussion of each new point.

Transitions are vital to effective speaking. If the introduction, body, and conclusion are the bones of a speech, the transitions are the sinew that holds the bones together. Without transitions, a speech may seem more like a laundry list of unconnected ideas than a coherent whole.

Outlining Speeches

Once you've honed your speaking purpose, collected your evidence, and organized your ideas, you are ready to create an outline for your speech. Outlines are used by novice and seasoned speakers alike, because all of us tend to be more effective when we have the basic sketch of our speech before us. Outlines provide a clear, very concise profile of the overall speech.

Often, beginning speakers think that an outline is unnecessary, but they're mistaken. A good outline provides you with a safety net in case you forget what you intend to say or in case you are disrupted by some unforeseen event such as a question or a disturbing noise. Outlines also allow you to make sure that you have organized your ideas well and have enough evidence to support your claims. Without an outline, speakers have only ideas in their heads or scribbled notes that may not reflect the order of ideas and may not include references to all evidence and transitions. Thus, speakers who wing it without outlines can be undermined if they have a lapse of memory—there's nothing to guide them back on track.

An outline is usually a skeleton of a speech. It is not and should not be the whole speech unless you are giving a manuscript speech, which we will discuss later in this chapter. In most cases, speakers who write out entire speeches sound canned or read the speech instead of communicating interactively with listeners. An effective outline has main headings for the introduction, body, and conclusion. Under each main point are subpoints, references to supporting material, and abbreviated transitions. If your speech includes quotations, statistics, or other evidence that must be presented with absolute accuracy, you should write the evidence in full, either on your outline or on separate index cards. In addition, your outline or index card should include the source and date of the evidence so that you can provide an oral footnote to listeners.

FIGURE 14.1
Sample Skeleton Outline

I. Introduction
   A. Attention: Would you vote for a system in which half of us work only one job and the other half of us work two and everyone gets equal rewards? No? Well that's the system that most families in this country operate under today.
   B. Thesis statement: Women's double shift in paid labor and homemaking and child care has negative effects on them personally and on marriages.
   C. Preview: In the next few minutes, I will show that the majority of married women work a double shift while their husbands work only a single shift. I will then trace the harmful effects of this inequitable division of labor.
II. Body
   A. The majority of married women today work two jobs: one in the paid labor market and a second one when they get home from their paid jobs.
      1. Most families today have two wage earners.
         a. Only 17% have one earner.
         b. The increase in working wives has been matched by only a 10% increase in husbands' work in the home—from 20% to 30% in 3 decades.
      2. Only 20% of husbands in two-worker families do 50% of the homemaking and child care.
         a. Example of chores couples do.
         b. Reasons husbands give for doing less: quotes (see separate cards).
      3. The trend for women to assume the majority of responsibilities for homemaking and child care holds true for all groups, but it does vary

somewhat among races, educational levels, and socioeconomic classes.

    a. Working-class husbands are likely to do more and to resent homemaking chores less than middle-class husbands.

        i. Example of Jacob and Ina.

        ii. Example of John and Jennifer.

    b. Better educated couples achieve a more balanced division of home labor, although women still do more than 50% (bar graph).

    4. Women's double shift doesn't vary regardless of how much income they earn or even if they earn more income than their husbands.

       a. Detailed example of Jeremy and Nancy—she earns 140% of his salary and still does 80% of the homemaking and child care.

       b. Statistics (study by Hochschild, with Machung, 1989).

Transition: Now that we've seen how the double shift works and how pervasive it is, let's consider its effects.

B. The double shift harms women's health and creates stress in marriages.

    1. Working a double shift harms women physically and psychologically.

       a. Undetailed examples of physical harm: sleep deprivation, reduced immunity to infections, susceptibility to illnesses.

       b. Researchers report higher levels of stress and unhappiness (see quotes on separate cards).

    2. The double shift women work also erodes marital satisfaction.

FIGURE 14.1 *(Continued)*

Constructing an outline is not difficult. A good outline simply weaves together all of the work that you've done in preparing, researching, and organizing your presentation. It then provides you with the information you need to make an effective presentation. Figure 14.1 shows a sample skeleton outline.

Some speakers prefer a less detailed outline, called a **key word outline.** As the name implies, a key word outline includes only key words for each point. Its purpose is to trigger the speaker's memory of each point. Figure 14.2 shows a key word outline for the double shift speech.

FIGURE 14.1 (Continued)

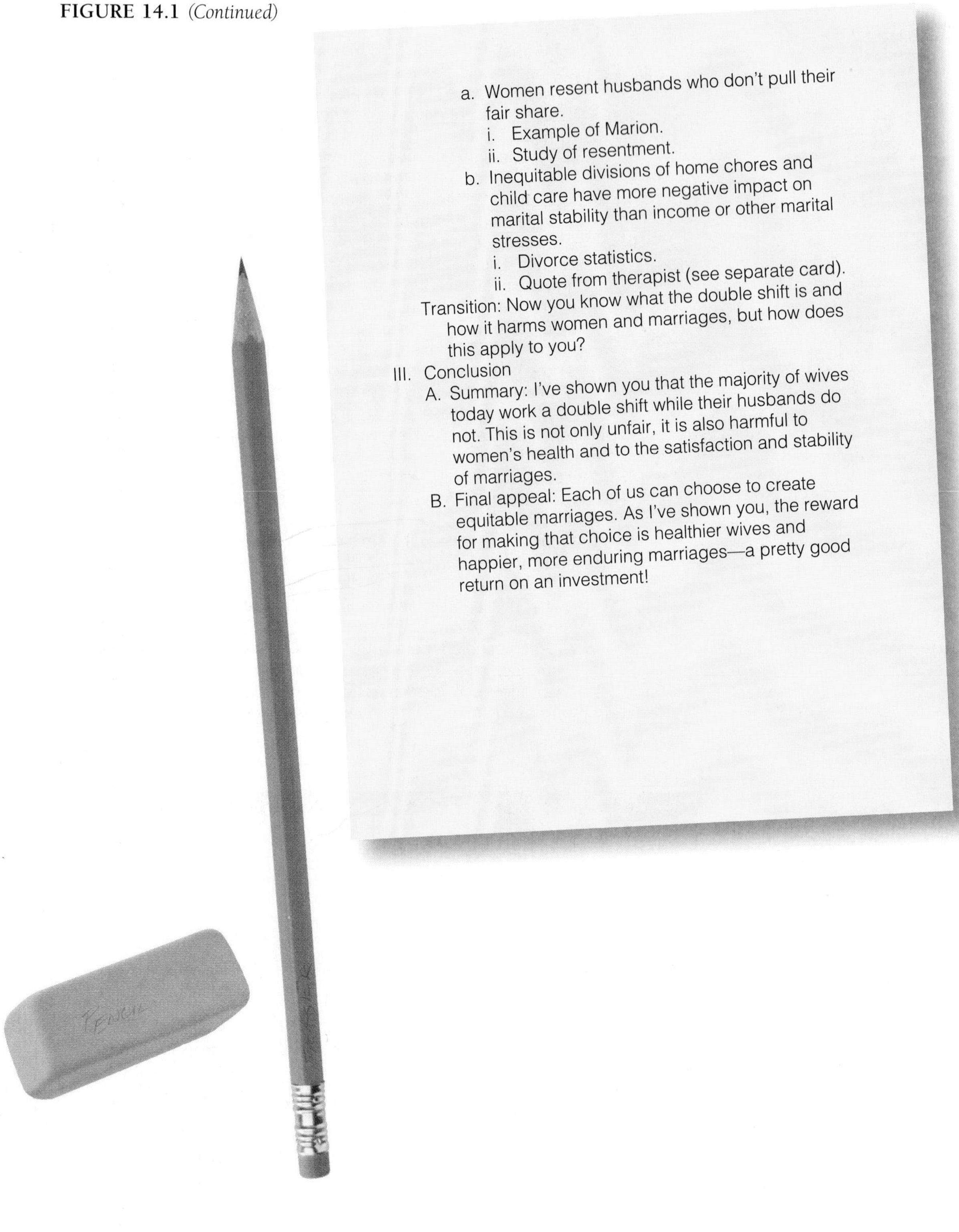

a. Women resent husbands who don't pull their fair share.
    i. Example of Marion.
    ii. Study of resentment.
b. Inequitable divisions of home chores and child care have more negative impact on marital stability than income or other marital stresses.
    i. Divorce statistics.
    ii. Quote from therapist (see separate card).
Transition: Now you know what the double shift is and how it harms women and marriages, but how does this apply to you?

III. Conclusion
A. Summary: I've shown you that the majority of wives today work a double shift while their husbands do not. This is not only unfair, it is also harmful to women's health and to the satisfaction and stability of marriages.
B. Final appeal: Each of us can choose to create equitable marriages. As I've shown you, the reward for making that choice is healthier wives and happier, more enduring marriages—a pretty good return on an investment!

FIGURE 14.2
Sample Key Word Outline

I. Introduction
    A. Half work one, half work two
    B. Effects—personal, on marriage
    C. Majority of married women; effects of inequity
II. Body
    A. Majority of married women—two jobs
        1. Two wage earners standard
            a. 17% single wage earner
            b. 10% increase in husbands' contribution
        2. 20% husbands assume half
        3. Pattern varies
            a. Class
                i. Jacob and Ina
                ii. John and Jennifer
            b. Education
        4. Women's double shift not tied to salary
            a. Jeremy and Nancy
            b. Hochschild study (see card)
    B. Effects
        1. Physical and psychological
            a. Sleep, illness, infection
            b. Stress unhappiness
        2. Marital satisfaction erodes
            a. Resentment
                i. Marion
                ii. Study (see card)
            b. Marital stability
                i. Divorce statistics (see card)
                ii. Therapist quote (see card)
III. Conclusion
    A. Unfair + health harms + marital stability and satisfaction
    B. Your choice—return on investment

PRESENTING PUBLIC SPEECHES

We turn now to the final aspect of public speaking— delivering a presentation to listeners. Delivery, or oral style, affects every aspect of speaking effectiveness from listeners' interest and retention to listeners' judgments of a speaker's credibility. We'll discuss the nature of oral style and then consider alternative styles of delivery.

Oral Style

Oral style involves speakers' visual, vocal, and verbal communication with listeners. Visual delivery concerns a speaker's appearance, facial expressions, eye contact, posture, gestures, movement during a presentation, and visual aids. Vocal aspects of delivery include volume, pitch, pronunciation, articulation, inflection, pauses, and speaking rate. Verbal delivery refers to word choices and sentence structure.

A speech is oral communication, not a spoken essay. A common mistake of speakers, both new and experienced, is to use written style, rather than oral style. The two modes of communication are distinct, and neither is effective if used in an inappropriate context.

There are three primary qualities of effective oral communication (Wilson & Arnold, 1974). First, it is more informal than written communication. Thus, speakers use contractions and sentence fragments that would be inappropriate in a formal written document. In oral communication, we are used to hearing short and even incomplete sentences. When giving oral presentations, simple sentences ("I have three points") and compound sentences ("I want to describe the current system of selling textbooks, and then I will propose an alternative that would be less costly for students") are more appropriate than complex sentences ("There are many reasons to preserve the Arctic National Wildlife Refuge, some of which have to do with endangered species and others with the preservation of wilderness environment, yet our current Congress is not protecting this treasure"). The informal character of oral style also means it's appropriate for speakers to use colloquial words and even slang in informal speaking contexts. However, speakers shouldn't use slang or jargon that might offend any listener or that might not be understood by some listeners.

Oral style should also be more personal than written. This implies that speakers may include personal stories and personal pronouns, referring to themselves as "I" rather than "the speaker." In addition, speakers should sustain eye contact with listeners and show that they are approachable. If you reflect on speakers you've found effective, you'll probably realize that they seemed personal and open to you.

"Dr. Carberry has been showing much more originality in his sermons lately, hasn't he?"

(Drawing by Chas. Addams; © 1935, 1963 The New Yorker Magazine, Inc.)

"MISSING THE BOAT" IN COMMUNICATION

Communication scholar Wen Shu Lee (1994) points out that many people for whom English is a second language don't understand what native speakers consider everyday idioms. Nonnative speakers may "miss the boat" if speakers use idioms such as "kicked the bucket," "chew the fat," "far out," "hit the road," "this car's a real lemon," "hangdog expression," "cooked goose," "hang a right," or "bail out."

The informality appropriate for speaking should not create barriers to understanding.

Third, effective oral style is more immediate and active than written style tends to be. This is important, since listeners must understand ideas immediately as they are spoken, whereas readers can take time to comprehend ideas. Immediacy is fostered by using short sentences (simple or compound) instead of complex sentences with multiple phrases. Immediacy also involves moving quickly instead of gradually to develop ideas. Rhetorical questions, interjections, and redundancy also enhance the immediacy of a speech. Reread the excerpts from Martin Luther King, Jr.'s speech on page 376, and notice his skill in repeating key phrases such as "now is the time." Also note Dr. King's use of simple sentences and his emphasis on personal language (I and we).

Notice the style of speakers you find effective, and you'll find it tends to be relatively immediate, informal, and personal. Contrast the communication style of speakers you find effective with the style of speakers you judge to be less effective. The latter group is likely to adopt a formal, impersonal, abstract style of communication. Noticing the differences will give you a clear understanding of the value of oral speaking style.

Styles of Delivery

Throughout this book, we've seen that communication occurs in contexts that influence what will be effective and ineffective. This basic communication principle guides a speaker's choice of a style of presentation. The style of speaking that's effective at a political rally is different from the style appropriate for an attorney's closing speech in a trial; delivering a toast at a wedding requires a different style than testifying before Congress. Each speaking situation suggests its own guidelines for presentational style, so speakers must consider the context when selecting a speaking style. There are four presentational styles, each of which is appropriate in certain contexts.

PERSONAL STYLE AND EFFECTIVE TEACHING

Teachers, like others who speak to large groups, are more effective when they come across as being personal. A substantial amount of research shows that teachers who seem warm and approachable, show interest in talking with students, maintain eye contact when lecturing, use humor in class, and touch students are better liked than teachers who are more impersonal. Personal style not only influences students' affection for teachers, but also increases motivation to study and learn. These effects have been found with students in courses in high schools, in colleges, and even in off-campus televised programs.

Sources: Christophel, D. M. (1990). The relationships among teacher immediacy behaviors, student motivation, and learning. *Communication Education, 39,* 323–340. Gorham, J., & Zakahi, W. R. (1990). A comparison of teacher and student perceptions of immediacy and learning. *Communication Education, 39,* 46–62. Hackman, M. Z., & Walker, K. B. (1990). Instructional communication in the televised classroom: The effects of system design and teacher immediacy on student learning and satisfaction. *Communication Education, 39,* 196–206. Mongeau, P. A., & Blalock, J. (1994). Student evaluations of instructor immediacy and sexually harassing behaviors: An experimental investigation. *Journal of Applied Communication Research, 22,* 256–272.

Impromptu Style   **Impromptu speaking** involves little preparation. Speakers speak "off the cuff," organizing ideas as they talk and working with evidence that is already familiar to them. You use an impromptu style when you make a comment in a class, answer a question you hadn't anticipated in an interview, or respond to a request to share your ideas on a topic. There is no time to prepare or rehearse, so impromptu speaking calls for thinking on your feet.

Impromptu speaking is appropriate when you know a topic well enough to organize and support your ideas without a lot of advance preparation. The president of a company, for instance, could speak off the cuff about the company's philosophy, goals, and recent activities. Similarly, politicians who have worked out their positions and familiarized themselves with evidence often speak in an impromptu style. Impromptu speaking tends to be highly informal, personal, and immediate—the best qualities of oral style. Yet impromptu speaking has the disadvantage of allowing less time to research and organize. Consequently, this is not an effective style when speakers are not highly familiar with topics and at ease in speaking in public.

Extemporaneous Style   Probably the most common presentational style today, **extemporaneous speaking** relies on preparation and practice, but actual words and nonverbal behaviors aren't memorized. Extemporaneous speaking (also called extemp) requires speakers to do research, organize

WAYS ORAL STYLE DIFFERS FROM WRITTEN STYLE

1. More personal pronouns
2. More variety in sentence lengths
3. More varied types of sentences
4. More simple sentences
5. More sentence fragments and phrases
6. More rhetorical questions
7. Repetition of words, phrases, and even sentences
8. Greater use of words with only one syllable
9. More contractions
10. More interjections
11. Greater use of colloquial, or informal, language
12. Greater use of connotative words
13. More euphony (attention to the sound of language)
14. More figurative language
15. More direct quotations
16. More familiar words

Source: Wilson, J. F., & Arnold, C. C. (1974). *Public speaking as a liberal art* (4th ed.). Boston: Allyn & Bacon.

ideas, select supporting evidence, prepare visual aids, outline the speech, and practice delivery. Yet, the speech itself is not written out in full. Instead, speakers construct an outline—either a skeleton or a key word outline.

Extemporaneous speaking involves a fine balance between too little and too much practice. Not rehearsing enough may result in stumbling, forgetting key ideas, and not being at ease with the topic. On the other hand, too much practice tends to result in a speech that sounds canned. The idea is to prepare and practice just enough to be comfortable with the material, yet still be natural and spontaneous in delivery. Extemporaneous speaking involves a conversational and interactive manner that is generally very effective with listeners. This probably is why the extemporaneous style is the most popular of all presentational modes.

Manuscript Style   As the name suggests, **manuscript speaking** involves speaking from a complete manuscript of a speech. After planning, researching, organizing, and outlining a presentation, a speaker then writes

Even in formal situations, openness and conversational style are appropriate. Notice the nonverbal behaviors of the speaker, Nelson Mandela.
(© Michael Geissinger/Comstock)

the complete word-for-word text and practices the presentation using that text or that text transferred to a teleprompter. The clear advantage of this style is that it provides total security to speakers. Even if a speaker gets confused when standing before an audience, she or he can rely on the full text.

The security provided by working with a full written text of a speech, however, is often offset by several disadvantages of manuscript speaking. First, this style restricts a speaker's ability to adapt on the spot to listeners. If someone looks puzzled, the extemporaneous speaker can elaborate an idea, but the manuscript speaker may be locked into the written text. This points to a second hazard of manuscript speaking—the tendency to read the speech instead of delivering it in an interactive manner. Reading limits the effectiveness of nonverbal communication—the inflection, eye contact, gestures, and facial expressions add dynamism to oral presentations. It's difficult to be animated and visually engaged with listeners when reading a manuscript.

BRAD

Most of my professors are pretty good. They talk with us in classes, and they seem to be really involved in interacting with students. But I've had several professors who read their notes—like I mean every day. They'd just come in, open a file, and start reading. I had one professor who almost never looked at us. It didn't feel like a person was communicating with us. I'd rather have read his notes on my own.

A third disadvantage is that it's difficult to adopt a truly oral style when relying on a manuscript. Only veteran manuscript speakers or speech writers can write a speech that has oral flavor. More often, a manuscript speech adopts written style and, thus, it isn't immediate, personal, and informal. Instead, the speech has complex, cumbersome sentences, formal language, and abstract vocabulary. Speakers who become locked into manuscripts run the risk of losing visual contact with their listeners, and this breaks the connection between them. In Western cultures, eye contact is one of the most important nonverbal aspects of effective public speaking.

Manuscript speaking is appropriate, and perhaps necessary, in a few specific situations. When the content of a speech must be precise and there is no room for adapting or rewording ideas, then a manuscript is advisable. The situations that require this are few and not part of most people's everyday lives. Official declarations, diplomatic agreements, and formal press statements are examples of contexts in which manuscript speaking may be advisable.

Memorized Style   The final presentational style is **memorized speaking,** which carries the manuscript style one step further. After going through all of the stages of manuscript speaking (preparing, researching, organizing, outlining, writing out the full text, and practicing), a speaker then commits the entire speech to memory. Thus, the speaker speaks from a manuscript that is in his or her head.

The advantages of this style are the same as those for manuscript speaking—an exact text exists so that everything is prepared in advance. However, there are serious disadvantages to memorizing. Because memorized speaking is based on a full written speech, there is the possibility that the presentation will reflect written, rather than oral, style. In addition, memorized speaking is risky because a speaker has no safety net in case of memory lapses. Speakers who forget a word or phrase may become rattled and unable to complete the presentation. Whereas a speaker using extemporaneous style and an outline would simply substitute a different word if the desired one didn't come to mind, a speaker who has memorized a speech may get stuck and be unable to continue if she or he forgets anything. Memorized style also has the potential to limit effective delivery. It is difficult for a speaker to sound spontaneous when she or he has memorized an entire speech. Because the speaker is preoccupied with remembering the speech, she or he can't interact fully with listeners. These drawbacks of memorized speaking explain why it isn't widely used or recommended.

Knowing the benefits and liabilities of each presentational style provides you with alternatives. For most speaking occasions, extemporaneous style is effective, since it combines good preparation and practice along with spontaneity. Although this style tends to be the most effective in the majority of speaking situations, there are exceptions. When deciding which style to use, carefully consider your own needs and speaking preferences, the nature of your presentation, the context in which you will deliver it, and your particular listeners.

Practice

Whichever presentational style you choose, practice is important. Ideally, you should begin practicing your speech several days before you plan to deliver it. During practice, you should rely on your outline as it will be when you actually deliver the speech. This ensures that you will be familiar with its layout and know where various materials are on the outline. You should also practice with visual aids and any other materials you plan to use in your speech so that you are comfortable working with them.

There are many ways to practice a speech. Usually, speakers prefer to practice alone initially so that they gain some confidence and comfort in presentation. You may find it helpful to practice in front of a mirror to see how you appear and to keep your eyes focused away from the outline. Practicing before a mirror is especially helpful in experimenting with

Practicing a speech in front of a mirror allows this speaker to monitor how she will appear to listeners. (© Anne Dowie)

different nonverbal behaviors that can enhance your presentational impact. Videotaping is another way to see yourself and work on aspects of delivery that need improvement. You should take breaks between practices so that you don't wind up memorizing the speech inadvertently.

When you've rehearsed enough to feel comfortable with the speech, it's a good idea to deliver it to other people. Ask friends to be listeners, and invite their suggestions on ways you can refine your presentation. Ask them if they can follow your organization; if they find your examples, statistics, and other evidence convincing; and if they perceive your delivery as personal, immediate, and informal. Also ask your listeners to give you feedback on your nonverbal communication: Are you maintaining good eye contact? Are your gestures, facial expressions, and movements appropriate? Do you use vocal inflections, changes in volume, and pauses effectively to accent your ideas?

Practice until you know your material well but haven't memorized it. *Then stop!* Overrehearsing is just as undesirable as not practicing enough. You want to preserve the freshness and spontaneity that is important in oral style.

SUMMARY

In this chapter, we concluded our discussion of public speaking. Building on Chapters 12 and 13, we discussed ways to organize and present public communication. We considered seven distinct patterns for ordering the ideas in a speech and explored how each pattern affects the residual message of a presentation. Which organizational structure is best depends on a variety of factors, including the topic, your speaking goal, and the listeners with whom you will communicate. These same factors influence decisions of whether to present one-sided or two-sided speeches.

We've also seen that there are different presentational styles and that each one has distinct advantages and liabilities. Effective delivery cannot be reduced to a universal formula. What is effective depends on particular speakers, contexts, listeners, and speaking goals. Different presentational styles are effective in different situations. What is constant is that delivery, like all aspects of public communication, should reflect sensitivity to ethical principles of communication, situations, listeners, and yourself. These considerations are the heart of all communication, whether it is public speaking or intimate conversation.

To make sure that you've thought through all important aspects of organizing, outlining, and delivery, review the checklist on pages 404–405.

FOR FURTHER REFLECTION AND DISCUSSION

1. Attend a public presentation, and keep notes of how the speaker organizes the speech. What is the overall pattern for the presentation? Did the speaker make a wise choice? Identify transitions in the speech and evaluate their effectiveness. Do the introduction and conclusion serve the appropriate goals in speaking?

2. To appreciate the difference between written and oral styles, do this: Using library references, find a volume of famous speeches and select two to analyze. Then select two formal essays to analyze (the Declaration of Independence, for example). Check the essays and speeches against the features of oral style summarized on page 399. Now deliver the essays orally. What happens? Are they effective as oral communication? Explain why or why not.

3. Have members of the class give short 1- to 2-minute impromptu speeches on their favorite activity or some other topic with which they are already familiar. Next, spend two days preparing an extemporaneous speech on the same topic. How do the two speeches differ in quality and effectiveness?

KEY TERMS

inoculation	impromptu speaking
transitions	extemporaneous speaking
key word outline	manuscript speaking
oral style	memorized speaking

CHECKLIST FOR ORGANIZING AND PRESENTING A SPEECH

1. If you didn't do the Everyday Application on pages 383–384, do it now.
   How could you structure your speech using each of the organizational
   patterns we discussed? Write out a thesis statement for each pattern.

   A. Time: _____

   _____

   B. Space: _____

   _____

   C. Topical: _____

   _____

   D. Comparative: _____

   _____

   E. Cause–effect: _____

   _____

   F. Effect–cause: _____

   _____

   G. Problem–solution: _____

   _____

   H. Motivated sequence: _____

   _____

2. Which pattern have you decided to use? _____

   A. List the two or three main points into which you've divided your topic:

   _____, _____, and _____

3. Explain your decision of whether to present a one-sided or two-
   sided presentation.

   I am using a _____-sided presentation because _____

   _____

   _____

4. Describe the three parts of your introduction:

   A. I will gain attention by _____

   _____

   B. My thesis statement is _____

   _____

   C. My preview is _____

   _____

5. Describe the transitions you've developed to move listeners from idea to idea in your speech.

   A. My transition from introduction to the body of the speech is: _____

   _____

   B. My transitions between major points in the body are

      1. _____

      _____

      2. _____

      _____

      3. _____

      _____

   C. My transition from the body to the conclusion of the speech is: _____

6. Describe the two parts of your conclusion:

   A. Restatement of thesis and major points: _____

   _____

   B. Concluding emphasis: _____

   _____

7. The delivery style I will use is _____

   because _____

   _____

8. I've practiced my speech

   A. On my own

   B. In front of others

   C. In front of a mirror

   D. In the room where I will deliver it

   E. On videotape

We've Come a Long Way

As I reflect on all that we've discussed, I find a central theme that unifies individual chapters and topics. The theme is that communication is an intricate tapestry woven from the threads of self, others, perceptions, relationships, contexts, culture, listening, and verbal and nonverbal language. Each thread has its own distinct character, and yet each thread is also woven into the complex, ever-changing tapestry of human communication. We've taken time to discuss each thread in its own right and then explored how it interweaves with other threads in particular communication situations.

Sometimes a particular thread stands out boldly, as individual threads sometimes do in fabric weavings. For instance, the thread of delivery is quite prominent in public speaking, while the thread of listening is more difficult to see. Yet, as we learned, to be effective, speakers must understand and adapt to their listeners. At other times, an individual thread blends so fully with other threads that we don't perceive it as separate from the overall pattern of the

(© Stewart Cohen/Tony Stone Images, Inc.)

(© Gary Conner/PhotoEdit)

(© Jeff Greenberg/PhotoEdit)

tapestry. Organization, for example, is present in interaction between friends as they decide what to talk about and how to sequence the topics. Yet in friends' conversation, the thread of organization is muted, while other threads, such as sensitive listening, stand out. The many threads that make up the tapestry of communication vary in intensity and prominence from one point in the tapestry to another, yet all are part of the whole.

To conclude our study of the communication tapestry, let's review what we've studied and what it means for us. The overall goal of this book was to explain and appreciate communication as an integral part of our everyday lives. We launched our journey in Chapter 1, which described the range of human communication and the modern academic field that bears its name. Chapter 2 allowed us to delve into the complicated process of perception so that we could understand how perception, thought, and communication interact. We learned that we seldom, if ever, perceive the full, raw reality around us. Instead, we perceive selectively—noticing only some things and overlooking others. The labels we use to name, classify, and evaluate our perceptions reverberate back into our consciousness to shape what we perceive and what it means to us. In fact, the great majority of the time, how we think, feel, and act are based not on objective realities in the external world, but rather on how we label our selective perceptions of it. This is normal, yet it can cause us trouble if we forget that we are responding to *our labels,* not to the world itself.

In Chapter 3, we traced the reciprocal relationship between communication and our sense of personal identity. As we interact with others and learn how they see us, we form initial concepts of who we are. At the same time, how we see ourselves influences how and with whom we communicate. In turn, the ways we interact and the people with whom we interact affect how our sense of self continues to evolve. The connection between identity and communication is continuous and cyclical.

Chapters 4 through 6 focused on primary forms of communication: listening, verbal communication, and nonverbal behavior. As we considered each topic, we examined what it involves and ways to improve our personal effectiveness as communicators. Particularly important to our understanding of these topics is the realization that people differ in their styles of listening and in how they communicate verbally and nonverbally. Awareness of differences in how various social groups communicate enables us to perceive others on their own terms. The understandings and skills we discussed in these chapters should serve you well throughout your life as you seek to interact effectively and sensitively with others in personal, social, and professional contexts.

The elaborate and fascinating relationships between culture and communication were the focus of Chapter 7. There we unmasked the subtle ways in which communication creates and sustains cultural beliefs, values, and practices. Just as important, we saw that cultures shape the forms and content of communication by telling us what is and is not important and what are appropriate and inappropriate ways of interacting with others. Understanding differences among cultures allows us to appreciate the distinct character of each one and to add to our own repertoire of communication skills.

The second half of the book extended the first seven chapters by weaving basic communication concepts and skills into communication in relationships, groups, and public situations. In Chapters 8 and 9, we explored interpersonal communication in general and also as it occurs in friendships and romantic relationships. The intimate bonds that grace our lives are communicative achievements, since we create and sustain them largely through interaction and the meanings we assign to it. Communication is the lifeblood of intimacy. In both dramatic forms, such as declarations of love and disclosure of secrets, and everyday "small talk," it is communication that continually breathes life and meaning into our relationships with others.

We moved to a quite different context in Chapters 10 and 11, which examined communication in small groups. There we learned what types of communication facilitate and hinder effective group discussion and what communication responsibilities accompany effective membership and leadership. We also studied the standard agenda for problem solving, which provides participants with an effective method of organizing group discussion.

The final three chapters of this book concentrated on public speaking, which we discovered is really enlarged conversation, more like than unlike everyday interaction. From the early stages of planning presentations, to researching and developing evidence, and finally to organizing, outlining, and practicing, public speaking involves skills that most of us already have and use in other communication situations. As is true for all interactions, good public speaking centers on others—the values, interests, knowledge, and beliefs of listeners guide what speakers can and cannot wisely say and how they develop and present their ideas. Effective public speaking, like effective everyday conversation, is a genuine interaction between people in which the views and values of all participants should be taken into account.

Whether we are talking to a friend, a co-worker, or an audience of 500 people, we rely on common basic ethical principles and communication skills. Among the most important is sensitivity to others and their perspectives. Because communication—by us and others—reflects cultures, perceptions, and personal identities, we need to discover how others see themselves and the topics they discuss with us. Another principle that is important in all communication situations is sensitive listening. When we listen mindfully to others, we gain insight into them and their perspectives so that we may communicate effectively with them.

Clarity and responsibility are earmarks of effective verbal and nonverbal communication. To be clear in our messages and to understand those of others, we must recognize the ambiguity and abstractness of communication and find ways to check with others to make sure we share meanings. Responsibility involves following ethical principles in our communication. In addition to respecting others and their positions, we should be careful to be accurate in making claims, whether in a public speech or in a private conversation. Any evidence that we use to support our ideas should be sound, and anything that we say should be respectful of others, including ways they differ from us. Whether we're talking to one other person in an intimate setting or a thousand people in a large auditorium, good communication is clear and responsible. Tentativeness and open-mindedness are ethical guidelines for interpreting others' verbal and nonverbal communication, since our perspectives may not coincide with those of people from different cultures and co-cultures.

Learning to appreciate many different people and communication styles enriches each of us.

(© David Bitters/The Picture Cube, Inc.)

Throughout *Communication in Our Lives,* we've seen that people differ in how they communicate and what they mean by various words and actions. The cornucopia of cultures and co-cultures in today's world gives rise to a fascinating range of communication styles. No way of communicating is inherently superior to any others; the differences result from diverse cultural heritages and practices.

Learning not to impose our own communication patterns and our culture's judgments on others and being open to styles of interaction that differ from our own allow us to enlarge who we are as individuals and enrich who we are as a collective. Curiosity, appreciation, and openness to unfamiliar ways of communicating are the foundation of a healthy pluralistic society in which each of us preserves our own distinct identity and, at the same time, each of us is part of and engaged with a larger whole.

If you have learned these principles and skills of human communication, then you have the foundation for being effective in personal, professional, and social settings. If you are committed to practicing and continuously enlarging the principles and skills introduced in this book, then you are on the threshold of a fulfilling life that promises engagement, adventure, personal growth, and joy.

GLOSSARY

abstract   Removed from concrete reality. Symbols are abstract because they are inferences and generalizations abstracted from a total reality.

acknowledgment   Second of three levels of interpersonal confirmation. Acknowledgment communicates that you hear and understand another's feelings and thoughts.

ambiguous   Unclear meaning. Symbols are ambiguous because their meanings vary from person to person, context to context, and so forth.

ambushing   Listening carefully for the purpose of attacking a speaker.

analogies   Type of comparison that uses metaphors, which indirectly assert likeness between two things.

arbitrary   Random or nonnecessary. Symbols are arbitrary because there is no necessary reason for any particular symbol to stand for a particular referent.

artifacts   Personal objects we use to announce our identities and personalize our environments.

assimilation   Occurs when people give up their own ways and take on the ways of another culture.

attachment styles   Patterns of parenting that teach children who they are, who others are, and how to approach relationships.

attributions   Causal accounts that explain why things happen and why people act as they do.

authoritarian leadership   A style of leadership in which a leader provides direction, exerts authority, and confers rewards and punishments on group members.

authority rule   Group decision-making method that occurs when some individual or group with authority tells a group what to do and the group ratifies the authority's decision.

beliefs   Assumptions about what is true, accurate, or factual. Beliefs may be false, even though they are regarded as true.

brainstorming   Group technique for generating possible solutions to a problem. Brainstorming encourages ideas to flow freely without immediate criticism.

chronemics   A type of nonverbal communication concerned with how we perceive and use time to define identities and interaction.

climate communication   One of three constructive forms of participation in group decision making. Climate communication focuses on creating and sustaining an open, engaged atmosphere for discussion.

co-cultures   Groups of people who live within a dominant culture, yet also are members of another culture that is not dominant in a particular society.

cognitive complexity   Determined by the number of constructs used, how abstract they are, and how elaborately they interact to create perceptions.

cognitive restructuring   A method of reducing communication apprehension that involves teaching individuals to revise how they think about speaking situations.

cohesion   The degree of closeness or feeling of esprit de corps among members of a group.

commitment   A decision to remain with a relationship. Commitment is one of three dimensions of enduring romantic relationships, and it has more impact on relational continuity than does love alone. It is also an advanced stage in the process of escalation in romantic relationships.

communication   A systemic process in which individuals interact with and through symbols to create and interpret meanings.

communication apprehension Anxiety associated with real or anticipated communication encounters. Communication apprehension is common and can be constructive.

communication climate   The overall feeling or emotional mood between individuals.

communication rules   Shared understandings of what communication means and what behaviors are appropriate in various situations.

comparisons   Form of evidence that uses associations between two things that are similar in some important way or ways.

compromise   Method of group decision making in which members work out a solution that satisfies each person's minimum criteria but that may not fully satisfy all members.

conflict   Exists when individuals who depend on each other express different views, interests, or goals and perceive their differences as incompatible or as opposed by the other.

consensus   Decision-making method in which all members of a group support a decision.

constitutive rules   Communication rules that define what communication means by specifying how certain communicative acts are to be counted.

constructivism   Theory that states that we organize and interpret experience by applying cognitive structures called schemata.

content level of meaning   One of two levels of meaning in communication. The content level of meanings is the literal, or denotative, information in a message.

covert conflict   Conflict that is expressed indirectly. Covert conflict is generally more difficult to manage constructively than overt conflict.

credibility   Willingness to believe in a person or to trust what a person says and does. Credibility exists in the minds of listeners, and they confer it, or refuse to confer it, on speakers.

criteria   Standards group members use to evaluate alternative solutions or decisions. Criteria should be established during stage three of standard agenda.

critical listening   Listening to analyze and evaluate the content of communication and/or the person speaking.

cultural calamity   Adversity that brings about change in a culture. Cultural calamity is one of four ways cultures change.

cultural relativism   Recognition that cultures vary in how they think, act, and behave, as well as in what they believe and value. Cultural relativism is not the same as moral relativism.

culture   Beliefs, understandings, practices, and ways of interpreting experience that are shared by a number of people.

defensive listening   Perceiving personal attacks, criticisms, or hostile undertones in communication where none are intended.

democratic leadership   A style of leadership that provides direction without imposing strict authority on a group.

demographic analysis   Form of audience analysis that focuses on general features that are common to a group of listeners.

derived credibility   The expertise and trustworthiness that listeners grant a speaker as a result of how the speaker communicates during a presentation.

diffusion   Borrowing from another culture. Diffusion is one of four ways cultures change.

direct definition   Communication that explicitly tells us who we are by specifically labeling us and reacting to our behaviors. Direct definition usually occurs first in families and also in interaction with peers and others.

downers   People who communicate negatively about us and who reflect negative appraisals of our worth as individuals.

dual perspective   The ability to understand another person's perspective, beliefs, thoughts, and/or feelings.

dyadic breakdown   The first stage of relational decay. Dyadic breakdown involves degeneration of established patterns, understandings, and routines that make up a relational culture and that sustain intimacy on a day-to-day basis.

dyadic negotiation   Stage in relational deterioration in which partners discuss problems and alternative futures for the relationship.

dynamic   Evolving and changing over time.

ego boundaries   Define where an individual stops and the rest of the world begins.

egocentric communication   An unconstructive form of group contribution that is used to block others or to call attention to oneself.

empathy   Ability to feel with another person—to feel what she or he feels in a situation.

endorsement   Third of three levels of interpersonal confirmation. Endorsement communicates acceptance of another's thoughts and feelings. Endorsement is not the same as agreement.

environmental factors   Elements of settings that affect how we feel and act. Environmental factors are a type of nonverbal communication.

ethnocentrism   The tendency to regard ourselves and our way of life as superior to other people and other ways of life.

evidence   Material used to interest, move, or persuade people. Types of evidence are statistics, examples, comparisons, quotations, and visual aids.

examples   Form of evidence that uses single instances to make a point, dramatize an idea, or personalize information. There are four types of examples: undetailed, detailed, hypothetical, and anecdotes or stories.

explorational communication   Stage in the escalation path of romantic relationships in which individuals explore various common interests and backgrounds that might provide a basis for further interaction.

extemporaneous speaking   Presentational style that includes preparation and practice, but actual words and nonverbal behaviors aren't memorized.

fantasy themes   Ideas that spin out in a group and capture its social and task themes.

feedback   Responses to a message that may be verbal or nonverbal or both. Feedback appeared first in interactive models of communication.

goal-focused analysis   Method of audience analysis that seeks information about listeners that relates directly to the speaker's topic and purpose.

grave dressing   Final stage in the deterioration of romantic relationships in which partners "put the relationship to rest."

group   Three or more individuals who interact over time, are interdependent, and follow shared rules of conduct in order to reach a common goal. One type of group is a team.

groupthink   Exists when members cease to think critically and independently about ideas generated by a group.

halo effect   Occurs when an expert in one area is assumed to also be an expert in other areas that may be unrelated to the individual's expertise.

haptics   Form of nonverbal communication that involves physical touch.

hearing   A physiological activity that occurs when sound waves hit our eardrums. Unlike listening, hearing is a passive process.

identity scripts Guides to action based on rules for living and identity. Initially communicated in families, identity scripts define our roles, how we are to play them, and basic elements in the plot of our lives.

impromptu speaking Involves little preparation. Speakers think on their feet as they talk about ideas and positions with which they are familiar.

indexing Technique of noting that statements reflect specific times and circumstances and may not apply to other times and/or circumstances.

individualism Pronounced Western value that holds that each person is unique and important and should be recognized for her or his individual activities.

informational listening Listening to gain and understand information. The focus of informational listening tends to be on the content level of meaning.

initial credibility The expertise and trustworthiness listeners grant a speaker before a presentation begins. Initial credibility is based on titles, positions, experiences, or achievements that are known to listeners before they hear a speech.

inoculation Immunization of listeners in advance against opposing ideas and arguments that they may later encounter.

intensifying communication Stage in the escalation of romantic relationships that increases the depth of a relationship by increasing personal knowledge and allowing a couple to begin creating a private culture. Also called euphoria.

interpersonal communication Deals with communication between people, usually in close relationships such as friendship and romance.

interpretation The subjective process of evaluating and explaining perceptions.

intrapersonal communication Communication with ourselves, or self-talk.

intrapsychic phase The second phase in disintegration of romantic relationships, this involves brooding about problems in the relationship and dissatisfactions with a partner.

invention The creation of tools, ideas, and practices. Invention is one of four ways cultures change.

investment Something put into a relationship that cannot be recovered should the relationship end. Investments, more than rewards and love, increase commitment.

invitational communication Second stage in the escalation phase of romantic relationships. In this stage, individuals signal they are interested in interacting and respond to invitations from others.

key word outline An abbreviated speaking outline that includes only key words for each point in a speech. The key words trigger a speaker's memory of the full point.

kinesics Body position and body motions, including those of the face.

laissez-faire leadership From the French term meaning "do nothing," this style of leadership is nondirective and sometimes leads to unproductive groups.

listening A complex process that consists of being mindful, physically receiving messages, selecting and organizing information, interpreting, responding, and remembering.

literal listening Listening only to the content level of meaning and ignoring the relational level of meaning.

loaded language An extreme form of evaluative language that relies on words that strongly slant perceptions and, thus, meanings.

manuscript speaking Presentational style that involves speaking from a complete manuscript of a speech.

memorized speaking Presentational style in which a speech is memorized word-for-word in advance.

mindfulness A concept from Zen Buddhism that refers to being fully present in the moment. Being mindful is the first step of listening and the foundation for all other steps.

mind map A holistic record of information on a topic. Mind mapping is a method that can be used to narrow speech topics and/or to keep track of information gathered during research.

mindreading Assuming we understand what another person thinks or how another person perceives something.

minimal encouragers Communication that gently invites another person to elaborate by expressing interest in hearing more.

monopolizing Hogging the stage by continuously focusing communication on ourselves instead of the person who is talking.

multilingual Ability to speak and think in more than one language or with more than one cultural perspective.

narrative speaking Rendering a story to share experiences, build community, pass on history, or teach a lesson.

neutralization One of four responses to relational dialectics. Neutralization involves balancing or finding a compromise between two dialectical poles.

noise Anything that interferes with intended communication.

nonverbal communication All forms of communication other than words themselves. Nonverbal communication includes inflection and other vocal qualities as well as several other behaviors.

norms Informal rules that guide how members of a culture think, feel, and act. Norms define what is normal, or appropriate, in various situations.

oral style Visual, vocal, and verbal aspects of the delivery of a public speech.

organizational culture Understandings about identity and codes of thought and action that are shared by members of an organization.

overt conflict Conflict that is expressed directly and in a straightforward manner.

paralanguage Communication that is vocal but does not include actual words. Sounds, vocal qualities, accents, and inflection are examples of paralanguage.

paraphrasing A method of clarifying others' meaning by reflecting our interpretations of their communication back to them.

participation Response to cultural diversity in which individuals incorporate some practices, customs, and traditions of other groups into their own lives.

particular others One source of social perspectives that individuals use to define themselves and guide how they think, act, and feel. The perspectives of particular others are the viewpoints of specific individuals who are significant to the self.

passion Intensely positive feelings and desires for another person. Passion is based on rewards from involvement and is not equivalent to commitment.

perception An active process of selecting, organizing, and interpreting people, objects, events, situations, and activities.

personal constructs Bipolar "mental yardsticks" that allow us to measure people and situations along specific dimensions of judgment.

personal relationship Defined by uniqueness, rules, relational dialectics, commitment, and embeddedness in contexts. Personal relationships, unlike social ones, are irreplaceable.

person-perception The ability to perceive another as a unique and distinct individual apart from social roles and generalizations.

perspective of the generalized other The collection of rules, roles, and attitudes endorsed by the whole social community in which we live.

physical appearance Physical features of individuals and the values attached to those features. Physical appearance is one type of nonverbal communication.

positive visualization A technique for reducing speaking anxiety in which an individual visualizes herself or himself communicating effectively in progressively challenging speaking situations.

power The ability to influence others. This is a feature of small groups that affects participation.

power over The ability to help or harm others. Power over others is usually communicated in ways that highlight the status and influence of the person using power over others.

power to The ability to empower others to reach their goals. Individuals who use power to help others generally do not highlight their own status and influence.

procedural communication One of three constructive ways of participating in group decision making. Procedural communication orders ideas and coordinates contributions of members.

process Something that is ongoing and continuously in motion, and for which it is difficult to identify beginnings and endings. Communication is a process.

prototypes Knowledge structures that define the clearest or most representative examples of some category.

proxemics A type of nonverbal communication that includes space and how we use it.

pseudolistening Pretending to listen.

psychological responsibility Responsibility to remember, plan, and coordinate domestic work and child care. In general, women assume psychological responsibility for child care and housework, even if both partners share in the actual doing of tasks.

punctuation Defining the beginning and ending of interaction or interaction episodes.

quality circle Group in which individuals from different departments or areas in an organization collaborate to solve problems, meet needs, or increase the quality of worklife.

quotation Form of evidence that uses exact citations of statements made by others. Also called testimony.

recognition Most basic kind of interpersonal confirmation. Recognition communicates awareness that another person exists and is present.

reflected appraisal Process of seeing and thinking about ourselves in terms of the appraisals of us that others reflect.

reframing One of four responses to relational dialectics. The reframing response transcends the apparent contradiction between two dialectical poles and reinterprets them as not in tension.

regulative rules Communication rules that regulate interaction by specifying when, how, where, and with whom to talk about certain things.

relational culture A private world of rules, understandings, and patterns of acting and interpreting that partners create to give meaning to their relationship. Relational culture is the nucleus of intimacy.

relational dialectics Opposing forces, or tensions, that are normal parts of all relationships. The three relational dialectics are autonomy/intimacy, novelty/routine, and openness/closedness.

relational listening Listening to support another person and/or to understand another person's feelings and perceptions. The focus of relational listening is on the relational level of meaning as much as it is on the content level of meaning.

relationship level of meaning One of two levels of meaning in communication. The relationship level of meaning expresses the relationship between communicators.

remembering The process of recalling what you have heard. This is the sixth part of listening.

resistance Response to cultural diversity that occurs when we attack the cultural practices of others or proclaim that our own cultural traditions are superior.

respect Response to cultural diversity in which an individual respects others' customs, traditions, values, and so forth even if the individual does not actively incorporate those into her or his own life.

responding Symbolizing your interest in what is being said with observable feedback to speakers during the process of interaction. This is the fifth of six elements in listening.

revising communication A stage in the escalation of romantic relationships that many, but not all, couples experience. Revising involves evaluating a relationship and working out any obstacles or problems before committing for the long term.

rules Patterned ways of behaving and interpreting behavior. All relationships develop rules.

schemata Cognitive structures we use to organize and interpret experiences. Four types of schemata are prototypes, personal constructs, stereotypes, and scripts.

scripts One of four cognitive schemata. Scripts define expected or appropriate sequences of action in particular settings.

segmentation One of four responses to relational dialectics. Segmentation responses meet one dialectical need while ignoring or not satisfying the contradictory dialectical need.

selective listening Focusing on only selected parts of communication. We listen selectively when we screen out parts of a message that don't interest us or with which we disagree, and also when we rivet attention on parts of communication that do interest us or with which we agree.

self A multidimensional process that involves forming and acting from social perspectives that arise and evolve in communication with others and ourselves.

self-disclosure Revealing personal information about ourselves that others are unlikely to discover in other ways.

self-fulfilling prophecy Acting in ways that bring about expectations or judgments of ourselves.

self-sabotage Self-talk that communicates we are no good, we can't do something, we can't change, and so forth. Self-sabotaging communication undermines belief in ourselves and motivation to change and grow.

self-serving bias Tendency to attribute our positive actions and successes to stable, global, internal influences that we control, and to attribute negative actions and failures to unstable, specific, external influences beyond our control.

separation One of four responses to relational dialectics. The separation response occurs when friends or romantic partners assign one pole of a dialectic to certain spheres of activities or topics and assign the contradictory dialectical pole to distinct spheres of activities or topics.

silence Lack of verbal communication or paralanguage. Silence is a type of nonverbal communication that can express powerful messages.

similes Direct comparisons that typically use either *like* or *as* to link two things.

skills training A method of reducing communication apprehension that assumes anxiety results from lack of speaking skills and, thus, can be reduced by learning skills.

social climbing The process of trying to increase personal status in a group by winning the approval of high-status members.

social comparison Involves comparing ourselves with others to form judgments of our own talents, abilities, qualities, and so forth.

social phase Part of relational disintegration in which partners figure out how to inform outsiders that the relationship is ending.

social relationship Unlike personal relationships, social ones tend to follow broad social scripts and rules, and members of them tend to assume conventional social roles in relation to one another. Social relationships, unlike personal ones, can be replaced.

social support Phase of relational decline in which partners look to friends and family for support during the trauma of breaking up.

specific purpose Behavioral objective, or observable response, that a speaker specifies as a gauge of effectiveness. The specific purpose reinforces more general speaking goals.

speech to entertain Speech in which the primary goal is to amuse, interest, or engage listeners.

speech to inform Speech in which the primary goal is to increase listeners' understanding, awareness, or knowledge about some topic.

speech to persuade Speech in which the primary goal is to change listeners' attitudes, beliefs, or behaviors and/or to motivate listeners to action.

standard agenda A logical seven-step method for making decisions.

standpoint theory Claims that a culture includes a number of social groups that differently shape the perceptions, identities, and opportunities of members of those groups.

static evaluation Assessments that suggest something is unchanging or static. "Bob is impatient" is a static evaluation.

statistics Form of evidence that uses numbers to summarize a great many individual cases or that demonstrates relationships among phenomena.

stereotypes Predictive generalizations about people and situations.

survey research Involves asking a number of people about their opinions, preferences, actions, or beliefs relevant to a speaking topic.

symbols Arbitrary, ambiguous, and abstract representations of other phenomena. Symbols are the basis of language, much nonverbal behavior, and human thought.

synergy A special kind of energy in groups that combines and goes beyond the energies, talents, and strengths of individual members.

system A group of interrelated elements that affect one another. Communication is systemic.

systematic desensitization Method of reducing communication apprehension that, first, teaches individuals how to relax physiologically and then helps them practice feeling relaxed as they imagine themselves in progressively difficult communication situations.

task communication One of three constructive forms of participation in group decision making. Task communication focuses on giving and analyzing information and ideas.

team A special kind of group that is characterized by different and complementary resources of members and by a strong sense of collective identity. All teams are groups, but not all groups are teams.

terminal credibility The cumulative expertise and trustworthiness listeners confer on a speaker as a result of initial and derived credibility. Terminal credibility may be greater or less than initial credibility, depending on how effectively a speaker communicates.

thesis statement The main idea of an entire speech. It should capture the key message in a concise sentence that listeners can remember easily.

tolerance Response to diversity in which a person accepts differences, although she or he may not approve of or even understand them.

totalizing Responding to persons as if one aspect of them is the total of who they are.

transitions Words and sentences that connect ideas and main points in a speech so that listeners can follow a speaker.

understanding Response to cultural diversity that assumes differences are rooted in cultural teachings and that no traditions, customs, and behaviors are intrinsically more valuable than others.

uppers People who communicate positively about us and who confirm with positive appraisals our worth as individuals.

values Views of what is good, right, and important that are shared by members of a particular culture.

visual aids Form of evidence that uses visual objects such as charts, graphs, photographs, and physical objects either to reinforce ideas presented verbally or to provide information in their own right.

voting Method of group decision making in which a decision is made based on the support of a certain number of group members. Some groups have simple majority rule, while others require two-thirds or three-fourths support.

vulture Extreme form of a downer. Vultures attack a person's self-concept and sense of self-worth. Vultures may be others who attack an individual or the individual who attacks herself or himself.

Acitelli, L. (1988). When spouses talk to each other about their relationship. *Journal of Social and Personal Relationships, 5,* 185–199.

Acitelli, L. (1993). You, me, and us: Perspectives on relationship awareness. In S. W. Duck (Ed.), *Understanding relationship processes, 1: Individuals in relationships* (pp. 144–174). Newbury Park, CA: Sage.

Adler, R., & Towne, N. (1993). *Looking out/looking in* (7th ed.). Fort Worth, TX: Harcourt Brace Jovanovich.

Alcoff, L. (1991, Winter). The problem of speaking for others. *Cultural Critique,* pp. 5–32.

Alexander, E. R., III. (1979). The reduction of cognitive conflict: Effects of various types of communication. *Journal of Conflict Resolution, 23,* 120–138.

Allen, M., Hale, J., Mongeau, P., Berkowitz-Stafford, S., Stafford, S., Shanahan, W., Agee, P., Dillon, K., Jackson, R., & Ray, C. (1990). Testing a model of message sidedness: Three replications. *Communication Monographs, 37,* 275–291.

Allen, M., Hunter, J., & Donahue, W. (1989). Meta-analysis of self-report data on the effectiveness of public speaking anxiety treatment techniques. *Communication Education, 38,* 54–76.

Andersen, M. L., & Collins, P. H. (Eds.). (1992). *Race, class, and gender: An anthology.* Belmont, CA: Wadsworth.

Andersen, P. (1993). Cognitive schemata in personal relationships. In S. W. Duck (Ed.), *Understanding relationship processes, 1: Individuals in relationships* (pp. 1–29). Newbury Park, CA: Sage.

Angelou, M. (1990). *I shall not be moved.* New York: Random House.

Argyle, M., & Henderson, M. (1984). The rules of friendship. *Journal of Social and Personal Relationships, 1,* 211–237.

Argyle, M., & Henderson, M. (1985). The rules of relationships. In S. W. Duck & D. Perlman (Eds.), *Understanding personal relationships: An interdisciplinary approach* (pp. 63–84). Beverly Hills, CA: Sage.

Aries, E. (1987). Gender and communication. In P. Shaver (Ed.), *Sex and gender* (pp. 149–176). Newbury Park, CA: Sage.

Axtell, R. (1990a). *Dos and taboos around the world* (2nd ed.). New York: Wiley.

Axtell, R. (1990b). *Dos and taboos of hosting international visitors.* New York: Wiley.

Ayres, J., & Hopf, T. S. (1990). The long-term effect of visualization in the classroom: A brief research report. *Communication Education, 39,* 75–78.

Bach, G. R., & Wyden, P. (1973). *The intimate enemy: How to fight fair in love and marriage.* New York: Avon.

Baine, D. (1986). *Memory and instruction.* Englewood Cliffs, NJ: Educational Technology Publications.

Baird, J. E., Jr. (1974). The effects of speech summaries upon audience comprehension of expository speeches of varying quality and complexity. *Central States Speech Journal, 25,* 124–135.

Baker, E. E. (1965). The immediate effects of perceived speaker disorganization on speaker credibility and audience attitude change in persuasive speaking. *Western Journal of Speech Communication, 29,* 148–161.

Barker, L., Edwards, R., Gaines, C., Gladney, K., & Holley, F. (1981). An investigation of proportional time spent in various communication activities by college students. *Journal of Applied Communication Research, 8,* 101–109.

Barnes, M. K., & Duck, S. (1994). Everyday communicative contexts for social support. In B. Burleson, T. Albrecht, & I. Sarason (Eds.), *Communication of social support* (pp. 175–194). Thousand Oaks, CA: Sage.

Baron, R. A., & Berne, D. (1994). *Social psychology* (7th ed.). Boston, MA: Allyn & Bacon.

Bartholomew, K., & Horowitz, L. M. (1991). Attachment styles among young adults: A test of a four-category model. *Journal of Personality and Social Psychology, 61,* 226–244.

Bass, B. M. (1990). *Bass and Stogdill's handbook of leadership: Theory, research, and managerial applications* (3rd ed.). New York: Free Press.

Bateson, M. C. (1990). *Composing a life.* New York: Penguin/Plume.

Baxter, L. A. (1984). Trajectories of relationship disengagement. *Journal of Social and Personal Relationships, 7,* 141–178.

Baxter, L. A. (1985). Accomplishing relational disengagement. In S. Duck & D. Perlman (Eds.), *Understanding personal relationships: An interdisciplinary approach* (pp. 243–265). Beverly Hills, CA: Sage.

Baxter, L. A. (1987). Symbols of relationship identity in relationship cultures. *Journal of Social and Personal Relationships, 4,* 261–279.

Baxter, L. A. (1988). A dialectical perspective on communication strategies in relationship development. In S. W. Duck, D. F. Hay, S. E. Hobfoll, W. Iches, & B. Montgomery (Eds.), *Handbook of personal relationships* (pp. 257–273). London: Wiley.

Baxter, L. A. (1990). Dialectical contradictions in relational development. *Journal of Social and Personal Relationships, 7,* 69–88.

Baxter, L. A. (1993). The social side of personal relationships: A dialectical perspective. In S. Duck (Ed.), *Understanding relationship processes, 3: Social context and relationships* (pp. 139–165). Newbury Park, CA: Sage.

Baxter, L. A., & Simon, E. P. (1993). Relationship maintenance strategies and dialectical contradictions in personal relationships. *Journal of Social and Personal Relationships, 10,* 225–242.

Beatty, M. J., & Behnke, R. R. (1991). Effects of public speaking trait anxiety and intensity of speaking task on heart rate during performance. *Human Communication Research, 18,* 147–176.

Beatty, M. J., Plax, T., & Kearney, P. (1985). Reinforcement vs. modeling theory in the development of communication apprehension: A retrospective analysis. *Communication Research Reports, 12,* 80–95.

Be civil. (1994, July 5). *Wall Street Journal,* p. A1.

Beck, A. (1988). *Love is never enough.* New York: Harper & Row.

Becker, C. S. (1987). Friendship between women: A phenomenological study of best friends. *Journal of Phenomenological Psychology, 18,* 59–72.

Bellah, R., Madsen, R., Sullivan, W., Swindler, A., & Tipton, S. (1985). *Habits of the heart: Individualism and commitment in American life.* Berkeley, CA: University of California Press.

Belsky, J., & Pensky, E. (1988). Developmental history, personality, and family relationships: Toward an emergent family system. In R. A. Hinde & J. Stevenson-Hinde (Eds.), *Relationships within families: Mutual influences* (pp. 193–217). Oxford, UK: Clarendon.

Benjamin, D., & Horwitz, T. (1994, July 14). German view: "You Americans work too hard—and for what?" *Wall Street Journal,* pp. B1, B6.

Berg, J. H. (1987). Responsiveness and self-disclosure. In V. J. Derlega & J. H. Berg (Eds.), *Self-disclosure: Theory, research, and therapy.* New York: Plenum.

Berger, C. R., & Bell, R. A. (1988). Plans and the initiation of social relationships. *Human Communication Research, 15,* 217–235.

Berger, P. (1969). *A rumor of angels: Modern society and the rediscovery of the supernatural.* Garden City, NY: Doubleday.

Berger, P., & Kellner, H. (1964). Marriage and the construction of reality: An exercise in the microsociology of knowledge. *Diogenes, 46,* 1–24.

Bergner, R. M., & Bergner, L. L. (1990). Sexual misunderstanding: A descriptive and pragmatic formulation. *Psychotherapy, 27,* 464–467.

Berne, E. (1964). *Games people play.* New York: Grove.

Bernstein, B. (Ed.). (1973). *Class, codes, and control,* (Vol. 2). London: Routledge & Kegan Paul.

Bingham, S. (Ed.). (1994). *Conceptualizing sexual harassment as discursive practice.* Westport, CT: Praeger.

Birdwhistell, R. (1970). *Kinesics and context.* Philadelphia: University of Pennsylvania Press.

Blumer, H. (1969). *Symbolic interaction: Perspective and method.* Englewood Cliffs, NJ: Prentice-Hall.

Blumstein, P., & Kollock, P. (1988). Personal relationships. *Annual Review of Sociology, 14,* 467–490.

Blumstein, P., & Schwartz, P. (1983). *American couples: Money, work, and sex.* New York: William Morrow.

Bolton, R. (1986). Listening is more than merely hearing. In J. Stewart (Ed.), *Bridges, not walls* (4th ed., pp. 159–179). New York: Random House.

Booth-Butterfield, M., & Booth-Butterfield, S. (1994). Communication anxiety and signing effectiveness: Testing an interference model among deaf communicators. *Journal of Applied Communication Research, 22,* 273–286.

Bormann, E. G. (1975). *Discussion and group methods: Theory and practice.* New York: Harper & Row.

Bormann, E. G., Putnam L. L., & Pratt, J. M. (1978). Power, authority and sex: Male response to female dominance. *Communication Monographs, 45,* 119–155.

Bostrom, R. N. (1988). *Communicating in public: Speaking and listening.* Santa Rosa, CA: Burgess.

Boulding, K. (1990). *Three faces of power.* Newbury Park, CA: Sage.

Bourhis, J., & Allen, M. (1992). Meta-analysis of the relationship between communication apprehension and cognitive performance. *Communication Education, 41,* 68–76.

Bowen, S. P., & Michal-Johnson, P. (1996). Gendered negotiation about safer sex. In J. T. Wood (Ed.), *Gendered relationships* (pp. 177–196). Mountain View, CA: Mayfield.

Bowlby, J. (1973). *Separation: Attachment and loss* (Vol. 2). New York: Basic Books.

Bowlby, J. (1988). *A secure base: Parent–child attachment and healthy human development.* New York: Basic Books.

Bowles, J. G. (1990, September 24). The human side of quality. *Fortune,* n.p.

Bozzi, V. (1986, February). Eat to the beat. *Psychology Today,* p. 16.

Bradbury, T. N., & Fincham, F. D. (1990). Attributions in marriage: Review and critique. *Psychological Bulletin, 107,* 3–33.

Bradley, B. (1978). *Fundamentals of speech communication: The credibility of ideas* (2nd ed.). Dubuque, IA: William C. Brown.

Brehm, S. (1992). *Intimate relations* (2nd ed.). New York: McGraw-Hill.

Brock-Utne, B. (1989). *Feminist perspectives on peace and peace education.* New York: Pergamon Press.

Buber, M. (1957). Distance and relation. *Psychiatry, 20,* 97–104.

Buber, M. (1970). *I and thou* (Trans. Walter Kaufmann). New York: Scribner.

Burgoon, J. K., Buller, D. B., Hale, J. L., & deTurck, M. A. (1984). Relational messages associated with nonverbal behaviors. *Human Communication Research, 10,* 351–378.

Burgoon, J. K., Buller, D. B., & Woodhall, G. W. (1989). *Nonverbal communication: The unspoken dialogue.* New York: Harper & Row.

Buss, A. H. (1980). *Self-consciousness and social anxiety.* San Francisco: W. H. Freeman.

Butler, H. E. (Trans.). (1950). *The institutio oratoria of Quintilian* (Vol. 3, book 7). Cambridge, MA: Harvard University Press.

Caldera, Y. M., Huston, A. C., & O'Brien, M. (1989). Social interactions and play patterns of parents and toddlers with feminine, masculine, and neutral toys. *Child Development, 60,* 70–76.

Campbell, K. K. (1989). *Man cannot speak for her.* New York: Prager.

Canary, D., & Stafford, L. (Eds.). (1994). *Communication and relational maintenance.* New York: Academic.

Cancian, F. (1989). Love and the rise of capitalism. In B. Risman & P. Schwartz (Eds.), *Gender in intimate relationships* (pp. 12–25). Belmont, CA: Wadsworth.

Capella, J. N. (1991). The biological origins of automated patterns of human interaction. *Communication Theory, 1,* 4–35.

Caspi, A., & Harbener, E. S. (1990). Continuity and change: Assortive marriage and the consistency of personality in adulthood. *Journal of Personality and Social Psychology, 58,* 250–258.

Cassirer, E. (1944). *An essay on man.* New Haven: Yale University Press.

Chesebro, J. W. (1995). Communication technologies as cognitive systems. In J. T. Wood & R. B. Gregg (Eds.), *Toward the 21st Century.* Cresskill, NJ: Hampton.

Christophel, D. M. (1990). The relationships among teacher immediacy behaviors, student motivation, and learning. *Communication Education, 39,* 323–340.

Cissna, K. N. L., & Sieburg, E. (1986). Patterns of interactional confirmation and disconfirmation. In J. Stewart (Ed.), *Bridges, not walls* (4th ed., pp. 230–239). New York: Random House.

Civickly, J. M., Pace, R. W., & Krause, R. M. (1977). Interviewer and client behaviors in supportive and defensive interviews. In B. D. Ruben (Ed.), *Communication yearbook, 1* (pp. 347–362). New Brunswick, NJ: Transaction Books.

Clair, R. P. (1993). The use of framing devices to sequester organizational narratives: Hegemony and harassment. *Communication Monographs, 60,* 113–136.

Clements, M. (1994, August 7). Sex in America today. *Parade,* pp. 4–6.

Cloven, D. H., & Roloff, M. E. (1991). Sense-making activities and interpersonal conflict: Communicative cures for the mulling blues. *Western Journal of Speech Communication, 55,* 134–158.

Condry, S. M., Condry, J. C., & Pogatshnik, L. W. (1983). Sex differences: A study of the ear of the beholder. *Sex Roles, 9,* 697–704.

Conrad, C. (1995). Was Pogo right? In J. T. Wood & R. B. Gregg (Ed.), *Toward the 21st Century.* Cresskill, NJ: Hampton.

Cooley, C. H. (1912). *Human nature and the social order.* New York: Scribner.

Cosby, P. (1973). Self-disclosure: A literature review. *Psychological Bulletin, 79,* 73–91.

Cox, J. R. (1989). The fulfillment of time: King's "I have a dream" speech (August 28, 1963). In M. C. Leff & F. J. Kaufeld (Eds.), *Texts in context: Critical dialogues on significant episodes in American rhetoric* (pp. 181–204). Davis, CA: Hermagoras Press.

Cronen, V., Pearce, W. B., & Snavely, L. (1979). A theory of rule-structure and types of episodes and a study of perceived enmeshment in undesired repetitive patterns ("URPs"). In D. Nimmo (Ed.), *Communication Yearbook, 3.* New Brunswick, NJ: Transaction Books.

Crowley, G. (1995, March 6). Dialing the stress-meter down. *Newsweek,* p. 62.

Cunningham, J. A., Strassberg, D. S., & Haan, B. (1986). Effects of intimacy and sex-role congruency on self-disclosure. *Journal of Social and Clinical Psychology, 4,* 393–401.

Cunningham, J. D., & Antill, J. K. (1995). Current trends in nonmarital cohabitation: The great POSSLQ hunt continues. In J. T. Wood & S. W. Duck (Eds.), *Understanding relationship processes, 6: Off the beaten track: Understudied relationships* (pp. 148–172). Thousand Oaks, CA: Sage.

Daly, J., & McCroskey, J. (Eds.). (1984). *Avoiding communication: Shyness, reticence, and communication apprehension.* Beverly Hills, CA: Sage.

Dance, F. E. X. (1970). The concept of communication. *Journal of Communication, 20,* 201–210.

Darnell, D. K. (1963). The relationship between sentence order and comprehension. *Speech Monographs, 30,* 97–100.

Davis, F. (1991). *Moving the mountain: The women's movement in America since 1960.* New York: Simon & Schuster.

Death toll from AIDS escalating (1991, January 21). *Dayton Daily News,* p. 4A.

DeFleur, M. L., & Ball-Rokeach, S. (1989). *Theories of mass communicaton* (5th ed.). White Plains, NY: Longman.

DeFrancisco, V. (1991). The sounds of silence: How men silence women in marital relations. *Discourse and Society, 2,* 413–423.

Delia, J., Clark, R. A., & Switzer, D. (1974). Cognitive complexity and impression formation in informal social interaction. *Speech Monographs, 41,* 299–308.

Deming, W. E. (1982). *Out of the crisis.* Cambridge, MA: Cambridge University Press.

Derlega, V. J., & Berg, J. H. (1987). *Self-disclosure: Research, theory, and therapy.* New York: Plenum.

Dickson, F. (1995). The best is yet to be: Research on long-lasting marriages. In J. T. Wood & S. W. Duck (Eds.), *Understanding relationship processes, 6: Off the beaten track: Understudied relationships* (pp. 22–50). Thousand Oaks, CA: Sage.

Dindia, K. (1994). A multiphasic view of relationship maintenance strategies. In D. Canary & L. Stafford (Eds.), *Communication and relational maintenance* (pp. 91–112). New York: Academic Press.

Dixson, M., & Duck, S. W. (1993). Understanding relationship processes: Uncovering the human search for meaning. In S. W. Duck (Ed.), *Understanding relationship processes, 1: Individuals in relationships* (pp. 175–206). Newbury Park, CA: Sage.

Duck, S. W. (1985). Social and personal relationships. In M. L. Knapp & G. R. Miller (Eds.), *Handbook of interpersonal communication* (pp. 655–686). Beverly Hills, CA: Sage.

Duck, S. W. (1990). Relationships as unfinished business: Out of the frying pan and into the 1990s. *Journal of Social and Personal Relationships, 7,* 5–24.

Duck, S. W. (1992). *Human relationships* (2nd ed.). Newbury Park, CA: Sage.

Duck, S. W. (1994a). *Meaningful relationships.* Thousand Oaks, CA: Sage.

Duck, S. W. (1994b). Steady as (s)he goes: Relational maintenance as a shared meaning system. In D. Canary & L. Stafford (Eds.), Communication and relational maintenance (pp. 45–60). New York: Academic Press.

Duck, S. W., & Wood, J. T. (Eds.). (1995). *Understanding relationship processes, 5: Confronting relationship challenges.* Thousand Oaks, CA: Sage.

Eadie, W. F. (1982). Defensive communication revisited: A critical examination of Gibb's theory. *Southern Speech Communication Journal, 47,* 163–177.

Eckman, P., Friesen, W., & Ellsworth, P. (1971). *Emotion in the human face: Guidelines for research and an integration of findings.* Elmsford, NY: Pergamon.

Egan, G. (1973). Listening as empathic support. In J. Stewart (Ed.), *Bridges, not walls.* Reading, MA: Addison-Wesley.

Ellis, A., & Harper, R. (1977). *A new guide to rational living.* North Hollywood, CA: Wilshire Books.

Entman, R. M. (1994). African Americans according to TV news. *Media Studies Journal, 8,* 29–38.

Ernst, F., Jr. (1973). *Who's listening? A handbook of the transactional analysis of the listening function.* Vallejo, CA: Addresso'set.

Estes, W. K. (1989). Learning theory. In A. Lessold & R. Glaser (Eds.), *Foundations for a psychology of education.* Hillsdale, NJ: Lawrence Erlbaum.

Evans, D. (1993, March 1). The wrong examples. *Newsweek,* p. 10.

Faludi, S. (1991). *Backlash: The undeclared war against American women.* New York: Crown.

Fehr, B. (1993). How do I love thee: Let me consult my prototype. In S. W. Duck (Ed.), *Understanding relationship processes, 1: Individuals in relationships* (pp. 87–122). Newbury Park, CA: Sage.

Fehr, B., & Russell, J. A. (1991). Concept of love viewed from a prototype perspective. *Journal of Personality and Social Psychology, 60,* 425–438.

Ferrante, J. (1992). *Sociology: A global perspective.* Belmont, CA: Wadsworth.

Ferrante, J. (1995). *Sociology: A global perspective* (2nd ed.). Belmont, CA: Wadsworth.

Fincham, F. D., & Bradbury, T. N. (1987). The impact of attributions in marriage: A longitudinal analysis. *Journal of Personality and Social Psychology, 53,* 510–517.

Fisher, B. A. (1987). *Interpersonal communication: The pragmatics of human relationships.* New York: Random House.

Fisher, J. D., & Byrne, D. (1975). Too close for comfort: Sex differences in response to invasions of personal space. *Journal of Personal and Social Psychology, 32,* 15–21.

Fitzpatrick, M. A. (1988). *Between husbands and wives: Communication in marriage.* Newbury Park, CA: Sage.

Fitzpatrick, M. A., & Best, P. (1979). Dyadic adjustment in relational types: Consensus, cohesion, affectional expression and satisfaction in enduring relationships. *Communication Monographs, 46,* 167–178.

Fletcher, G. J., & Fincham, F. D. (1991). Attribution in close relationships. In G. J. Fletcher & F. D. Fincham (Eds.), *Cognition in close relationships* (pp. 7–35). Hillsdale, NJ: Lawrence Erlbaum.

Fowers, B. J. (1991). His and her marriage: A multivariate study of gender and marital satisfaction. *Sex Roles, 24,* 209–221.

Fox-Genovese, E. (1991). *Feminism without illusions.* Chapel Hill, NC: University of North Carolina Press.

French, M. (1992). *The war against women.* New York: Summit.

Gabriel, S. L., & Smithson, I. (Eds.). (1990). *Gender in the classroom: Power and pedagogy.* Urbana, IL: University of Illinois Press.

Gaines, S., Jr. (1995). Relationships between members of cultural minorities. In J. T. Wood & S. W. Duck (Eds.), *Understanding relationship processes, 6: Off the beaten track: Understudied relationships* (pp. 51–88). Thousand Oaks, CA: Sage.

Gandy, O. H., Jr. (1994). From bad to worse—the media's framing of race and risk. *Media Studies Journal* (Special issue: Race—America's rawest nerve), *8,* 39–48.

Garner, T. (1994). Oral rhetorical practice in African American culture. In A. González, M. Houston, & V. Chen (Eds.), *Our voices: Essays in culture, ethnicity, and communication* (pp. 81–91). Los Angeles: Roxbury.

Gates, H. L. (1992). *Loose canons: Notes on the culture wars.* New York: Oxford University Press.

Gerstel, N., & Gross, H. (1985). *Commuter marriage.* New York: Guilford Press.

Gibb, C. (1969). Leadership. In G. Lindsey & E. Aronson (Eds.), *The handbook of social psychology* (2nd ed., pp. 205–282). Reading, MA: Addison-Wesley.

Gibb, J. R. (1961). Defensive communication. *Journal of Communication, 11,* 141–148.

Gibb, J. R. (1964). Climate for trust formation. In L. Bradford, J. Gibb, & K. Benne (Eds.), *T-group theory and laboratory method* (pp. 279–309). New York: Wiley.

Gibb, J. R. (1970). Sensitivity training as a medium for personal growth and improved interpersonal relationships. *Interpersonal Development, 1,* 6–31.

Gibbs, J. T. (1992). Young black males in America: Endangered, embittered, and embattled. In M. L. Andersen & P. H. Collins (Eds.), *Race, class, and gender: An anthology* (pp. 267–276). Belmont, CA: Wadsworth.

Gochenour, T. (1990). *Considering Filipinos.* Yarmouth, ME: Intercultural Press, Inc.

Goleman, D. (1990, December 25). The group and self: New focus on a cultural rift. *New York Times,* p. 40.

Goodrich, T. J., Rampage, C., Ellman, B., & Halstead, K. (1988). *Feminist family therapy: A casebook.* New York: W. W. Norton.

Gorham, J., & Zakahi, W. R. (1990). A comparison of teacher and student perceptions of immediacy and learning. *Communication Education, 39,* 46–62.

Gottman, J. (1993). The roles of conflict engagement, escalation or avoidance in marital interaction: A longitudinal view of five types of couples. *Journal of Consulting and Clinical Psychology, 61,* 6–15.

Gottman, J. M., & Carrère, S. (1994). Why can't men and women get along? Developmental roots and marital inequities. In D. Canary & L. Stafford (Eds.), *Communication and relational maintenance* (pp. 203–229). New York: Academic Press.

Gottman, J., Markman, H. J., & Notarius, C. (1977). The topography of marital conflict: A sequential analysis of verbal and nonverbal behavior. *Journal of Marriage and the Family, 39,* 461–477.

Gouran, D. S. (1982). *Making decisions in groups: Choices and consequences.* Glenview, IL: Scott, Foresman.

Griffin, K. (1991). *A first look at communication theory.* New York: McGraw-Hill.

Gronbeck, B. E., McKerrow, R., Ehninger, D., & Monroe, A. H. (1994). *Principles and types of speech communication* (12th ed.). Glenview, IL: Scott, Foresman.

Hackman, M. Z., & Walker, K. B. (1990). Instructional communication in the televised classroom: The effects of system design and teacher immediacy on student learning and satisfaction. *Communication Education, 39,* 196–206.

Hall, E. T. (1966). *The hidden dimension.* New York: Anchor.

Hall, E. T. (1968). Proxemics. *Current Anthropology, 9,* 83–108.

Hall, E. T. (1977). *Beyond culture.* New York: Doubleday.

Hall, J. A. (1978). Gender effects in decoding nonverbal cues. *Psychological Bulletin, 85,* 845–857.

Hall, J. A. (1987). On explaining gender differences: The case of nonverbal communication. In P. Shaver & C. Hendricks (Eds.), *Sex and gender* (pp. 177–200). Newbury Park, CA: Sage.

Hamachek, D. (1992). *Encounters with the self* (3rd ed.). Fort Worth: Harcourt Brace Jovanovich.

Hamilton, C. (1996). *Successful public speaking*. Belmont, CA: Wadsworth.

Hansen, J. E., & Schuldt, W. J. (1984). Marital self-disclosure and marital satisfaction. *Journal of Marriage and the Family, 46,* 923–926.

Haraway, D. (1988). Situated knowledges: The science question in feminism and the privilege of partial perspective. *Signs, 14,* 575–599.

Harding, S. (1991). *Whose science? Whose knowledge? Thinking from women's lives*. Ithaca: Cornell University Press.

Harris, T. J. (1969). *I'm OK, you're OK*. New York: Harper & Row.

Hayakawa, S. I. (1962). *The use and misuse of language*. New York: Fawcett Publications.

Hayakawa, S. I. (1964). *Language in thought and action* (2nd ed.). New York: Harcourt, Brace & World.

Hecht, M. L., Collier, M. J., & Ribeau, S. A. (1993). *African American communication: Ethnic identity and cultural interpretation*. Newbury Park, CA: Sage.

Hecht, M. L., Marston, P. J., & Larkey, L. K. (1994). Love ways and relationship quality in heterosexual relationships. *Journal of Social and Personal Relationships, 11,* 25–44.

Hegel, G. W. F. (1807). *Phenomenology of mind*. (Trans. J. B. Baillie). Germany: Wurzburg & Bamburg.

Heider, F. (1958). *The psychology of interpersonal relations*. New York: Wiley.

Helgesen, S. (1990). *The female advantage: Women's ways of leadership*. New York: Doubleday/Currency.

Hendrick, C., & Hendrick, S. (1988). Lovers wear rose colored glasses. *Journal of Social and Personal Relationships, 5,* 161–184.

Hendrick, C., & Hendrick, S. (1996). Gender and the experience of heterosexual love. In J. T. Wood (Ed.), *Gendered relationships* (pp. 131–148). Mountain View, CA: Mayfield.

Hendrick, C., Hendrick, S., Foote, F. H., & Slapion-Foote, M. J. (1984). Do men and women love differently? *Journal of Social and Personal Relationships, 2,* 177–196.

Henley, N. M. (1977). *Body politics: Power, sex and nonverbal communication*. Englewood Cliffs, NJ: Prentice-Hall.

Hershey, P., & Blanchard, K. (1993). *Management of organizational behavior: Utilizing human resources*. Englewood Cliffs, NJ: Prentice-Hall.

Higginbotham, E. (1992). We were never on a pedestal: Women of color continue to struggle with poverty, racism, and sexism. In M. L. Andersen, & P. H. Collins, (Eds.), *Race, class, and gender: An anthology* (pp. 183–190). Belmont, CA: Wadsworth.

Hochschild, A., with Machung, A. (1989). *The second shift*. New York: Viking.

Hofstede, G. (1980). *Cultural consequences: International differences in work-related values*. Beverly Hills, CA: Sage.

Hojat, M. (1982). Loneliness as a function of selected personality variables. *Journal of Clinical Psychology, 38,* 136–141.

Honeycutt, J. M., Woods, B., & Fontenot, K. (1993). The endorsement of communication conflict rules as a function of engagement, marriage and marital ideology. *Journal of Social and Personal Relationships, 10,* 285–304.

Houston, M. (1994). When black women talk with white women: Why dialogues are difficult. In A. González, M. Houston, & V. Chen (Eds.), *Our voices: Essays in culture, ethnicity, and communication* (pp. 133–139). Los Angeles: Roxbury.

Houston, M., & Wood, J. T. (1996). Difficult dialogues, expanded horizons: Communicating across race and class. In J. T. Wood (Ed.), *Gendered relationships* (pp. 39–56). Mountain View, CA: Mayfield.

Huston, M., & Schwartz, P. (1995). Relationships of lesbians and gay men. In J. T. Wood & S. W. Duck (Eds.), *Understanding relationship processes, 6: Understudied relationships: Off the beaten track* (pp. 89–121). Thousand Oaks, CA: Sage.

Huston, M., & Schwartz, P. (1996). Gendered dynamics in the romantic relationships of lesbians and gay men. In J. T. Wood (Ed.), *Gendered relationships* (pp. 163–176). Mountain View, CA: Mayfield.

Huston, T. L., McHale, S. M., & Crouter, A. C. (1986). When the honeymoon is over: Changes in the marriage relationship over the first year. In R. Gilmour & S. Duck (Eds.), *The emerging field of personal relationships* (pp. 109–132). Hillsdale, NJ: Lawrence Erlbaum.

Hyde, M. J. (1995). Human being and the call of technology. In J. T. Wood & R. B. Gregg (Eds.), *Toward the 21st Century*. Cresskill, NJ: Hampton.

Inman, C. C. (1996). Men's friendships: Closeness in the doing. In J. T. Wood (Ed.), *Gendered relationships* (pp. 95–110). Mountain View, CA: Mayfield.

Jackson, S., & Allen, J. (1990). *Meta-analysis of the effectiveness of one-sided and two-sided argumentation*. Paper presented at the International Communication Association. Montreal, Canada.

Jaffe, C. (1995). *Public speaking: A cultural perspective*. Belmont, CA: Wadsworth.

Janis, I. L. (1977). *Victims of groupthink*. Boston: Houghton-Mifflin.

Javidi, A., & Javidi, M. (1994). Cross-cultural analysis of interpersonal bonding: A look at East and West. In L. A. Samovar & R. E. Porter (Eds.), *Intercultural communication: A reader* (7th ed.). Belmont, CA: Wadsworth.

Johnson, C. B., Stockdale, M. S., & Saal, F. E. (1991). Persistence of men's misperceptions of friendly cues across a variety of interpersonal encounters. *Psychology of Women Quarterly, 15*, 463–465.

Johnson, D., & Johnson, F. (1991). *Joining together: Group theory and group skills.* Englewood Cliffs, NJ: Prentice-Hall.

Johnson, F. L. (1989). Women's culture and communication: An analytic perspective. In C. M. Lont & S. A. Friedley (Eds.), *Beyond the boundaries: Sex and gender diversity in communication.* Fairfax, VA: George Mason University Press.

Johnson, F. L. (1996). Women's friendships: Closeness in dialogue. In J. T. Wood (Ed.), *Gendered relationships* (pp. 79–94). Mountain View, CA: Mayfield.

Jones, E., & Gallois, C. (1989). Spouses' impressions of rules for communication in public and private marital conflicts. *Journal of Marriage and the Family, 51*, 957–967.

Jones, W. H., & Moore, T. L. (1989). Loneliness and social support. In M. Hojat & R. Crandall (Eds.), *Loneliness: Theory, research, and applications* (pp. 145–156). Newbury Park, CA: Sage.

Kaye, L. W., & Applegate, J. S. (1990). Men as elder caregivers: A response to changing families. *American Journal of Orthopsychiatry, 60*, 86–95.

Keeley, M. P., & Hart, A. J. (1994). Nonverbal behavior in dyadic interaction. In S. W. Duck (Ed.), *Understanding relationship processes, 4: Dynamics of relationships* (pp. 135–162). Thousand Oaks, CA: Sage.

Kelley, H. H. (1967). Attribution theory in social psychology. In D. Levine (Ed.), *Nebraska symposium on motivation* (Vol. 15, pp. 192–238). Lincoln: University of Nebraska Press.

Kelly, C., Huston, T. L., & Cate, R. M. (1985). Premarital relationship correlates of the erosion of satisfaction in marriage. *Journal of Social and Personal Relationships, 2,* 167–178.

Kelly, G. A. (1955). *The psychology of personal constructs.* New York: W. W. Norton.

Keyes, R. (1992, February 22). Do you have the time? *Parade,* pp. 22–25.

Kiesler, C. A., & Kiesler, S. B. (1971). Role of forewarning in persuasive communications. *Journal of Abnormal and Social Psychology, 18,* 210–221.

Kinlaw, D. C. (1991). *Developing superior work teams: Building quality and the competitive edge.* Lexington, MA: Lexington Books.

Klopf, D. W. (1991). *Intercultural encounters: The fundamentals of intercultural communication* (2nd ed.). Englewood, CO: Morton.

Knapp, M. L. (1972). *Nonverbal communication in human interaction.* New York: Holt, Rinehart & Winston.

Kochman, T. (1981). *Black and white styles in conflict.* Chicago: University of Chicago Press.

Kohlberg, L. (1958). *The development of modes of thinking and moral choice in the years 10 to 16.* Unpublished doctoral dissertation, University of Chicago.

Korzybski, A. (1948). *Science and sanity* (4th ed.). Lakeville, CT: International Non-Aristotelian Library.

Kurdek, L. A. (1993). The allocation of household labor in gay, lesbian, and heterosexual married couples. *Journal of Social Issues, 49,* 127–139.

La Gaipa, J. J. (1982). Rituals of disengagement. In S. W. Duck (Ed.), *Personal relationships, 4: Dissolving personal relationships.* London: Academic Press.

Lakoff, G., & Johnson, M. (1980). *Metaphors we live by.* Chicago: University of Chicago Press.

Langer, S. (1953). *Feeling and form: A theory of art.* New York: Scribner.

Langer, S. (1979). *Philosophy in a new key: A study in the symbolism of reason, rite, and art* (3rd ed.). Cambridge, MA: Harvard University Press.

Langston, D. (1992). Tired of playing monopoly? In M. L. Andersen & P. H. Collins (Eds.), *Race, class, and gender: An anthology* (pp. 110–119). Belmont, CA: Wadsworth.

Lasch, C. (1990, spring). Journalism, publicity and the lost art of argument. *Gannett Center Journal,* pp. 1–11.

Laswell, H. D. (1948). The structure and function of communication in society. In L. Bryson (Ed.), *The communication of ideas.* New York: Harper & Row.

Lau, B. (1989). Imagining your path to success. *Management Quarterly, 30,* 30–41.

Lea, M., & Spears, R. (1995). Relationships conducted over electronic systems. In J. T. Wood & S. W. Duck (Eds.), *Understanding relationship processes, 6: Understudied relationships: Off the beaten track* (pp. 197–233). Thousand Oaks, CA: Sage.

Leathers, D. G. (1976). *Nonverbal communication systems.* Boston: Allyn & Bacon.

Leathers, D. G. (1986). *Successful nonverbal communication: Principles and applications.* New York: Macmillan.

Lederman, L. (1990). Assessing educational effectiveness: The focus group interview as a technique for data collection. *Communication Education, 39,* 117–127.

Lee, J. A. (1973). *The colours of love: An exploration of the ways of loving.* Don Mills, Ontario: New Press.

Lee, J. A. (1988). Love-styles. In R. J. Sternberg & M. L. Barnes (Eds.), *The psychology of love* (pp. 38–67). New Haven, CT: Yale University Press.

Lee, W. (1994). On not missing the boat: A processual method for inter/cultural understandings of idioms and lifeworld. *Journal of Applied Communication Research, 22,* 141–161.

Le Poire, B. A., Burgoon, J. K., & Parrott, R. (1992). Status and privacy restoring communication in the workplace. *Journal of Applied Communication Research, 4,* 419–436.

Lewin, K., Lippitt, R., & White, R. K. (1939). Patterns of aggressive behavior in experimentally created "social climates." *Journal of Social Psychology, 10,* 271–299.

Lichter, S. R., Lichter, L. S., Rothman, S., & Amundson, D. (1987, July/August). Prime-time prejudice: TV's images of blacks and Hispanics. *Public Opinion,* pp. 13–16.

Lorde, A. (1992). Age, race, class, and sex: Women redefining difference. In M. L. Andersen & P. H. Collins (Eds.), *Race, class, and gender: An anthology* (pp. 495–502). Belmont, CA: Wadsworth.

Luft, J. (1969). *Of human interaction.* Palo Alto, CA: Natural Press.

Lumsden, G., & Lumsden, D. (1997). *Communicating in groups and teams* (2nd ed.). Belmont, CA: Wadsworth.

Lund, M. (1985). The development of investment and commitment scales for predicting continuity of personal relationships. *Journal of Social and Personal Relationships, 2,* 3–23.

Lytton, H., & Romney, D. M. (1991). Parents' differential socialization of boys and girls: A meta-analysis. *Psychological Bulletin, 109,* 267–296.

Major, B., Schmidlin, A. M., & Williams, L. (1990). Gender patterns in social touch: The impact of setting and age. In C. Mayo & N. M. Henley (Eds.), *Gender and nonverbal behavior* (pp. 3–37). New York: Springer-Verlag.

Malandro, L. A., & Barker, L. L. (1983). *Nonverbal communication.* Reading, MA: Addison-Wesley.

Maltz, D. N., & Borker, R. (1982). A cultural approach to male–female miscommunication. In J. J. Gumpertz (Ed.), *Language and social identity* (pp. 196–216). Cambridge: Cambridge University Press.

Mandelbaum, D. G. (Ed.). (1949). *Selected writings of Edward Sapir.* Berkeley: University of California Press.

McBath, J. H., & Burhans, D. T., Jr. (1975). *Communication education and careers.* Falls Church, VA: Speech Communication Association.

McCroskey, J. C. (1977). Oral communication apprehension: A summary of recent theory and research. *Human Communication Research, 4,* 78–96.

McCroskey, J. C. (1982). *Introduction to rhetorical communication* (4th ed.). Englewood Cliffs, NJ: Prentice-Hall.

McCroskey, J. C., & Mehrley, R. S. (1969). The effects of disorganization and nonfluency on attitude change and source credibility. *Speech Monographs, 36,* 13–21.

McGee-Cooper, A., with Trammel, D., & Lau, B. (1992). *You don't have to go home from work exhausted.* New York: Bantam.

McGuire, W. J. (1989). Theoretical foundations of campaigns. In R. E. Rice & C. K. Atkin (Eds.), *Public communication campaigns* (2nd ed., pp. 43–65). Newbury Park, CA: Sage.

Mead, G. H. (1934). *Mind, self, and society.* Chicago: University of Chicago Press.

Mehrabian, A. (1981). *Silent messages: Implicit communication of emotion and attitudes* (2nd ed.). Belmont, CA: Wadsworth.

Metts, S., Cupach, W. R., & Bejlovec, R. A. (1989). "I love you too much to ever start liking you": Redefining romantic relationships. *Journal of Social and Personal Relationships, 6,* 259–274.

Meyers, D. G. (1993). *Social psychology* (4th ed.). New York: McGraw-Hill.

Meyers, M. (1994). News of battering. *Journal of Communication, 44,* 47–62.

Miell, D. E., & Duck, S. W. (1986). Strategies in developing friendship. In V. J. Derlega & B. A. Winstead (Eds.), *Friendship and social interaction.* New York: Springer-Verlag.

Miller, E. (1974). Speech introductions and conclusions. *Quarterly Journal of Speech, 32,* 118–127.

Miller, G. R., & Parks, M. R. (1982). Communication in dissolving relationships. In S. W. Duck (Ed.), *Personal relationships 4: Dissolving personal relationships* (pp. 127–154). London: Academic Press.

Miller, J. B. (1993). Learning from early relationship experience. In S. W. Duck (Ed.), *Understanding relationship processes, 2: Learning about relationships* (pp. 1–29). Newbury Park, CA: Sage.

Mongeau, P. A., & Blalock, J. (1994). Student evaluations of instructor immediacy and sexually harassing behaviors: An experimental investigation. *Journal of Applied Communication Research, 22,* 256–272.

Monroe, A. H. (1935). *Principles and types of speech.* Glenview, IL: Scott, Foresman.

Montgomery, B. M. (1988). Quality communication in personal relationships. In S. W. Duck (Ed.), *Handbook of personal relationships* (pp. 343-366). New York: Wiley.

Motley, M. (1990). Public speaking anxiety qua performance anxiety: A revised model and an alternative therapy. *Journal of Social Behavior and Personality, 5,* 85–104.

Motley, M., & Molloy, J. (1994). An efficacy test of a new therapy ("communication-orientation motivation") for public speaking anxiety. *Journal of Applied Communication Research, 22,* 48–58.

Muehlenhardt, C. L., & Linton, M. A. (1987). Date rape and sexual aggression in dating situations: Incidence and risk factors. *Journal of Counseling Psychology, 34,* 186–196.

Mulac, A., Wiemann, J. M., Widenmann, S. J., & Gibson, T. W. (1988). Male/female language differences and effects in same-sex and mixed-sex dyads: The gender-linked language effect. *Communication Monographs, 55,* 315–335.

Murphy, B. O., & Zorn, T. (1996). Gendered interaction in professional relationships. In J. T. Wood (Ed.), *Gendered relationships* (pp. 213–232). Mountain View, CA: Mayfield.

Nardi, P. M., & Sherrod, D. (1994). Friendship in the lives of gay men and lesbians. *Journal of Social and Personal Relationships, 11,* 185–199.

Natalle, E. (1996). Gendered issues in the workplace. In J. T. Wood (Ed.), *Gendered relationships* (pp. 253–274). Mountain View, CA: Mayfield.

National Geographic. (1994, November 5). Public Broadcasting System, 7:30 P.M. EST.

Noller, P. (1986). Sex differences in nonverbal communication: Advantage lost or supremacy regained? *Australian Journal of Psychology, 38,* 23–32.

Noller, P. (1987). Nonverbal communication in marriage. In D. Perlman & S. Duck (Eds.), *Intimate relationships: Development, dynamics, and deterioration* (pp. 149–176). Newbury Park, CA: Sage.

Nussbaum, J. E. (1992, October 18). Justice for women! *New York Review of Books,* pp. 43–48.

Okin, S. M. (1989). *Gender, justice, and the family.* New York: Basic Books.

Olien, M. (1978). *The human myth.* New York: Harper & Row.

Olson, J. M., & Cal, A. V. (1984). Source credibility, attitudes, and the recall of past behaviors. *European Journal of Social Psychology, 14,* 203–210.

O'Meara, J. D. (1989). Cross-sex friendship: Four basic challenges of an ignored relationship. *Sex Roles, 21,* 525–543.

Orbe, M. P. (1994). "Remember, it's always the white's ball": Descriptions of African American male communication. *Communication Quarterly, 42,* 287–300.

Ostermeier, T. H. (1967). Effects of type and frequency of reference upon perceived source credibility and attitude change. *Speech Monographs, 34,* 137–144.

Park, M. (1979). *Communication styles in two different cultures: Korean and American.* Seoul: Han Shin.

Patterson, M. L. (1992). A functional approach to nonverbal exchange. In R. S. Feldman & B. Rime (Eds.), *Fundamentals of nonverbal behavior* (pp. 458–495). New York: Cambridge University Press.

Pearce, W. B., Cronen, V. E., & Conklin, F. (1979). On what to look at when analyzing communication: A hierarchical model of actors' meanings. *Communication, 4,* 195–220.

Pearson, J. C. (1985). *Gender and communication.* Dubuque, IA: William C. Brown.

Petronio, S. (1991). Communication boundary management: A theoretical model of managing disclosure of private information between married couples. *Communication Theory, 1,* 311–335.

Phillips, G. M. (1991). *Communication incompetencies.* Carbondale, IL: Southern Illinois University Press.

Phillips, G. M., & Wood, J. T. (1983). *Communication and human relationships.* New York: Macmillan.

Piaget, J. (1932/1965). *The moral judgment of the child.* New York: Free Press.

Pierson, J. (1995, February 17). Form + function. *Wall Street Journal,* p. B1.

Porter, K., & Foster, J. (1986). *The mental athlete: Inner training for peak performance.* New York: Ballantine.

Public pillow talk. (1987, October). *Psychology Today,* p. 18.

Puka, B. (1990). The liberation of caring: A different voice for Gilligan's different voice. *Hypatia, 5,* 59–82.

Quality circles help sharpen competitive edge. (1991, Winter). *The Scorpion: The official all-state legal supply employee publication.*

Quindlen, A. (1994, September 13). The image of a modern girl. *Raleigh News & Observer,* p. A9.

Raspberry, W. (1994, July 5). Major gains in minorities' grades at Tech. *Raleigh News & Observer,* p. A9.

Rawlins, W. K. (1981). *Friendship as a communicative achievement: A theory and an interpretive analysis of verbal reports.* Ph.D. dissertation. Philadelphia: Temple University.

Rawlins, W. K. (1994). Being there and growing apart: Sustaining friendships during adulthood. In D. Canary & L. Stafford (Eds.), *Communication and relational maintenance* (pp. 275–294). New York: Academic Press.

Reel, B. W., & Thompson, T. L. (1994). A test of the effectiveness of strategies for talking about AIDS and condom use. *Journal of Applied Communication Research, 22,* 127–141.

Reis, H. T., Senchak, M., & Solomon, B. (1985). Sex differences in the intimacy of social interaction: Further examination of potential explanations. *Journal of Personality and Social Psychology, 48,* 1204–1217.

Ribeau, S. A., Baldwin, J. R., & Hecht, M. L. (1994). An African-American communication perspective. In L. Samovar & R. Porter (Eds.), *Intercultural communication: A reader* (7th ed., pp. 140–147). Belmont, CA: Wadsworth.

Richmond, V. P., & McCroskey, J. C. (1992). *Communication: Apprehension, avoidance, and effectiveness* (3rd ed.). Scottsdale, AZ: Gorsuch Scarisbrick.

Riessman, C. (1990). *Divorce talk: Women and men make sense of personal relationships.* New Brunswick, NJ: Rutgers University Press.

Rohlfing, M. (1995). Doesn't anybody stay in one place anymore? An exploration of the understudied phenomenon of long-distance relationships. In J. T. Wood & S. W. Duck (Eds.), *Understanding relationship processes, 6: Understudied relationships: Off the beaten track* (pp. 173–196). Thousand Oaks, CA: Sage.

Root, M. P. P. P. (1990). Disordered eating habits in women of color. *Sex Roles, 22,* 525–536.

Rosenberg, M. (1979). *Conceiving the self.* New York: Basic Books.

Ruberman, T. R. (1992, January 22–29). Psychosocial influences on mortality of patients with coronary heart disease. *Journal of the American Medical Association 267,* 559–560.

Rubin, B. D. (1988). *Communication and human behavior* (2nd ed.). New York: Macmillan.

Ruddick, S. (1989). *Maternal thinking: Towards a politics of peace.* Boston: Beacon Press.

Rusbult, C. (1987). Responses to dissatisfaction in close relationships: The exit-voice-loyalty-neglect model. In D. Perlman & S. W. Duck (Eds.), *Intimate relationships: Development, dynamics, and deterioration* (pp. 109–238). London: Sage.

Rusbult, C. E., Johnson, D. J., & Morrow, G. D. (1986). Impact of couple patterns of problem solving on distress and nondistress in dating relationships. *Journal of Personality and Social Psychology, 50,* 744–753.

Rusbult, C. E., & Zembrodt, I. M. (1983). Responses to dissatisfaction in romantic involvement: A multidimensional scaling analysis. *Journal of Experimental Social Psychology, 19,* 274–293.

Rusbult, C. E., Zembrodt, I. M., & Iwaniszek, J. (1986). The impact of gender and sex-role orientation on responses to dissatisfaction in close relationships. *Sex Roles, 15,* 1-20.

Rusk, T., & Rusk, N. (1988). *Mind traps: Change your mind, change your life.* Los Angeles: Price Stern Sloan.

Sadker, M., & Sadker, D. (1986, March). Sexism in the classroom: From grade school to graduate school. *Phi Delta Kappan,* pp. 512–515.

Sallinen-Kuparinen, A. (1992). Teacher communicator style. *Communication Education, 41,* 153–166.

Samovar, L., & Porter, R. (1991). *Communication between cultures.* Belmont, CA: Wadsworth.

Samovar, L., & Porter, R. (Eds.). (1994). *Intercultural communication: A reader* (7th ed.). Belmont, CA: Wadsworth.

Samovar, L., & Porter, R. (1995). *Communication between cultures* (2nd ed.). Belmont, CA: Wadsworth.

SCA (Speech Communication Association). (1995). *Pathways to careers in communication.* Annandale, VA: Speech Communication Association.

Scarf, M. (1987). *Intimate partners: Patterns in love and marriage.* New York: Random House.

Schminoff, S. B. (1980). *Communication rules: Theory and research.* Newbury Park, CA: Sage.

Schramm, W. (1955). *The process and effects of mass communication.* Urbana, IL: University of Illinois Press.

Schutz, W. (1966). *The interpersonal underworld.* Palo Alto, CA: Science and Behavior Books.

Schwartz, T. (1989, January/February). Acceleration syndrome: Does everyone live in the fast lane nowadays? *Utne Reader,* pp. 36–43.

Sebeok, T. A., & Rosenthal, R. (Eds.). (1981). *The Clever Hans phenomenon: Communication with horses, whales, apes and people.* New York: New York Academy of Sciences.

Secord, P. F., Bevan, W., & Katz, B. (1956). The Negro stereotype and perceptual accentuation. *Journal of Abnormal and Social Psychology, 54,* 78–83.

Seligman, M. E. P. (1990). *Learned optimism.* New York: Simon & Schuster/Pocket Books.

Shannon, C., & Weaver, W. (1949). *The mathematical theory of communication.* Urbana, IL: University of Illinois Press.

Shattuck, T. R. (1980). *The forbidden experiment: The story of the wild boy of Aveyron.* New York: Farrar, Straus, & Giroux.

Sher, B., & Gottlieb, A. (1989). *Teamworks!* New York: Warner Books.

Shimanoff, S. B. (1980). *Communication rules: Theory and research.* Beverly Hills, CA: Sage.

Shotter, J. (1993). *Conversational realities: The construction of life through language.* Newbury Park, CA: Sage.

Sights, sounds, and stereotypes. (1992, October 11). *Raleigh News & Observer,* pp. G1, G10.

Simon, S. B. (1977). *Vulture: A modern allegory on the art of putting oneself down.* Niles, IL: Argus Communications.

Simons, G. F., Vázquez, C., & Harris, P. R. (1993). *Transcultural leadership: Empowering the diverse workforce.* Houston: Gulf.

Spain, D. (1992). *Gendered spaces.* Chapel Hill, NC: University of North Carolina Press.

Spencer, M. (1982). *Foundations of modern sociology.* Englewood Cliffs, NJ: Prentice-Hall.

Spencer, T. (1994). Transforming personal relationships through ordinary talk. In S. W. Duck (Ed.), *Understanding relationship processes, 4: Dynamics of relationships* (pp. 58–85). Thousand Oaks, CA: Sage.

Spender, D. (1989). *Invisible women: The schooling scandal.* London: Women's Press.

Spicer, C., & Bassett, R. E. (1976). The effect of organization on learning from an informative message. *Southern Speech Communication Journal, 41,* 290–299.

Spitz, R. (1965). *The first year of life.* New York: International Universities Press.

Spitzack, C. (1990). *Confessing excess.* Albany, NY: State University of New York Press.

Spitzack, C. (1993). The spectacle of anorexia nervosa. *Text and Performance Quarterly, 13,* 1–21.

Staley, C. C. (1988). The communicative power of women managers: Doubts, dilemmas, and management development programs. In K. Valentine & N. Hoar (Eds.), *Women and communicative power* (pp. 36–48). Annandale, VA: Speech Communication Association.

Stamp, G. H., & Sabourin, T. C. (1995). Accounting for violence: An analysis of male spousal abuse narratives. *Journal of Applied Communication Research, 23,* 284–307.

Stephenson, S. J., & D'Angelo, G. (1973). *The effects of evaluative/empathic listening and self-esteem on defensive reactions in dyads.* Paper presented to the International Communication Association, Montreal, Quebec, Canada.

Stets, J. E. (1990). Verbal and physical aggression in marriage. *Journal of Marriage and the Family, 52,* 501–514.

Stets, J. E., & Straus, M. A. (1989). The marriage license as a hitting license: A comparison of assaults in dating, cohabiting, and married couples. *Journal of Family Violence, 41,* 33–52.

Stone, R. (1992). The feminization of poverty among the elderly. In M. L. Andersen & P. H. Collins (Eds.), *Race, class, and gender: An anthology* (pp. 201–214). Belmont, CA: Wadsworth.

Strine, M. S. (1992). Understanding "how things work": Sexual harassment and academic culture. *Journal of Applied Communication Research, 20,* 391–400.

Suitor, J. J. (1991). Marital quality and satisfaction with the division of household labor across the family life cycle. *Journal of Marriage and the Family, 53,* 221–230.

Surra, C., Arizzi, P., & Asmussen, L. (1988). The association between reasons for commitment and the development and outcome of marital relationships. *Journal of Social and Personal Relationships, 5,* 47–64.

Swain, S. (1989). Covert intimacy: Closeness in men's friendships. In B. Risman & P. Schwartz (Ed.), *Gender and intimate relationships* (pp. 71–86). Belmont, CA: Wadsworth.

Sypher, B. (1984). Seeing ourselves as others see us. *Communication Research, 11,* 97–115.

Tannen, D. (1990). *You just don't understand: Women and men in conversation.* New York: William Morrow.

Tavris, C. (1992). *The mismeasure of woman.* New York: Simon & Schuster.

Taylor, B., & Conrad, C. (1992). Narratives of sexual harassment: Organizational dimensions. *Journal of Applied Communication Research, 4,* 401–418.

Thomas, V. G. (1989). Body-image satisfaction among black women. *Journal of Social Psychology, 129,* 107–112.

Thompson, E. H., Jr. (1991). The maleness of violence in dating relationships: An appraisal of stereotypes. *Sex Roles, 24,* 261–278.

Toffler, A. (1970). *Future shock.* New York: William Morrow.

Toffler, A. (1980). *The third wave.* New York: William Morrow.

Tolhuizen, J. H. (1989). Communication strategies for intensifying dating relationships: Identification, use, and structure. *Journal of Social and Personal Relationships, 6,* 413–434.

Trenholm, S. (1991). *Human communication theory* (2nd ed.). Englewood Cliffs, NJ: Prentice-Hall.

Triandis, H. C. (1990). Cross-cultural studies of individualism and collectivism. In J. J. Berman (Ed.), *Cross-cultural perspectives* (pp. 41–133). Lincoln, NE: University of Nebraska Press.

Trotter, R. J. (1975, October 25). "The truth, the whole truth, and nothing but . . ." *Science News, 108,* 269.

Underwood, H. G. (1977). Foundations in thought and values: How we differ. *Korea Journal, 17,* 6–9.

Upton, H. (1995, May 8). Peerless advice from small-business peers. *Wall Street Journal,* p. A14.

Villarosa, L. (1994, January). Dangerous eating. *Essence,* pp. 19–21, 87.

Vocate, D. (Ed.). (1994). *Intrapersonal communication: Different voices, different minds.* Hillsdale, NJ: Lawrence Erlbaum.

Walker, M. B., & Trimboli, A. (1989). Communicating affect: The role of verbal and nonverbal content. *Journal of Language and Social Psychology, 8,* 229–248.

Watzlawick, P., Beavin, J., & Jackson, D. D. (1967). *Pragmatics of human communication.* New York: W. W. Norton.

Weaver, C. (1972). *Human listening: Processes and behavior.* Indianapolis: Bobbs-Merrill.

Weber, S. N. (1994). The need to be: The socio-cultural significance of black language. In L. Samovar & R. Porter (Eds.), *Intercultural communication: A reader* (7th ed., pp. 221–226). Belmont, CA: Wadsworth.

Wells, W., & Siegel, B. (1961). Stereotyped somatotypes. *Psychological Reports, 8,* 77–78.

Werner, C. M., Altman, I., Brown, B. B., & Ginat, J. (1993). Celebrations in personal relationships: A transactional/dialectical perspective. In S. W. Duck (Ed.), *Understanding relational processes, 3: Social context and relationships* (pp. 109–138). Newbury Park, CA: Sage.

Werner, C., Altman, I., & Oxley, D. (1985). Temporal aspects of homes: A transactional perspective. In I. Altman & C. M. Werner (Eds.), *Home environments, 8. Human behavior and environment: Advances in theory and research* (pp. 1–32). Beverly Hills, CA: Sage.

West, C., & Zimmerman, D. H. (1987). Doing gender. *Gender and Society, 1,* 125–151.

West, J. (1995). Understanding how the dynamics of ideology influence violence between intimates. In S. W. Duck & J. T. Wood (Eds.), *Understanding relationship processes, 5: Confronting relationship challenges* (pp. 129–149). Thousand Oaks, CA: Sage.

Westefield, J. S., & Liddell, D. (1982). Coping with long-distance relationships. *Journal of College Student Personnel, 23,* 550–551.

Weston, K. (1991). *Families we choose: Lesbian, gays, kinship.* New York: Columbia University Press.

Wexner, L. B. (1954). The degree to which colors (hues) are associated with mood-tones. *Journal of Applied Psychology, 38,* 432–435.

What teens say about drinking. (1994, August 7). *Parade,* p. 9.

Whitbeck, L. B., & Hoyt, D. R. (1994). Social prestige and assortive mating: A comparison of students from 1956 and 1988. *Journal of Social and Personal Relationships, 11,* 137–145.

White, R., & Lippitt, R. (1960). *Autocracy and democracy.* New York: Harper & Row.

Whorf, B. (1956). *Language, thought, and reality.* New York: MIT Press/Wiley.

Wiemann, J. M., & Harrison, R. P. (Eds). (1983). *Nonverbal interaction.* Beverly Hills, CA: Sage.

Wilkie, J. R. (1991). The decline in men's labor force participation and income and the changing structure of family economic support. *Journal of Marriage and the Family, 53,* 111–122.

Williams, R. (1994). *The non-designer's design book: Design and typographic principles for the visual novice.* Berkeley, CA: Peachpit Press.

Wilson, J. F., & Arnold, C. C. (1974). *Public speaking as a liberal art* (4th ed.). Boston: Allyn & Bacon.

Winans, J. A. (1938). *Speechmaking.* New York: Appleton-Century-Crofts.

Wolf, N. (1991). *The beauty myth.* New York: William Morrow.

Wong, W. (1994). Covering the invisible "model minority." *Media Studies Journal* (Special issue: Race—America's rawest nerve), 8, 49–60.

Wood, J. T. (1982). Communication and relational culture: Bases for the study of human relationships. *Communication Quarterly, 30,* 75–84.

Wood, J. T. (1986). Different voices in relationship crises: An extension of Gilligan's theory. *American Behavioral Scientist, 29,* 273–301.

Wood, J. T. (1992a). *Spinning the symbolic web: Human communication as symbolic interaction.* New Jersey: Ablex.

Wood, J. T. (1992b). Telling our stories: Narratives as a basis for theorizing sexual harassment. *Journal of Applied Communication Research, 4,* 349–363.

Wood, J. T. (1993a). Diversity and commonality: Sustaining their tension in communication courses. *Western Journal of Communication, 57,* 367–380.

Wood, J. T. (1993b). Engendered relations: Interaction, caring, power, and responsibility in intimacy. In S. W. Duck (Ed.), *Understanding relationship processes, 3: Social context and relationships* (pp. 26–54). Newbury Park, CA: Sage.

Wood, J. T. (1993c). Enlarging conceptual boundaries: A critique of research on interpersonal communication. In S. P. Bowen & N. J. Wyatt (Eds.), *Transforming visions: Feminist critiques in communication studies* (pp. 19–49). Cresskill, NJ: Hampton.

Wood, J. T. (1993d). Gender and moral voice: From woman's nature to standpoint theory. *Women's Studies in Communication, 15,* 1–24.

Wood, J. T. (1994a). Diversity in dialogue: Communication between friends. In J. Makau & R. Arnett (Eds.), *Ethics of communication in an age of diversity.* Urbana: University of Illinois Press.

Wood, J. T. (1994b). Engendered identities: Shaping voice and mind through gender. In D. Vocate (Ed.), *Intrapersonal communication: Different voices, different minds..* Hillsdale, NJ: Lawrence Erlbaum.

Wood, J. T. (1994c). Gender and relationship crises: Contrasting reasons, responses, and relational orientations. In J. Ringer (Ed.), *Queer words, queer images: The construction of homosexuality.* New York: New York University Press.

Wood, J. T. (1994d). *Gendered lives: Communication, gender and culture.* Belmont, CA: Wadsworth.

Wood, J. T. (1994e). *Who cares? Women, care and culture.* Carbondale, IL: Southern Illinois University Press.

Wood, J. T. (1995a). Feminist scholarship and research on personal relationships. *Journal of Social and Personal Relationships, 12,* 103–120.

Wood, J. T. (1995b). *Relational communication: Continuity and change in personal relationships.* Belmont, CA: Wadsworth.

Wood, J. T. (1996a). *Everyday encounters: An introduction to interpersonal communication.* Belmont, CA: Wadsworth.

Wood, J. T. (Ed.). (1996b). *Gendered relationships.* Mountain View, CA: Mayfield.

Wood, J. T. (1997). *Communication theories in action.* Belmont, CA: Wadsworth.

Wood, J. T., Dendy, L., Dordek, E., Germany, M., & Varallo, S. (1994). Dialectic of difference: A thematic analysis of intimates' meanings for differences. In K. Carter & M. Presnell (Eds.), *Interpretive approaches to interpersonal communication* (pp. 115–136). New York: State University of New York Press.

Wood, J. T., & Duck, S. W. (1995a). Off the beaten track: New shores for relationship research. In J. T. Wood & S. W. Duck (Eds.), *Understanding relationship processes, 6: Understudied relationships: Off the beaten track* (pp. 1–21). Thousand Oaks, CA: Sage.

Wood, J. T., & Duck, S. W. (Eds.). (1995b). *Understanding relationship processes, 6: Understudied relationships: Off the beaten track.* Newbury Park, CA: Sage.

Wood, J. T., & Inman, C. C. (1993). In a different mode: Masculine styles of communicating closeness. *Journal of Applied Communication Research, 21,* 279-295.

Wood, J. T., & Phillips, G. M. (1990). The pedagogy of group decision making: Teaching alternative strategies. In G. M. Phillips (Ed.), *Small group communication: Theory and pedagogy.* New Jersey: Ablex.

Wood, J. T., Phillips, G. M., & Pedersen, D. J. (1986). *Group discussion: A practical guide to participation and leadership* (2nd ed.). New York: Harper & Row.

Woolfolk, A. E. (1987). *Educational psychology.* Englewood Cliffs, NJ: Prentice-Hall.

Wu, C., & Shaffer, D. R. (1988). Susceptibility to persuasive appeals as a function of source credibility and prior experience with attitude object. *Journal of Personal and Social Psychology, 52,* 677–688.

Wycoff, J. (1991). *Mind-mapping: Your personal guide to exploring creativity and problem-solving.* New York: Basic Books.

Zorn, T. (1995). Bosses and buddies: Constructing and performing simultaneously hierarchical and close friendship relationships. In J. T. Wood & S. W. Duck (Eds.), *Understanding relationship processes, 6: Understudied relationships: Off the beaten track* (pp. 122–147). Thousand Oaks, CA: Sage.

PLEASE GIVE US YOUR FEEDBACK

Thank you for using *Communication in Our Lives*. I hope you have enjoyed reading it and have found it valuable in your interpersonal, social, and professional interactions. In order to make the next edition even better, I'd like to know what you think about the book. Please give me your opinions on this edition by filling out the questionnaire below. When you're done, just fold and seal the questionnaire, and drop it into the mail (postage is already paid).

Thanks for your help!

     Julia T. Wood

1. In comparison to other textbooks you have read, is *Communication in Our Lives* better, about the same, or less effective?

2. What are the three topics or parts of the book that you found most useful?

3. Which parts did you find least useful?

4. Did you discuss the ideas presented in the "Communication Highlight" boxes? Did you find this feature useful?

5. Are there any other criticisms you have of this edition?

6. How can we improve the next edition?

7. Did you use a computer in conjunction with this class? If yes, what kind and for what purpose?

May we quote your answers to all of the above questions?   ◯ yes   ◯ no

Do you have a student commentary (like those included in this book) that you would like to have me consider using in the next edition? If yes, please type it up and send it to the address on the other side of this page. If your commentary is published, your privacy will be protected.

Name (optional) _____

School _____

Address _____

City/State/Zip _____

Internet address _____

Year in school and field of study _____